TurboTax® Deluxe

THE OFFICIAL GUIDE

For Tax Year 2000

Gail Perry, CPA

Osborne/**McGraw-Hill**

Berkeley   New York   St. Louis   San Francisco
Auckland   Bogotá   Hamburg   London   Madrid
Mexico City   Milan   Montreal   New Delhi   Panama City
Paris   São Paulo   Singapore   Sydney   Tokyo   Toronto

Osborne/**McGraw-Hill**
2600 Tenth Street
Berkeley, California 94710
U.S.A.

For information on translations or book distributors outside the U.S.A., or to arrange bulk purchase discounts for sales promotions, premiums, or fund-raisers, please contact Osborne/**McGraw-Hill** at the above address.

TurboTax® Deluxe: The Official Guide for Tax Year 2000

1234567890 AGM AGM 019876543210

ISBN 0-07-213083-0

Publisher	**Technical Editors**
Brandon A. Nordin	Bob Meighan, Renée George
Vice President and Associate Publisher	**Copy Editor**
Scott Rogers	Lunaea Weatherstone
Editorial Director	**Proofreader**
Roger Stewart	Andrea Fox
Acquisitions Editor	**Indexer**
Megg Bonar	Jack Lewis
Project Manager	**Computer Designer**
Laurie Stewart	Maureen Forys, Happenstance Type-O-Rama
Acquisitions Coordinator	**Series Designers**
Cindy Wathen	Jill Weil, Peter F. Hancik

This book was composed with QuarkXPress 4.11 on a Macintosh G4.

To Georgia and Katherine, my two shining
lights, who make everything worthwhile.

Contents

Part II   **Using TurboTax to Prepare Your Tax Return**

Part IV   Dealing with the IRS

Part V   **Good Tax Sense for the Future**

Acknowledgments

I hardly know where to start when it comes to thanking the people who worked to put this project together, with a timetable that, looking back, doesn't seem humanly possible. Throughout it all, everyone maintained a remarkable attitude of confidence, skill, and devotion to the project. Thanks above all to Megg Bonar, the first editor I ever knew when I began writing books seven years ago, who provided insights and guidance, and who put this whole project together and held it fast even when it appeared that it might be bursting at the seams.

Thank you to Bob Meighan and Renée George at Intuit who read every chapter for accuracy and consistency, and to Laurie Stewart, the project manager, and her team of book packagers—Lunaea Weatherstone, the copy editor, Maureen Forys, the typesetter, and Andrea Fox, the proofreader—all of whom burned more midnight oil than anyone in this profession ought to. Many thanks to Cindy Wathen at Osborne/McGraw-Hill, who kept the traffic flowing and managed to keep track of where all the parts of this book were located. Thank you also to Todd Stanley at Intuit, who kept me supplied with software and answers to my questions, and to Intuit's Stuart Heilsberg and Monica Muilenburg. Thanks also to Todd Santos at Intuit for his help in getting the cover exactly correct.

Introduction

I'm always curious to know what makes people purchase the books I write. Did you buy this book at the same time you bought the program because they seemed to go hand in hand? Is this the first time you've tried to prepare your tax return with a computer and you want to have a reference guide to help you? Did you buy the book first to read about the program, and then make your decision about whether or not to buy TurboTax? Did you use TurboTax in a prior year and wish you had a comprehensive manual to accompany the program? Did you try using the program for your 2000 tax return and find you had questions about some of the features TurboTax has to offer? No matter what your reason was for buying this book, feel free to visit http://www.osborne.com/ and fill out the short survey there to tell me why you did buy this book, I'd love to hear your reasons.

Although I may never know exactly what motivated you to make this purchase, I do know this: the people who read this book are people who want to figure out their tax return by themselves, without having to hire a tax professional. They believe that the process of preparing and filing a tax return ought to be simple and straightforward, and they are motivated by a goal of making the tax preparation process quick, easy, and inexpensive.

By acquiring TurboTax and this book, you've done just that. The nominal cost of the TurboTax program and this book hardly compares to what it would cost to hire a pro to prepare your return. And the ease of using TurboTax, coupled with the tax tips and rules provided in this book, will ensure that your tax preparation time is cut to a minimum.

Why I Wrote This Book

I agreed to write this book because I feel strongly that the taxpayers of this country should be able to sit down at their desks or kitchen tables and prepare their own tax returns. I believe people should be able to fill out and submit their tax forms without having to hire expensive accountants and without worrying that the numbers they put on the forms are wrong, or worse, that something awful will happen to them when the IRS sees the information on the forms.

I believe that our tax laws are too complicated, and that they are getting more complicated with each attempt of Congress to simplify the tax code. I believe that the instructions that accompany the tax forms are intentionally ambiguous, to cover every possible exception to the rules, and that, as a result, they are impossible to understand if you haven't been trained in the tax laws. Even trained professionals have difficulty understanding all the nuances of the tax code. I've seen repeated evidence that professional tax return preparers, when given a set of facts regarding a sample taxpayer, will produce tax returns with different results from the returns prepared by their peers.

I also believe that for the average taxpayer, the best possible chance you have of preparing a tax return that will be true and accurate, is to follow the steps in the TurboTax program and let the program prepare the tax forms for you. As easy as TurboTax is to use, there may still be situations in which you don't understand what the program is asking for. If you don't understand some of the steps in the program, this book will provide you with samples and solutions. This book is my attempt to assist taxpayers in the preparation of their tax returns, so that they can mail their forms and rest easy with the knowledge that they have done the best possible job at filling out their tax forms.

Book Organization

This book is organized into six parts, and each part is designed to give you a particular perspective about your taxes.

Part One: Getting Started

The first section of *TurboTax Deluxe: The Official Guide* tells you what has happened to taxes in the past year, and gives you pointers for assembling all the information you need so that when you get ready to prepare your tax return, you won't have to keep hopping up and down to find more receipts. In addition, you'll find a series of tax scenarios designed to explain the special tax rules that affect you—because every person, whether married or single, a parent, a business owner, or elderly, gets treated a little bit differently in the eyes of the IRS.

Part Two: Using TurboTax to Prepare Your Tax Return

Part Two provides the meat of the program—these chapters cover the ins and outs of entering all of your income and deductions into your tax program, so that TurboTax can do its job and produce a tax return you can be proud of. In these chapters you'll find tips for entering your information expeditiously and suggestions for maximizing your refund. You'll find warnings about how current tax savings can result in big tax liabilities down the road, you'll learn about tax credits that can slash your tax bill, and you'll learn about the variety of tax-deferred savings plans that are available to help you ease into retirement with a nice nest egg.

Part Three: Internet Resources to Help You File Your Taxes

Everyone keeps hearing that there is a wealth of information available on the Internet. The trick is knowing how to sift through all of the information to find what you're looking for. Part Three of this book does the sifting for you and shows you just where to look in cyberspace for tax forms and instructions, changes in the tax laws, and the latest tax news. And if you're ready to take the e-file plunge and prepare and file your tax return completely online, TurboTax is ready for you. Learn how Intuit's TurboTax for the Web is changing the way people prepare their tax returns.

Part Four: Dealing with the IRS

There are many ways in which we all deal with the IRS, some more tolerable than others. You deal with the IRS when you pay your taxes, and you deal with them when you wait, sometimes impatiently, for your refund. Sometimes you realize the information on your tax return needs to be changed, so you have to deal with the IRS for that too. And one of these days you may get a letter in the mail, informing you of a mistake or omission on your tax return, or telling you your tax return has been chosen for examination. The information in this section will tell you just what you need to know to approach the IRS with a calm air of confidence.

Part Five: Good Tax Sense for the Future

Paying taxes isn't something that happens only on April 15. Paying, and planning for your tax liability, should occur all year long, every year. Part of good tax planning includes keeping good tax records. You have more control over the amount of tax you owe than you may realize, and you can take many steps that will maximize your tax refund and also keep your hard-earned money a little closer to home.

Part Six: Appendixes

There are two appendixes at the back of the book in Part Six. One of them you may not need at all, and the other one you shouldn't do without.

Appendix A gives you information about purchasing a TurboTax federal or state tax program if you haven't done so already, and also provides pointers on installation of the program. If you've already installed your TurboTax program, you won't need any of the information in Appendix A.

Appendix B provides a series of worksheets and tax planning tools that will give you some great ideas on how to cut your taxes. Learn how effective a small investment in a Roth IRA can be for setting yourself or your children up for retirement. Learn how to value the used items you donate to charity, and figure out whether it's more cost effective to lease or purchase an automobile. Calculate the long-term tax effects of taking deductions for your home office, and figure out how much the tax will be if you convert a regular IRA to a Roth IRA. Visit http://www.osborne.com/ for fully interactive versions of these documents.

Conventions

There are particular elements in this book that will make your reading experience more valuable. Look for these features that call attention to particularly useful information:

Tip   *Tips provide you with quick explanations of tax rules.*

Note   *Notes provide explanatory information that may not be obvious from the program.*

Caution   *A caution contains extremely important information—cautions are not to be overlooked.*

 SAVE TIME   The Save Time icon provides you with ideas for how you can make your tax preparation process more efficient.

 SAVE MONEY   Items in this category will help you increase your deductions and cut your taxes.

GET SMARTER   Information tagged with the Get Smarter icon will provide you with insights into the tax laws and examples of how you can use the laws to your advantage.

New to TurboTax This Year

If you've used TurboTax in the past, you'll be interested to know that there are some new features that have been added to the program for the 2000 tax year. The most significant change is the new Automated Tax Return. The Automated Tax Return feature enables you to directly download information from your W-2 and 1099 forms over the Internet from the source that provided the forms. Your form must have been produced by a participating source, and you'll know if you qualify for this feature if your W-2 or 1099 forms indicate they are eligible for Intuit's Automated Tax Return.

Another new feature, Quick Cash, offers taxpayers the opportunity to get a loan, up to $5,000, based on their anticipated refund. The loan is deducted from the refund, so there is no up-front cost to the borrower.

New to Tax Laws This Year

As of the time this book went to press, there was no major tax legislation in 1999, even though members of Congress spent the better part of the year voting on various tax bills, including a repeal of the estate and gift tax and an end to the so-called marriage penalty. There was also talk of sweeping changes to individual retirement plans with regard to how much taxpayers can contribute each year, but there were no decisions that coincided with the deadlines for this book. The online tax sources mentioned in Chapter 12, particularly those that include links to tax laws or to current newspaper columns devoted to tax, are a good place to look if you are interested in following various tax measures as they make their way through the federal law-making maze.

Taxes and Tax Accountants

As I mentioned earlier in this introduction, one of the reasons I wrote this book was to help encourage people who don't need to hire accountants to prepare their own tax returns. That said, I will also say that there are many situations where it is helpful to contact a tax professional. The general rule to follow in tax preparation should be, if you don't know what to enter on your tax return, ask for help.

The first places you should go for help are this book and the onscreen help features in your TurboTax program. When you have exhausted those sources, if you are still in a quandary, try calling the IRS help line at (800) 829-1040. Although it has been said that IRS agents give much misinformation over the phone, I can attest to the fact that most of the people answering the phones at the IRS are very knowledgeable about taxes, and if they don't know the answer themselves will try to find someone who does. Much of what passes for misinformation provided by the IRS can be attributed to a miscommunication between the caller and the IRS representative, who are probably speaking in two different languages: the language of the tax novice versus the language of the tax pro. Wording the tax question so that the IRS helper on the phone can understand what you need to know is the hardest part of getting correct and useful information from the IRS.

If you don't feel you're finding what you need from the easy sources mentioned above, you can try communicating with Intuit online. The TurboTax Web site at http://www.turbotax.com/ includes online technical support, and you can also try looking for information at the other Internet sites mentioned in Chapter 12.

If you do decide you need to hire professional help, keep in mind the fact that you don't have to hire a tax accountant to prepare your entire tax return. You can prepare as much of the return as you feel capable of doing, then consult with a pro for those few thorny questions you can't seem to answer. Another option is to prepare your tax return yourself, then take the finished product to a tax professional for an analysis. Services such as these are more cost-efficient than hiring an accountant to do the work that you can do yourself.

About the Author

My career as an accountant began when I graduated from Indiana University with a degree in English and journalism, a minor in computer science, and a desire to work with numbers. My first job was as an accountant for a large Washington, D.C., law firm, and I was hooked. I returned to the Midwest and went back to school at Illinois State University where I took all the accounting courses I could stand, and then passed the CPA exam.

I spent the next several years in public accounting, learning the ropes of the tax profession, first at Deloitte & Touche in Chicago, then at smaller regional CPA firms in Indianapolis. Throughout all of my accounting experience, I found myself working with computers every chance I got, and writing up little manuals so the rest of the people in my firm would know how to do what I had learned.

I left public accounting seven years ago, with a contract to write my first book in one hand and a contract to teach computer courses (including TurboTax!) for the Indiana CPA Society in the other hand, and I haven't looked back. Fourteen books and countless computer classes later, I find I still get excited about the work I do and don't want to trade it for any other job.

A few years ago I was hired by Intuit to provide editorial guidance to the people who write the EasyStep Interview questions that appear in your TurboTax program. Although I knew how to use TurboTax to prepare tax returns before that experience, my immersion in the program has been complete since I started working with the Intuit team.

I'm the author of, among other titles, *Excel 2000 Answers,* published last year by Osborne/McGraw-Hill, *The Complete Idiot's Guide to Doing Your Income Taxes,* published by Alpha, and *Special Edition Using QuickBooks & QuickBooks Pro,* published by Que. I also write a weekly column about taxes for the *Indianapolis Star,* and I am the managing editor of an Internet site for the accounting profession, called AccountingWEB, located at http://www.accountingweb.com/. More than these accomplishments, however, I'm a mom and a wife, and wouldn't be anything if it weren't for that.

Getting Started

This first part of this book provides you with some insights into how the tax laws specifically affect you. You'll also learn about what has changed in the tax laws since last year, and you'll get some tips about how to get ready to prepare your tax return. This part includes the following chapters:

Chapter 1: *Tax Law Changes for 2000 and Beyond*

Chapter 2: *Assembling Your Tax Information Before You Begin*

Chapter 3: *Tax Scenarios*

Part One

Tax Law Changes for 2000 and Beyond

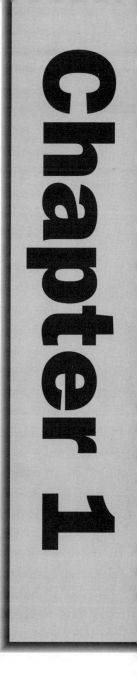

In This Chapter:

- *Changes That Affect Everyone*

- *Changes for the Self-Employed*

- *Changes for Investors in Retirement Funds*

- *Changes for College Students*

- *Changes for Parents*

- *Changes for Landlords*

Every year the tax laws change a bit—standard deductions and exemptions increase, marginal tax rates change, the Social Security threshold goes up. Other changes occur in the way information is presented on tax forms and the amounts of certain types of deductions. Changes in the tax laws for tax year 2000, most of them small and many of them unnoticeable, result in higher taxes for some and lower taxes for others. Each year, it seems, one group pays more, another group pays less, and just about everything washes out in the end.

Changes That Affect Everyone

The IRS makes changes every year to certain areas of the tax laws that result in more of the tax being shifted from the lowest income taxpayers to the wealthier taxpayers. These changes are built into the tax rules in the form of annual cost-of-living adjustments. You won't need to know these amounts for purposes of filling out your tax return—that's one of the reasons people use TurboTax, so they won't have to look up all the changes themselves. But just in case you're curious, here are the changes that went into effect for the year 2000. Every taxpayer is affected by at least some of these changes.

Note | *This chapter refers to tax information that may still be affected by year 2000 tax legislation. Even if some of the numbers in this chapter change as a result of late changes in the tax laws, you can be sure that TurboTax will incorporate all of the current data in the program that you use.*

Widening Tax Brackets

Taxpayers will experience a widening of the tax brackets in 2000, meaning more income will be taxed at lower rates, which will be a tax saving for everyone except those whose income already falls completely in the lowest (15 percent) tax bracket. Table 1-1 shows how changes in the tax brackets for 2000 will affect the way in which income is taxed compared to 1999.

For a single taxpayer with taxable income of $30,000, income tax in 1999 was $5,052, with $25,750 being taxed at 15 percent and the balance being taxed at 28 percent. The same taxpayer in 2000 pays $4,988, calculated by taking 15 percent of $26,250 (which is $500 more than last year's $25,750) and 28 percent of the balance.

Filing Status	Income Taxed at:			
	15%	**28%**	**31%**	**36%**
Single	$500	$1,100	$2,350	$5,200
Married Filing Jointly and Qualifying Widow(er)	$800	$1,900	$2,900	$5,200
Married Filing Separately	$400	$950	$1,450	$2,600
Head of Household	$600	$1,650	$2,650	$5,200

Table 1-1 • Change in Amount of Income Being Taxed

Standard Deduction Increases

The standard deduction increases each year, which means every taxpayer gets a slightly larger amount of basic reduction to income before tax is applied, thus lowering tax slightly. Table 1-2 shows the standard deductions for 1999 and 2000.

Filing Status	1999 Standard Deduction	2000 Standard Deduction
Single	$4,300	$4,400
Married Filing Jointly and Qualifying Widow(er)	$7,200	$7,350
Married Filing Separately	$3,600	$3,765
Head of Household	$6,350	$6,450
Taxpayers Claimed as Dependents on Another Tax Return	$700	$700

Table 1-2 • Increases in Standard Deductions from 1999 to 2000

The standard deduction is used in lieu of itemizing deductions. If your itemized deductions exceed the standard deduction amount, you should itemize instead of claiming the standard deduction.

Personal Exemptions Amounts Changing

You are entitled to deduct a personal exemption amount for yourself, your spouse (if married filing a joint return), and each of your dependents. In 1999, the personal exemption amount was $2,750 per person. For 2000, the personal exemption amount is $2,800.

Personal exemptions are phased out when income reaches certain levels. The income phase-out level is increasing each year, which results in more people being able to claim their full personal exemptions and a decrease in income tax for people who are affected by this change. Table 1-3 shows the 2000 change in the personal exemption phase-out limit.

Filing Status	1999 Personal Exemption Phase-Out	2000 Personal Exemption Phase-Out
Single	$126,600	$128,950
Married Filing Jointly and Qualifying Widow(er)	$189,950	$193,400
Married Filing Separately	$94,975	$96,700
Head of Household	$158,300	$161,150

Table 1-3 • Income Phase-Out for Personal Exemptions Deduction

Itemized Deduction Limitation

Taxpayers who make more than $128,950, or $64,475 if Married Filing Separately, will not be able to use the full amount of their itemized deductions. If your adjusted gross income is greater than the above amount, your itemized deductions will be reduced by the smaller of:

(a) 3 percent of the amount by which your adjusted gross income exceeds $128,950 (or $64,475)

or

(b) 80 percent of your itemized deductions, not including medical expenses, investment interest, casualty and theft losses, and gambling losses

For example, if your adjusted gross income is $140,000 and your itemized deductions, all of which are subject to the 80 percent test, total $17,000, your deductions will be reduced by the smaller of:

(a) 3 percent of ($140,000 − $128,950) = $332

or

(b) 80 percent of $17,000 = $13,600

In this situation, you will be allowed to deduct $17,000 − $332 or $16,668 of your itemized deductions.

The remainder of unused itemized deductions does not get carried over to future returns—it is lost forever.

In 1999, the itemized deduction limit was based on adjusted gross income that exceeded $126,600 (or $63,300), so this change represents an increase in allowable itemized deductions of as much as $70 (3 percent of the difference between $128,950 and $126,600) for higher income taxpayers. In the 36 percent tax bracket, this would translate into a potential tax saving of $25. As you can see, this does not represent a great change on the tax returns of taxpayers in this income bracket.

Social Security Threshold Changes

Once again the ceiling has been raised on how much a person can earn and still have Social Security tax extracted from his income. In 1999, the most income on which Social Security tax could be charged was $72,600. For 2000, the amount has increased to $76,200. With the Social Security tax rate at 6.2 percent, this means that taxpayers with income over $76,200 will pay an additional $223 in Social Security tax. Self-employed individuals at this income level will pay twice that amount.

Changes for the Self-Employed

Self-employed taxpayers who pay for their own health insurance (and aren't eligible to be covered at a place of employment or at their spouse's place of employment) may deduct 60 percent of their health insurance premiums as an adjustment on page 1 of the tax return. The remaining 40 percent may be combined with other medical expenses if you qualify for an itemized deduction for medical expense, otherwise the other 40 percent of health insurance premiums does not get deducted.

This 60 percent rule hasn't changed since 1999, but I mention it here because it is an area to watch. Present law has the self-employed health insurance adjustment remaining at 60 percent through 2001, then increasing to 70 percent in 2002 and 100 percent in 2003 and thereafter.

Congress has attempted to pass measures to speed up this timetable and let self-employed taxpayers take an adjustment for the full 100 percent of health insurance premiums sooner than 2003. So far these attempts have failed (and if they wait much longer the issue will be moot, since the 100 percent deduction will be allowed in three years anyway), but if you are a small business owner, you may want to pay attention to the attitude of the 2001–2002 Congress toward this legislation.

For more information about taking a deduction for health insurance premiums if you're self-employed, see the section "Income from Your Own Business" in Chapter 5.

Changes for Investors in Retirement Funds

One of the last issues to be debated in Congress in the fall of 2000 was the issue of increasing the amount of allowable income that may be deferred from taxation if it is invested in a retirement fund. The House passed a measure earlier in the year authorizing an increase from $2,000 to $5,000 for allowable annual contributions to IRAs, and an increase from $10,500 to $15,000 for allowable annual contributions to 401(k) plans.

As this book went to press, the Senate was still wrestling with the wording on their version of a similar bill, and but there was some uncertainty about whether or not President Clinton would sign such a measure. A change in allowable retirement contributions, if passed, would probably be phased in over a ten-year period, beginning in 2001. An excellent place to look on the Internet for information about recent tax legislation is the CCH Web site at http://www.tax.cch.com/. Click the Legislative Highlights link to find information about tax laws that have passed recently.

Changes for College Students Paying Back Loans

Those of you who have attended or are attending college and who have incurred loans associated with paying for your education will be happy to know that the amount of student loan interest you can deduct as an adjustment on page 1 of your tax return in 2000 has increased from $1,500 to $2,000.

The income levels for taking this deduction, unfortunately, have not been changed, so you are out of luck in deducting your student loan interest if your adjusted gross income exceeds $40,000 ($60,000 if Married Filing Jointly).

More information is available about the adjustment for student loan interest in Chapter 6.

Changes for Parents

The child tax credit is not new in 2000, but I'm mentioning it here because it is one of the most beneficial and yet most overlooked credits on the federal tax return. The child tax credit is a credit, not a deduction, which directly reduces your federal income tax by $500 for every dependent child under age 17 in your family.

As with many good things in the tax rules, this credit is not available to taxpayers in the higher income brackets. Single taxpayers begin to lose the child tax credit when taxable income reaches $75,000. Married taxpayers filing joint returns lose sight of the credit when their income goes over $110,000, and Married Filing Separately taxpayers find the credit starts to disappear when income exceeds $55,000.

You don't have to worry about applying this credit, because TurboTax will take care of that for you as long as you enter the ages of your dependent children when you enter their names and other information. If TurboTax doesn't know the ages of the children, it can't determine whether you qualify for this credit.

If you prepared your own tax return without the help of TurboTax in 1998 or 1999 and you had children who were under age 17 and who were your dependents, and you failed to claim the child tax credit, you should consider amending your tax return(s). More information about amending tax returns is available in Chapter 16.

Changes for Landlords

It was determined in 1999 that appliances, carpets, and furniture used in rental property should be depreciated over five years instead of the seven years that had appeared in tax publications and guides prior to 1999. Rather than stating that landlords should begin depreciating such property over a five-year period, effective as of a certain date or retroactive to a certain date, the IRS took the position that the previous publications had simply been in error and taxpayers who wanted to go back and amend tax returns to change the depreciable life of their rental property assets could do so.

If you filed a tax return during the past three years in which you claimed a seven-year life for depreciation on these types of rental property assets, you may file a Form 1040X to amend your previous returns to reflect the proper depreciation life of five years on these assets.

If you prefer, you may leave the assets as they are, being depreciated over seven years, and depreciate similar assets over five years from this point forward. The decision is yours and should be based on such factors as how much you would actually save by amending the prior tax returns, how long it will take you to amend the returns, and whether you want to allow the IRS to scrutinize these earlier returns by calling attention to them (by filing an amended return you provide the IRS with additional time in which they can examine your tax return).

For additional information on depreciating rental property assets, see the section "Income from Rental Property" in Chapter 5. For more information on amending tax returns, see Chapter 16.

Assembling Your Tax Information Before You Begin

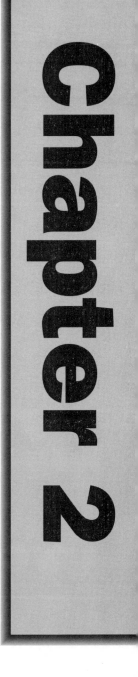

In This Chapter:

- *What Documents Show Evidence of Your Income*

- *What Documents Show Evidence of Your Expenses*

- *Organizing Your Information to Make Tax Time Easier*

S ome people begin preparation of their tax return with nothing more than a W-2 form in hand. Others start with a shopping bag full of receipts and documents, weeding and sorting as they go. You may fall into one of these categories, or you may be somewhere in between. The information in this chapter will guide you regarding the types of documents you will need to use in your tax return preparation, and will help you organize that information into some sort of useful order.

Documents That Identify Your Income

When you try to remember how much income you made last year, the first thing you probably think about is how much money you made at your job. For most people, income from employment is the single largest source of income. As far as your tax return is concerned, however, your job income may only be a starting point.

Income arrives in many mysterious forms, and Chapter 5 covers the proper way to report all types of income on your tax return. For now, your job is to collect and assemble all the proper documents that reflect the income you received during the year, so that the data entry part will be easy.

Tip   *One of the most important documents to have with you when you prepare your tax return is a copy of last year's tax return. Unless your lifestyle has changed drastically, you will find that if you follow along with last year's tax return, you will have an excellent guide for remembering all the information that you need to include with this year's return.*

W-2 Forms

You'll need to have all of your W-2 forms handy when you begin preparing your tax return. Every employer is required to provide employees with a W-2 form that summarizes the amount of income the employee earned during the year. Even if you only work for an employer for one day, the employer must provide you with a W-2 form.

The W-2 form, which is called Wage and Tax Statement, is sent to employees during the month of January. Employers are required to send or deliver all W-2 forms for the year 2000 by January 31, 2001. The IRS can penalize an employer who fails to perform this duty.

Not all W-2 forms look alike, and the one you receive may not look like the example shown in Figure 2-1, but somewhere on the form you receive from your employer you will see the heading: W-2 Wage and Tax Statement. You are required to attach a copy of each W-2 form you received to your federal and state tax return.

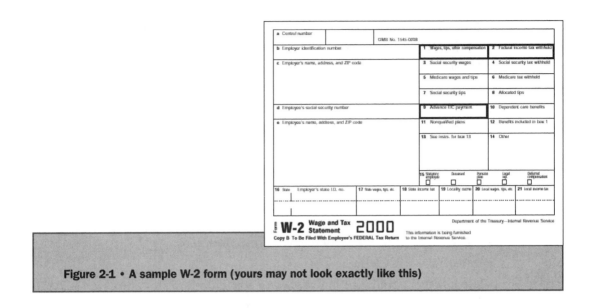

Figure 2-1 • A sample W-2 form (yours may not look exactly like this)

Repairing Damaged W-2 Forms

What happens if your W-2 form gets torn, or what if the ink gets smudged to a point where the form becomes illegible? What if the dog uses the form for a chew toy, or your child decides the boxes on the form would look nice colored with crayons?

Before you panic, keep in mind that the IRS already knows what information should appear on the W-2 form—your employer was required to send a copy of the company's W-2 forms to the Social Security Administration, and those folks at the SSA share information with the IRS. By attaching the form to your tax return you are simply providing a means of verifying the information that the IRS already has.

Somewhere on the W-2 form you will see the statement, "Copy B To Be Filed With Employee's FEDERAL Tax Return." The IRS doesn't care if it receives Copy B, Copy C, or Copy 2. If Copy B of the W-2 form is messy but can still be read, go ahead and attach the form to your return. If the Copy B is illegible but another copy of the form can be read, you can attach the Copy C (your copy), or one of the state copies (often the employer will provide you with an extra copy for the state). You can also make a photocopy of one of the other copies of your W-2 form and attach that to your federal tax return.

If the damage to your W-2 form is beyond repair, make your own W-2 form. Use a piece of paper and enter the following information, which is all the IRS really needs to see:

- Name, as it appears on the W-2 form
- Social Security number
- Employer name
- Wage information from Box 1
- Federal income tax information from Box 2
- Social Security wages from Box 3 (if different from Box 1)
- Social Security tax from Box 4
- State wages from Box 17 (if different from Box 1)
- State income tax from Box 18
- Local wages from Box 19 (if applicable and if different from Box 1)
- Local income tax from Box 21 (if applicable)

You can attach this statement to both your federal and state income tax returns in lieu of a W-2 form.

Replacing Lost W-2 Forms

If you lose your W-2 form, call the person responsible for payroll at the company where you work. The employer saves a copy of the form, and you can ask your employer to make a copy for you.

If your employer is unable or unwilling to make a copy for you, try asking over the phone for the information that appears on the form, and prepare a statement as described above.

Note   *Your employer is required to inform you of the information on your W-2 form. If your employer refuses to provide this information, you can contact the IRS at (800) 829-1040 and request that the IRS contact your employer on your behalf. Be prepared to provide the name, last known address, and phone number of the employer, as well as an estimate of your wages and withholdings from that employer and your dates of employment. The IRS will prepare and send Form 4598, Forms W-2, W-2P or 1099 Not Received or Incorrect, to the employer, requesting that your W-2 be sent to you.*

If your employer is out of business or for some reason cannot be reached, create a statement like the one described above, or download Form 4852, Substitute for Form W-2, Wage and Tax Statement, from the IRS at http://www.irs.gov/, using your best available information, such as information from a pay stub or from your deposit records.

Changing an Incorrect W-2 Form

Be sure to examine your W-2 form carefully. Occasionally the information on a W-2 is incorrect. In addition to checking all the numbers for accuracy (your final pay stub for the year is the best basis for comparison), check to make sure that it is your name that appears on the form, and that your Social Security number has been entered correctly.

If the Social Security number on your W-2 form is incorrect, it will be extremely difficult for the IRS to match your income with your tax return. This may seem like a good opportunity to avoid paying tax on some of your income. After all, the income is assigned to someone else's Social Security number, so the IRS can't trace it to you, right? Keep in mind the fact that it is *your responsibility* to report all of your income properly, and failure to do so can result in interest and penalties and even prosecution if it can be proven that you intentionally attempted to defraud the government. If there is an error in the Social Security number on your W-2 form, contact your employer immediately and ask that a corrected W-2 form (Form W-2c) be prepared and filed on your behalf.

Requesting a W-2 Form Before the End of the Year

If you leave your job and have no reason to believe you will be rehired, you don't have to wait until the next January to receive your W-2 form. If you submit a request in writing, your employer is required to provide you with your W-2 form within 30 days of the request.

W-2G Forms

There's another type of W-2 form that you might have received: the W-2G form. The "G" stands for "Gambling" and you should receive this form if you won more than $600 at one time from gambling. The W-2G may reflect tax withholding on your gambling winnings and because of this you will attach this form to your income tax return.

See Chapter 5 for information about requirements for reporting the income and offsetting losses from gambling.

1099 Forms

Even though most 1099 forms don't get attached to your tax return (there are exceptions, as noted below), you must gather up all of these forms and have them available when you begin preparing your tax return.

Income that you received during 2000 that was not reported to you on W-2 forms may be reported on 1099 forms. These 1099 forms reflect interest and dividend income, royalty payments, sales of homes and securities, proceeds from a retirement account, prizes, compensation for services, and more. Many 1099 forms look like the one shown in Figure 2-2; others take on the form of statements from banks or brokers, as described later in this chapter.

In most cases, the 1099 form will provide information about income you received but will not include information about tax withholding. The 1099 form is provided for your information. Occasionally there will be tax withholding reflected on a 1099 form. If your 1099 form shows federal or state tax withholding, the form must be attached to your income tax return.

When Is a 1099 Form Required?

Sometimes you will receive income during the year but will not receive a 1099 form. Not receiving the form does not alleviate your responsibility for reporting the income. It's possible that the person or organization paying you is not required to prepare a 1099 form. Table 2-1 shows when a 1099 form is required.

Type of Income	Threshold for 1099 Form
Interest	$10
Original issue discount	$10
Dividend	$10
Rent	$600
Royalties	$10
Non-employee compensation	$600
Substitute payments	$10
Sales of securities	All sales must be reported
Tax refunds, unemployment compensation	$10
Retirement proceeds	$10

Table 2-1 • Income Earned Over These Amounts Requires the Issuance of a 1099 Form

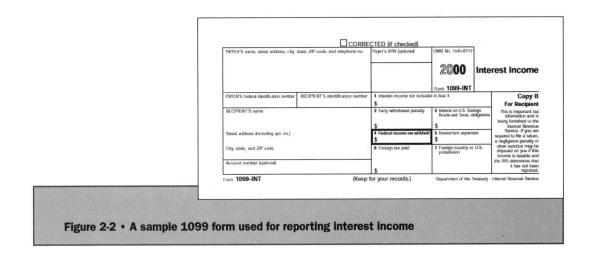

Figure 2-2 • A sample 1099 form used for reporting interest income

Although most 1099 forms do not get attached to your tax return, it is important to save these forms as evidence of the income you are reporting on your tax return. Chapter 18 discusses procedures for saving records and the length of time it is necessary to hold on to tax-related documents.

Bank Statements

A bank statement is a good place to look for a report of interest you earned on your savings. Banks will often forego issuing standard 1099 forms, like the one shown in Figure 2-2, because the information you need is right on the year-end bank statement.

Examine your statement from December 31, or the first statement you receive from your bank in January, to see if there is any interest income reported on the statement.

Caution   *If your savings are in a credit union account, the earnings on your money will probably be described as "dividends" on your year-end statement. Don't confuse this type of income with dividend income, which is described below. Earnings on a savings account, including an account held at a credit union, represent interest income.*

Keep the bank statement that shows your year-end interest income with your tax return documents.

Interest Expense on a Bank Statement

Some bank statements display interest expense that you paid on a loan from the bank. This information may be required for your tax return. Loans that represent funds borrowed for investment or for business purposes generate interest expense that may be deductible. Most other interest expense is not deductible. Keep these statements with your tax records as well.

Save Your Bank Statements

Your bank statements display all of the cash transactions that passed through your bank account during the year. The monthly bank statements may be an excellent source of documentation for your tax return, lending support to your claims of income you earned during the year.

Broker Statements

If you have an account with a broker, you will receive a year-end statement from the broker showing not only the past month's transactions, but also the information required for your tax return for the entire year.

The broker's statement may include such information as sales of securities, margin account interest expense, dividends earned, interest earned, and other distributions. Although the broker report typically does not get attached to your tax return, the information presented on this report will be used in the preparation of your tax return.

Tip   *Receipts and documentation describing your income and expenses aren't the only things required for successful tax preparation. You should gather the necessary tools so that when you actually sit down to prepare your return you will have everything you need. Tools you will want to have handy include: pencil and paper (in case you want to make some notes), stapler, calculator (for checking math on your handwritten statements), stamps and some big envelopes (if you're going to mail your tax return), file folders (for setting up a system for next year—see Chapter 18).*

Documents That Identify Your Expenses

Perhaps even more important than having the paper documents that support your claims of income is the need to have documentation supporting your expense deductions. Somehow the IRS always figures out how much income you should have reported, even if you forget to mention something. But the IRS isn't going to

help you figure out your deductions, nor will they take your word for it if you
don't have documentary support to back up your claims. Here's a rundown of the
types of receipts and other documents that will help substantiate the deductions
you take on your tax return.

Mortgage Statement

If you are a homeowner, you will want to include the final year-end statement
from your mortgage company with your tax documentation. This statement will
show the amount of interest you paid on your mortgage, and may show the real
estate taxes you paid as well. If a portion of your home is deductible as a home
office (see Chapter 5), you may find that the hazard insurance you pay on your
home, which should appear on this form, is deductible as well.

The year-end mortgage statement you receive is called Form 1098, and this
designation should appear somewhere on the form.

Check Register

If you want to demonstrate all the ways in which you spent money, the register in
your checkbook is one way you can put your paperwork where your mouth is.
Throughout the year, you enter all of your bank transactions in this little register
(you *are* diligent about making these entries, aren't you?). On the lines of your
check register, you indicate every check you write and every deposit you make.

The check register is an excellent resource for documenting your tax-related
expenses. Use a coding system (I use a red pen to check off transactions that are tax-
deductible) to keep track of which expenditures might qualify as tax deductions.

Which Items Should You Mark?   You can check off every item in your checking
register that might be tax-deductible, even if you're not sure you'll get to take the
deduction. For example, sometimes you won't know until the end of the year if
your medical expenses will amount to enough to qualify for a deduction. By marking
each medical expenditure, you can quickly summarize your medical expenses at the
end of the year to see if they add up to enough for a deduction. (Chapter 7 provides
more detail about the allowable deductions for medical expenses.)

This list is not exhaustive nor does it provide you with detail about individual
types of deductions, but it will give you a general idea of the common types of tax-
deductible items to mark in your check register:

- Expenses of moving to a new residence
- Medical expenses

- Student loan payments
- College tuition payments
- Retirement contributions
- Property taxes
- Income taxes
- Loan payments on money borrowed for investments
- Charitable contributions
- Business meals
- Expenses related to your job

Saving Cancelled Checks   If you don't have a corresponding receipt to provide documentation for a deductible expense, your cancelled check is the next best piece of evidence. Each month, when you reconcile your bank account, you can collect the cancelled check for each item you marked in your register and for which you don't have another receipt. You can wait until the end of the year to perform this task as well, but it may not seem so overwhelming if you save the checks on a monthly basis.

Saving Purchase Receipts

Telling the IRS to take your word for it that you made a deductible expenditure is not nearly as convincing as being able to hand them a paper receipt. The best kind of receipt includes the following information:

- Name and telephone number of the organization or person making the sale.
- Your name.
- The date of the transaction.
- A description of what the expenditure was for.
- The amount of the item.
- Some evidence that payment was made. This evidence can be a check number, a description of a credit card that was used, or the words "Paid in Full" stamped on the document with the date on which payment was made.

The more information that appears on the document, the more useful the document will be as evidence of a purchase having been made.

Often the purchase receipt or statement doesn't actually indicate that a payment has been made—for example, you may receive a bill in the mail from your doctor, but the bill doesn't indicate that you've made a payment. The statement is excellent evidence of the existence of the expense, but you should still hang on to your cancelled check so you have a way to prove that you actually made the payment.

You may be wondering, how much documentation is enough? Do you need to hang on to every little scrap of paper? Here are some general guidelines about the types of receipts and statements that constitute good and reliable evidence:

- **The original bill** for a service, such as a bill from your doctor, which describes the service performed and the date on which the service was performed.
- **A cash register receipt** for a purchase. Particularly desirable are receipts that include a description of the items purchased
- **A print-out** of a computer screen describing a purchase made online.
- **A price tag** from an article you purchased, such as the tag from an article of clothing.
- **The outer wrapper** from an item you purchased, such as the wrapper from a box of computer software, if there is a price evident on the wrapper.
- **A handwritten receipt** for a purchase. A signature of the seller or the printed name of the store on the receipt will give the receipt more weight.

You don't need to save more than one piece of evidence to substantiate a single purchase. For example, if you receive a descriptive bill from your doctor for medical services, and later receive a monthly statement for the same services, you don't need to save the monthly statement for your tax records in addition to the original bill.

Saving Credit Card Statements

Your monthly credit card statement is yet another form of evidence supporting payments that you have made. If you examine each of your credit card statements during the year, you may discover there are some expenses that will qualify as tax deductions.

Highlight the descriptions of purchases that are tax-deductible, and use the credit card statements just as you would cancelled checks, to demonstrate that you actually made a purchase for which you have a receipt.

If you use a debit card, your monthly bank statement may double as your credit card statement.

Receipts for Charitable Donations

I've assigned a special category for describing the rules for saving receipts for your charitable donations because the IRS has established special rules for these receipts. To find out if a contribution you make qualifies for a deduction, see the section "Charitable Contributions" in Chapter 7.

The rules for collecting receipts to support your deduction differ if your contribution is cash or if it is some form of property, and there are different rules depending on the value of the contribution.

Recordkeeping Rules for Cash Contributions

A cash contribution is a contribution that is made in any of the following ways:

- Cash
- Check
- Credit card
- Payroll deduction

There are separate rules depending on whether your contribution is less than $250 or if it is $250 or more.

Cash Contribution of Less Than $250   When the cash contribution you make is less than $250, you are required to keep one of the following pieces of evidence:

- Evidence of your contribution, which can include a cancelled check, a credit card statement, or a payroll voucher or stub supporting a payroll deduction. If you don't have any of these documents, you can simply write down the following information and keep it with your tax records:
  - For checks, write down the check number, amount of contribution, date the check cleared your account, and the organization to whom you made the contribution.
  - For credit card transactions, write down the amount of the contribution, the date of the transaction, and the organization to whom you made the contribution.
  - For payroll deductions, write down the amount of the deduction or the total amount deducted for the year, the date(s) on which the deduction was made, and the organization to whom you made the contribution.

- A letter or other document prepared by the charitable organization, stating the name of the organization, the date of the contribution, and the amount of the contribution.
- Other evidence of the contribution. This option is somewhat open to your discretion and can include such items as flyers, buttons, T-shirts, or other memorabilia handed out by the organization. You should also prepare a written memorandum that states the name of the organization, the date of the contribution, and the amount you contributed.

None of the above forms of evidence is required to be attached to your tax return. All of this information should be kept with your tax records for the year in which you made the contribution.

Cash Contributions of $250 or More   The rules get a bit stricter if your contribution is $250 or more. In order to claim a deduction for a cash contribution of $250 or more, you are required to obtain a written document from the charitable organization stating the amount of the contribution, as well as:

- A description of any goods or benefits you received in exchange for the contribution and an estimate of the value of those goods or services

or

- A statement to the effect that you did not receive any goods or services in exchange for the contribution

You are required to obtain this document on or before the earlier of the date on which you file your tax return or the due date (including extensions) of your tax return. In other words, you are not to wait to see if, three years down the road, your tax return is audited by the IRS before you attempt to obtain this document.

Recordkeeping Rules for Non-Cash Contributions

A non-cash contribution is a contribution of tangible property. This description can encompass nearly anything, but frequent types of non-cash contributions include:

- Clothing
- Household goods
- Books
- Computers and other electronic equipment
- Athletic equipment

For a more detailed list of the types of items that you can turn into tax-deductible contributions, along with a valuation for determining the amount of tax deduction you can take for these items, see "Non-Cash Charitable Contributions: Valuation Guide" in Appendix B.

The rules for collecting receipts to support your deduction for non-cash contributions vary depending on whether the contribution is valued at less than $250, less than $500, less than $5,000, or more than $5,000.

Non-Cash Contributions of Less Than $250   For non-cash contributions that are valued at less than $250, you are required to attempt to get a receipt from the organization to which you made the donation. The receipt should contain the name and location of the organization, the date of the donation, and, if possible, a description of the property donated.

The IRS understands that it might be impractical to get a receipt if the donation is made at a drop box or some other unattended facility.

Whether you have a receipt from the organization or not, you are also required to prepare a statement describing the item(s) donated. This document should contain the following information:

- The name and address of the organization to which the donation was made
- The date on which the donation was made
- The location at which the donation was delivered
- A detailed description of the donated item(s)
- An amount signifying the fair market value of the item(s) donated on the date of the donation
- The original cost or other basis of the item(s) donated
- The amount of the deduction you are claiming
- A description of any items or services you received in exchange for your donation
- A description of the terms of any conditions you may have attached as a requirement of the donation

This information stays with your tax records and does not get attached to your income tax return.

Non-Cash Contributions Valued Between $250 and $500   The rules for keeping documentation to support a non-cash contribution that exceeds $250 but is less than $500 are the same as those for the under-$250 donations with one notable exception: you are *required* to have a receipt or other statement from the organization to which you made the donation. This requirement is not optional for a donation in this range.

Note　*Multiple donations during the year to the same organization that are individually valued at under $250 but that cumulatively fall into the $250 to $500 range are not considered by the IRS to be donations of over $250. Each donation is considered individually.*

The receipt that you obtain from the charitable organization must be in your possession on or before the earlier of the date on which you file your tax return or the due date, plus extensions, of your tax return.

Non-Cash Contributions Valued Between $500 and $5,000　The receipt or statement that you are required to obtain for a non-cash contribution of $500 to $5,000 is the same as for a $250 to $500 contribution. The difference with a contribution in this range is in the area of information you need to generate yourself about the item(s) donated.

In addition to keeping a description of the item(s) donated, including the date and location of the donation and the value of the donation, you are also required to keep the following information:

- Date(s) on which the item(s) was (were) acquired
- The method by which the item(s) was (were) acquired (purchase, gift, and so on)
- How you determined the value of the donated item(s) (appraisal, thrift shop value, catalog value, comparable sales, and so on)

You are required to include this detailed information about these contributions on your income tax return.

Non-Cash Contributions of More Than $5,000　In additional to the types of documentary evidence supporting non-cash contributions that have been described previously, a contribution valued at more than $5,000 requires a signed appraisal that will accompany the tax return.

Note　*The fee you pay for an appraisal is considered to be a deductible expense; however, it does not increase the value of the charitable deduction. Instead, the fee is a miscellaneous deduction on Schedule A of your tax return. See Chapter 7 for more information about miscellaneous deductions.*

Organizing Your Tax Documents

The information presented in this chapter should give you all the information you need for assembling the paperwork necessary to supporting income and expenses you report on your tax return. To aid in the return preparation process, you can organize your receipts in the following order. Naturally, the more receipts you have, the more important this kind of organization becomes.

Order of Income Documents

You may not have all of these types of documents (most people don't), but you can use this list to organize the documents you do have. The order of documents in this list correlates with the order in which TurboTax will provide you with input screens for entering the information from these forms:

- W-2 forms
- 1099-INT forms for interest
- Bank statements
- 1099-DIV forms for dividends
- Broker statements
- 1099-MISC forms for non-employee compensation
- 1099-MISC forms for rents and royalties
- Schedules K-1 from partnerships, trusts, and S-corporations
- 1099-G forms showing state tax refunds or unemployment compensation received
- SSA-1099 forms for Social Security income
- 1099-R forms for retirement income
- 1099-MISC and W-2G forms for prizes and gambling and other non-categorized income

Order of Expense Documents

Keep in mind that some of these documents and receipts may not result in deductions on your tax return. Chapter 7 provides extensive detail about the types of items that you can deduct. Meanwhile, you can use this list to help organize the receipts you have:

- Year-end mortgage statement
- Check register
- Cancelled checks where that is the best evidence of a deduction
- Receipts from (potentially) deductible purchases
- Credit card statements
- Receipts for charitable contributions

Most of these documents will not actually get attached to your income tax return, but it will be necessary for you to save this documentation with your return (see Chapter 18).

Tax Scenarios

In This Chapter:

- *Scenarios for Single Taxpayers*

- *Scenarios for Married Taxpayers*

- *Scenarios for Taxpayers with Children*

- *Scenarios for Business Owners*

- *Scenarios for Elderly Taxpayers*

There are many aspects of tax preparation that are the same no matter what type of taxpayer you are. For example, everyone has to provide name and address information and sign the tax return. Everyone needs to report income earned throughout the year. Remarkably, the list of similarities pretty much ends there. The types of adjustments, deductions, exemptions, and credits that can be claimed, and the type and amount of tax that is owed, varies from one type of taxpayer to another, and the changes are based on such factors as marital status, parental status, employment status, age, and income level.

Scenarios for Single Taxpayers

Single taxpayers face a particular set of tax rules that will affect some of the decisions made in the tax planning process. A single taxpayer should be familiar with the unique tax rules that apply to this status and take advantage of that knowledge during the course of the year.

Tax Brackets for Single Taxpayers

The amount of income tax that you, as a single taxpayer, will be required to pay is based on the amount of money you earn. Tax rates are graduated, meaning they increase as your income level increases. You should be aware of the rate of income tax you will have to pay and the income level cut-offs for changes in the tax rate.

For example, suppose you earn $25,000 during the year and you are contemplating making a charitable contribution that will be large enough to enable you to itemize your deductions. At your level of income, your income is taxed at 15 percent, so your deductions generate a 15 percent tax saving. A contribution of $3,000 will provide $450 in tax relief. But wait! You're about to change jobs and increase your pay—next year you expect your income to be over $40,000. At the new level of income, your income tax rate jumps to 28 percent. If you wait until after the first of the year to make your contribution, you will see a tax saving of $840. Look at all the money you will save by waiting to make your contribution!

The federal income tax for a single taxpayer is calculated as follows:

- The first $26,250 of taxable income is taxed at 15 percent. This is true no matter how much you make.
- Your taxable income over $26,250 is taxed at 28 percent until your income reaches $63,550.

- Your taxable income over $63,550 is taxed at 31 percent until your income reaches $132,600.

- Your taxable income over $132,600 is taxed at 36 percent until your income reaches $288,350.

- All of your taxable income over $288,350 is taxed at 39.6 percent.

These rates apply to income earned in 2000. Tax rates have been decreasing in recent years. The cut-off levels change each year, typically increasing, meaning the lower tax rates apply to a greater amount of income each year and thus overall federal tax rates are slightly lower each year.

From a TurboTax standpoint, you don't have to know these rates for purposes of preparing your income tax return, because TurboTax will calculate your tax for you. As you can see, however, in the previous example, it makes sense to know the rates yourself so you can make intelligent decisions based on the rate of tax you pay.

Exemptions

Most taxpayers are entitled to claim one exemption apiece and one for each of their dependents. If you are elderly (over age 65) the rules for exemptions change and you should see the scenarios for elderly taxpayers described later in this chapter. If you have dependents, see the scenarios for taxpayers with children later in this chapter.

Sometimes single taxpayers, especially young taxpayers such as college students, can be claimed as an exemption by someone else. For example, you may live on your own at school, but your parents may still be paying your bills and supporting you.

If you can be claimed as an exemption on someone else's tax return you are not entitled to claim your own exemption. Therefore if your parents claim you on their tax return, or if another relative is caring for you and claims your exemption, you may not take your own exemption. If you are living with someone, even if that person is not a relative, and you can be claimed as a dependent on that person's tax return, you may not claim your own exemption.

Note that the rule states that you cannot claim your own exemption if you *can be* claimed as a dependent on someone else's tax return. Even if the person entitled to your exemption doesn't claim you, you cannot claim your own exemption because you are not entitled to it.

When preparing your tax return in TurboTax, you will be asked if you can be claimed as a dependent on someone else's tax return (Figure 3-1).

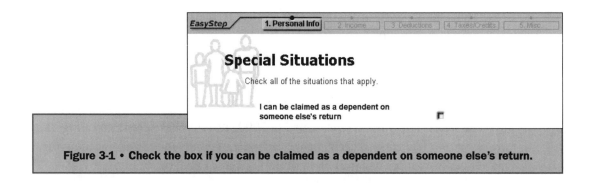

Figure 3-1 • Check the box if you can be claimed as a dependent on someone else's return.

If you missed this question in TurboTax and need to find the part of the tax return where you enter this exemption information, click the Personal Info option on the Progress Bar at the top of your screen. When the EasyStep Navigator appears, click the Special Situations option under the heading, About You and Your Family. The screen that opens will include the check box about being claimed as a dependent on someone else's return.

When Can You Claim Someone as a Dependent?

We often think of dependents in terms of babies and small children who are living at home. But there are other situations where someone can be considered a dependent. The basic rules state that, to be a dependent, a person must meet five tests:

- The gross income test: The dependent cannot have more than $2,700 in income for the year. (Exception: This rule can be ignored if the dependent is your child and is under 19 years of age by the close of the year or, if the child is a full-time student, under 24 years old by the end of the year.)

- The support test: You must pay for at least one half of the living expenses of the dependent during the year. Living expenses include food, lodging, medical bills, vacations, clothes, books, and so on. (Exception: In situations where two or more people share the support of a dependent, or where one person agrees to give up the dependency exemption to another as in the case of a divorce where the supporting parent lets the non-supporting parent claim the exemption, this rule can be overridden.)

- The relationship or member of the household test: The dependent must be a lineal descendant (child, grandchild, great-grandchild, stepchild, adopted child), a sibling (including step-siblings), or a lineal ancestor (parent, grandparent, great-grandparent, including step-ancestors), niece, nephew, aunt, uncle, in-law. Also included in this relationship group is anyone else, related or not, who lived in your home for the entire year, other than your spouse.

- The joint return test: You cannot claim a person as a dependent if that person is filing a joint return with someone else.
- The citizenship test: A dependent must be a U.S. citizen, a national, a resident of North America, or an alien child whom you have adopted and who lived with you for the entire year.

Typical Deductions

Single taxpayers have the same potential for deducting items on their tax returns that other taxpayers face, but there are certain reductions to income that seem to occur more frequently among single taxpayers than among their married counterparts. Here are some deductions beyond the typical deductions (such as mortgage interest and state income taxes) to consider if you are single. Check the index for the area of the book that covers these deductions and adjustments in more depth.

- **Moving expenses.** Many people move, but single people often find themselves more mobile and are often likely to change geographic locations several times during their careers. A move that is related to employment can generate an adjustment to income and as a result can reduce income tax.
- **College loan interest expense.** Single people who are paying off loans for college expenses may be able to take an income adjustment for the interest on these loans.
- **Alimony.** Single taxpayers who were once married may find themselves paying alimony to a former spouse. Alimony reduces the income of the person making the payments and at the same time increases the income of the recipient.
- **Employee business expenses.** Job-related expenses that aren't reimbursed by your employer can turn into deductions for those who have enough deductions to itemize.

Additional Taxes

There may not be much in the way of tax expense that the single taxpayer will incur and the married taxpayer will not, but one possible exception to this rule is the self-employment tax. Married people are sometimes less likely to venture in the direction of self-employment—maybe the risk seems too great when there are two or more people to support in a family. In any case, it seems that more single than married people experiment with self-employment and as a result face the self-employment tax.

Self-employment tax is actually Social Security and Medicare tax in disguise. The problem with self-employment tax is that there is no employer to pick up half of the tax bill, as there is when you are employed. So self-employed people must pay twice the amount of Social Security and Medicare as their employed counterparts. This tax is hefty and often a surprise to the newly self-employed person.

Available Credits

Credits available to the single person include the foreign tax credit for taxes paid to another country (most often occurs on foreign investments), and the new education credits (lifetime learning credit and Hope Scholarship credit).

The child tax credit is available to taxpayers who have or are caring for children, and the adoption credit is available to taxpayers who adopt a child. If you are single and have a child or children, you may qualify for the Head of Household tax status, which will provide you with lower tax rates. See Chapter 4 for details about which filing status applies to you.

National Averages

The latest statistics published by the IRS are for 1997 tax returns. For single taxpayers, Table 3-1 shows the percentage of tax returns reporting income in various ranges.

1997 Taxable Income	Percent of Single Taxpayers
$1 to $20,000	63%
$20,000 to $40,000	25%
$40,000 to $50,000	5%
$50,000 to $75,000	5%
$75,000 to $100,000	1%
Over $100,000	1%

Table 3-1 • Average Income for Single Taxpayers

Scenarios for Married Taxpayers

There is a special tax rate that applies to married taxpayers, and there are rules that apply only to married taxpayers. Congress has been attempting to change some of the tax rules that apply to married taxpayers, but for the year 2000 there is no change, other than a slight change over last year in the tax brackets.

Tax Brackets

As described in the single taxpayer section, taxes are computed based on marginal tax rates. The more you make, the higher your tax, but the tax builds, so that, for example, in 2000, the first $43,850 a married couple filing jointly earns is always taxed at the lowest tax rate (15 percent), the next $62,100 the couple earns is taxed at 28 percent, and so on. The tax brackets vary depending on whether you are married and filing a joint tax return or married and filing separate tax returns.

The federal income tax for the year 2000 for married taxpayers filing a joint tax return is calculated as follows:

- The first $43,850 of taxable income is taxed at 15 percent. This is true no matter how much you make.
- Your taxable income over $43,850 is taxed at 28 percent until your income reaches $105,950.
- Your taxable income over $105,950 is taxed at 31 percent until your income reaches $161,450.
- Your taxable income over $161,450 is taxed at 36 percent until your income reaches $288,350.
- All of your taxable income over $288,350 is taxed at 39.6 percent.

The federal income tax for the year 2000 for married taxpayers filing a separate tax return is calculated as follows:

- The first $21,925 of taxable income is taxed at 15 percent. This is true no matter how much you make.
- Your taxable income over $21,925 is taxed at 28 percent until your income reaches $52,975.
- Your taxable income over $52,975 is taxed at 31 percent until your income reaches $80,725.

- Your taxable income over $80,725 is taxed at 36 percent until your income reaches $144,175.
- All of your taxable income over $144,175 is taxed at 39.6 percent.

As mentioned in the single taxpayer section, from a TurboTax standpoint, you don't have to know these rates for purposes of preparing your income tax return, because TurboTax will calculate your tax for you.

What Is the Marriage Tax Penalty?

You've probably heard the phrase, marriage tax penalty, and you may recall there was much hoopla in Congress during 2000 when senators and representatives attempted to do away with this tax nightmare, but just what is the marriage penalty? The term "marriage penalty" refers to the extra tax burden that is placed on married couples where both spouses earn income that is subject to tax.

If only one spouse works, there is typically no marriage penalty, and in fact there is frequently a tax benefit over a pair of single taxpayers where only one works.

When both spouses in a married couple work, the marginal tax rates work to the disadvantage of the couple. Referring to the previous section for taxes in a married filing jointly situation, the first spouse is taxed at the lowest rate, with all income up to $43,850 being taxed at 15 percent. Any income over that amount, including all income of the second spouse if the combined income exceeds $43,850, is taxed at 28 percent or higher—almost double the tax on the first spouse's income!

If the spouses filed their tax returns as two single individuals, each spouse would be taxed on the first $26,250 at 15 percent, so when you combine the income of the spouses, up to $52,500 is taxed at 15 percent instead of just the first $43,850.

Many members of Congress have tried to change this tax so that the rate is the same no matter what the marital status. So far, attempts to change this rule have been unsuccessful.

Exemptions

When a married couple files a joint return, one exemption is claimed for each spouse, so there are at least two exemptions claimed on the tax return.

Typically, married people who file separately each claim their own exemption. The situation can arise, however, in which one spouse supports both members of the couple, even though they are living separately, in which case the spouse providing the support would claim both exemptions.

Typical Deductions

Although there are many deductions that apply to all taxpayers, and many deductions that most people never qualify for, there are a few deductions that seem to apply more frequently to married couples than to other taxpayers. Check the index for the area of the book that covers these deductions and adjustments in more depth.

- **Mortgage interest expense.** Of course many single taxpayers own homes, and many married people do not, but statistics show that married taxpayers are the most likely homeowners. That means the potential exists for deductions for mortgage interest expense and…
- **Property tax.** The property tax deduction goes hand in hand with the mortgage interest expense deduction.
- **Charitable contributions.** Married couples sometimes find themselves with a bit of disposable income, especially if both spouses work. Where there is extra income, sometimes there is an opportunity for making donations.

Additional Taxes

Spend a little time with a tax-savvy married person and you'll probably get an earful about the additional taxes that affect married people. The marriage penalty, discussed earlier in this chapter, affects nearly every married couple in which both spouses have income. At present there is no way to control or bypass this higher tax rate.

Another tax that is creeping onto the tax return landscape is the alternative minimum tax. This tax was designed to make sure taxpayers who receive beneficial tax treatment on some of their income and deductions still pay what the government feels is their fair tax rate. Taxpayers affected by this tax (and TurboTax will compute the tax automatically if it applies to you) may find that the alternative minimum tax not only increases the amount of income tax that must be paid, but the tax may have the effect of diminishing the benefit of tax credits to which you are otherwise entitled. Congress has been studying this side effect of the alternative minimum tax with the intent of minimizing the negative impact on tax credits.

Available Credits

Married taxpayers may find they can take advantage of various tax credits that will reduce the amount of tax that has been computed on taxable income. The following credits may be available to you. Check the index of this book for detailed information about these credits.

- Adoption credit
- Child tax credit
- Education credits (lifetime learning and Hope Scholarship)
- Foreign tax credit
- Credit for prior year minimum tax

National Averages

The latest statistics published by the IRS are for 1997 tax returns. For married taxpayers, Tables 3-2 and 3-3 show the percentage of tax returns reporting income in various ranges.

1997 Taxable Income	Percent of Joint Filers
$1 to $20,000	17%
$20,000 to $40,000	25%
$40,000 to $50,000	12%
$50,000 to $75,000	24%
$75,000 to $100,000	11%
Over $100,000	11%

Table 3-2 • Average Income for Married Taxpayers Filing Jointly

1997 Taxable Income	Percent of Separate Filers
$1 to $20,000	44%
$20,000 to $40,000	39%
$40,000 to $50,000	8%
$50,000 to $75,000	7%
$75,000 to $100,000	1%
Over $100,000	1%

Table 3-3 • Average Income for Married Taxpayers Filing Separately

Scenarios for Taxpayers with Children

Taxpayers with children can qualify for special tax benefits. There are exemptions, deductions, and credits that have been added to the tax laws specifically to benefit parents who care for children. Your tax filing status (single, married filing jointly, and so on) doesn't determine whether you have children, but it is possible that the existence of children in your life may have an effect on what filing status you use.

Single and married filing separately taxpayers have the option of using the Head of Household filing status. This filing status provides lower tax rates to those who qualify.

Tax Brackets for Head of Household

Whether or not you have children, if you file as a single or married taxpayer, the tax brackets stay the same as those used by your childless counterparts. There is one additional tax status available to certain taxpayers and that is the Head of Household status. To use the Head of Household status, you must meet these requirements:

- You must be unmarried as of the last day of the year. Being unmarried doesn't necessarily mean you must be single. Separated spouses may qualify as unmarried if their separation is recognized by state law under a divorce or separate maintenance decree.
- You paid more than half the cost of keeping up your home during the past year.
- A qualifying person must live with you in your home for more than half the year. Generally speaking, qualified people include lineal relatives. Typically, you must be entitled to claim an exemption for the person who qualifies you for the credit.

As mentioned, the tax rates for Head of Household taxpayers are a bit lower than those for single taxpayers.

The federal income tax for a Head of Household taxpayer is calculated as follows:

- The first $35,150 of taxable income is taxed at 15 percent. This is true no matter how much you make.
- Your taxable income over $35,150 is taxed at 28 percent until your income reaches $90,800.

- Your taxable income over $90,800 is taxed at 31 percent until your income reaches $147,050.
- Your taxable income over $147,050 is taxed at 36 percent until your income reaches $288,350.
- All of your taxable income over $288,350 is taxed at 39.6 percent.

Exemptions

Taxpayers with children are entitled to not only their own exemptions, but these taxpayers also qualify for an exemption for each child claimed as a dependent.

TurboTax will make this determination when you enter the dependent information for your children.

Typical Deductions

Certain deductions seem to crop up frequently for taxpayers with children. These can include:

- **Student loan interest.** Parents with children in college, or parents with children who have recently completed college, may be paying off student loans and may thus qualify for the adjustment for student loan interest.
- **Medical expenses.** If there are children in the house, there are more people who can require medical attention; there may be orthodontic expenses, eye care, broken limbs, and many other kinds of unexpected medical events that can lead to deductions for medical expenses. The deduction for medical expenses is limited to the amount of expenses that exceed 7.5 percent of your adjusted gross income, so many people without an extraordinary amount of expenses will not qualify for this deduction.
- **Charitable contributions.** Families with children are families with outgrown clothes, and these clothes are a prime source of charitable contributions for those who itemize their deductions.

Available Credits

There are some specific credits that relate to families with children, and the sentiment in Congress these days is to continue to offer credits in this area. If you are a taxpayer with children, you may be able to reduce your tax substantially by taking advantage of some of these credits.

- **The earned income credit** is for people who work and who have earned income (income from a job or self-employment). Generally speaking, this credit applies to people with income under $27,413 and who have a child who lives with them, or $31,152 if more than one child lives with them. There are circumstances where a person without a child may claim this credit, but your income must be lower than $10,380 for you to claim the credit.
- **The child tax credit** reduces your tax by $500 per child under age 17.
- **The child and dependent care credit** reduces your tax by a percentage of the expenses you pay for the care of your child or other dependent while you work.
- **The Hope Scholarship credit** reduces your tax by a percentage of the college tuition that you pay for your dependent child. This credit applies to tuition paid for the first two years of college and only if the student is at least a half-time student.
- **The lifetime learning credit** also reduces tax by a percentage of the tuition payments you make. The credit may not be used if you claim the Hope Scholarship credit in the same year, but this credit applies to any college costs, and it applies to any member of the family, not just your dependent child.

National Averages

The latest statistics published by the IRS are for 1997 tax returns. For taxpayers claiming the Head of Household status, Table 3-4 shows the percentage of tax returns reporting income in various ranges.

1997 Taxable Income	Percent in This Range
$1 to $20,000	59%
$20,000 to $40,000	28%
$40,000 to $50,000	6%
$50,000 to $75,000	5%
$75,000 to $100,000	1%
Over $100,000	1%

Table 3-4 • Average Income for Taxpayers Filing as Head of Household

Scenarios for Business Owners

Special tax circumstances apply to taxpayers who own their own businesses. This section will give you some pointers about what you should expect and watch out for from a tax standpoint if you are a business owner.

Tax Brackets

Your tax filing status and thus your tax brackets are not affected at all if you are a business owner. Base your tax filing status on your marital status and on whether or not you are supporting children, then the income taxes are computed accordingly.

Exemptions

Exemptions are not affected by your status as a business owner. You will claim the exemption for yourself, your spouse if you are married and filing a joint return, and your dependents.

Typical Deductions

If you own your own business, you incur many expenses necessary to keeping that business running. These expenses will often result in deductions on the business form of your tax return (Schedule C, Schedule E, Schedule F, for example). The "Income from Your Own Business" section in Chapter 5 explains in detail the deductions available to business owners. Meanwhile, keep in mind the following general deductions that all represent categories of expenses you should keep track of during the year:

- Advertising and promotional expenses
- Costs relating to sales of goods
- Employee expenses, including employee benefits and payroll expenses
- Repairs and other expenses relating to the maintenance of your business location
- Automobile and other transportation expenses
- Interest and taxes relating to your business

The above list is certainly not exhaustive, but is meant to give you a general idea of the types of expenditures that qualify as business deductions.

Additional Taxes

One of the most unpopular areas of the tax return to the self-employed person is the section on "Other Taxes." If you own your own business, you bear the brunt of both your own share and what would be your employer's share of Social Security and Medicare taxes. These taxes are barely noticed by the typical employee—the employee share is withdrawn from wages before the employee ever sees his paycheck, and the employer share is rarely even discussed with the employee. The result is that many employees never think of the employer's portion of their contributions to the Social Security and Medicare funds as coming from their own pockets.

Many a self-employed person, however, is aware of just how much money is siphoned off for these programs. The self-employed person is forced not only to pay double the share of an employee earning the same amount of money, but must take that double share out of his own earnings—an experience that can be particularly startling for the self-employed person who is new to the business and is caught off guard.

The typical employee receives money from a job after the tax withholding has occurred, computes income tax on Form 1040 after the end of the year, and may have to pay a bit extra to go along with the tax return but truthfully hopes for and even expects a refund each spring. Alternatively, the self-employed person finds that, between federal income tax, self-employment tax, and state income tax, nearly 50 percent of the income earned in the business must be reallocated to the various tax collection offices. It's a confusing system for many of our country's entrepreneurs.

The self-employment tax, which is the same thing as the Social Security and Medicare taxes, is computed by multiplying the first $76,200 of net self-employment income (your business income less deductible business expenses) by 15.3 percent. Income over $76,200 is taxed at 2.9 percent and there is no cap on the amount of income that is taxed at this lower rate. The base amount of income that is taxed at 15.3 percent increases each year.

Available Credits

There are a few credits that may be of interest to business owners. Farmers and other business owners who utilize off-road vehicles may qualify for the gasoline tax credit. This credit provides a reduction of income tax resulting from the excise taxes paid on fuel for off-road vehicles.

The benefit of the credit is somewhat diluted on the tax return for the year in which the credit is claimed because the benefit of the credit must be added back into income and subjected to income tax.

Two other credits that may interest business owners are the work opportunity tax credit and the welfare to work credit. These credits provide a tax credit to employers who hire individuals from certain target groups, including welfare recipients, ex-felons, certain veterans, and high-risk youths. You will want to consult with a welfare or social service office to make sure the employee qualifies under the program if you are interested in pursuing this credit.

National Averages

The latest statistics published by the IRS are for 1997 tax returns. Table 3-5 shows the percentage of tax returns reporting income from self-employment in various ranges and the average amount of self-employment income for each range.

1997 Adjusted Gross Income	Self-Employed Taxpayers	Self-Employment Income
$1 to $20,000	38%	$6,357
$20,000 to $40,000	24%	$8,910
$40,000 to $50,000	9%	$8,389
$50,000 to $75,000	13%	$12,313
$75,000 to $100,000	7%	$16,579
Over $100,000	9%	$43,357

Table 3-5 • Number of Tax Returns Reporting Self-Employment Income and Average Amount of Net Self-Employment Income per Return

Scenarios for Elderly Taxpayers

For the year 2000, the IRS defines an elderly taxpayer as anyone who turns 65 on or before January 1, 2001. There are certain tax rules that are designed specifically to benefit elderly taxpayers, including a tax credit and special exemptions.

Tax Brackets

Your tax filing status and thus your tax brackets are not affected if you are considered to be an elderly taxpayer. Base your tax filing status on your marital status, then the income taxes are computed accordingly.

Retirement Income

Special rules affect elderly people as a result of the fact than many elderly people are drawing on Social Security, pensions, and retirement plans. The income from these sources is taxable in various degrees, and TurboTax will assist you in figuring out just how much is subject to income tax.

See the "Retirement Income" section of Chapter 5 for information about how to report these various types of retirement income.

Standard Deduction

If you do not itemize your deductions but instead take a standard deduction, and if you qualify as an elderly or blind taxpayer, you are entitled to deduct an extra standard deduction amount on your tax return. For the year 2000, the extra standard deduction is $850 per incident of blindness and per elderly taxpayer if you are married. Single and head of household taxpayers are entitled to an extra exemption of $1,100 per incident of blindness and age.

Typical Deductions

Elderly taxpayers who own homes are entitled to the mortgage interest and property tax deductions. However, it is often the case that elderly taxpayers have finished paying off their mortgage and only the property tax remains as a potential deduction. Many people stop itemizing their deductions on their federal tax returns once their mortgage is paid off due to the fact that they don't have enough other deductions to make itemizing worthwhile. Although a taxpayer may no longer be able to itemize for federal purposes, many states allow itemizing.

Elderly taxpayers frequently have more medical expenses than younger taxpayers and thus may be eligible to take a deduction for medical expenses if they itemize. In addition to the medical expenses incurred in regular trips to the doctor and prescription drugs, elderly taxpayers may find they have long-term care expenses such as nursing home fees, hospitalization expenses, and the cost of ambulatory aids such as canes and walkers.

Social Security recipients have Medicare costs deducted from their Social Security checks. These payments constitute a form of health insurance and are thus deductible as a medical expense.

Available Credits

There is a credit for the elderly and disabled, which is available for elderly or disabled taxpayers who fall beneath a certain income level. The credit is at most 15 percent of income, but phases out when income exceeds certain levels, and this phase-out depends on your filing status. TurboTax will determine if this credit applies to you and will calculate it for you.

Using TurboTax to Prepare Your Tax Return

In this part of the book you'll learn how TurboTax can help you streamline the process of preparing your tax return. In addition, you'll pick up tips along the way that will help you cut your tax bite to a minimum. This part includes the following chapters:

Getting Started with TurboTax

In This Chapter:

- *Using the TurboTax Interview*

- *Switching Between Interview and Forms*

- *Using Last Year's Tax Return*

- *Importing from Quicken and QuickBooks*

- *Entering Personal Information*

Chapter 4

Before you can begin entering the numbers in your tax return, you need to provide some vital statistics. Not only do you need to enter your name, address, and Social Security number, but you will also enter information about your dependents and your job.

This chapter will show you how to get around in the TurboTax Interview, and guide you in entering the start-up information so the rest of your tax return will go smoothly.

Using the TurboTax Interview

The face of the TurboTax Interview remains fairly stable throughout the program. Once you get accustomed to finding your way around on one interview screen, the rest will seem familiar. The interview is designed to lead you through the preparation of your income tax return, beginning with the personal information that heads up each tax form, such as name and Social Security number. The interview then leads you through entering income, deductions, taking tax credits, and calculating your tax. Finally, there are some planning features you can use to help prepare yourself for future taxes.

Navigating Around Your Tax Return

Across the top of the interview window is the EasyStep Progress Bar, which groups the sections of your tax preparation into major categories, as shown here:

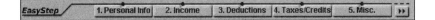

Clicking a topic in the Progress Bar displays the EasyStep Navigator, a scrollable list displaying all the information that will be covered in your tax return, shown in the illustration on the next page. Each item in the list gets checked off as it is covered. Click an item to go right to that part of the interview.

Clicking any item in the Progress Bar provides you with the entire scrollable list. For example, if you want to verify that you entered a W-2 form correctly, you don't necessarily have to click the Income topic in the Progress Bar. You can click any Progress Bar title, then scroll up or down until you find the information you want.

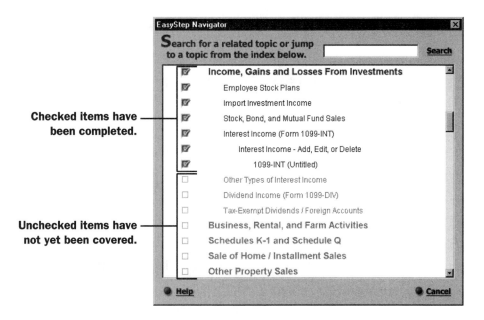

Checked items have been completed.

Unchecked items have not yet been covered.

Searching for Tax Return Topics

If you're not sure which topic to choose from those in the EasyStep Navigator, or if you're not sure where the topic you want is listed, you can perform a search to find what you are looking for. Enter a word or phrase describing the topic you want in the Search text box, and then click the Search button at the top of the EasyStep Navigator, as shown here:

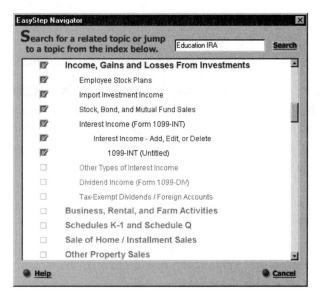

A window will appear displaying search results, as shown in the following illustration. Sometimes you may only get a few results from your search; other times you may get a lengthy scrollable list. Each result will include a description of where the item can be found in the EasyStep Navigator. If you want to get to the screen for one of the items quickly, click the item, and then click the Jump To button. The interview screen containing the information for which you searched will be displayed. If the topics displayed are not what you were searching for, enter a different word or phrase in the Search text box and search again.

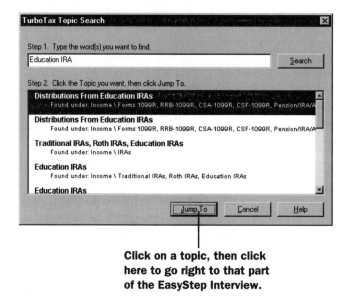

Click on a topic, then click
here to go right to that part
of the EasyStep Interview.

To return to the place where you left off previously, open the EasyStep Navigator, find where the checkmarks left off, and click the next unchecked topic.

Jump to Another Section of the Tax Return

Although the makers of TurboTax recommend that you prepare your tax return by following the interview in the order in which it was designed, you can use the Progress Bar and the EasyStep Navigator to move to different sections of your tax return.

For example, you may realize that you misspelled your street name and need to return to the Personal Info section of the return. Or you may want to jump ahead and enter a portion of the Girl Scout cookies you bought as a charitable contribution deduction, before you forget. By clicking the Progress Bar and opening the EasyStep Navigator, you can easily jump to another section of the tax return. Scroll through the list to find the section you want, and then click that section name. When you have finished with that section, return to where you left off by reopening the EasyStep Navigator and returning to the place where the checkmarks end, as shown here:

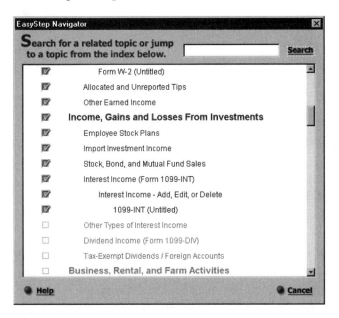

Viewing Your Forms

As you work, entering information into the TurboTax Interview screens, TurboTax is diligently filling out all of the necessary tax forms that you will need to send to the IRS. You can view these forms, their completion in progress, at the bottom of your TurboTax Interview screen, as shown in the following illustration. Each time you enter a number or other piece of information, the form is updated and, if necessary, recalculated. You can scroll through the form at the bottom of your screen to see how the calculations appear. In fact, you can even enter information directly on this form, although this is not recommended as all the steps to entering information are covered in the interview screens. If you want to hide the form, simply click the Hide button.

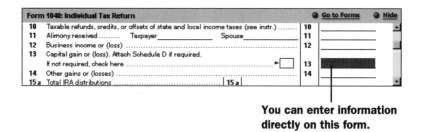

You can enter information
directly on this form.

If the form does not appear at the bottom of the interview screen, click the
Show Tax Form button, shown here:

Show Tax Form

Viewing Your Tax Summary

In the top-right corner of the EasyStep Interview window, TurboTax keeps a
running balance of the tax that you owe or the refund that is expected with your tax
return, as shown below in the illustration on the left. Every time you enter an
amount that affects the bottom line, this number changes. You can quickly view a
brief summary of the detail behind the number by placing your mouse right over
the number. A small box will appear, as shown in the illustration below on the right:

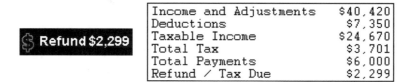

Income and Adjustments	$40,420
Deductions	$7,350
Taxable Income	$24,670
Total Tax	$3,701
Total Payments	$6,000
Refund / Tax Due	$2,299

$ Refund $2,299

- **Income and Adjustments** is your adjusted gross income—all the income that
  appears on page 1 of your income tax return, reduced by adjustments such as
  deductible contributions to an IRA, a deduction for student loan interest,
  moving expenses, and certain deductions relating to self-employed individuals.
  (More information about adjustments to income is available in Chapter 6.)

- **Deductions** are your personal exemptions plus your standard deduction or
  itemized deductions entered thus far. (Itemized deductions are covered in
  Chapter 7.)

- **Taxable Income** is the result after subtracting your deductions from your
  adjusted gross income.

- **Total Tax** is the total amount of tax that has been computed thus far on your tax return.
- **Total Payments** is the amount you entered for tax payments.
- **Refund/Tax Due** represents the difference between the total tax and the total payments.

All of the amounts in the summary box are subject to change as you enter more numbers in your tax return.

For more detail about your tax computation so far, click the tax/refund amount that appears in the upper-right corner of the interview screen. Your click will produce a printable Tax Summary window that provides a bit more information about your tax return. Included at the bottom of this window is an indicator telling you which type of 1040 form you will need to file. TurboTax makes this decision automatically depending on how you meet the requirements for each form.

Which Type of 1040 Is for You?

There are three types of 1040 forms that taxpayers file; the choice of forms is determined by marital status, income level, and whether or not you have dependents or plan to itemize. TurboTax will figure out which form is right for you and prepare the correct form, but just for your information, here is how the determination is made.

The requirements for using the 1040EZ form are as follows:

- Your filing status is Single or Married Filing Jointly.
- You (and your spouse) are not age 65 or older on 1/1/2001.
- You (and your spouse) are not blind as of 12/31/2000.
- You claim no dependents on your tax return.
- You do not itemize your deductions.
- Your taxable income (income minus exemptions and standard deduction) is less than $50,000 (standard deductions for 2000 are $4,400 for Single and $7,350 for Married Filing Jointly).
- Your only sources of income are wages, salaries, tips, unemployment compensation, taxable scholarships and fellowships, and taxable interest income of no more than $400.
- You didn't receive any advance earned income credit payments (see Chapter 8 for more information about the earned income credit).

If you don't meet the requirements for the 1040EZ, you may be able to use the 1040A, if the following conditions are met:

- You do not itemize your deductions.
- Your taxable income (income minus exemptions and standard deduction) is less than $50,000 (standard deductions for 2000 are $3,675 for Married Filing Separately, $6,450 for Head of Household, and $7,200 for Qualifying Widow(er); the others are mentioned above).
- Your only sources of income are wages, salaries, tips, IRA distributions, pensions and annuities, taxable Social Security and railroad retirement benefits, unemployment compensation, taxable scholarships and fellowships, interest income, or dividends.
- Your only credits are child and dependent care credit, earned income credit, credit for the elderly or disabled, the adoption credit, an education credit, or the child tax credit.

If you don't meet the requirements for the 1040EZ or the 1040A, you must file Form 1040. TurboTax will figure all of this out for you and choose the proper form, as the following illustration shows:

Tax Summary	2000
► Keep for your records	

Name (s)	SSN
Lucy L Johnson	123-45-6789

Total income	40,420.
Adjustments to income	
Adjusted gross income	40,420.
Itemized/standard deduction	7,350.
Personal exemptions	8,400.
Taxable income	24,670.
Tentative tax	3,701.
Additional taxes	
Total credits	
Other taxes	
Total tax	3,701.
Total payments	6,000.
Estimated tax penalty	
Refund	2,299.
Balance due	

Which Form 1040 to file?
You must use Form 1040A or Form 1040 because you had a dependent.

[Print]   [Close]   [Help]

Click the Tax | Refund amount in the upper-right corner of your screen to produce this window. This tells you which type of 1040 you will need to file.

Getting Help from Your TurboTax Program

Should you have questions about the tax rules while using your TurboTax program, there is ample onscreen assistance. There is a list of frequently asked questions at the right side of each interview screen. If you have a question, chances are good that the answer may appear here. Click a question and the Help window displaying the answer will appear, as shown in Figure 4-1.

At any time while working in the TurboTax Interview, you can click the Help button on the right side of the screen and open the Help window. The Help window contains access to the government instructions that accompany printed tax forms, many IRS publications that provide more detail than the instructions for the forms, the text of Mary Sprouse's *Money Income Tax Handbook*, as well as options for online support. (Some of these sources are only available in the Deluxe version of TurboTax.)

Click one of these questions to see the answer.

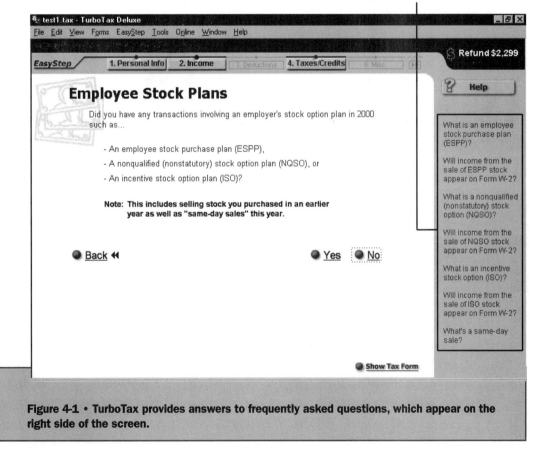

Figure 4-1 · TurboTax provides answers to frequently asked questions, which appear on the right side of the screen.

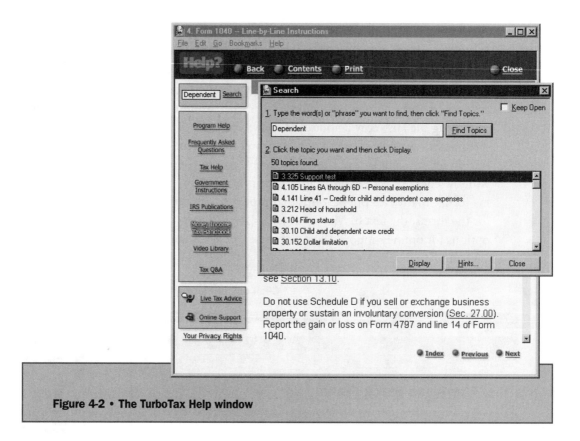

Figure 4-2 • The TurboTax Help window

To use the Search feature within the Help window, click the name of the source or publication in which you want to search (see Figure 4-2), then enter the word or phrase for which you want to search in the Search field at the top-left corner of the window. Click the Search button and you will either see a screen displaying help on your chosen topic or a list of choices for different help options from which you can select. If your search produced many results, choose from the list provided and click Display.

Exit TurboTax and Return Later

If you don't have enough time to prepare your entire tax return at one sitting, you can close TurboTax by choosing File | Exit TurboTax from the menu (or pressing ALT-F4), as shown on the next page. You will be asked if you want to save your file; answer Yes.

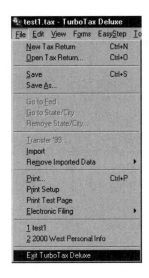

The next time you open TurboTax, your tax file will open right at the screen where you left off.

Switching from Interview to Forms, and Back Again

The TurboTax EasyStep Interview asks you all the questions necessary to prepare a complete tax return. You never have to look at the actual tax forms until the return is finished, at which time you should print out a copy of the tax form for your records and, if you choose to mail your return to the IRS, a copy for that purpose as well.

You may want to take a look at your actual tax forms if:

- You want to see where the numbers are going
- You want to get a sense of the whole picture
- You want to enter some information directly on the forms
- You are comfortable enough with the forms that you prefer to prepare your return without the help of the interview (not recommended, as the interview makes sure you don't leave anything out)

To look at your tax forms, click the Go To Forms button at the bottom of your EasyStep Interview screen, as shown on the next page, (the tax form must be showing at the bottom of the screen for you to see this button), or choose Forms | Go To Forms from the menu.

Go to Forms

Once on the Forms screen, you can ask to view any of the forms in your tax return by first clicking the Open A Form button at the top of the screen, as shown here:

Open a Form

In the window that appears (shown in the following illustration), choose Show My Return to view a list of the forms that are in progress for your tax return, or choose Open A Form to view a list of all the forms that TurboTax is capable of producing. Click a form that you want to view, then click Open to view that form.

```
Open Form                                      [x]
┌─ Options ──────────────────────────────────────┐
│  ● Show My Return   ○ Open a Form               │
└────────────────────────────────────────────────┘
┌────────────────────────────────────────────────┐
│ Federal Information Worksheet (NOT DONE)      ▲ │
│ Form W-2 (Untitled): Wage & Tax Statement       │
│ Tax Payments Worksheet                          │
│    Schedule B -- 1099-INT (Untitled) (NOT DONE) │
│ Form 1040A: Individual Tax Return               │
│ Schedule 1: Interest & Dividend Income          │
│ Form 1040ES 1&2: Estimated Tax Vouchers         │
│ Form 1040ES 3&4: Estimated Tax Vouchers         │
│ Form 1040X: Amended Tax Return (NOT DONE)       │
│ Forms W-2 & W-2G Summary                        │
│ Carryover Worksheet                             │
│ Planner: Summary Information                     │
│ Planner Information & Wages (NOT DONE)          │
│ Planner Investment Income                      ▼ │
└────────────────────────────────────────────────┘
        [ Open ]    [ Remove ]    [ Done ]
```

When more than one form is open, you can switch among open forms by choosing Window from the menu, then clicking on the name of the form you want to view (all open forms appear at the bottom of the Window menu). Alternatively, choose Window | Tile or Window | Cascade to see all the open forms on your screen simultaneously.

To close a form that you no longer want to view, click the Close Form option at the top-right corner of the form, shown on the left in the illustration below. Return to the interview, right where you left off, by clicking the Back To Interview option at the top of the form screen, which is shown on the right in the illustration below.

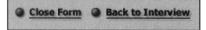

Referring to Last Year's Return

Probably the best single resource for preparing your 2000 income tax return is last year's tax return. Most people don't make a lot of changes in their financial activities from year to year. If you had interest income last year, chances are you will have it again this year. If you itemized your deductions last year, you'll probably itemize again this year. Last year's return can provide you with a guided tour to what you can expect for this year's tax return.

And while having last year's tax return by your side will help remind you of what kind of information you will be entering in this year's return, an even better tool is to have prepared your tax return using TurboTax last year.

One of the first questions you'll encounter in your TurboTax program is whether you want to transfer information from last year, as shown in the following illustration.

Click the Transfer From Last Year option. TurboTax will search for your 1999 tax file and import basic information, including:

- **Personal information** such as name, address, Social Security number, and information about your dependents
- **Business information** such as the name and address and type of your business, ending inventory from last year, carryovers of unused items from last year (such as home office expenses that couldn't be deducted because they exceeded last year's business income), depreciation information, names of partnerships, S-corporations, estates, or trusts in which you have an ownership interest

- **Carryover amounts** such as unused charitable contribution deductions, credits unused from last year, overpayment of taxes that was to be applied to your 2000 tax return
- **Investment information** such as the names of stocks on which you received dividends last year, the names of banks that paid you interest, the names of mutual funds in which you owned shares

If you prepared more than one tax return with TurboTax for 1999 (for example, you prepared your tax return and also that of your child), you will see a list showing each of the 1999 tax returns that are on your computer and are available for transfer. Click the name of the return that contains the information that should be transferred, then click the Transfer From Last Year button and the transfer process will begin. It only takes seconds to transfer information to your 2000 return.

If you used TurboTax for your 1999 tax return, but you have changed computers since last year's return, a Select Return To Transfer From window will appear asking you to indicate the location of your 1999 tax file, as shown in the following illustration. If your tax file is on a floppy disk, you will enter **a:** in the Look In field of this window. If the file is on your hard drive, indicate the folder in which the file is located. Select the tax return to open, then click Open to transfer the information to your 2000 tax return.

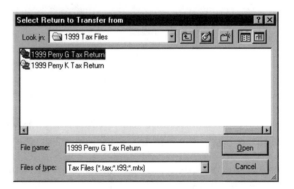

When you indicate the location of your tax file, the filename will appear in the center of this window. Click the filename, then click the Open button to begin the transfer process.

Special Tips for Quicken and QuickBooks Users

Quicken is a computer program that helps you manage your personal finances. More than simply a computerized checkbook, Quicken enables you to balance your accounts, produce reports about your finances, track investments, monitor your retirement accounts, prepare budgets, and generally keep a handle on all of your personal financial transactions.

QuickBooks is an accounting program for the small business. Equally useful in keeping the books for a corporation with 100 employees as it is in tracking finances for a one-person business, QuickBooks provides full bookkeeping services, including invoicing, bill paying, payroll and payroll taxes, inventory, time tracking and job costing (in the Pro version only), budgeting, and a full range of financial reporting.

If you use either of these programs—both made by Intuit, the maker of TurboTax—you can easily import information into your income tax return. The amount of tax preparation time you save can be enormous, depending on how much data is entered in these programs. If you are self-employed, for example, and you keep the records for all of your business income and expenses in QuickBooks, and that is your only source of income and deductions for your tax return, you could conceivably prepare your entire tax return in less than half an hour.

Importing from Quicken

If you use Quicken version 98, 99, or 2000, you can import information directly into your tax return. For example, if you have been tracking your investments in Quicken, recording the sales of your stock throughout the year, this information can be transferred directly to your Schedule D (Capital Gains & Losses) where the proper tax will be computed. Or if you have income from rental property that should flow to your Schedule E, as long as that income has been entered in Quicken, you can transfer it directly without having to go back and compute how much rent you received each month.

Before you can perform the import from Quicken, you must make sure all of the tax-related categories that you use in Quicken have been assigned to the appropriate tax lines of your tax return. This may seem like a tedious process if you haven't done it before, but after it's been done once, the tax assignments will carry forward to the future, even if you upgrade to another version of Quicken.

The fastest way to make tax line assignments in Quicken is to open the Tax Link Assistant by choosing Taxes | Tax Link Assistant from the Quicken menu. This menu choice is available in Quicken version 2000—in previous versions, press CTRL-C to open the Category and Transfer List, then click the Tax Link button that appears on the button bar. In the Tax Link Assistant window that appears (shown in the illustration below), click a category on the left, then click the tax form line on the right on which the amount from that category should appear on your tax return. If you want to start all over, click the Clear All Assignment button to clear all previously entered tax lines. Click the Clear Assignment button to remove the tax line assignment from the selected category.

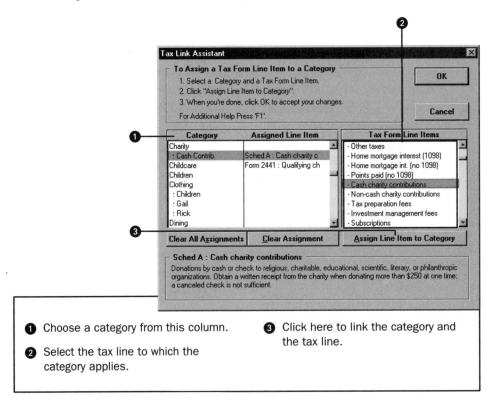

❶ Choose a category from this column.

❷ Select the tax line to which the category applies.

❸ Click here to link the category and the tax line.

When TurboTax asks which programs you want to import from, check the box for Quicken. If you are importing from Quicken for your personal data and QuickBooks for your business data, click both boxes. If you use another finance program, such as Microsoft Money, click the Other Financial Software option.

Caution *When your tax return has been completed, make sure there is no duplication of amounts. It's easy to enter information in TurboTax, forgetting that you imported the same information from Quicken.*

SAVE TIME Don't think that you have to assign every category that you use in Quicken to a tax line. In fact, many categories probably won't qualify for tax line treatment. For example, if you keep track of how much you spend on groceries, clothes for your children, or video rentals, these types of expenses don't get tax line assignments because they won't generate tax deductions. Only income- and tax-related expenses should receive tax line assignments.

Importing from QuickBooks

If you use QuickBooks version 6, 99, or 2000, you can perform a transfer of information directly into TurboTax, just as you can from Quicken. And just as with Quicken, you need to take the time in QuickBooks to assign all categories to the appropriate tax lines.

In QuickBooks, there are a few different ways in which you can assign tax links to your accounts, but here is the quickest way I have found to make the tax assignments:

1. Open the Chart of Accounts (CTRL-A).
2. Click the Reports button that appears in the Chart of Accounts window.
3. Choose Income Tax Preparation List from the Reports list.
4. In the window that appears, double-click any account name, and the Edit Account window will appear for that account.

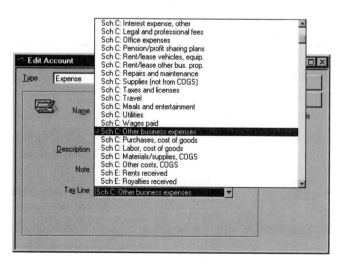

5. Click the drop-down arrow in the Tax Line field, as shown in the previous illustration, to choose the tax line that should be associated with that account.

You can perform these steps for any of the accounts in your Chart of Accounts, and watch your progress as you assign accounts to tax lines.

When TurboTax asks which programs you want to import from, check the box for QuickBooks. If you are importing from QuickBooks for your business data and Quicken for your personal data, click both boxes.

Entering Personal Information

You will be asked to enter some basic information about your filing status, your name and address, your occupation, and your dependents. You will find if you transferred information from last year's return, all this information will already be entered for you, and you simply need to confirm the data and make changes if any of the information has changed since last year.

Choose a Filing Status

Your *filing status* depends on your personal and family status. The purpose of indicating a filing status is to determine which tax rates will be used for computing your income tax. Table 4-1 shows the different tax brackets for each filing status for the year 2000.

	Income Taxed at:				
Filing Status	**15%**	**28%**	**31%**	**36%**	**39.6%**
Single	$0 to $26,250	$26,251 to $63,550	$63,551 to $132,600	$132,601 to $288,350	Over $288,350
Married Filing Jointly	$0 to $43,850	$43,851 to $105,950	$105,951 to $161,450	$161,451 to $288,350	Over $288,350
Married Filing Separately	$0 to $21,925	$21,926 to $52,975	$52,976 to $80,725	$80,726 to $144,175	Over $144,175
Head of Household	$0 to $35,150	$35,151 to $90,800	$90,801 to $147,050	$147,051 to $288,350	Over $288,350
Qualifying Widow(er)	$0 to $21,925	$21,926 to $52,975	$52,976 to $80,725	$80,726 to $144,175	Over $144,175

Table 4-1 • Marginal Tax Brackets for 2000

Your filing status is typically determined as of the last day of the calendar year. If you were single for all of 2000 but got married on New Year's Eve, your filing status would be one of the married statuses (Married Filing Jointly or Married Filing Separately), not Single.

Tip *Tax rates are not the only thing affected by the filing status you use. If you receive Social Security benefits, the amount of benefits on which you are taxed is in part determined by your filing status (see "Retirement Income" in Chapter 5 for more information). Some tax credits, such as the earned income credit, the tax credit for the elderly and disabled, the credit for child and dependent care, the education credits, and the adoption credit, are available to married taxpayers only if they file a joint tax return (Chapter 8 explains these credits). If you are married, the allowable loss you can take on rental property that you own can be affected by your filing status (see "Income from Rental Property" in Chapter 5 for more information).*

Sometimes you have a choice in selecting a filing status. The descriptions below explain how to determine the filing status available for you.

Single   Perhaps the easiest filing status to determine, you are *single* if you are not married, have no children, or were not made a widow or widower within the past two years.

Married Filing Jointly   You can use the Married Filing Jointly filing status if you were married as of December 31, 2000, you are not legally separated under a decree of divorce or separate maintenance as of December 31, 2000, and neither spouse was a nonresident alien at any time during 2000 (but see the note that follows). Most married couples use the Married Filing Jointly filing status; however, there are occasions when the Married Filing Separately status can be more advantageous. If you qualify for the Married Filing Jointly status, you are allowed to use the Married Filing Separately status if you prefer.

Note   *A married couple that includes a nonresident alien spouse can elect to file jointly if they agree to be taxed in the United States on all of their income, no matter the country of origin, and if they agree to make certain books and records available to the IRS for examination. In addition, a one-time election to file a joint return can be made in the year in which the nonresident alien spouse becomes a resident of the United States.*

Married Filing Separately   Married couples are required to file separate tax returns if both their tax years do not end on the same date (a tax year typically ends on December 31, but it is possible to apply to the IRS for a different tax year end) or if they are legally separated under a decree of divorce or separate maintenance on the last day of the tax year. If the couple is separated on the last day of the tax year, but there is no legal separation agreement, they are allowed to file jointly.

Head of Household   An individual qualifies for the Head of Household status if he or she maintains a household which, for more than half of the tax year, is the principal place of residence of anyone eligible to be claimed as a dependent by the taxpayer. (An exception to the dependent rule is that it does not apply to someone eligible to be claimed as a dependent under a multiple support agreement, which is discussed under "Entering Dependents" later in this chapter.) In order to qualify for the Head of Household status, a taxpayer cannot be married as of the last day of the tax year or is separated under a decree of divorce or separate maintenance. A married person will be considered to be separated and eligible for the Head of Household status if the taxpayer's spouse was not a member of the household for the last six months of the year.

Qualifying Widow(er)   A taxpayer qualifies for the Qualifying Widow(er) filing status for two years following the year of death of the spouse if, during those years, the taxpayer maintains a household that is the principal residence for his or her child, and if the taxpayer is eligible to claim that child as a dependent. The Qualifying Widow(er) status is not available if the taxpayer remarries during the two-year eligibility period.

Enter or Verify Name, Address, Social Security Number

Believe it or not, one of the most important screens you must fill out for your tax return is the screen on which you enter your name, address, and Social Security number, shown in the illustration on the following page. If you transferred information from last year's return, this information will be filled out for you, but you must be sure to verify that everything on this screen is correct.

If you are filing a joint return, typically the husband's name appears first, then the wife's. It doesn't matter in which order you place these names, but you should follow the same order year after year.

The birth date you enter does not appear on your tax return. The reason for entering the birth date is so that the TurboTax program will be able to compute the year in which you turn age 65 (in which case you may be entitled to additional tax benefits) or if you are a child (in which case special tax rates may apply).

If your Social Security number is incorrect on this screen, the number will be incorrect on every form in your tax return, and your return will not be processed correctly. *Make sure* that the Social Security number is exactly correct.

The address you enter should match the address at which you live when you are filling out your tax return, even if that address is not the address at which you lived during 2000. If the IRS needs to contact you for additional information, or if they are expected to send a refund check to you in the mail, they will need your current address. If you use a post office box, you can enter that as your mailing address, but the IRS prefers that you use a street address if possible.

By the way, the telephone number that TurboTax requests is optional. This information will not appear on your federal tax return. However, it's possible that your state tax return requires a phone number, in which case, if you use TurboTax for your state return, the number you enter here will be printed on that return.

Answering Questions

A small collection of facts (shown in the following illustration) will determine the course that certain areas of your tax return preparation will take. Check off any boxes that apply to you or your spouse, and TurboTax will take care of the rest.

EasyStep	1. Personal Info	2. Income	3. Deductions	4. Taxes/Credits	5. Misc.

Special Situations

Check all of the situations that apply.

	Simon	Gail
Can be claimed as a dependent on someone else's return	☐	☐
Was in the U.S. Armed Forces (active, reserve, or Nat. Guard) in 2000.	☐	☐
Is permanently and totally disabled as **defined for Schedule R**	☐	☐
Is legally blind	☐	☐
Died before filing this return	☐	☐

● Back ◀◀   ● Continue

Can you be claimed as a dependent on someone else's return?   The amount of standard deductions you are eligible to claim may be limited if this situation applies to you. Furthermore, you are not eligible to claim a personal exemption for yourself if someone else can claim you as a dependent. If the person who is eligible to claim you as a dependent chooses not to claim you, you are still precluded from claiming the exemption for yourself.

Were you in the U.S. Armed Forces in 2000?   Certain tax rules apply to members of the armed forces, and TurboTax will take care of applying those rules if you check this box. For example, you are allowed a deduction for moving expenses if your role as a member of the armed forces requires you to move, even if you don't meet the time and distance tests that go along with a deduction for moving expenses. Also, members of the military who are on duty outside the United States and Puerto Rico receive an automatic two-month extension of time in which to file their tax returns without having to file any form to request the extension.

Are you permanently and totally disabled?   You may be eligible for the tax credit for the permanently and totally disabled. The criteria for making this claim are

- A doctor must certify in writing that your condition has lasted or will last a year or more or that it is terminal.
- As a result of your condition, you must be unable to "engage in any substantial gainful activity." For example, you must be unable to hold down a regular, ongoing job for which an impartial employer would be willing to pay.

Were you declared legally blind on or before 12/31/00?   The definition of legal blindness is that your corrected vision in your best eye is no better than 20/200 or your field of vision is 20 degrees or less. You must have this condition verified in writing by your doctor. If you qualify as legally blind, you are eligible for an additional exemption on your tax return.

Did the taxpayer pass away before filing this return?   If the taxpayer or spouse passed away before the return was filed, you will be asked for the date of death. TurboTax will take care of including the proper forms with the return, will enter the word "Deceased" in the name section of the return, along with the deceased taxpayer's name, and will make the appropriate indication in the signature area. If there is a refund check to be issued, it will be issued in the name of the surviving spouse.

Note   *If the taxpayer passed away and the person filing the return and to whom a refund should be paid is not the surviving spouse, you will need to obtain Form 1310, Statement of Person Claiming a Refund Due a Deceased Taxpayer, and attach this form to the tax return. TurboTax does not prepare this form, but you can download the form at http://www.irs.gov/, or you can call the IRS at (800) 829-3676 and request a copy of the form.*

Entering Dependents

For each dependent you enter, you can take an *exemption*. An exemption is like a deduction—it reduces your income and thus your tax. For 2000, each exemption reduces your income by $2,800. This amount may be reduced, however, if your income exceeds these thresholds: $193,400 for joint or surviving spouse taxpayers, $161,150 for head of household, $128,950 for single, and $96,700 for married filing separately.

If you know you have dependents, you can proceed through the TurboTax dependents section pretty quickly. You will be asked to enter the name, Social Security number, birth date, type of dependent (choose from child who does or does not live with you, other dependent, or person who is not a dependent but who qualifies you for the earned income credit, described in Chapter 8), and the relationship you have with the dependent, as shown here:

But first you must know if the person actually qualifies as a dependent. To be a dependent, a person must pass five tests. TurboTax will lead you through an analysis of these steps if you select the Guide Me option at the beginning of the dependent area of the interview.

1. **The Gross Income Test.** The person must have earned less than $2,800 during 2000. This amount changes each year. However, you can skip this test if the person is your child and that child either is under 19 years old by 12/31/00 or is a full-time student under 24 years old. Your child can have any amount of income and still be your dependent, as long as the other rules are met.

2. **The Support Test.** You must have provided more than 50 percent of the support for the person. Support includes food, lodging, medical bills, vacations, clothes, books, and so on. There are two exceptions to this rule:

   - You can agree to give your right to the dependency claim to someone else. For example, if the person is the child of divorced parents, the parents can agree as to which of them will claim the child as a dependent, no matter who provided the support. This agreement is made on IRS Form 8332 and is signed by the person giving up the right to make the claim. The form gets attached to the tax return of the person claiming the child as a dependent.

- In some cases, the support of a relative will be shared among several family members, and they will sign a legal document called a multiple support agreement that states who can list the person as a dependent on whose tax return.

3. **The Relationship or Member of the Household Test.** The person must be related to you in one of the following ways:
   - Lineal descendant (child, grandchild, great-grandchild, step-lineal descendants such as stepchildren, and adopted children included).
   - Sibling (including step- and half-siblings).
   - Lineal ancestor (parent, grandparent, great-grandparent, step-lineal ancestors included).
   - Niece, nephew, aunt, or uncle of blood, step-, or adopted relatives—no relations by marriage allowed (for example, your mother's brother counts, but not his wife).
   - In-laws.
   - Anyone else, related or not, who lived in your home for the entire year (but not your spouse). A foster child who lived with you for the entire year would fit in this category.

4. **The Joint Return Test.** The person must not file a joint tax return for 2000.

5. **The Citizenship Test.** The person must be a citizen, national, or resident of the United States, a resident of Canada or Mexico, or an alien child whom you have adopted and who lived with you for the entire year.

Entering Income into TurboTax

In This Chapter:

- *Using TurboTax's New Automated Tax Return*

- *Entering Income from W-2 Forms*

- *Entering Sales of Stock*

- *Entering Interest and Dividend Income*

- *Entering Income from Your Business*

- *Entering Income from Your Rental Property*

- *Entering Income from Your Farm*

- *Entering Income from K-1 Forms*

- *Selling Your Home*

- *Recording Retirement Income*

- *Entering Miscellaneous Income*

The reason we file tax returns is to inform the government of the income we earned during the year. In 1913, the year of the first income tax form 1040, this process was so simple that the entire form, including instructions, covered four pages. Were people's lives really so much less complicated than ours are now? No matter how many different kinds of income you had, or from what sources, everything could be reported on three pages (the fourth page was the instructions). Today, we sometimes complete dozens of forms for our tax return, and the instructions for the tax forms fill books.

We could linger over discussions of what happens to the tax laws once Congress gets involved, but those issues would fill a separate book. For the matter at hand, we need to comply with the existing laws and get all of your income reported properly on your tax return. That's where this lengthy chapter comes in. There are so many different types of income, it's unlikely every section will apply to you. Feel free to skip around this chapter and pick the parts you need. To make it simple for you, the income issues are addressed in the same order here as they are presented in the TurboTax program.

Using TurboTax's New Automated Tax Return

The new Automated Tax Return from TurboTax is a process whereby you can automatically download information from your W-2 and 1099 forms directly to your tax return. All of the information from the form will be entered on your tax return.

You can easily tell if you are eligible to use this service by looking at your W-2 form or your last paycheck stub. If the statement "TurboTax Automated Tax Return" appears on the form or stub, you can electronically download the information to your tax return. You must have an Internet connection to perform this operation. If required, TurboTax will provide you with a complimentary dial-up Internet account for purposes of preparing your tax return (a window will appear in which you can indicate that you already have an Internet account or you can select the complimentary account).

If you answer Yes when asked if you want to use the TurboTax Automated Tax Return feature, TurboTax will present you with a list of information providers who are participating in the Automated Tax Return program. Choose the provider named on your W-2 or 1099 form, then enter the requested information (see Figure 5-1).

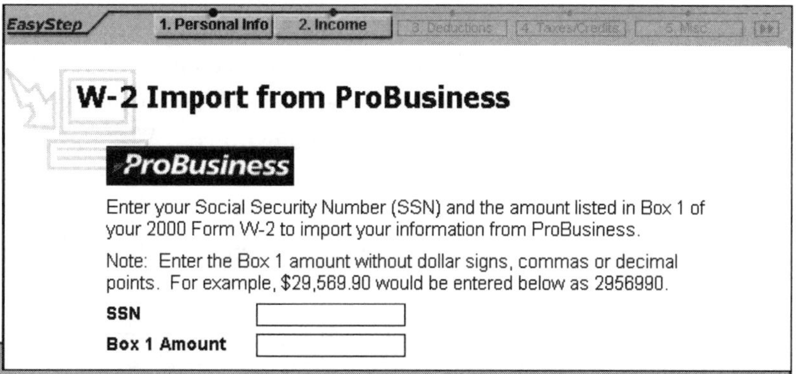

W-2 Import from ProBusiness

ProBusiness

Enter your Social Security Number (SSN) and the amount listed in Box 1 of your 2000 Form W-2 to import your information from ProBusiness.

Note: Enter the Box 1 amount without dollar signs, commas or decimal points. For example, $29,569.90 would be entered below as 2956990.

SSN

Box 1 Amount

Figure 5-1 • Enter the information requested (which may include a password that will have been provided to you), then click Continue to activate the automatic transfer.

It's possible this new Automated Tax Return process will forever change the way most people prepare their tax returns. For taxpayers without complicated tax schedules, like the itemized deductions and business schedules, this is the first major step down the road to the future of tax return preparation: the ten-minute tax return.

W-2 Income from Your Job

Employers are required to mail W-2 forms to their employees by the end of January each year. The W-2 form, Wage and Tax Statement, summarizes the income you earned and the amounts of tax and other deductions you had withheld from your pay as an employee during the prior year.

The first thing you should do when you receive a W-2 form in January or early February is verify, if possible, that all the information on the form is correct. You can compare the amounts on the form to the amounts on your final paycheck of the year. When checking the W-2 form, check your Social Security number and the spelling of your name to make sure there are no mistakes. If there are any mistakes on the form, let your employer know immediately so a revised form can be issued.

This W-2 document is your evidence that you have paid your taxes during the year. If the information on the form is erroneous, the IRS may not be able to link your tax payments with your tax liability so it's important to have the correct information represented.

Entering Details from Your W-2s into TurboTax

The W-2 form is filled with little boxes containing numbers and codes. The detailed explanations in this section will describe what the information in each of those boxes represents. Follow along on your W-2 form, entering information from each box into the appropriate field in TurboTax (as shown in Figure 5-2). The descriptions for each box will agree with the descriptions that appear on your W-2 form—the illustrations will show where the information should be entered in TurboTax.

Box a: Control number   Sometimes this box on the W-2 form is left blank. The control number is not a relevant part of your tax return; however, if you plan to file your return electronically, you need to enter the control number, if it exists, when you enter other W-2 information. The control number is a reference number for your employer.

Void   If this box is checked on your W-2 form, you are using the wrong W-2 form. A check here means your employer issued a revised W-2 form to take the place of this one, which was filed erroneously. Search through your documents and see if you can find the real W-2. If this is all you have, contact your employer and let him know you received the wrong form.

Box b: Employer's identification number   This is like a Social Security number for your employer's company—the number is unique to the company. Electronic filing demands that you enter this number in TurboTax. If you're filing a paper return, you don't have to worry about entering this, but it won't hurt if you do.

Box c: Employer's name, address, and ZIP code   Electronic filers will have to enter this information. Others can do so if they desire, but it is not required. Entering at least the employer's name is recommended in order to distinguish this from any other W-2 forms you enter.

Box d: Employee's (taxpayer's) Social Security number   Double-check and triple-check this number. If your Social Security number has been entered incorrectly on your W-2 form, contact your employer and get a new W-2 form issued.

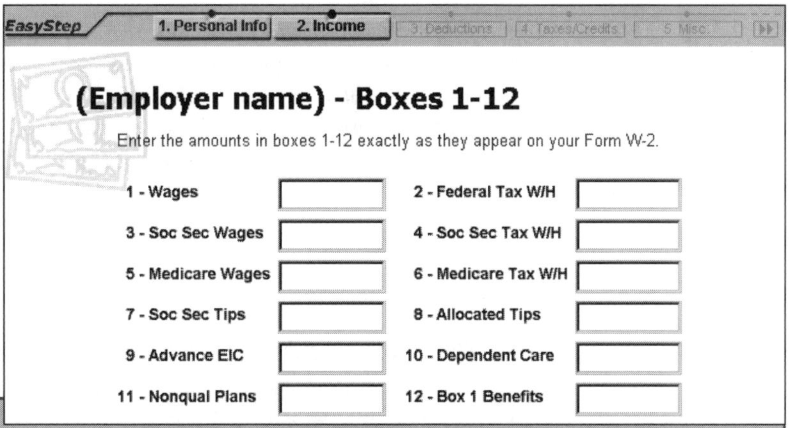

Figure 5-2 • Follow along with your W-2 form while you enter information into TurboTax.

Box e: Employee's (your) name and address Check the name and address on the W-2 form and make sure you didn't receive someone else's W-2 form. Then verify that your name and address, as TurboTax has entered it in the screen shown next, exactly agrees with the information on your W-2 form. If you have moved or changed your name since the W-2 form was issued, you should still enter information here that agrees exactly with the W-2.

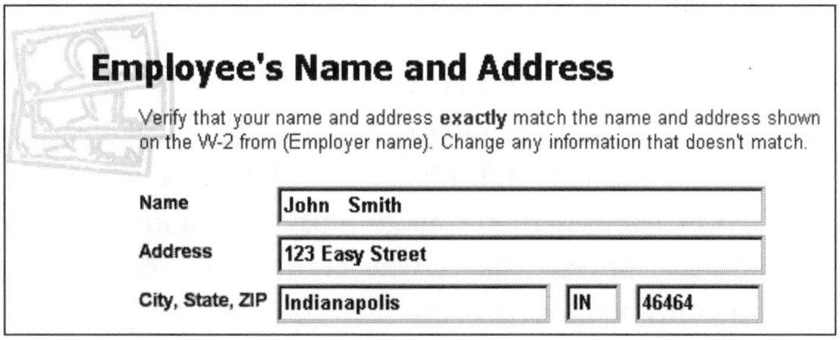

Box 1: Wages, tips, other compensation This box shows how much you earned last year. You probably didn't receive all of this, due to tax withholding and perhaps some other withholdings, but this is the amount on which you will be taxed.

Tip   *You can round the numbers you enter in TurboTax. The IRS offers the option of rounding your numbers to the nearest dollar. You can enter cents if you like, but the cents are completely optional. If you choose to round your numbers, round them like this: Any number that contains 50 cents or more gets rounded up to the next dollar. Any number containing less than 50 cents does not get rounded up. Note that if you don't round the numbers, TurboTax will accept the numbers you enter, including cents, but the numbers will be rounded to dollars on the actual tax forms.*

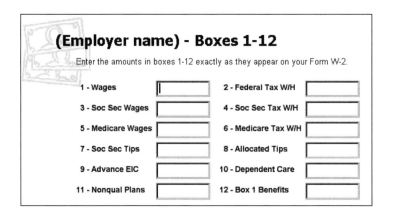

Box 2: Federal income tax withheld   This is the amount of federal income tax your employer has already sent to the IRS on your behalf. This amount, plus any other amounts paid in estimated payments or withheld from other jobs, will be compared to the tax that is computed on your tax return, and the difference will either be refunded to you or owed by you.

Box 3: Social Security wages   This amount will differ from your box 1 amount on your W-2 form if you had tax-deferred deductions, such as a contribution to a 401(k) plan, withheld from your gross pay. The contribution is not subject to income tax in the current year, which is why it is not included in box 1, but it is subject to Social Security and Medicare tax.

Box 4: Social Security tax withheld   The tax shown in this box is paid to the Social Security Administration to pay retirement and other benefits to today's Social Security recipients.

The maximum Social Security tax you can pay for 2000 is $4,724 (this amount increases each year). If you have more than one employer during 2000, you may have paid too much Social Security tax. The excess will be treated as income tax withholding and will be applied to your 2000 income tax. If you have paid enough tax through withholding or estimated payments to cover your income tax for 2000, the excess Social Security tax will be refunded to you.

Box 5: Medicare wages and tips   Typically, this amount is the same as your Social Security wages, with the exception being that the Social Security wages that appear on your 2000 W-2 form cannot exceed $76,200 in 2000, whereas the Medicare wages have no ceiling.

Box 6: Medicare tax withheld   The Medicare tax is 1.45 percent of all of the wages that you earned. There is no maximum amount of Medicare that can be withheld. In case you are wondering, you are not entitled to a medical expense deduction for the Medicare that is withheld from your wages, even though this amount represents a type of health insurance.

Box 7: Social Security tips   If you work in an environment where you receive tips and report the amount you receive to your employer, your employer will show the amount you reported in this box. The sum of box 3 and box 7 cannot exceed $76,200 in 2000.

Box 8: Allocated tips   This amount represents tips that your employer allocates to you based on his receipts.

Box 9: Advance EIC payment   If you are eligible for the earned income credit (see Chapter 8), and your employer gives you an advance on this credit, the amount of the advance goes in this box on the W-2.

Box 10: Dependent care benefits   An amount in this box represents the amount paid by your employer under a dependent care assistance program at your place of employment. This number may include the value of dependent care provided by your employer, the pre-tax money you set aside for dependent care, or the dependent care benefits paid by your employer on your behalf. An amount in excess of $5,000 in this box will also be included in boxes 1, 3, and 5 and will be subject to income tax, Social Security tax, and Medicare tax.

Box 11: Nonqualified plans   An amount in this box represents a distribution you received from a nonqualified retirement plan. Distributions from nonqualified plans are subject to tax, thus the amount shown here has been included in your income in box 1 or in your Social Security and Medicare wages in boxes 3 and 5.

Box 12: Benefits included in box 1   The amount in this box represents taxable benefits your employer paid to you or provided you with during the year. This includes items such as education reimbursements, the value of your personal use of a company car, or membership in a social club. You don't have to show the amount in box 12 on your tax return: it's already included in your total wages. However, you may not be responsible for taxes on some of this amount even though it has been included in your income. Ask for a statement from your employer itemizing what makes up this number, and then determine if any of this amount represents an expense you can deduct, such as a business-related expense that might qualify as a miscellaneous itemized deduction.

Box 13: Codes   Any amount that appears in box 13 of your W-2 form will have a letter code from A to T listed next to it. Enter in TurboTax the letter as well as the amount of each item that appears here.

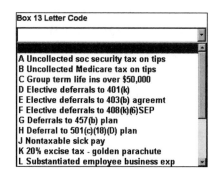

Some of the coded items in box 13 will result in changes to your tax return. TurboTax will automatically transfer the amounts you enter to the proper lines and tax forms, but here's what you can expect:

- **Code A.** An amount accompanied by this code represents Social Security tax on tips that was not withheld from your pay and for which you are now liable. The amount will be added to the other taxes on your tax return.

- **Code B.** An amount accompanied by this code represents Medicare tax on tips that was not withheld from your pay and for which you are now liable. The amount will be added to the other taxes on your tax return.

- **Code C.** This amount represents the cost of group term life insurance exceeding $50,000. You are required to pay tax on this amount and it has already been included with your income in box 1 of the W-2.

- **Codes D through H.** Amounts coded with these letters represent amounts you contributed to retirement plans. These amounts are not subject to income tax in this year—the tax will be paid at the time you withdraw the money from your retirement fund.

- **Code J (there is no Code I).** An amount accompanied by this code represents sick pay you received during the year. The amount is not taxable and is listed here for your information only.

- **Code K.** An amount accompanied by this code represents a 20 percent excise tax on excess "golden parachute" payments to key corporate employees. This tax will be included with income tax withheld in box 2, and the income associated with this tax has been added to your wages in boxes 1, 3, and 5.

- **Code L.** An amount accompanied by this code represents business expenses, such as travel or meals, for which you have been reimbursed. The amount is not taxable and is here for your information only.

- **Code M.** An amount accompanied by this code represents Social Security tax on your group term life insurance that exceeds $50,000. The amount will be added to the other taxes on your tax return.

- **Code N.** An amount accompanied by this code represents Medicare tax on your group term life insurance that exceeds $50,000. The amount will be added to the other taxes on your tax return.

- **Code P (there is no Code O).** An amount accompanied by this code represents moving expenses for which your employer reimbursed you. This amount has been included in your income in box 1. You may be entitled to take a moving expense deduction for this amount that will offset the effect of the income.

- **Code Q.** An amount accompanied by this code represents the value of housing, subsistence, and combat zone compensation paid to military personnel. Although this amount does not get included in your income, it will be taken into consideration to determine your eligibility to receive the earned income credit.

- **Code R.** An amount accompanied by this code represents employer contributions on your behalf to a medical savings account. If the amount is subject to tax, it will be included in your income in boxes 1, 3, and 5.

- **Code S.** An amount accompanied by this code is a salary reduction for an employee contribution to a SIMPLE retirement plan. This amount is not subject to income tax in this year—the tax will be paid at the time you withdraw the money from your retirement fund.

- **Code T.** If your employer provided adoption benefits, the amount will be coded with a T. TurboTax will ask you some questions later in the interview and make the appropriate calculations to determine if any of this amount is taxable.

Box 14: Other   This box contains miscellaneous informative messages from your employer. Your employer may use this space to report benefits that the company paid on your behalf that didn't fit into any of the categories in box 13. Typically, the amounts reported here are for your information only and will have no effect on your tax return. If you're not sure what an amount in this box represents, ask your employer for details.

(Employer name) - Box 14

Enter the descriptions and amounts that are in box 14 of your Form W-2.

Box 14 Description	Amount

Box 15: Check boxes   Some of these boxes might be checked on your W-2 form. Information from these boxes doesn't go anywhere on your income tax return; however, some of these checks may have a ripple effect on other areas of your tax return. For example, if the Pension Plan box is checked, your contributions to an IRA may be limited. If the Deferred Compensation box is checked, the amount of contribution you can make to a deferred income plan may be limited (see the Save Money sidebar on the following page). Check the boxes on your TurboTax screen just as they are checked on your W-2 form.

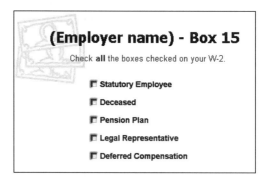

(Employer name) - Box 15

Check **all** the boxes checked on your W-2.

☐ **Statutory Employee**

☐ **Deceased**

☐ **Pension Plan**

☐ **Legal Representative**

☐ **Deferred Compensation**

Box 16: State   The name of the state in which your income is taxable appears here. Unless you live in a state that doesn't require you to file a state income tax return (Alaska, Florida, Nevada, South Dakota, Washington, Texas, and Wyoming), you should file a state income tax return for this state. If you have more than one state listed on your W-2 form, you probably have to file a state income tax return for each state. You can acquire TurboTax software for each state in which you need to file a return. You can purchase the software online and download it right to your computer at http://www.turbotax.com/, or you can call TurboTax at (800) 224-1047 and purchase the software over the phone, in which case the program will be mailed to you.

(Employer name) - Boxes 16-18

	16- State	Employer's State ID No.	17 - State Wages	18 - State Income Tax
First State	IN			
Second State				

Box 17: State wages, tips, etc.   The amount in box 17 of your W-2 form represents income that was earned in the state shown in box 16.

Box 18: State income tax   Box 18 contains the amount of state income tax that was withheld from your wages during 2000. If you itemize your deductions on your federal tax return, TurboTax will carry this amount to the state and local income taxes area of your federal Schedule A.

SAVE MONEY   **Avoid Double Tax on Excess Deferred Contributions**
If the total of amounts coded D through H in box 13 of your W-2 exceeds $10,500, you have the option of withdrawing the excess amount from your retirement plan by April 15. It's wise to withdraw the excess contribution if you can—otherwise you will pay tax on the excess contribution this year and again when you withdraw the amount in your retirement. Any taxpayer who participates in more than one tax-deferred retirement plan can run into this problem. Check with your employer for information on implementing such a withdrawal (but don't wait until April 14—your employer will need a little advance notice). There are times when the combined allowable contributions to tax-deferred retirement plans can exceed $10,500 and not cause an increase to your taxable income. If your contribution exceeds $10,500 and you participate in more than one retirement plan, or if you participate in a tax-sheltered annuity plan, or if you're just not sure if the excess contribution is tax-deferred, check with a tax professional.

Box 19: Locality name   If you had local taxes withheld (city taxes, county taxes, and so on), the name of the local taxing authority appears here. You may have to prepare a separate income tax return for the locality. In some states, the local taxes are paid right along with the state taxes on the state income tax return. If you use TurboTax to prepare your state income tax return, and the local taxes are a part of the state return, these taxes will be computed automatically, assuming you enter the name of the locality properly. TurboTax provides a list of recognized localities for which it will prepare the proper local tax return. Click the Help button, then perform a Search for **locality**. The search produces one result relating to "locality fields on form W-2" (see illustration). Displaying this option will produce a list of the locality codes recognized by TurboTax.

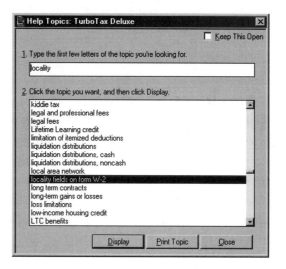

Box 20: Local wages, tips, etc.   This is the amount of income that was earned in the locality shown in box 19.

Box 21: Local income tax   This is the amount of local income tax that was withheld from your wages during 2000. If you itemize your deductions on your federal tax return, TurboTax will carry this amount to the state and local income taxes area of your federal Schedule A.

If You Need to Change Any W-2 Information

If you made a mistake on one of your W-2 forms, or if you neglected to enter one of your W-2 forms, you can return to the W-2 part of your TurboTax EasyStep Interview at any time.

To change a W-2 or to add a new W-2, follow these steps:

1. Click the Income option on the Progress bar at the top of your TurboTax screen. The EasyStep Navigator window will open.
2. Click on the Form W-2 – Add, Edit, or Delete option.

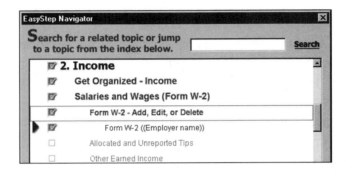

3. To edit a W-2 that has already been entered, click on the name of the employer, then click the Edit button.
4. To add a new W-2, click the Enter New W-2 option.
5. When you are finished, you can return to the place in the EasyStep Interview where you left off by opening the EasyStep Navigator again, then scrolling down until you find the place where the checkmarks stop. Click on the first unchecked item.

Reporting Sales of Stock, Mutual Funds, and Other Investments

If you sell any of your investments, the transaction is subject to income tax and must be reported on your tax return. It doesn't matter if you made a profit or experienced a loss, the transaction itself must be reported, and then the tax benefits or costs will be weighed.

Not everything you sell counts as an investment and qualifies for capital gain treatment, which is a lower tax rate than the rate at which you pay tax on other income. Capital gain property encompasses items that are held for investment, such as stocks, bonds, and collectibles. If something you own turns into an investment, it will also receive capital gain treatment, even if it wasn't originally acquired as an investment. For example, that Lionel train collection you've been storing in your cellar for 50 years was purchased for fun when you were a kid. Sell it today and you will have a large taxable gain, but the gain will receive favorable tax treatment in the form of the lower capital gain tax.

Capital Gain Tax Rates

Different tax rules apply to income from sales of investments as compared to other forms of income you report on your tax return. The timing of the sale has a substantial effect on the tax treatment, as investments that are owned for one year or less do not receive the favorable treatment.

Sales of investments are grouped into categories of long-term and short-term. The lower capital gain tax rates apply only to long-term sales of investments.

Long-Term Capital Gains

Long-term capital gains are gains (profits) on the sale of capital assets (assets held for investment) that have been owned for more than 12 months. Short-term capital gains are gains on assets owned for 12 months or less.

Long-term capital losses are losses on assets owned for more than 12 months. Long-term capital losses are combined with long-term capital gains to produce a net long-term capital gain or loss. If the result of this computation is a gain, the tax is calculated at the lower capital gain tax rates. If the net result is a loss, the long-term loss is combined with any net short-term loss, and the total deduction for capital losses is limited to $3,000 for 2000. Any unused loss is carried forward to future years, until such time as it is used up.

The tax rates on net long-term capital are as follows:

- A maximum of 20 percent if your highest marginal tax rate is 28 percent or higher
- A maximum of 10 percent if your highest marginal tax rate is 15 percent

You can tell what your marginal tax rate is by determining where your income falls in the tax rate tables. Compare your taxable income (place your mouse over the Tax Due or Refund calculator at the top-right corner of your TurboTax screen to see a pop-up box that will tell you your taxable income), and then examine Table 5-1. If your taxable income is beneath the threshold shown in Table 5-1, your maximum capital gain tax is 10 percent. If your income is over the threshold, your maximum capital gain tax is 20 percent.

```
          $ Tax Due $6,310

Income and Adjustments    $62,000
Deductions                $10,115
Taxable Income            $43,485
Total Tax                  $6,021
Total Payments                 $0
Refund / Tax Due          $-6,310
```

Filing Status	Taxable Income Threshold
Single	$26,250
Married Filing Jointly or Qualifying Widow(er)	$43,850
Married Filing Separately	$21,925
Head of Household	$35,150

Table 5-1 • Taxable Income at Which Tax on Capital Gains Increases to 20 percent

Entering Basic Information About the Investment

In order for the TurboTax program to assess tax properly, you will need to provide basic information when you describe the sale of an investment. This information includes:

Stock, Bond, and Mutual Fund Sales

Complete the following information. Enter a specific description such as 100 shares ABC stock or ABC - 100 Sh.

Description [   ]

Net Sales Price [   ]   Date Sold [   ]

Cost or Basis [   ]   Date Acquired [   ]

What Type of Sale? [Normal sale ▼]

- A general description of the property that was sold

- The date on which the property was acquired (you can enter VAR for variable if the property was acquired over time, such as shares of stock in a company that experienced stock splits over the years)

Note | *If you enter VAR, TurboTax will treat the sale as long-term. You can force a short-term sale, if that is applicable, by choosing Force Short-Term in the What Type Of Sale field.*

- The date on which the property was sold
- The original cost, increased by any commissions or other fees associated with the purchase
- The sales price, including sales commissions and any other fees associated with the sale

Personal Assets and Personal Investment Assets

There is a fine line distinguishing personal assets from personal investment assets. A personal asset is something you own and use, and would own whether or not it had any investment value. An asset held for investment is something you purchased solely because of its value as an asset and the hope that it will generate a profit at some point in the future.

The reason we make this distinction is that you are not allowed to take a deduction for a loss on the sale of a personal asset. For instance, if you purchased a Ford Mustang convertible in 1964 and you have cared for the car all these years and the car is still in like-new condition, you have a valuable asset on your hands that you will be able to sell for much more than the $2,500 to $3,000 you paid for it in your youth. But the car is a personal asset, not an investment. That doesn't mean you get out of paying tax on the income when you sell your car. The profit on the sale is a taxable transaction and the gain will be given long-term capital gain treatment. But say instead you purchased a family car three years ago for $20,000 and in 2000 you sold the car for $11,000. Do you have a $9,000 capital loss to report? No way. The IRS doesn't want to hear about your personal losses, only the gains.

Selling Stock

When you sell shares of stock, you must indicate the date purchased, date sold, cost, and sales price of the stock. This may all seem very straightforward, but there are times when this information can get a bit complicated.

For example, if you sell some but not all of the shares of stock you own in a corporation, you have the choice of which specific shares you sell. You can choose to sell the shares you bought first, which may generate long-term treatment and lower tax rates, or you may want to sell shares you bought more recently because they were more expensive and will generate a loss or a smaller gain. You may have some capital losses that you won't be able to deduct this year because they exceed $3,000, but you can sell certain shares of stock that will generate a gain that can be offset against the loss, thus making the gain essentially tax-free.

Examine the cost of the shares of stock you own and consider the tax ramifications of selling shares with different costs to make an intelligent decision about which shares to sell.

Note   *Be advised that if you decide to choose the specific shares you want to sell, and those shares are held by a stockbroker, it is your responsibility to advise the broker of which shares you want sold.*

Selling Shares of Mutual Funds

If you purchase shares in a mutual fund over a period of time, or if you have dividends reinvested in such an account, you may think you have an accounting nightmare when you try to calculate the gain or loss on the sale of shares. Every month there are purchases in the account from the reinvested dividends, and each purchase carries its own basis and purchase date.

See "Selling Shares in Mutual Funds" in Chapter 19 for detailed information about how to value your shares and also how you can manage the shares to exert control over the gain or loss you incur when selling them.

Selling Other Investments

Because nearly everything you sell for a gain results in a taxable transaction, you must keep on top of sales all year. It's easy to remember that you sold stock or mutual funds—your year-end broker statements will remind you. But what about selling some of your antiques at the flea market or cleaning out the closets on eBay? Those items require recordkeeping and diligence.

Anything you sell should be catalogued, with the original purchase date (or an estimate, if that is the best you can do), the original cost (again, an estimate if necessary), the date of sale, and the sales cost. Any costs associated with the sale (a fee to the online agent or costs to repair the item before it can be sold) get deducted from the sales cost when computing your gain.

All personal items you sell for a profit must be reported on Schedule D, and TurboTax will show you the way. Gains on sales of personal items are subject to income tax at the favorable, capital gain tax rates. (Losses on such sales are not deductible and don't get included on your tax return.) These items will be reported later in the program, on a screen called Sale Of Other Investment Or Personal Property (see Figure 5-3).

Interest Income

Interest income represents earnings from your investments in banks, credit unions, and other financial institutions, in the form of savings accounts and other interest-bearing accounts, investments in bonds, and loans owed to you. Most interest income is reported to you on Form 1099-INT. Your form may look like the one shown here, or it may be a bit different, depending on the whims of the issuer.

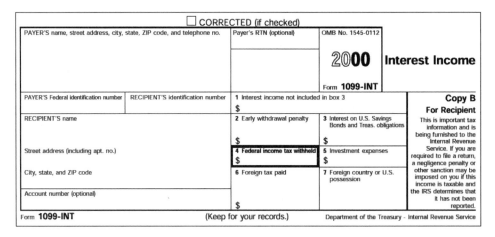

You only need one 1099 form from each of your interest-bearing investments, but sometimes you may receive duplicates. Occasionally an institution will send out a year-end statement that purports to be a 1099-INT, and they will send a separate 1099-INT form as well. This doesn't mean you have to report the income twice! In fact, check closely to make sure you don't duplicate the income—it's easy to do when you receive more than one form.

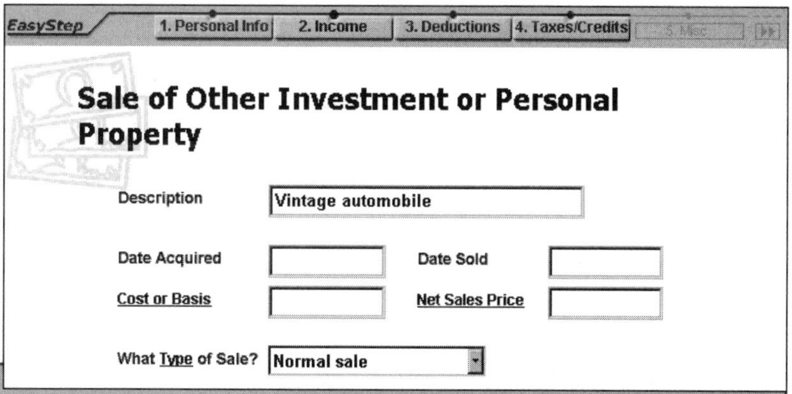

Figure 5-3 • Indicate all the particulars about your sale of a personal property item.

The IRS gets copies of the 1099 forms. Also, they cross-reference the forms with your tax return. If you fail to report some of your 1099 interest or dividend income, chances are good that the IRS will catch the discrepancy between their copies of forms and the amount you reported. The IRS may contact you and ask you to resolve the difference between their records and yours.

Note *If you earned less than $10 in interest or dividend income from an investment, you may not get a 1099 form in the mail. The companies that paid the interest and dividends aren't required to send you a 1099 unless the amount you earned is at least $10. This doesn't mean you don't have to report the income from these low-paying investments! It's your responsibility to know what you earned and report everything on your income tax return, whether or not you receive a statement in the mail.*

Interest Income Not Reported on Form 1099-INT

If you receive interest on a personal loan, you probably won't receive a 1099 form. You must still report the income on your income tax return. List it with your other interest income, as shown in Figure 5-4.

Interest Income from Seller-Financed Mortgages

If you sold your home on a contract to someone and you are receiving periodic payments on that contract, those payments include interest income. When you enter that income in TurboTax, you will be asked for the name, address, and Social

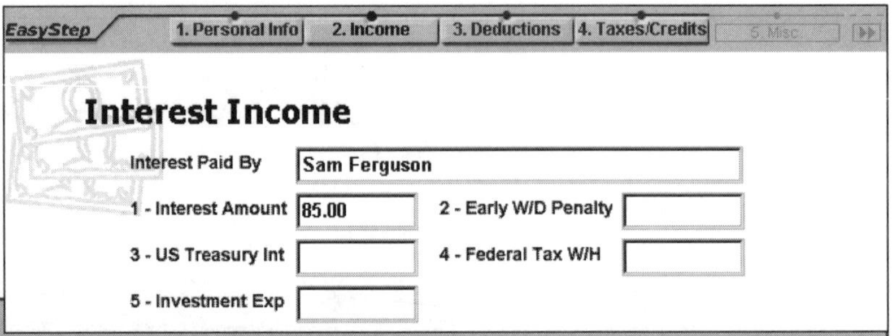

Figure 5-4 • Enter interest income received on personal loans just as you would interest earned at the bank.

Security number of person who paid you the interest, in addition to the amount you received. The IRS needs this information because presumably the person paying you will take a mortgage interest deduction for this amount on his or her Schedule A. There must be a way for the IRS to tie these two amounts together.

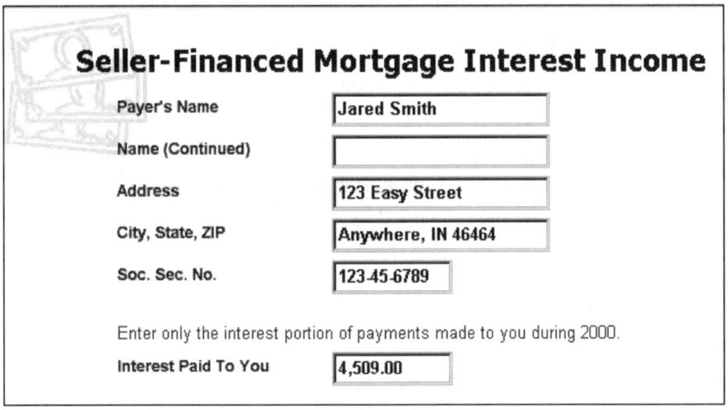

Tax-Exempt Interest

Some interest income is exempt from federal income taxation. This favored status applies primarily to income from investments in state or local municipal bonds. Interest earned on municipal bonds is usually exempt from state income tax as well as federal income tax, if the bond was issued in your state. In the screen shown in Figure 5-5, you should check the first check box if the interest is exempt from federal income tax. If the interest is exempt from state income tax because the interest was earned on a municipal bond that was issued in your state, enter the two-letter abbreviation for your state in the space provided on the actual Schedule B form in the lower portion of your TurboTax screen.

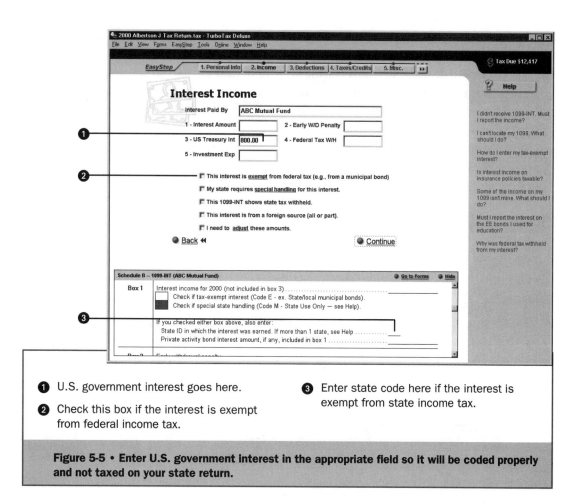

① U.S. government interest goes here.

② Check this box if the interest is exempt from federal income tax.

③ Enter state code here if the interest is exempt from state income tax.

Figure 5-5 • Enter U.S. government interest in the appropriate field so it will be coded properly and not taxed on your state return.

If you earned interest that is exempt from federal income tax, you may be wondering why you need to report the earnings on your tax return. The IRS uses information about your tax-exempt interest for a few calculations:

- Some tax-exempt interest you earn is used to determine whether or not you can take an IRA deduction.

- Some tax-exempt interest you earn is used to determine your alternative minimum tax (see Chapter 9 for more information on this tax).

- The amount of tax-exempt interest you earn is used to calculate how much of your Social Security income is taxable.

Some interest is exempt on state tax returns but not on your federal return. Interest earned on investments in U.S. Treasury bonds, bills, notes, and zero coupon Treasury bonds is taxable on your federal income tax return but exempt from state and local income taxation. When you enter the interest earned on these investments, be sure to place the amount in the US Treasury Int area so it will be coded properly for your state tax return (see Figure 5-5). If you plan to prepare your state tax return manually, make sure you remember to deduct this amount on the appropriate line of your state tax return.

Dividend Income

Dividend income represents distributions of earnings from your investments in corporations in the form of stock ownership. Dividends are usually paid in cash but can be paid in additional stock or in property. If your investments earned dividends during 2000, you should receive a 1099-DIV form in early 2001 indicating the amount of your dividends for the year. A sample 1099-DIV form is shown in Figure 5-6.

Sometimes dividends are reported on your broker's year-end statement and that statement will take the place of the small dividend form.

☐ CORRECTED (if checked)

PAYER'S name, street address, city, state, ZIP code, and telephone no.		1 Ordinary dividends $ 2a Total capital gain distr. $	OMB No. 1545-0110 **2000** Form **1099-DIV**	**Dividends and Distributions**
PAYER'S Federal identification number	RECIPIENT'S identification number	2b 28% rate gain $	2c Unrecap. sec. 1250 gain $	**Copy B For Recipient**
RECIPIENT'S name		2d Section 1202 gain $	3 Nontaxable distributions $	This is important tax information and is being furnished to the Internal Revenue Service. If you are required to file a return, a negligence penalty or other sanction may be imposed on you if this income is taxable and the IRS determines that it has not been reported.
Street address (including apt. no.)		**4 Federal income tax withheld** $	5 Investment expenses $	
City, state, and ZIP code		6 Foreign tax paid $	7 Foreign country or U.S. possession	
Account number (optional)		8 Cash liquidation distr. $	9 Noncash liquidation distr. $	

Form **1099-DIV** (Keep for your records.) Department of the Treasury - Internal Revenue Service

Figure 5-6 • An annual form like this summarizes the dividends you received from one company for the year.

Entering Dividends Reported on 1099 Forms

You can follow along on the 1099-DIV form you receive and enter the information right onto the TurboTax screen. There is a box on the screen for each box on the form. Each 1099-DIV gets entered separately.

Taxable Dividend Income

Payer	ABC Company		
1 - Ordinary Divs	350.00	2a - Capital Gains	
2b - 28% Tax Gain		2c - Sec 1250 Gain	
2d - Sec 1202 Gain		3 - Nontax Distrib	
4 - Federal Tax W/H		5 - Investment Exp	

Be sure to check the appropriate boxes if any of the situations listed at the bottom of the screen apply, such as U.S. government interest included in your dividends (this can happen if you own shares in a mutual fund that invests in U.S. government instruments). If you check any of these boxes, the next screen will ask for the necessary information.

Note *If your dividends include capital gain distributions (box 2a of the 1099-DIV), this amount is long-term capital gain that will be carried to your Schedule D and grouped with other gains and losses on assets. This amount will be taxed at the favorable capital gain tax rate (see "Capital Gain Tax Rates" previously in this chapter). If you are looking for capital gains with which to offset capital losses that exceed the $3,000 per year limit on how much loss you can deduct, this is one source to consider.*

Accounting for Stock Dividends

Sometimes companies issue stock to their shareholders in the form of stock splits. In a stock split, the shareholders receive a quantity of stock shares based on how many shares they own. For example, a 2-for-1 split occurs when a company gives you one stock share for every one that you own. After the transaction, you have twice as many shares as before the split, thus the concept of 2 for 1. Stock splits are not taxable transactions, because you have not gained anything of value. You owned 100 shares, now you own 200 shares, but the value of the new shares is half the value of the old shares, so the total value of your portfolio has not changed.

When a stock split occurs, the *basis* in your stock changes. If you bought 100 shares for $20 per share and now you own 200 shares because of a stock split, the basis in each share drops to $10. When you sell the shares you will compare the sales price to your basis of $10 per share to determine your gain or loss.

Stock splits do not get reported on a 1099-DIV and you don't have to report the split on your tax return.

Income from Your Own Business

People who work for themselves, either full- or part-time, report their income and related expenses on Schedule C, Profit or Loss From Business. (Farmers report their income and related expenses on Schedule F, Profit or Loss From Farming. Farming business is covered later in this chapter.) If your business is small, with receipts of $25,000 or less and no more than $2,000 in business expenses, you may be able to file Schedule C-EZ. TurboTax will make the determination as to which business form you will need to file.

When you work for yourself, you are considered to be either a sole proprietor or an independent contractor. If you are an independent contractor (see next section), you may perform services for someone else who pays you for those services, but that person does not employ you.

Are You an Employee or an Independent Contractor?

The IRS closely examines relationships between business owners and the people who work for them to determine if the workers are supposed to be treated as employees or as independent contractors. The IRS has developed a 20-point checklist to help define the independent contractor, but there is no hard and fast rule.

Although the decision to call someone an employee or an independent contractor is somewhat subjective, the general rule is that if you have control over how, when, and where you perform a job, you are probably an independent contractor. If the person who pays you controls your work, you are probably an employee. The more of these 20 points that you can answer positively, the more likely it is that you will be considered an employee:

- Does your boss give you instructions that you have to obey?
- Does the company you work for provide you with training?

- Are your services integrated into the regular business operation of the place where you work?
- Is it a requirement that you, personally, provide the services?
- Are you prohibited from subcontracting the work?
- Is the business relationship an ongoing one?
- Does the person for whom you work set your hours?
- Are you required to work full time for one organization?
- Is your work performed at the premises of the person who pays you?
- Does your boss tell you in what order to perform your tasks?
- Must you submit reports (oral or written) summarizing your work progress?
- Do you receive payment at regular intervals, such as weekly or monthly?
- Do you get reimbursed for business and travel expenses?
- Does the person you work for provide your tools and supplies?
- Do you have no significant investment in the tools required to perform your job?
- Is your work relationship such that you will never incur a loss from the services you provide?
- Are you prohibited from working for more than one company or person at a time?
- Are you prohibited from making your services available to the general public?
- Is it the company's responsibility if you don't meet the specifications of your contract?
- If you cause damage, is the company for which you work responsible?

Entering Income Reported on 1099 Forms

If it is determined that you perform services as an independent contractor, or if you operate a nonservice business yourself, the IRS expects you to enter your income on Schedule C. Some of your income may be reported to you on 1099-MISC forms, and TurboTax provides a special section where you can enter the income reported on these forms.

One timesaving advantage of using this section of the interview to fill in the information about your 1099-MISC is that TurboTax will remember this information next year. The names of the people and companies who report the amount they pay you in this manner will already be entered in the program.

The 1099 forms are information forms that you keep with your records—you don't have to turn these forms over to the IRS like you do your W-2 forms. The exception to this rule is that if the person or company issuing the 1099-MISC form withholds tax from your pay, that tax withholding will be reported on the 1099-MISC form (see Figure 5-7), and you should attach the 1099-MISC form to your tax return as evidence of the withholding.

The IRS receives copies of the 1099-MISC forms. Although the 1099 forms are not listed individually on your Schedule C, the IRS will scrutinize the amount of income you report on your Schedule C and they will notice if the amount you report as income on your tax return isn't at least as much as the amount of income that was reported to you on 1099-MISC forms.

If you received 1099-MISC forms relating to your business, enter them in TurboTax in this manner:

1. If you are married filing a joint tax return, identify to which spouse the 1099-MISC applies.
2. Enter the name of the person or company making the payment.

An amount here represents income tax withholding. If an amount appears here, you must attach this form to your Form 1040.

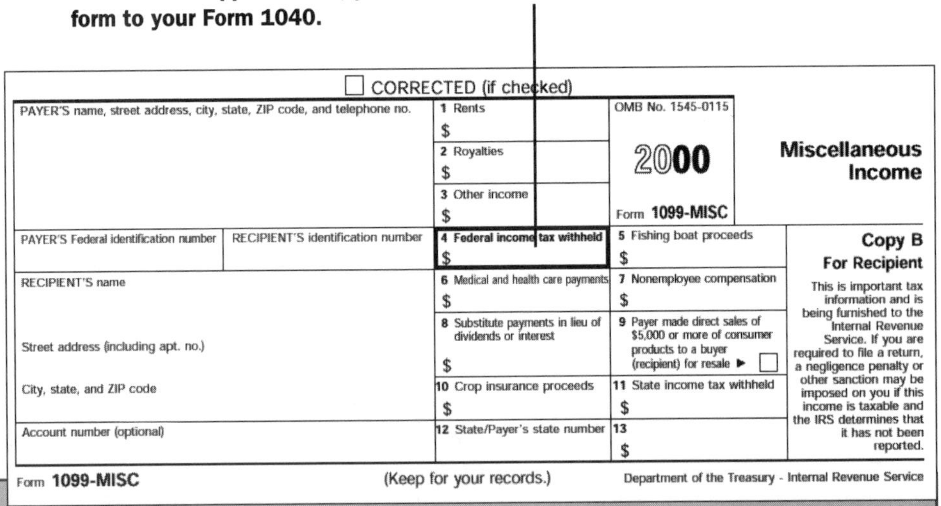
☐ CORRECTED (if checked)

PAYER'S name, street address, city, state, ZIP code, and telephone no.

1 Rents $

2 Royalties $

3 Other income $

OMB No. 1545-0115

2000

Form 1099-MISC

Miscellaneous Income

PAYER'S Federal identification number

RECIPIENT'S identification number

4 Federal income tax withheld $

5 Fishing boat proceeds $

RECIPIENT'S name

6 Medical and health care payments $

7 Nonemployee compensation $

Street address (including apt. no.)

8 Substitute payments in lieu of dividends or interest $

9 Payer made direct sales of $5,000 or more of consumer products to a buyer (recipient) for resale ▶ ☐

City, state, and ZIP code

10 Crop insurance proceeds $

11 State income tax withheld $

Account number (optional)

12 State/Payer's state number

13 $

Copy B For Recipient

This is important tax information and is being furnished to the Internal Revenue Service. If you are required to file a return, a negligence penalty or other sanction may be imposed on you if this income is taxable and the IRS determines that it has not been reported.

Form 1099-MISC (Keep for your records.) Department of the Treasury - Internal Revenue Service

Figure 5-7 • Transfer the amounts from your 1099-MISC to TurboTax.

3. Follow along with your 1099-MISC, entering the amount from each box into the appropriate areas on the EasyStep Interview screens.

ABC Company - Boxes 1-8

Payer's Name	ABC Company
Account Number	

1 - Rents		5 - Fishing Boat	
2 - Royalties		6 - Medical Pmts	
3 - Other Income		7 - Nonempl Comp	1,200.00
4 - Fed Income Tax		8 - Substitute Pmts	

4. Associate the 1099-MISC income with your Schedule C. Because there may be situations where you enter information from a 1099-MISC on another area of your tax return, you must specifically associate this income with the schedule on which it is to appear. In this case, you must identify the Schedule C to which this income belongs.

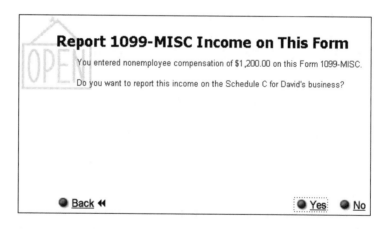

Report 1099-MISC Income on This Form

You entered nonemployee compensation of $1,200.00 on this Form 1099-MISC.

Do you want to report this income on the Schedule C for David's business?

● Back ◄◄   ● Yes   ● No

Caution   *If you don't associate a 1099-MISC with a specific tax form (such as your Schedule C), the income will not be included on your tax return.*

You Didn't Receive a 1099-MISC

A business is required to prepare a 1099-MISC form if the services it pays for are $600 or more. If you are a business consultant who charges a client $595 for a consulting project, the client is not required to prepare a 1099-MISC for your services. If you charge $600, you are required to provide your Social Security number or federal identification number to the client, and the client, if it is a corporation, is required to provide you with a 1099-MISC.

Sometimes people just don't get around to preparing and mailing the 1099-MISC forms. Small businesses, in particular, that don't have many 1099-MISC forms to fill out may decide not to bother sending the forms. Even though the business may be required to prepare such a form for you, it's not a crisis if you don't receive the form. You must still report the income on your tax return, whether or not you have a piece of paper documenting the income.

The business that fails to prepare these required forms is liable for a penalty of $50 per unfiled form, but that is between the business and the IRS. As long as you report the income properly on your tax return, you don't need to be concerned with the fact that you didn't receive a form in the mail.

Entering Other Income

Enter other income you received in your business by entering the entire amount in the TurboTax field Receipts Or Sales Not Reported On Form 1099-MISC.

You can provide details on the income entered in the above screen by double-clicking in the field and filling in the Supporting Details window that appears. You have the option of including this supporting schedule with your tax return or simply keeping it for your records. The IRS doesn't require details on the source of your receipts, but you are welcome to send this schedule with your tax return. The schedule can include narrative information in addition to a list of names and amounts. Note that if you file your return electronically, the supporting schedule will not be included with your tax return.

Supporting Details

Check this box to **NOT** print this supporting details .... ► ☐

Schedule C (Sales)/Other receipts

Description	Amount
Misc Income earned Jan-Mar	2,300.00
Misc Income earned Apr-June	2,000.00
Misc Income earned July-Sept	6,000.00
Misc Income earned Oct-Dec	1,700.00
4 Items	**Total** 12,000.00

Sort Delete Line Insert Line Remove Print Close Help

Cash versus Accrual Accounting

When you enter business income on Schedule C, you are asked if your business uses the cash or the accrual method of accounting. Most people who use Schedule C for their small business use the cash method of accounting for reporting their business income and expenses, but that method is not a requirement. If you filed Schedule C in prior years, you already have an accounting method in place. Look at last year's Schedule C to see which box was checked. If this is your first year for using Schedule C, the following discusses your options for methods for reporting your income and expenses. If you are just beginning your business, it would be wise to talk to an accountant about accounting methods. Once you make a decision to use an accounting method, you must request permission from the IRS to change. Note: If you don't keep written records of your income and expenses, you are required to use the cash method of accounting.

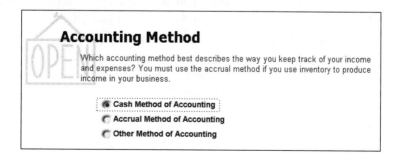

Cash Method

Using the cash method of accounting, you report income in the year you receive it and expenses in the year you pay for them. In other words, when the cash is in your hands, you report it as income. When the cash leaves your hands, you report the expense. If you sell items in December 2000 and don't receive the money for the sale until January 2001, the income belongs on your 2001 income tax return. If you incur a business expense in November 2000, receive the bill in December 2000, but don't pay for the expense until January 2001, the expense is a deduction on your 2001 income tax return.

Accrual Method

With the accrual method of accounting, you report income in the year it is earned, even if you don't receive it in that year. Using the accrual method, if you perform some work in December 2000 and don't get paid for your work until January 2001, the income belongs on your 2000 tax return. If you purchase some business supplies in December 2000 but don't pay for them until January 2001, the expense for the supplies is a deduction on your 2000 income tax return.

Entering Business Expenses

The cost of doing business is not something you have to bear alone. The IRS allows business owners to take deductions for the regular expense of conducting a trade or business. Expenses such as payroll, rent, auto expenses, supplies, and insurance all contribute to the operation of a business.

Business expenses are used to reduce your business income and thus your tax. By subtracting your business expenses from your business income (which TurboTax will do automatically), you lower the amount of income on which your income tax is computed. Furthermore, business income is subject to the self-employment (Social Security) tax, and business deductions reduce this tax as well.

No one tells you how much you are allowed to spend on your business. Know, though, that the IRS watches out for unusually high business expenses and compares your deductions to national averages. If something seems out of line, the IRS has the right to question your deduction and ask for documentation to support the amount. Make sure that you keep clear and accurate records of all of your business expenditures.

Inventory

If you keep an inventory on hand, the cost of the inventory items that you sell is a deductible expense. How you determine that cost can be a complicated accounting issue, especially if you have either a large quantity or a large variety of inventory items. The first issue you must disclose on your tax return is how you determine the cost of your inventory items.

The Cost of Your Inventory   Most people use the cost method of valuing their inventory because it is the easiest method. Choose from one of the following methods of valuation and apply this method to your entire inventory.

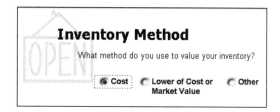

- **Cost.** Choose Cost if you value your inventory at the actual cost that you paid for it or the actual cost incurred in building the item.
- **Lower Of Cost Or Market Value.** Choose this method if you keep track of the market value of your inventory and choose the lower of the two amounts (cost or market) for your method of valuing the inventory. If you use this method, you must determine the value of each item in your inventory, comparing its cost to the market value and choosing the lower amount.
- **Other.** If neither of the two preceding methods applies to you, choose the Other option. Attach a statement to your tax return (just write out a paragraph and put it behind your Schedule C when you assemble your return) describing how you have valued your inventory.

Note   *If you reported inventory on last year's tax return, you have already made a determination as to how you will treat the cost of your inventory items. If you have changed methods of costing your inventory, you must indicate this information on your tax return and attach a statement explaining how and why you made the change.*

Inventory Value

What was the value of your inventory at the...

Beginning of 2000 [　　　　]   End of 2000 [　　　　]

☑ I Didn't use the same method to value my inventory at the end of 2000 as I did at the beginning of 2000.

Note: If you did change the method you use to value your inventory, attach an explanation to your tax return.

Valuing Your Inventory   When you enter the value of your inventory, you are required to enter the value as of the end of the year 1999 and the value as of the end of the year 2000 (see Figure 5-8). TurboTax will compare the two numbers to determine the change in your inventory, and your deduction for inventory cost will reflect this change.

The method you choose for determining the cost of your inventory will help you in calculating the actual value of your inventory. Once you decide the cost of each item in inventory, you must determine which items actually remain in your inventory and which ones got sold.

There are three methods of determining the value of your closing inventory. You should choose the method that most closely represents the actual value of your inventory items. Once you pick a method, you must stick with that method. If you decide you have a business reason for changing the method of valuation, you must request approval from the IRS to change your method.

- **Specific identification.** If you've been able to track each item in your inventory and know the cost of each item as you sell it, you can specifically identify the cost of the items remaining in your ending inventory. This is the most precise way of measuring the value of your inventory. Computers have made the specific identification method much more viable for companies, even those with a large inventory.

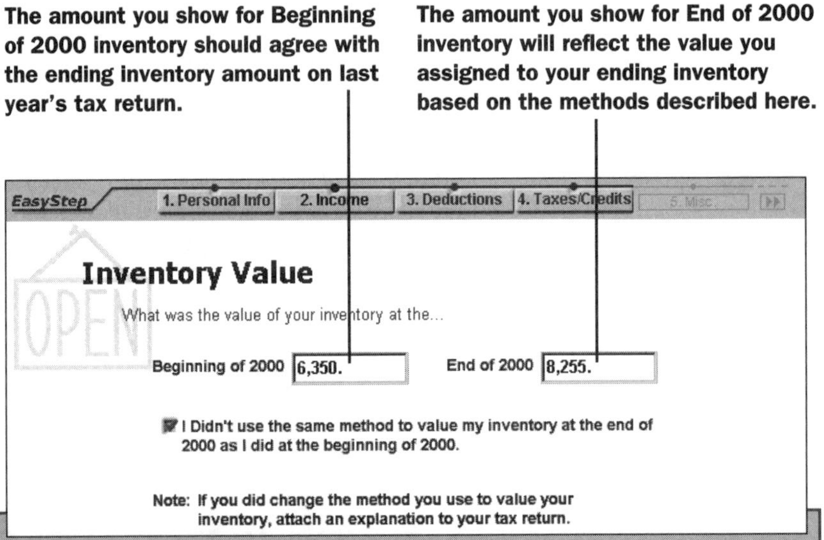

The amount you show for Beginning of 2000 inventory should agree with the ending inventory amount on last year's tax return.

The amount you show for End of 2000 inventory will reflect the value you assigned to your ending inventory based on the methods described here.

EasyStep	1. Personal Info	2. Income	3. Deductions	4. Taxes/Credits	5. Misc

Inventory Value

What was the value of your inventory at the...

Beginning of 2000 `6,350.`   End of 2000 `8,255.`

☑ I Didn't use the same method to value my inventory at the end of 2000 as I did at the beginning of 2000.

Note: If you did change the method you use to value your inventory, attach an explanation to your tax return.

Figure 5-8 • Enter the value you assigned to your inventory.

- **FIFO.** FIFO stands for first-in-first-out. If you can't specifically identify the cost of each item in your inventory, or if there are so many inventory items it would take too much time to figure out the individual cost of each item, you can value your inventory using this method. With FIFO, you assume that the first inventory items you purchased (first in) are the first ones you sold (first out). Therefore, the cost of items remaining in your inventory at the end of the year is represented by the cost of the last inventory items you bought, even if this isn't precisely true. A food store is a good example of a business that would embrace this method. The oldest perishable food items are the ones the business will try to sell first, before they turn bad.

- **LIFO.** LIFO stands for last-in-first-out. Using this method, you assume that the last inventory items you purchased (last in) are the first items you sold (first out). Therefore, the cost of items remaining in your inventory at the end of the year is represented by the cost of the earliest items you purchased. If you go to a hardware store where the items on the back of the shelf are covered with dust and the items on the front of the shelf are shiny and new, it's a safe bet the hardware store owner should be using the LIFO method for valuing his inventory.

Material Participation in Your Business   A complicated area of tax law surrounds the concept of material participation. The IRS needs to know if you materially participated in your business. If you didn't, you are considered a passive owner of the business and the expenses you incur in your business are limited to the income you report for your business and other similar activities. Additional expenses that cannot be deducted will be carried over to future years where they can be offset against business income.

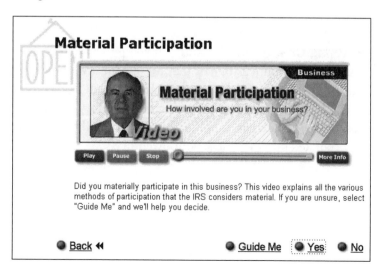

To be considered a material participant in your business, you must meet one of these tests:

- You, or your spouse, participated in the business for more than 500 hours during 2000.
- You are basically the only person who participates in this activity.
- You participated in the business for more than 100 hours during 2000, and no one else participated more in the business than you did (someone else could, however, participate an equal amount of time as you).
- You participated in several Schedule C–type businesses for more than 100 hours during 2000, and your total time in these businesses adds up to more than 500 hours for 2000.
- You met the material participation test for five of the past ten tax years. If the business still exists, you are a material participant this year even if you don't meet any other tests. This rule is for people who retire but are still marginally active in their business. But the IRS is more flexible about determining material participation if your business involves a service that you provide. See the next point, which discusses personal service businesses.
- If your business involves performing a personal service such as accounting, law, writing, architecture, music, engineering, medicine, or consulting—something that requires your personal service in order to accomplish the job—you need only to have materially participated in the business for any three of the past ten years to continue material participation in the current year.
- You participated in the business on a "regular, continuous, and substantial" basis. This last-chance test is subjective, and whether or not you meet this test is completely up to the IRS.

Entering Cost of Goods Sold   If you purchase items for your inventory, then resell them to your customers, the cost of your inventory items that you sell will simply be the cost of the inventory purchases you made during the year. If you have a hand in producing or altering the inventory items before you sell them, the cost of labor, materials, supplies, shipping, and other related costs will be incorporated into the cost of your inventory.

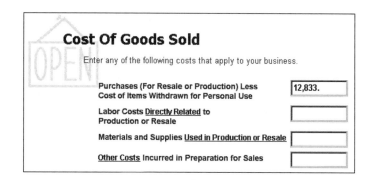

Cost Of Goods Sold

Enter any of the following costs that apply to your business.

Purchases (For Resale or Production) Less
Cost of Items Withdrawn for Personal Use   `12,833.`

Labor Costs <u>Directly Related</u> to
Production or Resale

Materials and Supplies <u>Used in Production or Resale</u>

<u>Other Costs</u> Incurred in Preparation for Sales

You will enter all of the costs associated with your inventory for the year, even though some of the inventory items may remain on hand and have not been sold yet. TurboTax will calculate the actual cost of the items you sold by adjusting the cost of inventory acquired or produced during 2000 with the change in inventory from the end of the year last year to the end of the year 2000.

General Business Expenses

Expenses are the cost of operating your business. Everyone's business is different, and the types of expenses that you claim as deductions for your business vary depending on what kind of business you have. TurboTax lists common types of deductions (see Figure 5-9) that appear as separate lines on the Schedule C tax form, where your business income and deductions appear. You are not limited to the deductions that you see listed here. After entering information on the expense screens provided by TurboTax, you will be given an opportunity to enter "other deductions," where you can provide a detailed list of expenses not previously deducted.

| EasyStep | 1. Personal Info | 2. Income | 3. Deductions | 4. Taxes/Credits | 5. Misc. |

Business Expenses

Advertising	`653.`	Mortgage Interest	
Bad Debts		Other Interest	
Commissions		Legal/Prof Fees	`250.`
Depletion		Office Expense	`425.`
Empl Benefits		Pension Plans	
Insurance	`370.`		

Figure 5-9 • Fill in the blanks to show the various expenses related to your business.

Business Travel Expenses   Airplane, bus, train, taxi, limousine, car rental—any form of transportation other than your personal automobile expense (which has its own category) while traveling overnight is summarized here. Also allowed as travel expense are lodging, baggage handling, cleaning and laundry expenses, valet service, telephone expenses (business calls only), tips, and any ordinary, necessary, and reasonable expense incurred while traveling overnight. Do not include meals in this category.

If you mix business with pleasure when you travel, be prepared to separate the business portion of your expenses from the personal portion. If another family member travels with you, the expenses incurred for that family member are not business expenses unless the family member is working for you in your business.

Meals and Entertainment   Meals and beverages relating to the operation of your business, including meals while traveling, tickets to athletic events and theaters, and hunting and fishing trips, are deductible expenses. The deduction for expenses in this category is limited to 50 percent of the amount you spent on these expenses during 2000. Enter the full amount of your meals and entertainment expenses on the first line of this screen (see Figure 5-10), and TurboTax will take care of computing the 50 percent limitation.

Certain exceptions apply to the 50 percent rule for deducting meal expenses. The Department of Transportation has issued special rules for airline personnel, interstate truck drivers, and merchant marines—their meals fall under a 60 percent deductible rule. Certain other meals are 100 percent deductible. This includes meals you provide to your employees at company events. The 100 percent rule also applies to meals that you provide to employees and independent contractors if the meals are included in the W-2 forms and 1099-MISC forms of these workers.

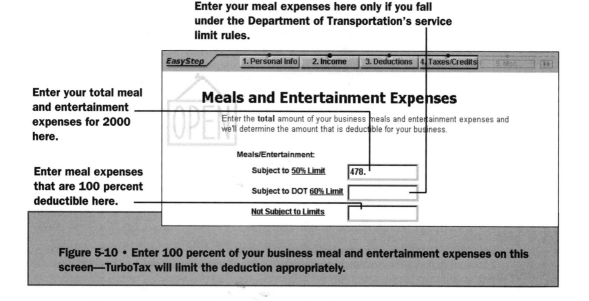

Enter your meal expenses here only if you fall
under the Department of Transportation's service
limit rules.

Enter your total meal
and entertainment
expenses for 2000
here.

Meals and Entertainment Expenses

Enter the **total** amount of your business meals and entertainment expenses and
we'll determine the amount that is deductible for your business.

Enter meal expenses
that are 100 percent
deductible here.

Meals/Entertainment:

Subject to <u>50% Limit</u>　478.

Subject to DOT <u>60% Limit</u>

<u>Not Subject to Limits</u>

Figure 5-10 • Enter 100 percent of your business meal and entertainment expenses on this screen—TurboTax will limit the deduction appropriately.

The meals that you deduct must be directly related to your business or associated with your business. This means that you need to be able to prove that you derive some business benefit from providing the meals. You should keep a record of all your meal expenses, such as names of people who were present, the date, place where meal was provided, cost of the meal, and the business purpose. Save receipts whenever possible.

Taking a Home Office Deduction

In addition to the benefit of being able to meet your children at the door with a plate of warm cookies when they come home from school, there are tax advantages to working from home. Many of the amounts you would spend anyway on operating your home become deductible business expenses when your home is your office. And a portion of those expenses that would be deducible as itemized deductions on your Schedule A—such as mortgage interest and property taxes—are still deductible, only they are deducted on Schedule C instead of on Schedule A. Why does it matter if you take the deduction on Schedule A or Schedule C, as long as you get the deduction?

There are a few benefits that come with reporting deductions on Schedule C:

- Items that are deductible on Schedule C generally carry over to your state income tax return, so you get a reduction of state as well as federal income taxes as a result of these deductions.

- By pulling items out of your itemized deductions, you might reduce your itemized deductions to the level where the standard deduction is higher than the itemized deductions, thus giving you the benefit of using the standard deduction while still allowing you to reduce your income by your other deductions (because they're on Schedule C). The end result is higher deductions for you.

- If you have the opportunity to shift deductions from Schedule A to Schedule C, you will be able to reduce your self-employment tax.

- You may not even have enough deductions to itemize on Schedule A, or your filing situation may prevent you from doing so (for example, if you are using the Married Filing Separately status, both spouses must agree to itemize or neither can do so). If you don't itemize, the only way you will get the benefit of deductions for home mortgage interest and property tax is if you take the deductions on Schedule C.

See Chapter 7 for more information about itemizing.

Note *Home is where you place your doormat. The home office deduction is not limited to people who own their own houses. You can take a home office deduction for the office space in a house or apartment that you rent, your condominium, your houseboat or trailer, or any other place you call home.*

Who Qualifies for the Home Office Deduction?

In order to take a deduction for the business use of your home, certain rules must be followed:

- The area of your home designated as a home office must be used *regularly*, on an ongoing basis, for your business. Occasional use of the home office will not count toward making the office expenses deductible.

- If you have another place of business in addition to your home office, the home office must be the place where the most important part of your business takes place. If you perform all of your work outside of the home, but use the home for the bookkeeping and administrative functions of your work, you will meet the requirements for claiming a home office.

- The area you use for a home office must be used *exclusively* for work. If the home office is used for work as well as for personal use, the deduction will be disqualified.

Note   *Your home office deductions may be limited. Expenses for the use of your home as a business can only be deducted on your tax return if they do not exceed the net income of your business. In other words, the home office deduction cannot generate a loss on your business tax form. Any home office expense that you are not able to deduct this year will carry over and you may deduct the expense next year, assuming your business generates enough income to offset the expense.*

Deductible Home Office Expenses

The amount of home office expense you can deduct is calculated by taking a percentage of the normal expenses of running your home. The percentage is derived by determining how much of your home space is used for your office compared to the entire space in the home. You can calculate this percentage in one of two ways. Either use the square feet of the office compared with the square feet of the entire home, or, if the rooms in your home are all approximately the same size, count the number of rooms you use for your office and compare that to the number of rooms in your entire home. Enter the numbers, square feet or rooms, into the appropriate boxes on the TurboTax screen, and TurboTax will calculate the percent for you.

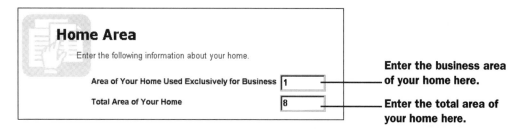

You will also be asked to enter the percent of profit you derive from the business you conduct at your home. If you work in more than one location, this amount will be something less than 100 percent. This percentage may limit the amount of home office deduction you can claim this year.

The types of expenses you can deduct relating to your home office include:

- Mortgage interest
- Property tax

- Rent
- Utilities (gas, electric, water, and sewer)
- Repairs
- Insurance
- Depreciation
- Cleaning

When you enter your home office expenses, you must indicate if the expense is direct or indirect. *Direct expenses* are those expenses that relate specifically to your home office. If you paint the walls or repair the electrical wiring in the part of the home used as your office, that is a direct expense and the entire amount will be treated as a home office expense.

Direct and Indirect Expenses

Enter this home's <u>direct and indirect</u> expenses.

	Direct Expenses	Indirect Expenses
Casualty Losses		
Mortgage Interest		2,000.
Real Estate Taxes		1,200.
Excess Mortgage Interest		
Insurance		450.
Repairs & Maintenance		270.
Utilities		1,146.
Other Expenses		

Note The main telephone line that comes into your house is considered a personal expense, even if you use the phone primarily for business. The cost of long distance telephone charges may be deducted as a business expense, but the monthly cost for having the phone in the house is not deductible. A second phone line that is dedicated 100 percent to your business is fully deductible.

Expenses that relate to the entire home must be allocated to the home office, based on the percentage of space used for the office. These are *indirect expenses* because they don't relate exclusively to the office. Most of your home expenses, such as mortgage interest, real estate tax, homeowner's insurance, trash pickup, utilities, and furnace repair, are indirect expenses.

> **Note** *When you enter home office expenses that would be otherwise allowed as itemized deductions, such as mortgage interest and property tax, TurboTax will take the personal portion of this expense that is not used on your business expense form and transfer it automatically to your itemized deductions form. Do not enter the expense again when you enter your itemized deductions for mortgage interest and real estate tax.*

The Effects of Depreciating Your Home

Rather than deducting in the year of purchase the cost of an asset you expect to use for several years, you deduct the cost over the years during which you will use the asset in your business. This process of deducting over several years is called *depreciation*.

If you claim a deduction for the business use of a home that you own, you must take a deduction for depreciation expense on the portion of the home being used for business. This generates a nice deduction in the years in which you operate the business, but taking this deduction may result in a taxable gain when you sell the house.

TurboTax will calculate the depreciation expense for you when you enter the date you began using the home for business and the cost of the home. TurboTax will also keep track, year after year, of the amount of depreciation you claim on your home, and you may have to pay tax on a portion of the gain on the home in the year in which you sell the home.

If you sell a home that has been depreciated as a home office, the gain on the home, to the extent that you have taken depreciation deductions, will be taxed as ordinary income, just as if you sold some other business asset, such as a computer or something from your inventory. The special tax treatment that allows many people to sell their home without paying tax on the gain (see "Selling Your Home" later in this chapter) does not apply to the portion of a home that is being used as a business.

The Audit Risk Associated with Home Office Deductions

Years ago, people thought that taking a home office deduction on your tax return raised an immediate red flag, and you might as well just call up the IRS when you mail your return and set up an appointment for an audit, it was that likely that your return would be examined.

Times have changed. With so much of the workforce moving into home offices, the IRS has relaxed the rules for deducting home office expenses and is not calling these returns up for examination like it once did.

There is always a risk that your tax return will be examined, no matter what type of deductions you claim, because the IRS does perform random audits. But the home office deduction by itself is no longer triggering audits. As long as you keep accurate records and fill out your return correctly, it won't matter if you get audited or not. If you are entitled to a deduction, an audit won't take that deduction away.

Entering Auto Expenses

If you drive your vehicle for business purposes, the cost relating to use of the vehicle is considered a tax-deductible expense. Driving a vehicle for business means driving to business-related locations other than your office and back home.

Note *The rules explained here relate not only to auto and truck expense on your Schedule C, but also for similar expenses you may incur as an employee. If you drive your car for your job, you are entitled to a deduction for your automobile expense. If your employer reimburses you for auto usage, it is generally assumed that the reimbursement will not be included in your income and you will not have a need to take a deduction for the expenses. If you choose to deduct your auto expenses even though your employer reimbursed you for these expenses, you will have to include this reimbursement with your income from your job.*

Here are some examples of deductible driving events that will enable you to claim a tax deduction for your vehicle expense:

- Driving from job #1 to job #2
- Using your car to run errands to and from your job site
- Calling on clients, customers, and sales leads
- Driving to and from home and a temporary work site (temporary means less than two months)
- Driving from home to any business location if your home is the principal place of work

Commuting from home to your principal job site is not considered business use of the car. Mileage for commuting is not included in any computations for determining the business portion of your car usage.

There are two ways in which vehicle expense can be computed. You can use the *standard mileage* option or you can use the *actual expense* option. Generally speaking, you can choose the method that gives you the best tax deduction.

If you own your vehicle, and you decide to use the actual expense method in the first year your vehicle qualifies as a business vehicle, you must stay with that method for the business life of the car. You can't switch over to the standard mileage method. If you choose to use the standard mileage method in the first year, you can switch to the actual expense method later if you like.

If you lease your vehicle, you are only entitled to use the standard mileage method if you choose to do so in the first year of the lease, and you must continue to use that method for the duration of the lease term.

Using the Standard Mileage Options

Keep track of the miles you drive during the year—not just the business-related miles, but all the miles you drive. Certain vehicle-related expenses are deductible based on the percentage of business use of the vehicle, which means you must know the total number of miles you drove during the year as well as the number of miles you drove for business.

Enter in TurboTax the total number of miles you drove for the year, the business miles, and the commuting miles. If you drove more than one vehicle for business, you will make these entries again later for the second vehicle.

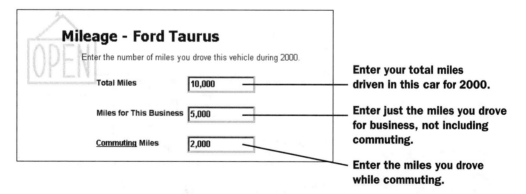

Whether you plan on using or are eligible to use the standard mileage method or the actual expense method, you must enter the mileage information.

Using the Actual Expense Option

You don't have to make the decision yourself as to whether you should use the standard mileage option or the actual expense option. If you enter all the information for both options, TurboTax will calculate both and tell you the deduction you will get for each method. If you are eligible to choose between the methods, you can select the one that will give you the best tax deduction.

Enter your actual auto expenses, including gas, oil, repairs, and so on (see Figure 5-11), and TurboTax will do the work for you. If an expense, such as car washes or new floor pads, doesn't fall into one of these categories, use the Other category. You can always double-click the Other field to create a detailed list of the items you put into this category. If you leased your car, TurboTax will give you an opportunity to enter the leased car expenses.

Note   *If you are contemplating leasing a car that you will use for business purposes and are curious about the tax effects of leasing versus buying, see "Automobile, Buy versus Lease" in Appendix B of this book, and work through the five-year plan for leasing and buying a car to see which method will provide you with the financial results you desire.*

If you pay property or excise taxes on your vehicle as part of your annual registration, don't enter that amount here. TurboTax will give you an opportunity to enter that amount later.

| EasyStep | 1. Personal Info | 2. Income | 3. Deductions | 4. Taxes/Credits | 5. Misc |

Vehicle Expenses - Ford Taurus

Enter **all** that apply.

Gasoline	2,000.	Vehicle Insurance	350.
Oil	148.	Registration/ License Fees	120.
Tires		Garage Rent	
Repairs/ Maintenance	260.	Other Expenses	175.

Figure 5-11 • Enter all of your vehicle expenses on this screen.

When computing the actual expense method of determining deductible auto expenses, you have the option of taking a deduction for depreciation on your vehicle. To make this calculation, you will need to enter the cost of the vehicle. TurboTax will make the calculation for you and advise you of your options for choosing between the standard mileage and the actual expense method.

Miscellaneous Vehicle Expenses

No matter which method you choose for deducting vehicle expenses, you are entitled to take a deduction (see Figure 5-12) for certain vehicle expenses that relate specifically to your business:

- **Business Parking Fees.** Enter the parking fees you paid during 2000 that relate specifically to your business use of the vehicle.
- **Business Tolls.** Enter the tolls you paid during 2000 that relate specifically to your business use of the vehicle.
- **Business Local Transportation.** Enter any taxi, bus, commuter train, or other local transportation expenses other than commuting expense that relate specifically to your business.
- **Property Tax Portion Of Auto Reg. Fees.** If you live in a state where property or excise tax is paid at the time you register your vehicle, enter the full amount of tax you paid here. TurboTax will compute the personal portion of this tax and carry the amount over to your Schedule A.
- **Total Interest Paid On Vehicle.** If you have a loan on your vehicle and are paying interest with your payments, enter the total amount of interest you paid for this vehicle during 2000. TurboTax will compute the business portion of the interest.

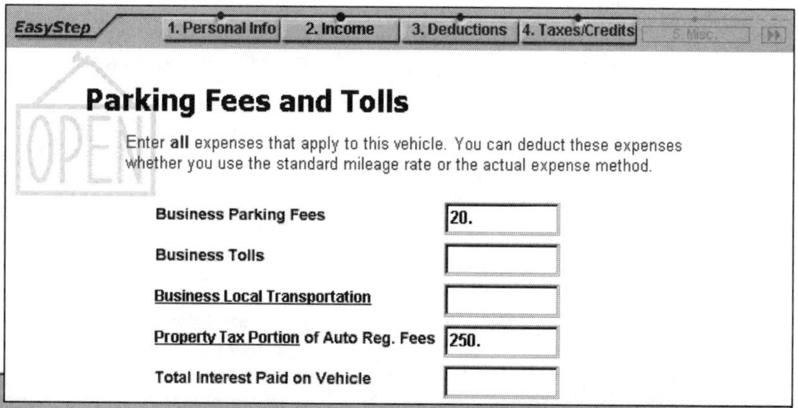

Figure 5-12 • These expenses are allowed as a deduction whether you use the standard mileage rate or the actual expense method.

Entering Information About Business Assets

Business assets are items you buy for your business that you expect will last for several years. A house can be a business asset if you're in the business of renting property (covered later in this chapter under "Income from Rental Property") or using your house for business purposes. A piece of furniture can be a business asset, and so can a car or a computer. Office supplies aren't depreciable assets because they wear out too quickly. Supplies get deducted in the year in which they are purchased.

Some assets last almost forever and can't be depreciated. Land, for example, is an asset that lasts forever. If you buy a house that you plan to use for rental property and the cost of the house includes the land on which the house stands, you have to separate the cost of the land from the cost of the house before you depreciate the house.

So that you don't have to guess how many years an asset is going to last, the IRS has produced asset groupings, summarized in Table 5-2, which provide the life expectancies for depreciable assets.

Life Expectancy Category	Type of Assets
3-year property	Breeding hogs, racehorses (at least 2 years old), and old horses (at least 12 years old when placed in service).
5-year property	Automobiles and light purpose trucks, computer equipment, and office equipment such as typewriters, calculators, and copiers. Appliances, such as stoves and refrigerators, carpets, and furniture used in rental property.
7-year property	Office furniture, tools, business equipment that doesn't fit in the 5-year class, and horses that don't fit in the 3-year class.
10-year property	Trees and vines bearing fruits or nuts, and assets used in petroleum refining.
15- and 20-year property	Sewers, treatment plants, telephone distribution plants, and communication equipment.
27.5-year property	Residential rental property.
31.5-year property	Commercial real estate property placed in service before May 13, 1993.
39-year property	Commercial real estate property placed in service after May 12, 1993.

Table 5-2 • Life Expectancies for Depreciable Assets

When you enter an asset in TurboTax, you will be asked to choose the type of asset from a descriptive list. Once you have made this choice, you can answer the questions about whether you used the asset exclusively for business and what percent of the asset was used for your business, and then TurboTax will take care of calculating the actual depreciation deduction on your behalf.

Section 179 Deduction

The IRS offers businesses the opportunity to take what amounts to a full deduction for business assets purchased during the year. The maximum deduction under Section 179 for 2000 is $20,000, which means that you can take a deduction of up to $20,000 of the cost of assets you purchased during the year.

Technically, the Section 179 deduction is a process by which you take an early deduction for the depreciation that you would have claimed over future years. Keep in mind that if you sell the asset before the depreciation period (see Table 5-2) would have ended, you will have to reclaim as income the portion of the Section 179 deduction to which you weren't entitled.

TurboTax will tell you if the asset you entered qualifies for the Section 179 deduction, then it will give you the option of claiming this deduction. Section 179 is optional and some taxpayers might prefer to stretch their depreciation deductions over future years instead of taking the deduction all at once. If you know you're going to sell the asset in two years, it may make sense not to take the Section 179 deduction. Also, you cannot use a Section 179 deduction to generate a loss in your business. If you claim a Section 179 deduction and your business shows a loss, the portion of the Section 179 deduction that is included in the loss will be carried over to next year's tax return.

Selling Business Assets

When a business sells an asset, the sale gets reported on a special form, Form 4797, Sales of Business Property. TurboTax will fill out this form and include it with your tax return if you indicate that you have sold a business asset. Profits on the sale of business assets are subject to tax, and losses on these sales are deductible.

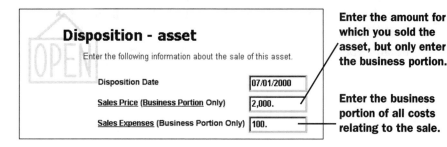

Disposition - asset

Enter the following information about the sale of this asset.

Disposition Date	07/01/2000
Sales Price (Business Portion Only)	2,000.
Sales Expenses (Business Portion Only)	100.

Enter the amount for which you sold the asset, but only enter the business portion.

Enter the business portion of all costs relating to the sale.

You will be asked to enter the date on which you sold or otherwise disposed of an asset (disposition date), the amount for which you sold the asset, and any expenses, such as sales commissions, that relate to the sale. From there on, TurboTax will take care of entering the information about the asset on the property forms.

Income from Rental Property

If you own real property (land or building) and rent it to others, the resulting income you receive and expenses you pay generally must be included on your tax return. You may own a property that is exclusively used for rental, or you may own a vacation home that you use yourself and also rent to others. Both types of property are addressed in this section.

Full-time Rental versus Vacation Rental

The IRS has set out rules that will help you determine how to report the income and expenses from your rental property, and TurboTax will help you make your way through those rules. If you own a property that is used full-time as rental property, the entire amount of income and related expenses will get reported on your tax return. If your property is rented for less than the entire year or if you share the property with your tenants, using it some of the year for your own personal purposes, different rules apply. You may not even have to report your rental income at all!

The 14-Day Rule

If you own a second home (a vacation cottage, a condo in the city, a houseboat, for example), and you rent the property to someone else for *no more than 14 days* during the year, you don't have to report the rental income to the IRS. Likewise, any expenses that you might incur on the property during those 14 days cannot be reported on your tax return as any kind of a tax deduction.

TurboTax will ask you to enter a description of your rental property and then to enter how many days the property was rented. If you enter 14 or fewer days, TurboTax will remove all reference to the rental property from your tax return because you are not required to report the rent on this property as income.

Number of Days Used

Enter the number of days you rented this House out to others and the number of days you used it for <u>personal purposes</u>, if any.

Note: Only count the days it was rented and used during 2000.

Number of Days Rented Out   `12`

Number of Personal Days Used   `25`

Staying in Your Own Rental Property

If you own a piece of rental property and use the property personally for more than the greater of 14 days or 10 percent of the total days the property was rented during the year, the IRS requires that you report the rental income and expenses relating to this property on your tax return, but you will only be entitled to deduct expenses up to the amount of your rental income. Expenses that exceed income can be carried over to future years and applied against future rental income.

Entering Rental Income

If you received rental income on 1099 forms, you can enter those amounts when prompted, just as the entry of 1099-MISC income was described in the section on "Entering Income Reported on 1099 Forms" earlier in this chapter. After entering 1099 information, you will be asked to enter the rest of your rental income. Enter the full amount of rent you received for 2000 (excluding any amount you already entered from 1099 forms). If you would like to produce a detailed schedule showing all the sources of your rental income, either for your records or to attach to your tax return that goes to the IRS, double-click this space.

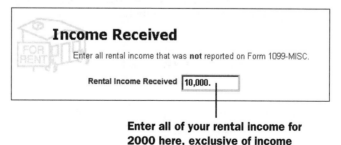

Income Received

Enter all rental income that was **not** reported on Form 1099-MISC.

Rental Income Received   `10,000.`

Enter all of your rental income for 2000 here, exclusive of income reported on 1099-MISC forms.

There are a few confusing items related to collecting rent, and the IRS has made some rules to alleviate the confusion:

- Security deposits that you ultimately intend to return to the tenant are not rent. Do not report them with your rental income. Likewise, don't report them as expenses when you return them at the end of the lease term. Security deposits of this nature never appear on your tax return.

- Security deposits that you intend to use as the last month's rent are rent and you should report them as rent income in the year in which you receive them, assuming you are a cash basis taxpayer.

- Payments you receive from tenants that represent reimbursement for repairs or costs of utilities should be added to your rental income. You will deduct the offsetting expense with your other expenses, so the net effect on your bottom line is zero.

- Sometimes tenants make improvements to dwelling units in lieu of paying the rent. For example, in exchange for your tenant painting his apartment perhaps you let him skip a month's rent. You should record the missed rent as rent income, and then deduct the same amount as the cost of painting the apartment.

Entering Rental Expenses

TurboTax provides fill-in-the-blank screens where you can enter the expenses associated with your rental property. Follow along, entering your expenses in each appropriate field. Ideally, you will have prepared a spreadsheet or a journal that shows you what your expenses were for all of 2000, and you can follow along, entering the information directly onto the TurboTax screen.

Travel includes the cost of your transportation (other than auto) to check up on the property.

Include property taxes you paid as well as payroll taxes paid on behalf of employees.

Common Expenses

Enter your rental expenses for this House.

Advertising	75.		Management Fees	
Travel (Not Auto)			Repairs	650.
Cleaning/Maint.	120.		Supplies	340.
Commissions			Taxes	1,200.
Insurance	450.		Utilities	1,575.
Professional Fees				

Be careful! Don't try to deduct the following items, which aren't allowed as deductions for rental property on your income tax return:

- **Points paid on the purchase of real estate.** You can deduct the points; it just takes a long time. You have to divide the amount of the points over the number of years in the mortgage loan and deduct that portion of the points each year. However, if you pay off the loan early, the remaining undeducted points are fully deductible in the year the mortgage debt is satisfied.

- **Personal portion of repair and maintenance and other expenses.** Some of your "personal" expenses are still deductible, such as property taxes and mortgage interest (on Schedule A as itemized deductions); others, such as utilities and cleaning services, are nondeductible. You must prorate your expenses between rent time and personal time if you used the property personally for a portion of the year. Personal time includes letting a relative stay there rent-free.

Expenses that might fall into the category of Other Rental Expenses include:

- Cost of collecting rent and evicting a tenant
- Bank charges
- Business gifts
- Deposits that were refunded (if you previously included them in income)
- Lawn service
- Legal and accounting fees
- Office expenses
- Wages paid to employees
- Postage
- Extermination and pest control
- Long-distance telephone calls to check up on your property or to talk with prospective tenants and their references
- Cost of film and developing photos of the property used for advertising purposes
- Subscription costs for magazines and newspapers relating to the rental industry or the local area where the property is located
- Casualty and theft losses

Depreciating Rental Property

There was a time when you could buy a house, use it as rental property, and deduct the cost of the house (depreciate it) over as few as 15 years. The rental market hasn't been so attractive for a long time. Now the house gets depreciated over 27.5 years.

To depreciate your rental property, you must know the *adjusted basis* of the property. Generally speaking, the adjusted basis is the cost plus the cost of improvements.

Whenever you buy or convert a piece of property to use as rental property, keep track of the adjusted basis of the property. Start with your cost, including nondeductible fees associated with the sale (legal fees, title search, and so on). As you continue to own the property over the years and you add permanent improvements, such as a room addition, new furnace, and landscaping, keep track of these items as well. All permanent improvements not only get depreciated along with the rental property itself, but affect the basis when you sell the property. Also keep track of any depreciation expense that you have claimed on your tax returns for this property. Depreciation deductions reduce the basis for purposes of computing your gain or loss on a sale of the property.

If you use TurboTax for all the years you own and rent the property, TurboTax will keep track of all of your basis adjustments for you.

Depreciating Furniture and Appliances

There are special rules associated with depreciation of furniture and appliances in rental property. Prior to 1999, the IRS required landlords to depreciate furniture, carpets, appliances, and similar items used in rental property over a seven-year period. In 1999, it was declared that such property should be depreciated over a five-year period.

When you enter these items in TurboTax, they will be depreciated over five years. For items acquired prior to 1999, which you are presumably depreciating over seven years, you can amend previous tax returns and change the amount of depreciation you claimed to the greater amount that would be allowed with a five-year cycle. See Chapter 16 for information on how this amending process works. Unless you have a lot of items that fall into this five-year class, you may feel it is not worthwhile to spend the time amending your returns. You will ultimately receive the entire amount of depreciation on the items—it's just going to take seven years if you acquired the items prior to 1999.

Nondeductible Losses from Rental Property

If your rental expense exceeds your rental income, the IRS limits you to $25,000 per year as a loss on all your combined rental properties. This $25,000 limitation is based on the assumption that you "actively participate" in the management of the rental property. If you just collect the checks and a management company takes complete care of your property, including paying the bills and making decisions about the maintenance of the property and who to rent to, the IRS is not likely to agree that you actively participate in the management.

If you don't actively participate in the management of the property, your losses are restricted to the point where you can only deduct the losses from rental property if you have passive income against which to offset them. (Passive income is income such as dividend and interest income, income from ownership in a limited partnership, discussed later in this chapter—basically, passive income is income earned while you sleep.)

The $25,000 allowance for rental losses is reduced by $1 for every $2 of adjusted gross income in excess of $100,000. When your adjusted gross income reaches $150,000, the allowance is completely phased out. So, if you file as married filing jointly and your adjusted gross income is $130,000, the $25,000 rental loss allowance is limited to $10,000 ($25,000 reduced by half of $30,000, the amount by which your AGI exceeds $100,000), or $25,000 − $15,000 = $10,000. This means that you would only be entitled to deduct $10,000 of loss from rental property in the current year.

The unused portion of your rental loss gets carried over to the next year. TurboTax will calculate the current year deduction and the carryover. If you use TurboTax to prepare your tax return next year, the carryover amount will be there, waiting for you.

Income from Farming Operations

The IRS has developed special tax forms for farmers. There are two forms from which to choose, depending on the type of farmer you are. If you operate the farm yourself, you will fill out Schedule F, Profit or Loss From Farming. If you own the land but rent it out to someone else to farm, you will fill out Form 4835, Farm Rental Income and Expenses. You must identify to TurboTax which form you are qualified to use (see Figure 5-13).

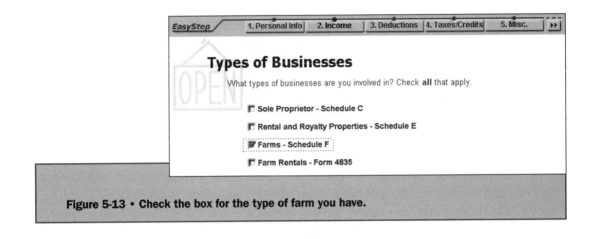

Figure 5-13 • Check the box for the type of farm you have.

Farm Return Due Date

If at least two-thirds of your gross income from all sources for 2000 is derived from farming, or if at least two-thirds of your gross income for 1999 was derived from farming, your filing due dates for your 2000 income tax return are as follows:

- **March 1, 2001.** File your entire 1040 by March 1 and pay the entire tax due with the tax return, and no estimated tax payments are due for the entire year.
- **April 16, 2001.** If you prefer to wait and file your 1040 on April 16, like the rest of the country, it's okay with the IRS. However, be advised that all of your estimated tax for 2000 is due by January 16, 2001. You need only make one payment of estimated tax for the entire year.

The amount of estimated payment due for 2000, if you choose to pay the 2000 estimate on January 16, 2001, is the smaller of two-thirds of your total tax for 1999, or 100 percent of the total tax shown on your 1998 income tax return. This assumes that at least two-thirds of your income for 1998 and 1999 was from farming. If you are contemplating estimating your tax for 2001, increase each of these years by one.

Note   *If you have withholding from a job, or if you are married and your spouse has withholding, and the withholding is sufficient to cover two-thirds of your tax for 2000, you do not need to make an estimated payment.*

If your farming income isn't expected to be two-thirds of your total income for 2000 (and it wasn't two-thirds of your income for 1999), then this special program for paying all of your estimated tax in one payment is not available to you. You will be required to pay quarterly estimated taxes throughout the year and file your return by April 16, 2001, like the rest of us.

Entering Farm Income

Report all income from sales of farm products or livestock, machine hire, and distributions from cooperatives.

CCC Loans

If you receive a Commodity Credit Corporation (CCC) loan and use crops to secure the loan, you may elect to report the proceeds of the loan as income in the year you received the loan instead of waiting until you sell the crop.

The only catch in choosing to report CCC loan proceeds as income in the year of receipt instead of in the year the pledged crop is sold is that once you make a choice in how to report CCC loan proceeds, you are required to continue that process for all years to come. Occasionally the IRS will allow a change in method if you can present a valid business reason for making such a change, but generally you will continue reporting the loan as income from here on.

If you choose to report your CCC loan proceeds as income rather than loans, you must attach a statement to your tax return indicating that you are making an election under IRC section 77(a). You can easily make this election right in TurboTax by following these steps:

1. Double-click the space where you enter the loan proceeds (see Figure 5-14). A Supporting Details statement will appear.

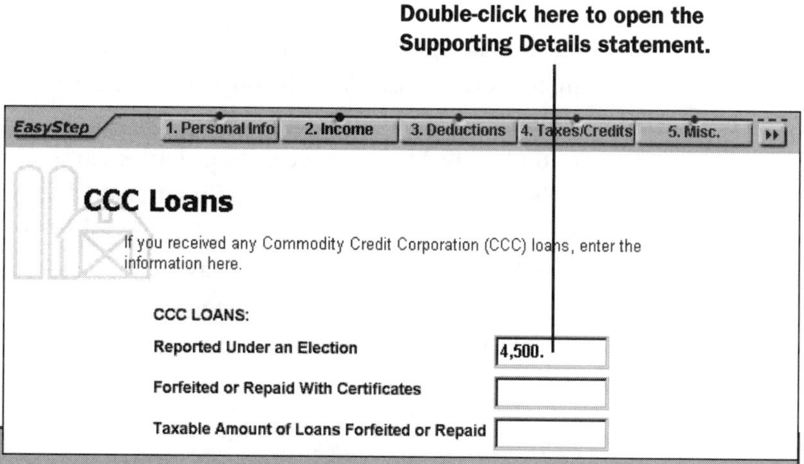

Double-click here to open the Supporting Details statement.

EasyStep	1. Personal Info	2. Income	3. Deductions	4. Taxes/Credits	5. Misc.

CCC Loans

If you received any Commodity Credit Corporation (CCC) loans, enter the information here.

CCC LOANS:

Reported Under an Election   `4,500.`

Forfeited or Repaid With Certificates

Taxable Amount of Loans Forfeited or Repaid

Figure 5-14 • Enter CCC loan proceeds here.

2. Enter the following text: **Taxpayer hereby elects to report CCC loan proceeds in the year of receipt under the provision of IRC section 77(a). Total loan proceeds:** and then enter the amount in the column at the right.

3. Click Close to close the statement. The statement will print with your tax return or will be dispatched with your return if you file electronically.

Farm Income Averaging

As a farmer, you have the right to average your income over the past three years. This method is advantageous if your tax rate this year is higher than it has been in the past three years. You can choose how much of your 2000 income you wish to spread over the three prior years. The amount you choose will be divided equally over the three previous years and the tax will be calculated at the tax rate that was in effect for each of those years.

The option for choosing to average your farm income is presented later in the program, when you get ready to calculate your taxes. The screen you see will ask you to identify how much of each type of income (ordinary, capital gain, and gain on the sale of farm property) you wish to average. It is recommended that you print a copy of your return without averaging first, then try the averaging and see whether this method will be beneficial to you.

Average Your Farm Income

The first step in averaging your income is to make a decision about just how much of your farm income you want to average. You must consider your ordinary income from your farming operations separately from any capital gains that arose from farming.

Amount of ordinary farming income subject to averaging	15,000.
Amount of capital gain income from farming subject to averaging	
Amount of capital gain income that is section 1250 gain	

You must have copies of your three prior tax returns with you in order to enter the necessary information for income averaging. You will be asked some questions about the information presented on these three prior tax returns, and that information will be used to perform the income averaging calculations.

1996 Tax Calculation Information

Enter the following information from your 1997 return.

Your Filing Status in 1997	Married filing joint
Your Taxable Income in 1997	42,005.
Your Income Tax in 1997	8,955.
If you filed Form 1040 in 1996, enter:	
The Amount on Your 1997 Form 1040, Line 13	12,522.
The Amount on Your 1997 Form 4952, Line 4e	

Entering Expenses Relating to Farming

The cost of running your farm is deductible. That cost includes the type of items nearly every business has, such as office supplies, copying expenses, computer expenses, bank fees, and so on. But many expenses are unique to the farming business. Here's a checklist of some of the items you may be able to deduct as a farmer:

- Branding tools
- Breeding fees

- Conservation expenses
- Crop dusting
- Dues to farm organizations
- Explosives
- Fence repair
- Fertilizer for crops
- Food for animals
- Ginning
- Harnesses
- Hay
- Pasture rental
- Rent paid in crops
- Room and board provided to laborers
- Seed
- Storage
- Subscriptions to farm publications
- Tractor and machine hire
- Veterinarian bills

Depreciating Farm Property

You can check back to the section on "Entering Information About Business Assets" for a refresher on depreciating property, but there are some extra rules just for farmers.

Depreciating Livestock

Farm animals are depreciable assets if you purchased them. If you raised an animal from birth, there is no purchase price and no depreciable basis.

Different animals have different depreciable lives, according to the rules set out by the IRS, which are displayed in Table 5-3.

Besides depreciating livestock, farms have other assets that are unique to the business, and these assets have their own unique depreciable lives. When you enter a depreciable asset for your farm, make sure that the correct number of years has been chosen for this asset.

Animal	Depreciable Life
Cows (dairy or breeding)	5 years
Goats	5 years
Sheep	5 years
Hogs	3 years
Racehorses (if over 2 years old when placed in service)	3 years
Racehorses (if 2 years old or younger when placed in service)	7 years
Horses other than racehorses (older than 12 years)	3 years

Table 5-3 • Depreciable Lives for Farm Livestock

Note   *Some farms buy egg-laying chickens, harvest the eggs for a year or so, then sell the chickens and get new chickens. Poultry that you plan to sell during the current year or next year gets deducted in the year of purchase rather than depreciated.*

You can see where TurboTax determined the life of the asset by scrolling down on the form at the bottom of your EasyStep Interview screen and examining the number described as the Asset Class (see Figure 5-15). If the life TurboTax has used to calculate depreciation is incorrect, you can change to the correct life right on the form. You will be asked if you want to override the number calculated by TurboTax, and when you say yes, your depreciation will be recalculated based on the life you give.

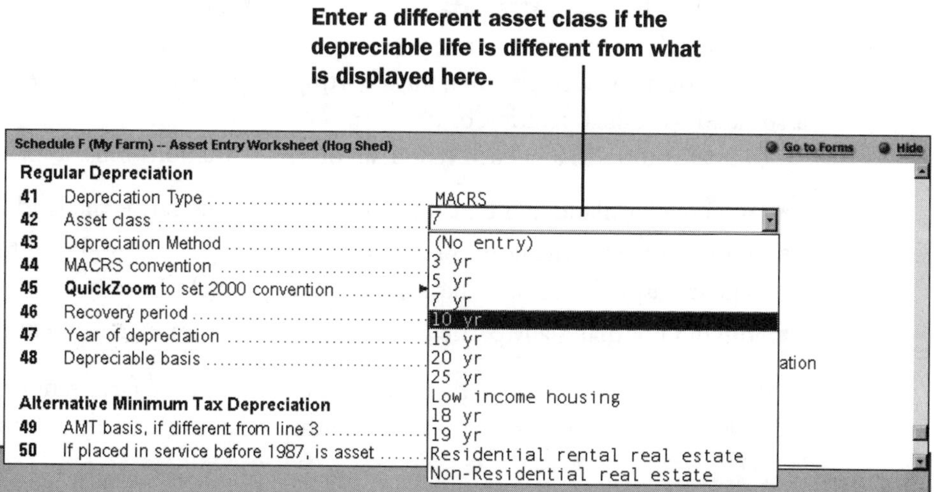

Enter a different asset class if the depreciable life is different from what is displayed here.

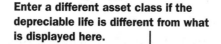

Schedule F (My Farm) -- Asset Entry Worksheet (Hog Shed)		● Go to Forms ● Hide

Regular Depreciation
41   Depreciation Type .... MACRS
42   Asset class 7
43   Depreciation Method .... (No entry)
44   MACRS convention .... 3 yr
45   **QuickZoom** to set 2000 convention .... ▶ 5 yr
                                                    7 yr
46   Recovery period .... 10 yr
47   Year of depreciation .... 15 yr
48   Depreciable basis .... 20 yr
                                                    25 yr
                                                    Low income housing
Alternative Minimum Tax Depreciation   18 yr
49   AMT basis, if different from line 3 .... 19 yr
50   If placed in service before 1987, is asset ...... Residential rental real estate
                                                    Non-Residential real estate

Figure 5-15 • Scroll down to view the asset class.

Table 5-4 displays the standard life expectancies for typical items of farm equipment.

Equipment	Depreciable Life
Single-purpose agricultural structures, such as hog sheds, chicken coops, and the like	10 years
Cotton ginning equipment	7 years
Drainage facilities	15 years
Farm buildings (such as barns)	20 years
Farm machinery	7 years
Fences	7 years
Fruit- or nut-bearing trees and vines	10 years
Grain bins	7 years
Greenhouses	10 years
Over-the-road tractors	3 years
Trucks	5 years

Table 5-4 • Depreciable Lives for Typical Items of Farm Equipment

Income or Expense of Farm Rental

A farm rental is a situation where you are paying someone to farm your land for you, but you are still responsible for reporting all of the income and expenses associated with the operation of the farm.

To treat your farm as a farm rental, all of these situations must apply:

- You own farmland and rent it to someone else who farms the land for you.
- Your income for the farm is based on crops or livestock produced by the tenant, just as if you were farming the land yourself.
- You did not materially participate in the operation or management of the farm.

If these criteria are met, you are required to file a special farm rental tax form, Form 4835. The information that goes on this form is essentially a duplicate of the information that you would enter on the regular farm income form, Schedule F; it's only your status as a landlord that is different.

TurboTax will walk you through the forms for entering income and expenses from your farm rental in exactly the same way it would through entering income and expenses for a Schedule F. When asked to enter the income from production, for example, you will enter the total of all income from production of crops and livestock on your farm. You can double-click the space where this amount appears if you want to prepare a statement showing the details of your income.

Production and Cooperative Income

Enter the amount of income you received from these sources.

Income From Production	7,400.
Total Income From Cooperative Distributions	
Taxable Income From Cooperative Distributions	

List all of your farm rental expenses, depreciation of farm assets, auto expenses associated with your farm, just as described in the previous section, "Entering Expenses Relating to Farming."

Enter Your Farm Rental Expenses

Chemicals		Freight	
Conservation Exp		Gasoline	
Custom Hire	650.	Insurance	1,200.
Employee Benefits		Mortgage Int	
Feed	4,955.	Other Interest	
Fertilizers			

Note *If you simply received rent from the tenant and did not have an interest in the crops or livestock, you will treat the farm rent as any other rent (see the section on "Income from Rental Property" earlier in this chapter).*

K-1 Income from Partnerships, S Corporations, Trusts

If you are a partner in a partnership, a shareholder of an S corporation, or the beneficiary of a trust or estate, you should receive a tax form in the mail called Schedule K-1. All amounts that appear on the K-1 form get transferred directly into TurboTax, and the tax program knows exactly where each amount should appear on your tax return.

Entering Partnership Information

When entering income from a partnership K-1 form, you will have the opportunity to check off boxes that correspond to the lines that are filled in on your K-1.

Depending on the boxes that you check, TurboTax will then present you with the appropriate screens for entering information from your form. For example, if you indicated that you have information entered on lines 4a through 4f, when you checked the boxes, as shown in the previous illustration, TurboTax will then present you with a screen specifically used for entering information from those lines. The screens you see will correspond exactly with the lines on your K-1.

ABC Partnership - Lines 4a Through 4c

Enter the following information as shown on lines 4a through 4c of the Schedule K-1 received from ABC Partnership.

Line 4a(1) - Interest	120.
Line 4a(2) - U.S. Bonds (Included in Interest)	
Line 4b - Dividends	
Line 4c - Royalties	

If there is an amount on line 15(a) of your partnership K-1, indicating income from self-employment, be aware that this income will be subject to self-employment tax in addition to income tax. The self-employment tax is a combination of the Social Security and Medicare taxes. TurboTax will compute this tax for you.

ABC Partnership - Lines 15a Through 15c

Enter the following information as shown on lines 15a through 15c of the Schedule K-1 received from ABC Partnership.

Line 15a - Net Earnings or Loss From Self-Employment	1,600.
Line 15b - Gross Farming or Fishing Income	
Line 15c - Gross Nonfarm Income	

☐ I am a general partner.

Passive Activities

It is important to note whether or not you materially participate in the operation of the partnership (see "Material Participation in Your Business" earlier in this chapter). If you do not materially participate in the partnership, your income or loss from this enterprise is considered *passive* and as such receives special tax treatment.

Compare the amount on line 3 with the total losses allowed. If the loss on line 3 is greater than the total losses allowed on line 11, a carryover of the difference exists.

All Other Passive Activities		
2 a Activities with net income (Worksheet 2, column (a)) ... **2 a**		
b Activities with net loss (Worksheet 2, column (b)) ...... **b**		
c Prior year unallowed losses (Worksheet 2, column (c)) . **c**		
d Combine lines 2a, 2b, and 2c.................................	**2 d**	
3 Combine lines 1d and 2d. If the result is net income or zero, all losses are allowed, including any prior year unallowed losses entered on line 1c or 2c. Do not complete Form 8582. Report the losses on the forms and schedules normally used. If this line and line 1d are losses, go to Part II. Otherwise, enter -0- on line 9 and go to line 10	**3**	-12,250.

Figure 5-16 • Examine Form 8582 for unused passive activity loss.

A passive activity, as defined by the IRS, is any activity involving the operation of a trade or business in which you do not materially participate. A trade or business is defined as an activity that:

- Involves the conduct of a trade or business in which deductions would be allowed but for the fact that the activity is passive
- Is conducted in anticipation of starting a trade or business
- Involves research or experimental expenditures that are deductible

A rental property is not considered a trade or business unless you are in the business of working with rental properties.

You are allowed to deduct losses from a passive activity only to the extent that they can be offset with income from passive activities. Excess loss is carried forward to the following year and on into future tax returns until either there is enough passive income against which to offset the loss or you extinguish your interest in the passive activity.

When you enter income and losses from passive activities on your tax return, TurboTax will identify them as such because you will indicate that you do not materially participate in the activity. TurboTax will then take care of grouping together all income and losses from passive activities to determine what gets reported on this year's tax return and what, if anything, gets carried forward to next year.

If you used TurboTax last year and you had a net loss from passive activities, TurboTax will bring that loss forward into this year's tax return and incorporate that loss with other passive activity income and losses from the current year. If you did not use TurboTax for the preparation of last year's tax return, you should examine your 1999 return to see if there is a Form 8582, Passive Activity Loss Limitations. If this form exists in last year's tax return, examine the form to see if there was any unused passive activity loss (see Figure 5-16). Unused loss will carry forward to your 2000 tax return.

You can indicate to TurboTax that a passive loss carryover exists, and then fill in the required information on the Passive Loss Carryovers screen. There are worksheets that accompany the passive loss form from last year. These worksheets are part of the preparation process for this form and should accompany your records of last year's tax return. You will need to examine those worksheets to obtain the information you need for this form.

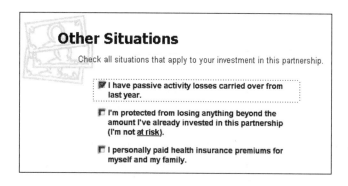

Entering S Corporation Information

An S corporation is a corporation that does not pay tax. Instead, the shareholders of the corporation report their share of the corporation's income and deductions on their tax returns and pay the tax at their tax rates.

If you are a shareholder in an S corporation, you will receive a K-1 form, similar to the partnership form. The K-1 form you receive from an S corporation will summarize your income and loss for the corporation. Just as with a partnership, TurboTax will ask you to indicate by checking boxes which lines are filled in on the

K-1 and then you will be presented with screens on which you can enter your share
of the amounts from the S corporation.

ABC Corporation - Choose Which Lines

Look at the Schedule K-1 you received from ABC Corporation and check those
lines with an amount.

☐ Lines 4a Through 4f

☐ Lines 5 and 6

☐ Line 7

☐ Lines 8 and 9

☐ Lines 10 and 11

☐ Lines 12a Through 12c

☐ Line 13

☐ Lines 14 Through 23

Self-Employment Taxes of S Corporation Shareholders

If you are a shareholder in an S corporation, and you materially participate in the
corporation, you should keep in mind the rules about self-employment income from
the corporation. Shareholders of S corporations are not subject to self-employment
tax on the income of the corporation. If, however, you perform personal services for
the corporation, the IRS expects you to be paid a salary by the corporation. Such a
salary should be an amount appropriate to what you would receive if you were
employed by any other employer for the same job, and your Social Security and
Medicare taxes will be withheld from your salary.

Entering Trust and Estate Information

If you are the beneficiary of an estate or trust, you will receive a K-1 form showing
your share of income and expenses of the estate or trust. The amounts on the form
must be reported on your tax return. As with the other K-1 forms, TurboTax will
ask you to indicate by checking boxes which lines of the K-1 have been filled in,
and you will then be prompted to enter the information from the K-1 form into
the appropriate areas of TurboTax.

Larsen Family Trust - Choose Which Lines

Look at the Schedule K-1 you received from Larsen Family Trust and check those lines with an amount.

☐ Lines 1 Through 4c

☐ Lines 5a Through 6d

☐ Lines 7 Through 10

☐ Line 11

☐ Lines 12a Through 13g

☐ Lines 14a Through 14h

Selling Your Home

The rules have changed in recent years, and most people will find that if they sell their personal residence for a profit they will not have to face a tax bill.

Under the old rules, which were changed in 1997, people would sell one house at a gain, and roll that gain into the purchase of a new, presumably more expensive house by lowering the basis of the new house by the amount of the gain, and repeat that cycle until they sold their last house. If the homeowner was over age 55 when the last house was sold, there was a special rule that allowed taxpayers to avoid tax on the first $125,000 in profit. Those rules are gone, and new, much more taxpayer-friendly rules have taken their place.

Under present law, the entire gain (profit) on the sale of a personal residence up to $250,000 ($500,000 if married filing a joint tax return) is excluded from tax if the following rules are met:

- You cannot have excluded from tax the gain on a sale of another home within the two years leading up to the sale of the current home.
- You must have owned the home for at least two of the five years leading up to the date of the sale.
- You must have lived in the home as your primary residence for at least two of the five years leading up to the date of the sale.

Note *The two-year tests for owning and living in the house do not have to be met with continuous time, nor do they have to be met simultaneously. For example, you could have lived in the house for one year, then you took a temporary one-year assignment for your job that placed you in a different geographic location, then you returned and lived in the house for one more year, and finally you sold the house. You would meet both the ownership test and the use test for this house.*

Here's a special situation: If you don't meet the use and ownership tests when you sell the home, the exclusion of gain will be prorated based on the actual number of days the home was used and owned as a principal residence if the owner of the home was required to move due to a change in place of employment, health, or some other unforeseen circumstances (to be determined by the IRS). TurboTax will ask that you enter the actual number of days during which you (and your spouse, if applicable) lived in the house as your main home and the number of days that you owned the home. The maximum amount of exclusion to which you are entitled ($250,000 or $500,000 if married filing jointly) will then be prorated based on the number of days you enter.

Count the Number of Days of Use

Enter the number of days **each** of you lived in this house as your main home. Only count from five years before the date you sold the house.

Number of Days Used by James	452
Number of Days Used by Laura	452

For example, if you are single, and you owned and lived in your home for only 200 days, and were forced to sell the home due to a change in employment, your maximum exclusion would be 200 divided by 730 (the total number of days in two years) times $250,000, or $68,493. As long your *gain* on the house doesn't exceed this amount, you will be able to exclude the entire gain from taxation. If you sold the house for a gain of $85,000, you would be required to pay tax (at capital gain tax rates) on the difference between $85,000 and $68,493, or $16,707.

Determining Your Gain on the Sale of Your Home

TurboTax can only do so much of the legwork in helping you determine the gain on the sale of your home. In order to calculate the gain (or loss) when you sell the home, you must provide TurboTax with three numbers: the selling price of the home, the expenses of the sale, and the adjusted basis in the home.

Selling Price of Your Home

The selling price is the price that the buyer pays for the home. It doesn't matter if you don't see the cash from the sale—for example, the money from the buyer may go to your bank to pay off your mortgage on the home—the entire selling price is the amount that you need to enter in the program. Typically, you can find this amount right at the top of your real estate closing statement. Do not adjust the amount for any selling expenses—the selling expenses get entered separately.

Selling Price

Enter the <u>selling price</u> of your home. Include any amounts that went toward paying off your old mortgage but do not include the price of any <u>personal-type</u> property you sold with your home. If you received Form 1099-S, this amount is reported in box 2.

Selling Price `120,000.`

Selling Expenses on the Sale of Your Home

There are several types of expenses that fall into the category of selling expenses. TurboTax expects you to enter one number, but you may want to double-click on the area where this number gets entered and prepare a detailed list of the selling expenses, so you will have this information stored with your tax return. To the extent that you had any of these selling expenses, they will appear on the seller's side of your closing statement.

Expenses of Sale

Enter expenses of sale incurred when you sold your home. Examples include commissions or broker's fees, advertising fees, legal fees, title insurance, transfer taxes, geological surveys, or loan charges (including points) you paid on the buyer's behalf.

Expenses of Sale `450.`

Typical selling expenses include:

- Advertising
- Building inspection fee

- Credit report
- Document creation fee
- Expenses you pay on buyer's behalf
- Insect inspection
- Inspection fees
- Legal fees
- Notary fee
- Real estate commission
- Recording fees
- Survey
- Title insurance
- Transfer fee
- Transfer stamps

Adjusted Basis of Your Home

The adjusted basis is the key number in determining how much gain you made on selling your home. This is probably the most confusing amount to calculate because over the years amounts will have been added to and subtracted from this number to arrive at a final adjusted basis.

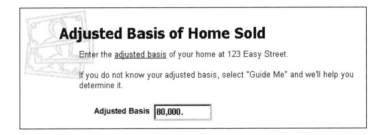

To determine the adjusted basis, start with your original cost of the home (can be found on your original closing statement), and *add* to the cost these items:

- Costs of the purchase (many of these items will duplicate those on the previous list of selling expenses, only in this case they are expenses that you paid when you bought the home and they will appear on the purchaser's side of your closing statement)
- Real estate taxes of the seller that you paid at the purchase and for which you were not reimbursed
- Major improvements such as room additions, furnace, central air-conditioning

- Permanent landscaping such as trees, shrubs, and perennials
- Appliances that stay with the house (value these at the lower of their cost or fair market value at the time of the sale)
- Major repairs such as a new roof
- Wall to wall carpeting
- Insulation
- Assessments for sidewalks, sewer, streetlights, and so on

After adding these items to the cost of your house in order to determine the adjusted basis, you must *deduct* these items:

- Any deduction on any tax return for a casualty or theft relating to the home (not to your possessions in the home)
- Depreciation allowed or allowable (even if you didn't claim a deduction)
- Real estate taxes that the seller paid on your behalf at the time you purchased the home

Retirement Income

Income in retirement comes in all shapes and colors, and some of it is taxable, some is not. With a little help from you, TurboTax will determine which types of retirement income are taxable and to what extent.

Retirement income that can be fully taxable includes:

- Proceeds from employer-contributed pension plans
- Proceeds from tax-deferred IRAs, Keoghs, SEP-IRAs, and SIMPLE plans

Retirement income that can be partially taxable includes:

- Proceeds from non-tax-deferred, employee-contributed pension plans
- Proceeds from nondeductible IRAs if you have deductible IRAs
- Social Security (and Railroad Retirement) benefits—the amount taxed depends on your income level when you receive the benefits

Retirement income that is not taxed includes:

- Proceeds from totally nondeductible IRAs
- Proceeds from Roth IRAs
- Social Security (and Railroad Retirement) benefits if your income is below the designated threshold

Social Security Benefits

If you receive Social Security benefits, you will receive a Form SSA-1099, which summarizes how much you received in benefits during the year. Enter the amounts exactly as they appear on the SSA-1099 and TurboTax will take care of determining how much, if any, of this income is taxable. In addition, if you itemize your deductions, TurboTax will transfer the amount of Medicare premiums included on this form to the medical expenses section of your itemized deductions schedule.

Social Security Payments

Total the amounts shown on **all** copies of Forms SSA-1099 and RRB-1099 that you received and enter the totals below. **Don't** include forms for which you later received corrected copies.

	James	Laura
Form SSA-1099, box 5		
Form RRB-1099, box 5		
Federal Tax Withheld, SSA-1099, box 6 & RRB-1099, box10		
Medicare B Premiums Withheld		

Pension Income

Income from pension and annuity plans is taxable if either your employer contributed to the plan or you made contributions to the plan that were deducted from your taxable income. You will receive a Form 1099-R reporting your retirement income. Frequently, this form will list the taxable portion of the income.

Follow along with your 1099-R, entering the amounts from each box of the form into your TurboTax program, and TurboTax will determine how much of the income, if any, is taxable to you.

Excelsior Fund - Boxes 1-2

1 - Gross Distribution `3,000.00`

2a - Taxable Amount `3,000.00`

2b - Check Boxes

☐ Taxable Amount Not Determined

☐ Total Distribution

IRA Income

An Individual Retirement Account (IRA) is like a savings account except that you aren't supposed to touch it until you reach age 59½. Sometimes contributions to an IRA can be deducted from your taxable income in the year you make the contribution, so that you don't pay tax on the contributions until you actually withdraw the money when you retire. See Chapter 6 for details about making contributions to IRAs and other types of tax-deferred retirement accounts.

If your IRA contributions were deducted from your income when you made the contributions, amounts withdrawn from your IRA are added to your income and subject to tax when you withdraw them. The way an IRA was meant to work is that you contribute up to a maximum of $2,000 of earned income per year to your IRA account, and you can deduct the amount you contribute on your income tax return, so you don't have to pay income tax on the amount you contribute. Then, when you retire, you start withdrawing money from the account. As you withdraw money from your IRA, you pay income tax on it. If your income tax rate in your retirement years is lower than your rate was when you were working, so much the better—your withdrawals from your IRA get taxed at the lower rate.

In 1987, Congress started restricting the amount of tax-deductible contributions you could make to your IRA based on your income. The IRA deduction was disallowed for many taxpayers. Taxpayers could still contribute each year to the account, but many people lost the benefit of the tax deduction and tax deferral. There is much discussion in Congress about easing these restrictions and thus making IRAs more attractive to more investors. See Chapter 1 for a brief discussion of what is happening on this front.

When you are ready to withdraw money from your IRA, you must examine your records of deposits to the account to determine how much of your contributions were deducted on your tax returns. If all the money you put in the IRA was tax deductible, everything you take out of the fund will be taxable. If none of your contributions were tax-deductible, only the earnings on the money in the fund will be subject to tax at the time of withdrawal. If a portion of your contributions were deductible and a portion not, you must prorate the money coming out of the fund to determine how much will be subject to tax.

Rollovers from an IRA

You can take money out of your IRA temporarily without paying tax on it, either for purposes of transferring the money to a different account or even as a short-term loan. You are only allowed to take money from your IRA once per year. You have 60 days from the date you withdraw the money to redeposit it or place it in a new IRA account to avoid being taxed on the withdrawal. Don't miss the 60-day date—check your calendar carefully. There are no exceptions to this rule, and the tax is high. Not only do you pay regular income tax on any money you withdraw and do not redeposit, but you are also required to pay a 10 percent penalty on the money.

IRA Withdrawals Before Age 59^1/2

You can withdraw penalty-free funds from your IRA for medical expenditures that exceed 7.5 percent of your adjusted gross income. The amounts withdrawn are subject to income tax if the amounts were tax deferred when originally contributed to your IRA, but the 10 percent early withdrawal penalty does not apply. In addition, you can withdraw penalty-free amounts from your IRA to pay medical insurance if you are out of work and receiving unemployment compensation for at least 12 consecutive weeks.

You can also withdraw penalty-free funds from your IRA up to $10,000 (a lifetime amount) for use in purchasing a home. This provision is for *first-time homebuyers* only, their children, and ancestors. A first-time homebuyer is defined as someone who has not owned a home that was used as a principal residence during the past two years.

Also, you can withdraw penalty-free funds from your IRA to be used for the cost of higher education for yourself, your spouse, a child, or grandchild, including tuition, fees, books, supplies, room and board, and equipment.

IRA Withdrawals After Age 59^1/2

You are eligible to withdraw penalty-free funds from your IRA once you reach age 59^1/2. You don't have to begin withdrawing amounts when you reach this age. However, you must begin withdrawing funds from your IRA by April 1 of the calendar year following the year in which you reach age 70^1/2. In other words, if you turned 70^1/2 in May 2000, you must begin making withdrawals from your IRA by April 2001.

Note that waiting until early 2001 to make a withdrawal for 2000 will result in two withdrawals in 2001 (the 2000 required amount and the 2001 required amount).

When you begin withdrawing from your IRA, you must choose between withdrawing the entire balance or making periodic distributions. You make this choice on the date on which your distributions will begin. However, you don't have the option of withdrawing your entire balance even after making periodic distributions.

Figuring Your Minimum Distribution   Typically, an annual distribution from your IRA is determined by dividing the entire balance in all of your IRA accounts as of December 31 of the preceding year by your *applicable life expectancy.* (There are special rules if the beneficiary of your IRA is not your spouse and is more than ten years younger than you.) The distribution does not have to be made annually, but can be made in regular (monthly, quarterly) installments instead.

The applicable life expectancy is a number of years determined by examining tables prepared by the IRA. The number is either:

- The IRA owner's remaining life expectancy (if the payments are for your life only)
- The remaining joint life expectancy of the owner and his designated beneficiary (if the payments are for the lives of you and your designated beneficiary)
- The remaining life expectancy of the IRA's beneficiary (if the owner dies before distributions have begun)

Fortunately, you don't have to figure out your life expectancy yourself—the IRS has already done it for you. The Life Expectancy Tables are available on the Internet at http://www.irs.gov/prod/forms_pubs/pubs/p5909901.htm. Use Life Expectancy Table I if you are determining your life expectancy singly. Use Life Expectancy Table II if you are determining your life expectancy jointly.

Once you determine the life expectancy figure, the computation for calculating your required distribution is as follows:

1. IRA total account balance as of 12/31 of the year *before* the year in which you turned $70^1/_2$. (If you turned $70^1/_2$ in May 2000, this amount is the IRA balance as of 12/31/1999.)
2. Life expectancy figure (as determined from the IRS tables).

Divide (1) by (2). If you turned $70^1/_2$ in 2000, the result of this computation is the amount that must be withdrawn from the IRA by April 1, 2001. Note that the withdrawal that is due by 4/1/01 is to be deducted from the IRA account balance for the purpose of determining the 12/31/00 balance (for the year 2 withdrawal), even if the actual withdrawal doesn't occur until 2001.

Other Forms of Income

The general rule, of course, is that every amount of income you receive must be recorded on your tax return, one way or another. But some types of income don't fall into the main categories. This section covers various types of miscellaneous income, all of which fall into the general "Other Income" category on your tax return.

Gambling Income

You are required to record gambling winnings on your tax return. You may receive a form W-2G documenting the winnings. Casinos, race tracks, and other organizations sponsoring events at which you can gamble are required to issue a W-2G form to people who win amounts that exceed certain thresholds. For example, if you win $1,200 or more at the slot machine, you'll receive a W-2G form. If you win at least 300 times your wager at the race track, and that amount exceeds $600 after deducting your wager, the race track will issue a W-2G. Certain winnings are subject to withholding. For example, lottery winnings that exceed $5,000 are subject to withholding at 28 percent. If there has been any tax withheld from your winnings, you will receive a W-2G form.

The IRS receives copies of the W-2G form and will expect the amount you report on your tax return to equal or exceed the amount on W-2G forms it receives.

If your winnings were small, you won't receive a form, but you must report the income just the same. In TurboTax, you are asked if you receive the W-2G form, but if you read the small print (see Figure 5-17), you will see that you should answer this question Yes, no matter what your source of gambling winnings, even if you didn't receive a form. This is the only place in TurboTax where you can report your gambling winnings, so enter all winnings here, whether or not you received W-2G forms. Taxable gambling winnings can include money won in a lottery, the proceeds from an office football pool, money won in a bet with your neighbor, the value of a car won in the church raffle. Anything or any amount you win that is a result of a wager or a bet is considered to be taxable gambling winnings.

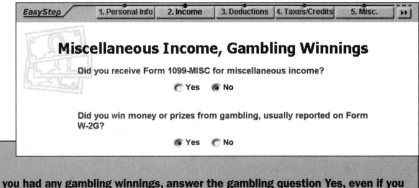

Figure 5-17 • If you had any gambling winnings, answer the gambling question Yes, even if you didn't receive a W-2G form.

If you received a W-2G form, follow along on your form to enter information into TurboTax. If you won money gambling but didn't get the form, sit tight. Another screen will appear later on asking you for your gambling winnings.

Ballantine Park - Boxes 1-14			
1-Gross Winnings	2,000.00	8-Cashier	
2-Federal Tax W/H		10-Window	
3-Type of Wager		11-First ID	
4-Date Won		12-Second ID	
5-Transaction		13-State Abbr	
6-Race		13-State ID No.	
7-Identical Winnings		14-State Tax W/H	

You are entitled to take a deduction for amounts you spent gambling to the extent that you had gambling winnings. In other words, if you spent $1,500 gambling and won $500, you will report the $500 as Other Income, and you will be able to deduct $500 of your gambling costs as an itemized deduction. See Chapter 7 for more information about deducting the cost of gambling.

Enter the amount of gambling winnings not reported to you on Form W-2G here.

Total Income Summary

Based on your entries, your total income is $60,609.

Wages and Salaries	$0
Interest and Dividends	$5,500
Income (Loss) - Schedule C	-5,611.
Income (Loss) - Schedule E	$17,825
Income (Loss) - Schedule F	$0
Taxable Retirement Income	$0
Net Gains and Losses	$40,445
Other Income (Loss)	$2,450
Total Income	$60,609

● Back ◄◄   ● Continue

Form 1040: Individual Tax Return		● Go to Forms ● Hide
19	Unemployment compensation	19
20 a	Social security benefits	20 a	
b	Taxable amount (see instructions)	20 b
21	Other income. List type and amount ..... SEE STMT _____	21	2,450. 🔍
22	Add the amounts in the far right column for lines 7 through 21.	
	This is your **total income** .... ►	22	60,609.
Adjusted Gross Income		

Prize Winnings

You are required to report the value of prize winnings on your income tax return. If you won cash, you will report the amount of cash you received. If you won a tangible item, such as a car or a trip or a toaster, report the fair market value of the prize as your income. Fair market value means what the item is worth if you try to sell it or what you would have to pay for it if you tried to buy it at a store. Examples of taxable prize winnings include prizes won at state fairs, essay contest prizes, cash awards given at work, prizes won on a radio or television game show.

Other Income Statement		
and Long-Term Care Insurance Contracts		
10 Refunds or reimbursements of deductions claimed in a prior year:		
a Reimbursement for deducted medical expenses		
b Refunds of deducted taxes (other than state or local inc. taxes) *(enter description and amount)* _____		
c Recapture of deducted moving expenses		
d Reimbursement for deducted casualty or theft loss	2,000.	
e Reimbursement for deducted employee business expenses		
f Other refunds or reimbursements		
11 Recoveries of bad debts deducted in a prior year		
12 Jury duty pay		
13 Bartering income not reported elsewhere		
14 Income from the rental of personal property		
15 Other taxable income:		
Gambling Income	450.	
Prize Winnings	300.	

Some prizes are not taxable. To avoid taxation on a prize, four tests must be met:

- The prize must be an award for a religious, charitable, scientific, education, artistic, literary, or civic achievement.
- You must have been selected to win the prize without taking any action yourself to enter a contest in which the prize was awarded.
- You cannot be required to render future services as a condition for receiving the prize.
- You must *give up* the prize by transferring it to a governmental unit or to a tax-exempt charitable, religious, or education organization of your choice. The prize must be transferred before being used, and a written statement is generally required that provides a description of the prize; the name and address of the organization to receive the prize; the donor's name, address, and identification number; and it must be signed and dated by the donor.

Hobby Income

If you attempt to operate a business, and that business loses money year after year, you run the risk of the business being treated as a hobby. If you have a little hobby where you make a bit of money, but your expenses exceed your income, the hobby is a hobby and not a business.

The official rule is that when a business that is trying to make money has expenses that exceed the income of the business for three of five consecutive years, the IRS deems the business to be a hobby and does not allow deductions for the losses generated by the business. In other words, if your business costs more to operate than it earns in revenue, but you do it anyway because you like it, you must report the revenue as income, and you are entitled to deduct your expenses, but only to the extent of your income. If the hobby earns $1,000 and you spent $1,500, your deduction is limited to $1,000. The deduction is included as a miscellaneous itemized deduction.

Any money you make from your hobby is subject to income tax. The money gets reported as other income on your tax return. Deductions relating to that hobby income may be taken as miscellaneous deductions if you itemize (see Chapter 7), but only to the extent that they don't exceed the hobby income.

Enter the income from your hobby here. Offsetting expenses may be entered as miscellaneous itemized deductions.

Other Income Statement		
and Long-Term Care Insurance Contracts		
10 Refunds or reimbursements of deductions claimed in a prior year:		
a Reimbursement for deducted medical expenses		
b Refunds of deducted taxes (other than state or local inc. taxes) *(enter description and amount)* _____		
c Recapture of deducted moving expenses		
d Reimbursement for deducted casualty or theft loss		2,000.
e Reimbursement for deducted employee business expenses		
f Other refunds or reimbursements		
11 Recoveries of bad debts deducted in a prior year		
12 Jury duty pay		
13 Bartering income not reported elsewhere		
14 Income from the rental of personal property		
15 Other taxable income:		
Gambling Income		450.
Prize Winnings		300.
Hobby Income		220.

Jury Duty

If you receive jury duty payments, you must report the amount you receive as income. If you turned the payments over to your employer in exchange for your employer paying you your regular salary for the day(s) of jury duty, you must still record the jury pay as income, but you will be entitled to deduct the amount you gave to your employer. Indicate on the form provided in TurboTax that you received such payments.

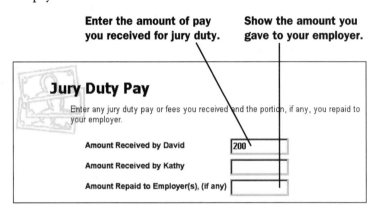

Scholarship Income

Sometimes income from scholarships is taxable, but most of the time it is not. Nontaxable scholarship money is money received for tuition and fees to attend school, or fees, books, supplies, and equipment required for courses at a specific educational institution. Amounts you receive for room and board are not tax exempt.

Amounts received for services required as a condition of the scholarship are taxable. This should include amounts received for teaching and research.

The taxable portion of scholarship money gets reported as Other Income in TurboTax. Answer Yes when asked if you received taxable scholarship, fellowship, grant, or stipend income.

Alimony

The alimony payments a divorced spouse receives are subject to income tax if *all* of the following requirements are met:

- The payments are in cash or something equivalent, like a check or a direct deposit to a bank account.
- Payments are required as a result of a divorce or separation decree.
- Payments totaling more than $15,000 per year continue for at least three years.
- The divorce or separation decree does not designate that the payments are not subject to income tax by the recipient and are not deductible by the payer (such as in the case of child support or a lump sum settlement).
- The recipient and the payer of alimony cannot be members of the same household at the time payments are made.
- There is no requirement to continue payments after the death of the recipient.
- The recipient and the payer do not file a joint return with each other.

If only some of the above requirements are met, the alimony payments are not taxable nor can the person making the payments take a deduction.

If you received taxable alimony payments, report all payments as income in the year received. Your former spouse will take a deduction for the payments and will report your Social Security number to the IRS, so the IRS will be aware of the payments you have received.

Alimony or Spousal Support Received

Enter the amount of <u>alimony</u> (spousal support) payments you or your spouse received in 2000.

Don't include amounts you received in 1999 or 2001 even if they were for 2000.

Alimony Received in 2000 by...

David [   ]

Kathy [12000]

Some payments and transfers between separating spouses don't count as alimony. For example:

- You can write an agreement into your divorce decree stating that the alimony payments won't be treated as taxable income to the recipient and the payer won't be entitled to a deduction for alimony.

- Payment of your spouse's legal fees relating to the divorce is not considered alimony.
- Child support is not alimony.
- A lump-sum property settlement is not alimony.
- Payments made out of the goodness of your spouse's heart, but not required by your decree, are not alimony.
- If your spouse owns the home in which you live and makes payments on the home, those payments are not considered to be alimony.

Unemployment Compensation

There was a time, years ago, when unemployment compensation—money you get from the federal or state government to hold you over while you're out of work and looking for a job—was not taxable. But tax laws have changed, and now you have to pay income tax on your unemployment compensation just like any other type of income.

You should receive form 1099-G from the government telling you how much unemployment compensation you received during 2000. Enter the amount that appears on the form on the screen for 1099-G information.

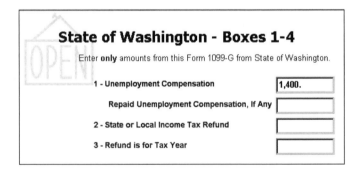

Income You Don't Have to Report to the IRS

Believe it or not, there are actually a few types of income that are not subject to tax:

- **Company benefits.** If you receive health, vision, and dental insurance from your employer, or a holiday gift valued at under $25, these benefits are not subject to income tax and don't have to be reported on your tax return. If your employer provides food at work, this is not taxable to you. The value of company parties and excursions is not taxable to the employees.

- **Gifts received.** You are not liable for tax nor do you need to report on your tax return the value of any gifts that you receive. The person giving the gift may be subject to gift tax, but that event does not affect you.

- **Inheritance.** You are not liable for income tax on any inheritance that you receive. This is not to say that there is no tax on inheritances. The estate pays the tax, before you get the inheritance. If you are a beneficiary of an estate that is earning money on investments while the estate is being settled, you may be subject to tax on these earnings and you will receive a K-1 form to reflect your share of income.

Reducing Your Income with Adjustments

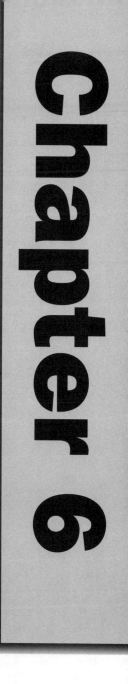

In This Chapter:

- *Adjustments for IRAs, 401(k)s, and Other Tax-Deferred Retirement Plans*

- *Adjustments for Medical Savings Accounts*

- *Adjustments for the Self-Employed*

- *Adjustments for Moving Expenses*

- *Adjustments for Student Loan Interest*

- *Adjustments for Alimony*

Adjustments are very similar to itemized deductions except everyone is entitled to claim adjustments, even if they don't qualify to itemize deductions. Adjustments are shown on page 1 of your tax return, and they are especially nice because adjustments pass through to your state tax return. Depending on the state you live in, if you get to reduce your federal income with an adjustment, your state income will be reduced also, whereas many states don't permit itemized deductions.

Tax-Deferred Retirement Plans

The premise behind a tax-deferred retirement plan begins with the attractive idea that you can defer paying income tax this year on the amount of money you contribute to a retirement plan. The money is invested and grows, tax-free, until you begin withdrawing the money when you retire. Frequently, people pay a lower marginal tax rate when they retire than they do when they are working, so the tax-deferred plan provides the added benefit of the income being taxed at a lower rate than it would be if it were taxed today.

For example, while working and drawing a regular pay check, you may be paying tax at a marginal tax rate of 28 percent, 31 percent, or higher. At retirement, many people resort to a lifestyle where expenses are fixed (either their house has been paid for or they rent property with a fixed monthly rate), and they have a fixed income based on revenue from a pension fund, Social Security, income from investments, and so on. Often the income in retirement is less than it was when the taxpayer was working full time, and, thus, the income may be taxed at a lower marginal tax rate—perhaps 15 percent. Income put aside in a tax-deferred fund while you are working misses being taxed at 28 percent or higher and is instead taxed years later at 15 percent. Not only do you save 13 percent or more on income tax, but the money has had years in which to grow as an investment and is worth more in the future than when you first invested it.

Another point to consider when planning for retirement is that income placed in some sort of savings environment, where it can grow, untouched, for many years, benefits from the effects of compounding interest, where interest is earned not only on the original investment but also on the previously earned interest. The more you can put away in the early years, the richer your savings fund will be, due to the fact that the earnings will have had a longer time in which to grow. Save $10,000 today and invest at 5 percent for 30 years and you will have a fund worth over $43,000. Save $333 per year for 30 years ($10,000 total), invested at 5 percent, and you will have a fund worth slightly over $23,000 in 30 years.

There are several types of tax-deferred plans available, so surely there's one for you. The different plans allow varying amounts of contributions based on your income or the type of job you have. All of these plans include a clause whereby you must pay a penalty if you withdraw the funds too early, so when you contribute to a tax-deferred plan, make sure you can afford to lock away that money for several years.

Keogh, SEP, and SIMPLE Plans

If you operate your own business, you have the option to establish and contribute to a Keogh, SEP, or SIMPLE retirement plan.

The Keogh Plan

The Keogh plan is a pension or profit-sharing plan available only to self-employed individuals and their employees.

Note   *Participation in a Keogh plan, which is based on your net income from self-employment, does not negate your privilege to make tax-deductible contributions toward an IRA.*

There are two options for the structure of the Keogh plan: it can be a profit-sharing plan or a defined benefit plan. If the Keogh plan is a profit-sharing plan, the self-employed Keogh participant can contribute the smaller of $30,000 or 25 percent of net self-employment income. If the plan is a profit-sharing plan, the contribution is limited to 15 percent of net self-employment income.

The computations for making contributions to a Keogh can be somewhat complicated. Fortunately, TurboTax will take care of this for you by examining the net income on your business tax form (Schedule C) and calculating the maximum amount that you can contribute. If you let TurboTax go ahead and calculate this contribution, then you can decide if you want to contribute the maximum amount or something less.

On the Contributions screen (see Figure 6-1), check the Maximize box for the type of plan you have, then scroll down in the form that appears at the bottom of the screen to see what that maximum amount is. If you can't afford to make the maximum contribution this year, you can enter a different amount in the space above.

As with most retirement plans, there is a penalty for early withdrawal of funds from the Keogh plan. An authorized withdrawal can occur at age $59\frac{1}{2}$ or beyond. A withdrawal of funds before then faces not only income taxation but also a 10 percent penalty. In addition, an early withdrawal of funds from a Keogh plan prohibits you from making contributions to the plan for five years.

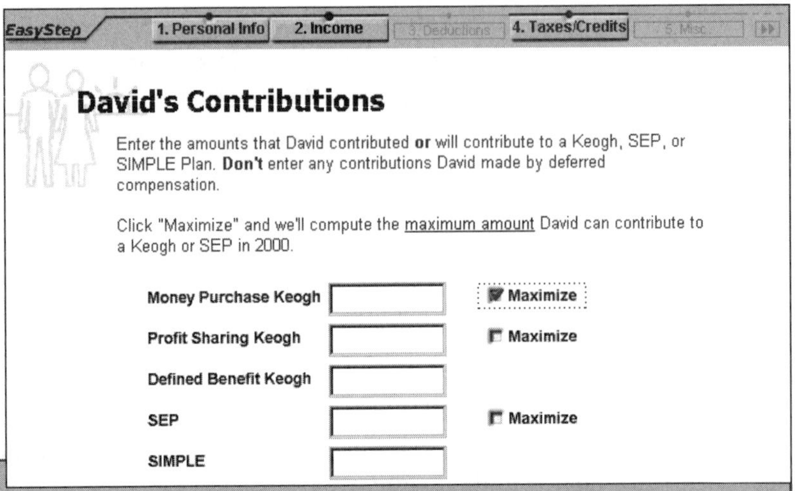

Figure 6-1 • Check the Maximize box if you want TurboTax to calculate the highest amount you are allowed to contribute to your plan.

SEP Plans

A Simplified Employee Pension Plan (SEP) is a retirement plan for self-employed individuals and their employees. Even if you're not self-employed, your employer may have set up an SEP in which you participate. An SEP is like a company retirement plan and an IRA combined, and your employees generally must be able to participate in the plan. Employers may contribute the lesser of up to 15 percent of your salary (generally, this is limited to $170,000 maximum for 2000) or $30,000 to the plan each year, and participants are entitled to contribute up to $2,000 each year.

As a self-employed individual, you can have TurboTax calculate the maximum SEP contribution available by checking the Maximize box on the Contributions screen. If you are employed by a company that has an SEP plan and you intend to make a contribution of some amount up to $2,000, you can enter the amount you plan to contribute on the line provided, as shown here:

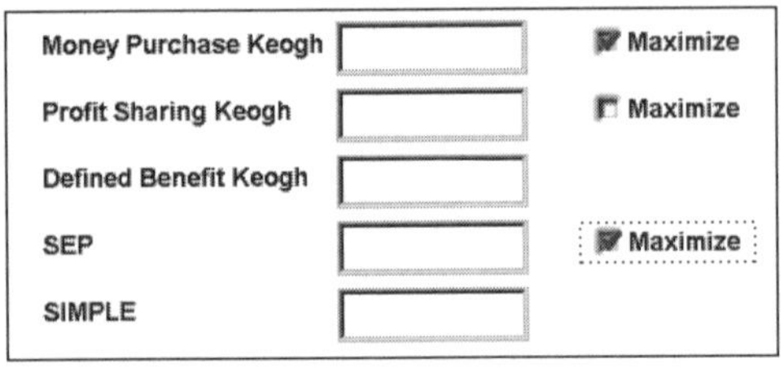

SIMPLE Plans

SIMPLE stands for Savings Incentive Match Plan for Employees, and as the name implies, this is a retirement savings plan that is a matching plan. Employees have the right to contribute up to $6,000 per year in a SIMPLE plan (this limit may increase in future years), and employers may make matching contributions in an amount up to 3 percent of the employee's salary.

If you are a participant in a SIMPLE plan, enter the exact amount you plan to contribute on the Contributions screen in TurboTax, shown here:

Click "Maximize" and we'll compute the maximum amount David can contribute to a Keogh or SEP in 2000.

Money Purchase Keogh		☐ Maximize
Profit Sharing Keogh		☐ Maximize
Defined Benefit Keogh		
SEP		☐ Maximize
SIMPLE	3,500.	

Contributions to 401(k) and 403(b) Plans

The 401(k) plan is named after the section of the Internal Revenue Code that authorizes the plan. An employer can offer employees the right to participate in a company-sponsored 401(k) plan. If such a plan exists at your workplace, you may have the right to participate by designating that your employer withhold a certain amount from your wages and place that amount in the plan. Some employers provide contributions to such a plan themselves in addition to the employee contributions.

The 403(b) plan is similar to a 401(k) except that it is offered exclusively to employees of nonprofit institutions such as schools, hospitals, museums, research institutes, and foundations.

Employee contributions to a 401(k) or 403(b) plan are not subject to current income tax as long as they are held in the plan. Money withdrawn from the plan is subject to taxation under rules described in the "Retirement Income" section of Chapter 5.

There is no special entry that you need to make in TurboTax regarding your contribution to a 401(k) or 403(b) retirement plan. The amount you contributed during the year will appear on your W-2 form and will be entered when you enter your other W-2 information. But since the retirement contribution is actually deducted from your income that is reported on your W-2 form, you don't need to enter the amount as an adjustment on your tax return.

Contributions to an IRA

An Individual Retirement Account can take on several forms. There is the traditional IRA, which until a few years ago was the only IRA available. Now there is also the Roth IRA and the Education IRA. The IRA accounts form a strange family because each of the accounts is very different from its brothers, and each account attracts a different kind of investor.

In a nutshell, the traditional IRA provides an option for a tax-deferred investment as well as a vehicle for tax-deferred savings. The Roth IRA provides lower- and middle-income taxpayers with an opportunity to invest tax-free in an account that, if they like, will outlive them and pass on, tax-free, to their heirs. The Education IRA is not a retirement account at all, but rather a means of rerouting money to children and grandchildren for use as college tuition. Contributions to an Education IRA are not reported on your tax return, but distributions from the account do get entered on your return in the same section with other IRA contributions.

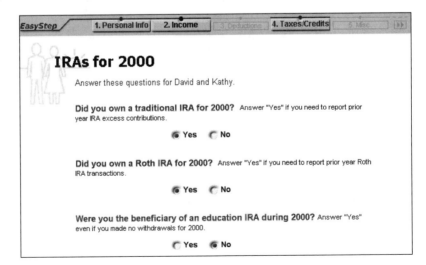

Deductible Contributions to a Traditional IRA

An IRA is a retirement savings account into which certain taxpayers can contribute up to $2,000 annually. Deductible contributions result in a deferment of tax on the amount contributed, and earnings in the account accumulate in a tax-deferred state until money is withdrawn from the account, at which time it is subject to income tax.

Note   *An IRA isn't just any savings account. You have to set up your IRA with a bank or stock brokerage firm—an organization, known as a custodian, that can ensure that the account meets the requirements set by the IRS. Furthermore, the contribution to your IRA must be made on or before the due date of your tax return, including extensions. Contributions for 2000 will need to be made on or before April 16, 2001 (or by the extended due date if you extend the due date of your tax return).*

The main obstacles standing in the way of taking a deduction for an IRA contribution are participation in a retirement plan at work and making too much money. If neither you nor your spouse participate in a retirement plan at work, the rules state that you are entitled to contribute up to $2,000 per year per spouse, assuming at least one of the spouses has *earned income* at least equal to the amount of the contribution. Earned income is income that you work for, such as income from an employer or your own business. Unearned income is income from investments, gifts, prizes, rental property (unless renting property is your main business), sales of stocks, and so on.

Because the annual IRA contribution is limited to the lower of a maximum of $2,000 per person or the person's earned income, if you make only $1,500 for the year, your IRA contribution will be limited to $1,500.

If either you or your spouse is a participant in a retirement plan at work, the rules for IRA contributions get a bit sticky. Limits on the amount you can deduct are based on your income and your filing status. Tables 6-1 and 6-2 show how the limits are applied. Fortunately, TurboTax does all of these calculations for you.

GET SMARTER   If your income falls in the phase-out range and your deductible IRA contribution is limited, you are not prohibited from contributing $2,000, you are just prohibited from *deducting* your entire contribution. It is only your deduction, not your contribution that is limited.

Filing Status	Adjusted Gross Income Range[1]				
	$0 to $10,000	$10,000 to $32,000	$32,000 to $42,000	$42,000 to $52,000	$52,000 to $62,000
Single or Head of Household	Maximum deduction	Maximum deduction	Deduction phases out	No deduction	No deduction
Married Filing Jointly or Qualifying Widow(er)	Maximum deduction	Maximum deduction	Maximum deduction	Maximum deduction	Deduction phases out
Married Filing Separately	Deduction phases out	No deduction	No deduction	No deduction	No deduction

[1] This doesn't take into account your IRA contribution and deductible student loan interest

Table 6-1 • IRA Deduction for Taxpayers Participating in a Retirement Plan at Work

Filing Status	Adjusted Gross Income Range[1]						
	$0 to $10,000	$10,000 to $32,000	$32,000 to $42,000	$42,000 to $52,000	$52,000 to $62,000	$62,000 to $150,000	Over $150,000
Single or Head of Household	Maximum deduction	Maximum deduction	Maximum deduction	Maximum deduction	Maximum deduction	Maximum deduction	Maximum deduction
Married Filing Jointly[2]	Maximum deduction	Maximum deduction	Maximum deduction	Maximum deduction	Maximum deduction	Deduction phases out	No deduction
Married Filing Jointly or Separately;[3] Qualifying Widow(er)	Maximum deduction	Maximum deduction	Maximum deduction	Maximum deduction	Maximum deduction	Maximum deduction	Maximum deduction
Married Filing Separately[3]	Deduction phases out	No deduction	No deduction	No deduction	No deduction	No deduction	No deduction

[1] This doesn't take into account your IRA contribution and deductible student loan interest
[2] Spouse is covered by a retirement plan at work
[3] Spouse is not covered by a retirement plan at work

Table 6-2 • IRA Deduction for Taxpayers Not Participating in a Retirement Plan at Work

If your income is in the phase-out range, as shown in Tables 6-1 and 6-2, your IRA contribution is limited to 20 percent of the high number in the phase-out range less your income, rounded up to the nearest $10. For example, if you are single and a participant in a company retirement plan, and your income is $35,000, your deductible contribution would be limited to 20 percent of ($42,000 to $35,000) or $1,400.

EasyStep	1. Personal Info	2. Income	3. Deductions	4. Taxes/Credits	5. Misc.

Traditional IRA Contributions

In "Regular Contribution," enter your <u>contributions</u> to traditional IRAs for 2000. Include any contributions you later <u>recharacterized</u> as, or <u>converted</u> to, a <u>Roth</u> IRA. **Don't** include any contributions you made directly to a Roth IRA that you later recharacterized as a traditional IRA. Include any SEP or SIMPLE **excess contributions** for 2000, and **exclude** any amounts already entered on Schedule K-1 worksheets.

In "Recharacterized Contribution," enter any contributions to a traditional IRA that you recharacterized as a Roth IRA. Don't enter any contribution to a traditional IRA that was part of a conversion to a Roth IRA. Don't include any earnings or losses in this amount.

	David	Kathy
Regular Contribution		2,000.
Recharacterized Contribution		

Enter the full amount of your contribution, even if you are unable to take a deduction for this amount.

Note | *The IRS requires that you provide the basis of your IRA account balance. The basis is not the entire value of the account nor is it the total amount of contributions you have made to the account. Instead, the basis is the total amount of nondeductible contributions you have made to the IRA account. If you have deducted all of your IRA contributions on previous tax returns, your basis is zero.*

EasyStep	1. Personal Info	2. Income	3. Deductions	4. Taxes/Credits	5. Misc.

Traditional IRA Basis

Enter David's and Kathy's total <u>IRA basis</u> for 1999 and earlier years, if any.

Note: IRA basis is NOT IRA value. You have a basis ONLY if any prior year contributions were nondeductible.

Basis for 1999 and Earlier Years:

Amount, David [   ]

Amount, Kathy [   ]

NonDeductible Contributions to an IRA

There is no prohibition on making a contribution to an IRA. Anyone with earned income of at least $2,000 can make an IRA contribution for up to that amount (and another $2,000 for your spouse, even if the spouse does not work, as long as your earned income equals or exceeds the amount of the contribution). The only prohibition is on deducting the contribution. The tables in the previous section show how deductions are limited.

If you decide to make a nondeductible contribution to your IRA, you should keep the following thoughts in mind:

- The nondeductible contribution does not lower your taxable income or your tax.
- The earnings in the IRA account are tax-deferred, even if the contribution was not.
- You must keep careful records of how much of your contributions over the years was deducted and how much was not. When you begin withdrawing funds, you will prorate the withdrawals based on a percentage determined by the nondeductible and deductible contributions over the year, so that some of the money withdrawn each year will be taxed and some will not.

Excess IRA Contributions

If you contributed too much to your IRA for 2000, either because you contributed more than the allowed $2,000 or because it turned out your earned income was less than $2,000, which limited your allowable contribution, you have two choices. You can withdraw the excess contribution by April 16, 2001, and not face any penalty, or you can leave the money where it is, but then you will be required to pay a tax on the excess contribution.

Note   *If you decide to withdraw the excess contribution to your IRA, be sure to also withdraw all earnings associated with the contribution—otherwise those earnings will be considered an excess contribution.*

The tax on an excess contribution is 6 percent of the excess contributions and earnings thereon.

When you enter your IRA contribution, TurboTax will be able to tell if your IRA contribution is too high and you will be advised as to how much of the IRA contribution is excess. Should you decide to withdraw the excess contribution before the due date of your tax return, you can do so, then go back and change the amount of contribution listed for your IRA.

Excess Contributions for 2000

Based on the information you've entered, we've determined that Kathy's excess contributions to an IRA for 2000 are $100.00.

The Roth IRA

The Roth IRA has only been around for two years and has gotten more press than any other tax issue I can remember. The Roth IRA is a simple, straightforward retirement alternative that appeals to many taxpayers. This special IRA gives low- and middle-income taxpayers the ability to save money for retirement now and pay no tax later on the earnings of that money.

Contributions to a Roth IRA are not deductible under any circumstances. The contributions to a Roth are subject to the same $2,000 limitation as with a traditional IRA. In other words, you can contribute a maximum of $2,000 per year to any one IRA or to all IRA accounts combined.

EasyStep | 1. Personal Info | 2. Income | 3. Deductions | 4. Taxes/Credits | 5. Misc. | ▶▶

2000 Roth IRA Contributions

Enter any contributions you made directly to a Roth IRA for tax year 2000, **including** any contributions that you later recharacterized as a traditional IRA.

Don't include any distributions from traditional IRAs that you converted to Roth IRAs, or any contributions you made to a traditional IRA which you later recharacterized as a Roth IRA. Also, **exclude** any amounts already entered on Schedule K-1 worksheets.

Regular Roth Contribution:

Amount, David   `2,000.`

Amount, Kathy   `[          ]`

Because Roth IRAs are still so new and many people have questions about how these accounts are structured, I've set out the main rules here:

- The Roth IRA is an individual retirement account to which contributions are entirely nondeductible and on which the earnings are entirely nontaxable, assuming the rules of the account are abided by.

- An IRA that is to be treated as a Roth IRA must be designated as a Roth IRA when the account is established.
- The annual contribution to a Roth IRA is limited to a maximum of $2,000, and the annual combined contribution to all IRA accounts cannot exceed $2,000.
- You are allowed to make a contribution to a Roth IRA if you are married filing a joint return and your adjusted gross income is under $160,000. All other taxpayers may make a contribution to a Roth if their adjusted gross income is under $110,000, except married filing separately taxpayers who lived with their spouse during the year, and they can only contribute to a Roth if their AGI is under $10,000.
- If, prior to December 31, 2000, you convert funds to a Roth IRA, only to discover at the end of the year that your income exceeds the $100,000 ceiling so you are not eligible to make the conversion, you can transfer the amount back to your traditional IRA before the due date of your tax return, including extensions, without any negative tax consequences. Any income earned in the Roth IRA account while the converted funds were in the account must also be transferred to the traditional IRA. The transfer between accounts must be directly from one account to the other—you cannot withdraw the funds personally, as you can with a traditional IRA rollover.

| EasyStep | 1. Personal Info | 2. Income | 3. Deductions | 4. Taxes/Credits | 5. Misc. | ▶▶ |

Roth IRA Contribution Recharacterized

Enter any contributions to a Roth IRA that you recharacterized as a traditional IRA. This includes traditional IRA contributions that you recharacterized as a Roth IRA then recharacterized back to the traditional IRA. Enter only **recharacterized contributions,** not any conversions from traditional IRAs.

Don't include any earnings or losses in this amount.

Recharacterized Contributions:

Amount, David [   ]

Amount, Kathy [   ]

- There is a phase-out for annual contributions to a Roth IRA beginning with an adjusted gross income of $150,000 for joint filers, $95,000 for all other filers except married filing separately taxpayers who lived with their spouses at any time during the year, and their phase out begins at $10,000. Married filing separately taxpayers who did not live with their spouse are barred from contributing to a Roth IRA. If your income is within the phase-out range for Roth contributions, your allowable contribution will be less than $2,000. TurboTax will advise you if the contribution you indicated is too high.

David's Excess 2000 Roth IRA Contributions

We've determined that David's excess contributions to a Roth IRA for 2000 is $1,210.00.

- Taxpayers may combine all Roth IRA amounts (conversion as well as original contribution) in a single account.
- Distributions from a Roth IRA may not be made before the end of the five-year period beginning with the first year *for which* a contribution is made. In other words, if you make your first contribution in April 2001 for the tax year 2000, the first withdrawal could be after 2005. If your April 2001 contribution is for the year 2001, the first withdrawal can occur after 2006. This five-year rule is in effect for both original contributions as well as conversions to Roth IRAs (see the next section).
- If traditional IRA amounts are converted to a Roth IRA, and if those amounts were includable in gross income at the time of the conversion, any portion of the converted amount that is withdrawn from the Roth IRA prior to the participant reaching age $59\frac{1}{2}$ is subject to a 10 percent penalty on the amount withdrawn.

Conversions to a Roth IRA

You may convert funds from traditional IRA accounts to a Roth IRA, as long as your adjusted gross income for the year does not exceed $100,000. For purposes of this computation only, all components of adjusted gross income are included without regard for the effects of including the income from the conversion. In other words, sometimes when you increase your adjusted gross income (as you would if you were adding the amounts from the conversion), certain losses may not be allowed. For purposes of computing, if your AGI does not exceed $100,000, these losses will be allowed, even though once you add in the converted funds, the losses may be disallowed.

If traditional IRA amounts are converted to a Roth IRA, and if those amounts were includable in gross income at the time of the conversion, any portion of the converted amount that is withdrawn from the Roth IRA prior to the participant reaching age 59½ is subject to a 10 percent penalty on the amount withdrawn.

If, prior to December 31, 2000, you convert funds to a Roth IRA, only to discover at the end of the year that your income exceeds the $100,000 ceiling so you are not eligible to make the conversion, you can transfer the amount back to your traditional IRA before the due date of your tax return, including extensions, without any negative tax consequences. Any income earned in the Roth IRA account while the converted funds were in the account must also be transferred to the traditional IRA. The transfer between accounts must be directly from one account to the other—you cannot withdraw the funds personally, as you can with a traditional IRA rollover.

If you converted funds from a traditional IRA to a Roth IRA in 1998, you had the special opportunity to spread the effect of the tax on this conversion over four years. If you took advantage of this opportunity, you must report various amounts from your 1998 tax return on your 2000 tax return so that the proper amount of tax may be assessed in 2000 (see Figure 6-2).

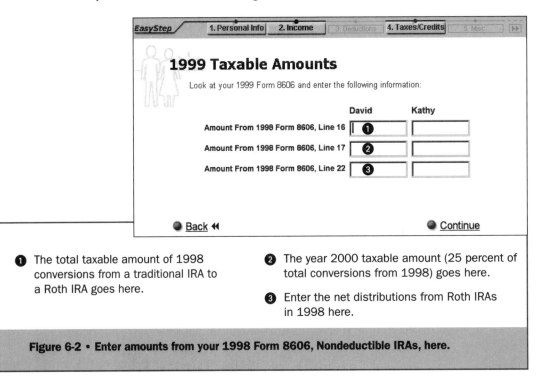

Figure 6-2 • **Enter amounts from your 1998 Form 8606, Nondeductible IRAs, here.**

Medical Savings Accounts

The Medical Savings Account (MSA) is a tax-free account that operates much like an IRA except that you can take money out of it (tax-free) to pay for your medical expenses that aren't covered by health insurance.

The MSA is available to self-employed individuals and employees of small businesses (50 or fewer employees) and is set up through your health insurance provider.

The MSA works like this:

- You make tax-free contributions to the account (an income-earning account maintained by your health insurance provider).

- The maximum contribution amount is 65 percent (for individual coverage) or 75 percent (for family coverage) of your plan's deductible (which must be at least $1,500 if you are single and $3,000 if your coverage is for more than one member of your family). You determine how much of this 65 or 75 percent you contribute during the year.

- Your MSA contribution cannot exceed the net income from the self-employed business for which the MSA was established.

- At any time during the year, you can make a request to receive reimbursement from your MSA (or have your MSA actually make payments for you) for medical expenses that are not covered by the health insurance plan (such as items that fall within your deductible amount).

- Earnings on amounts in the MSA account are not taxed, provided the amounts are used for qualified medical expenses.

- All money left in the plan at the end of the year carries over to the next year. The money in the plan belongs to you forever.

- You don't have to use the money in your MSA for health expenses. You can let the money grow, like a retirement plan, and begin withdrawing funds for any purpose, subject to income tax but no penalty, at age 65.

- You have until April 16, 2001, to set up and fund an MSA for 2000.

Adjustment for MSA Contributions

Distributions from your MSA, which are reported to you on Form 1099-MSA, must be recorded in TurboTax, but are not subject to tax, as long as the distributions were made within the allowable guidelines of the MSA plan.

Enter the total amount you withdrew from your MSA account during 2000 here. This amount should correspond with the amount on the 1099-MSA provided by your account administrator.

EasyStep	1. Personal Info	2. Income	3. Deductions	4. Taxes/Credits	5. Misc.

MSA Account - Boxes 1-5

1 - Gross Distribution — `375.00`

2 - Earnings on Excess Contributions

3 - Distribution Code
- 1-Normal distribution
- 2-Excess contributions
- 3-Disability
- 4-Death

4 - FMV on Date of Death

5 - Medicare+Choice MSA ☐

The contributions you make to your MSA are allowed as adjustments on your tax return. When entering MSA contributions, you must indicate the business with which the MSA account is associated.

EasyStep	1. Personal Info	2. Income	3. Deductions	4. Taxes/Credits	5. Misc.

Employer or Business

Enter the name of the employer or business where you have a high deductible health plan (HDHP).

Employer or Business Name `David's Consulting Business`

This Worksheet Is For ⦿ David ◯ Kathy

You must also indicate the type of coverage provided by the MSA—this information will enable TurboTax to determine what percentage of your contribution you are entitled to deduct. As long as you stay within the prescribed guidelines regarding the percentage of your plan's deductible that is allowed as a contribution, and as long as you have self-employment income at least as high as your MSA contribution, you will be able to deduct the full amount of your contribution.

EasyStep | 1. Personal Info | 2. Income | 3. Deductions | 4. Taxes/Credits | 5. Misc. | ▶▶

Type of Coverage

What type of <u>high deductible health plan</u> (HDHP) coverage did David have with David's Consulting Business?

● <u>Back</u> ◀◀   ● <u>Self-Only Coverage</u>   ● <u>Family Coverage</u>

You must provide the amount of your contribution, the amount of your plan's deductible, the number of months during 2000 that your plan was in effect, and the wages or net income from the business associated with this plan. TurboTax will then calculate your allowable contribution and compare amounts. You will be advised if an excess contribution was made. You are allowed to withdraw any excess MSA contribution before the due date of your tax return and avoid a penalty.

EasyStep | 1. Personal Info | 2. Income | 3. Deductions | 4. Taxes/Credits | 5. Misc. | ▶▶

MSA Contribution Worksheet

Enter the contribution David made to an MSA during the time period David was covered by the high deductible health plan (HDHP) through David's Consulting Business. Also, tell us about the health plan.

David's MSA Contribution	1,000.
Annual Deductible Amount	1,500.
Number of Months This Plan Was in Effect	12
Wages or Earnings From David's Consulting Business	15,000.

Warning About MSA Accounts

There is one feature of the MSA you must be careful about. If you find yourself covered by another medical plan (perhaps you decide to give up self-employment and take a job with an employer who provides healthcare, or perhaps you marry someone who has a health plan under which you can be covered), any amounts remaining in your MSA account are subject to income tax and a 15 percent penalty.

A bit of careful planning can circumvent this tax and penalty situation. If you expect to begin receiving healthcare coverage from another source, and this coverage will negate the tax-free benefits of your MSA, stop making contributions to your MSA, and use up the amounts that are in the account to pay for medical expense before your new plan becomes effective.

Adjustments for the Self-Employed

Self-employed individuals may not feel they are entitled to many tax breaks: they pay a higher tax than many other taxpayers due to the fact that they pay self-employment tax at twice the rate of employed taxpayers. But of course there are benefits to being in business for yourself, and one of them comes in the form of some special tax adjustments just for self-employed taxpayers.

Adjustment for Self-Employment Tax

Self-employment tax is another name for the Social Security and Medicare taxes. The difference is that when you pay Social Security and Medicare taxes, you are only paying half of your liability—your employer pays the other half. When you pay self-employment tax, you pay your full share of these taxes, so you actually pay double what employees pay.

Self-employment tax is assessed against net income from self-employment. Typically this translates into the net income at the bottom of your Schedule C or Schedule F. You may also have self-employment income passing through to you from an interest in a partnership.

If you are subject to the self-employment tax, which will be computed by TurboTax and will appear on Schedule SE, you are entitled to take a deduction from your income for half of the amount of the tax, as shown in Figure 6-3. The deduction doesn't reduce the amount of self-employment tax you must pay because the income on your business tax form is not affected by this deduction.

You don't have to make any special entries on the TurboTax screens to take advantage of this self-employment tax adjustment. TurboTax calculates the adjustment automatically and places the amount on page 1 of your tax return.

Adjusted Gross Income		
23 IRA deduction (see instructions)	**23**	2,000.
24 Student loan interest deduction (see instructions)	**24**	
25 Medical savings account deduction	**25**	1,000.
26 Moving expenses	**26**	1,520.
27 One-half of self-employment tax	**27**	1,095.
28 Self-employed health insurance deduction (see instr.)	**28**	1,440.
29 Self-employed SEP, SIMPLE, and qualified plans	**29**	3,500.
30 Penalty on early withdrawal of savings	**30**	

Figure 6-3 • TurboTax calculates half of the self-employment tax and shows that as an adjustment to your income on page 1 of your tax return.

Adjustment for Medical Insurance

If you are self-employed, you are entitled to take an adjustment for your cost of medical insurance. For the year 2000, the self-employed person can take 60 percent of the cost of medical insurance as an adjustment to income on page 1 of the tax return. Under present law, this percentage will remain the same for 2001, then increase to 70 percent in 2002 and 100 percent in 2003 and thereafter. Congress has floated the idea of speeding up this deduction timetable but as of yet no legislation has occurred to change this schedule.

When you enter the income and expenses associated with your self-employment, you will be asked if you paid for any health insurance coverage in 2000. When you enter the amount you paid in health insurance (as shown in Figure 6-4), TurboTax will compare this amount to your net business income to ensure you are entitled to take the full adjustment of 60 percent of your insurance. The allowable adjustment will be entered on page 1 of your tax return.

The adjustment for health insurance is limited to the amount of self-employment income you report on your tax return, less the amount of self-employment tax you deduct and less any deductible contribution to a Keogh, SEP, or SIMPLE plan.

Note   *If you were eligible to participate in a group health plan through your employer during any months of the year, or if your spouse was eligible to participate in such a plan during any months of the year, you are not entitled to take the self-employed medical insurance deduction for those months, even if you elect not to participate in the group plan.*

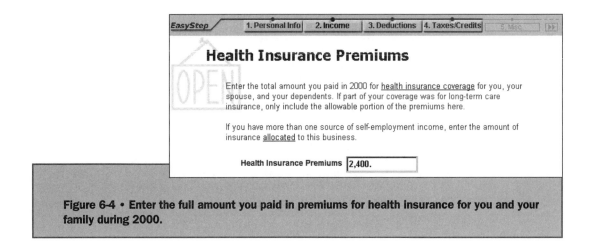

Figure 6-4 • **Enter the full amount you paid in premiums for health insurance for you and your family during 2000.**

The balance of any medical insurance cost that is not deducted as an adjustment on page 1 of the tax return is allowed as an itemized deduction on Schedule A (see Chapter 7 for more information about deducting medical expenses). You must be able to itemize your deductions, of course, and to claim the deduction for medical expenses in order to take advantage of this deduction.

Moving Expenses

You can take an adjustment for the expenses of a move to a new home if you meet the following tests:

- Your move has to be job-related. If you're moving to a new home because you like the climate, your friends live nearby, the new home has a bigger backyard, you wanted to get away from your former neighbors, or any other non–job-related reason, that's okay, as long as you're changing jobs as well. The new job can be a job for a new company, or it can be a transfer within the company for which you already work.

- The new job must be at least 50 miles farther from your old home than the old job was. If the move is to your first job, the new home must be at least 50 miles from your old home.

Distance Test

Enter total miles from your **old** home to your old and new workplaces. If you are certain that the difference between these two numbers is 50 miles or more, you can enter reasonable estimates.

Miles to OLD workplace [12]   Miles to NEW workplace [765]

- You must stay in your new location, working full-time at a job for at least 39 weeks during the first 12 months after you move. You don't have to stay at the same job for all those 39 weeks, but you have to continue working in the same geographical area if you want to take the deduction.
- You can take the adjustment for moving expenses if you are self-employed, but in that case you have to work full-time for 39 weeks of the first 12 months *and* 78 weeks of the first 24 months.

Moving Expenses You Can Deduct

Determining that you are eligible to deduct moving expenses is only half the battle. There are limitations on what types of moving expenses you can deduct. Moving expenses you can deduct as an adjustment on page 1 of your tax return include:

- The cost of packing and moving your household goods and personal belongings from the old home to the new home. This does not include the cost of shipping new furniture that is purchased in the location of the new home.
- The cost of travel and necessary overnight lodging while moving your family members to the new home, including the cost of overnight lodging for one night after you arrive at the location of the new home if you are not able to move in immediately.
- The cost of storing and insuring household goods and personal belongings within any period of 39 consecutive days after the day your things are moved from your former home and before they are delivered to your new home.
- The cost of connecting and disconnecting utilities at both homes.
- The cost of transporting pets to the new home.

TurboTax provides one screen for entering moving expenses. All deductible moving expenses are to be entered on this screen (see Figure 6-5). Double-click any space to create an itemized statement.

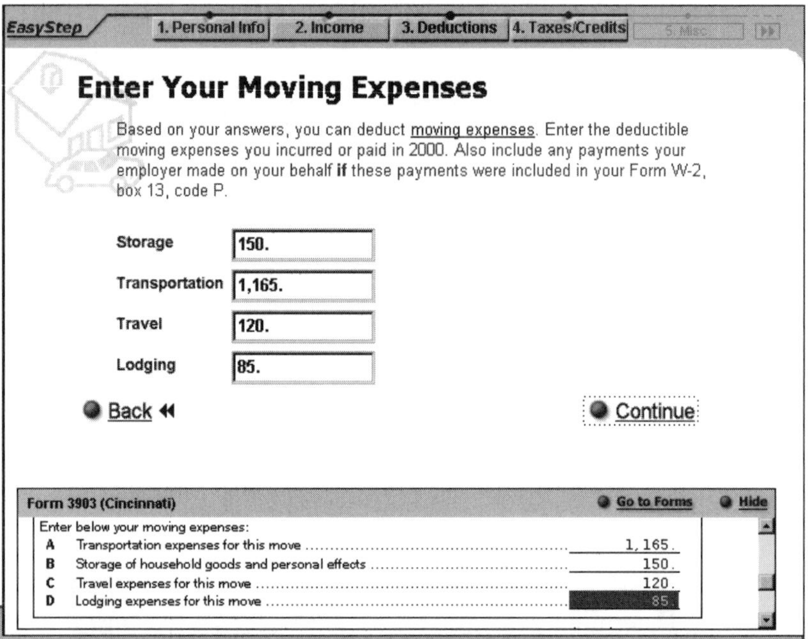

Figure 6-5 • This is the only screen on which you can enter moving expenses, so summarize all of your deductible expenses here.

If you drive your car as part of your move (as opposed to having the car shipped), you can either deduct your actual expenses for the car, including gas and oil, but not including repairs, maintenance, insurance, or depreciation, or you can take a deduction for the miles you drove associated with the move, at 10 cents per mile. In either case, you can deduct any parking fees and tolls you incurred in association with the move.

When to Deduct Moving Expenses

If you move and pay for the move all in the same year, there is no controversy over when to take a deduction for the expense. If your move straddles two years, or if you move in one year and pay for the expenses in a different year, you can choose whether to deduct the moving expenses in the year they were incurred or in the year they were paid.

NonDeductible Moving Expenses

The previous section discussed the moving expenses you can deduct, but just in case you have any lingering questions about what is allowed as a deduction, here is the IRS list of items you are not allowed to deduct. It's interesting to note that until 1994 most of these items were allowed as moving expense deductions.

- Any part of the purchase price of your new home
- Car tags and a driver's license in the new location
- Expenses of buying or selling a home
- Expenses of acquiring or breaking a lease
- Loss on the sale of your home
- Losses from disposing of memberships in clubs
- Meal expenses associated with house hunting and moving
- Penalties for early disposition of a mortgage
- Pre-move house-hunting expenses
- Real estate taxes
- Refitting carpets and draperies
- Security deposits, including any given up as a result of the move
- Storage charges other than those incurred in transit
- Temporary living expenses in the new location

Employer Reimbursement for Moving Expenses

Employers who reimburse employees for moving expenses are supposed to include the reimbursement as part of your wages on your W-2 form and indicate same on the form. If the reimbursement is for moving expenses that are nondeductible (such as a reimbursement for the sales commission you paid when you sold your house), the employer should withhold tax on that portion of the reimbursement.

If your employer reimbursed you for moving expenses and included the amount in your wages in Box 1 of your W-2 form, there may be mention in Box 14 of how much was reimbursed. In this case, you will want to deduct your moving expenses so that you can offset at least some of this income.

If the employer has not included your moving reimbursement with the wages on your W-2 form, you are precluded from taking a deduction for moving expenses associated with the reimbursement. In this situation, employers frequently show the moving reimbursement in Box 13 of the W-2 form and code the amount with the letter P, which represents moving expenses for which you were reimbursed but which were not included in your wages.

Student Loan Interest

You can take an adjustment for up to $2,000 of interest paid on qualified education loans. The amount will increase to $2,500 in 2001. The adjustment applies to education loans paid during the first 60 months that interest payments are required on the loan (excluding months in which the loan is in forbearance or has been deferred).

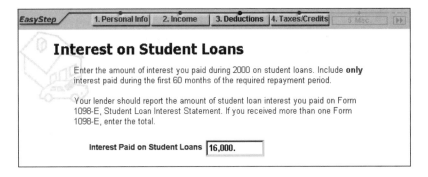

What Interest Expenses Can You Deduct?

A qualified education loan is a loan incurred to pay for qualified higher education expenses of the taxpayer, spouse, or any dependent. Qualified education expenses include tuition, fees, room and board, books, and supplies. The expenses must be incurred in relation to attending a postsecondary educational institution or vocational school and the student must be pursuing a degree, certificate, or similar credential.

Who Qualifies for the Deduction?

During the years in which the adjustment can be taken, the taxpayer claiming the interest deduction must not be claimed as a dependent on another taxpayer's tax return. Also, the taxpayer who claims the interest deduction must be the person who is legally liable for the debt. If the debt is taken out in the parent's name and the child is paying the loan (or vice versa), there is no interest deduction.

You are not allowed to claim the deduction if your adjusted gross income is over $55,000, or $75,000 if you are married filing a joint return. The deduction begins to be phased out when income exceeds $40,000, or $60,000 for married filing jointly.

Alimony

Alimony is money paid to a spouse or former spouse as a result of a court-ordered decree such as a separate maintenance agreement or a divorce decree. If you pay alimony, you can take an adjustment on page 1 of your tax return for the amount you pay. (If you receive alimony, report the amount as income, as described in the "Alimony" section of Chapter 5.)

As a payer of alimony, it is your responsibility to provide the IRS with the recipient's Social Security number. You will be liable for a $50 penalty and your deduction can be disallowed if you fail to provide this information.

Before entering your alimony costs as an adjustment, make sure the following requirements have been met:

- The payments must be required by a divorce decree, separate maintenance agreement, or a written agreement incident to the divorce or separation.
- The legal document requiring the alimony payment can't designate the amount as something other than alimony (child support, for example).
- You can't file a joint tax return with the recipient of the alimony, nor can the two of you live in the same household.
- Payments must be made in cash or checks as opposed to property.
- Payments will not continue if the recipient dies.

Reducing Your Income with Deductions

Chapter 7

In This Chapter:

- *Reducing Income with Medical Deductions*

- *Reducing Income with Tax Deductions*

- *Reducing Income with Interest Deductions*

- *Reducing Income with Deductions for Charitable Contributions*

- *Reducing Income with Casualty and Theft Losses*

- *Reducing Income with Miscellaneous Deductions*

Itemized deductions, which get listed on Schedule A of your tax return, are available to all taxpayers to the extent that the total itemized deductions exceed the standard deduction available to taxpayers. Itemized deductions are a means of lowering the income on which you pay tax, so that certain basic expenditures, such as the cost of medical care and the cost of housing, are not subject to income tax.

Note that the types of deductions covered in this chapter are organized in order of their appearance on the Schedule A tax form where they get reported, which is not exactly the same order in which these deductions appear in TurboTax. If you're following along in this book while entering information in your TurboTax program screen by screen, you may need to hop around a bit in this chapter.

Which Taxpayers Can Itemize?

To be able to itemize, you must have deductions higher than the standard deduction for your filing status. It doesn't make any sense to itemize otherwise—if the standard deduction is higher than your accumulated itemized deductions, you get a higher deduction by taking the standard. Standard deduction amounts increase each year. Standard deductions for 2000 for the various filing statuses are as follows:

- Single—$4,400
- Married Filing Jointly—$7,350
- Married Filing Separately—$3,675
- Head of Household—$6,450
- Qualifying Widow(er)—$7,350

Caution   *The exception to the rule of not itemizing if your deductions don't exceed the standard deduction occurs when you are married filing a separate return and your spouse itemizes. In such a case, you are required to itemize also, even if your itemized deductions are less than the standard deduction.*

If your itemized deductions exceed your standard deduction, you shouldn't hesitate to use your itemized deductions to reduce your tax burden. There was a time when itemized deductions were closely scrutinized by the IRS and thought of as a red flag that would draw unwanted attention to your tax return. Now the types of deductions that once lent themselves to stretching of the truth have been weeded out; the main deductions available to taxpayers are those that can be documented by public or electronic evidence. Since there is little room for exaggerating the amounts on itemized deductions, the IRS seems less concerned that tax cheating is going on in this area and so taxpayers should not feel discouraged from itemizing.

GET SMARTER   If you're not sure if you have enough deductions to itemize, there's no harm in filling out the screens in TurboTax. The program will calculate your total itemized deductions and if the standard deduction is higher, that's what will be used on your tax return. Not only will you get a chance to see how close your itemized deductions come to the standard deduction, but if you use TurboTax next year, all the entries you made for itemized deductions this year will carry over so you won't have to enter them again. For example, if you list the organizations to which you made charitable contributions, the names of the organizations will appear again next year—you won't have to type them again, and the list may serve as a reminder to help you organize your information for next year's return.

Medical Expenses

The medical expenses you can deduct are expenses for yourself, your spouse, and all of your dependents.

To take a deduction for medical expenses as part of your itemized deductions, your total medical expenses must add up to more than 7.5 percent of your adjusted gross income. For example, if you earn $40,000 a year, you must have at least $3,000 (7.5 percent of $40,000) worth of medical expenses before you can begin taking a deduction in this area. That first $3,000 will not be deducted—only the expenses you incur over 7.5 percent of your AGI are allowed as a deduction on your tax return. TurboTax will tell you exactly how much you need to enter in medical expenses to take a deduction. The amount shown by TurboTax (see Figure 7-1) is based on the income you have entered so far. If you expect to enter more income or offsetting expenses at a later time, this number may change.

If you don't come close to passing this test, you don't have to bother filling in the medical expenses section of your tax return. If you think you might have a chance of taking the deduction, go ahead and enter your expenses. TurboTax will figure out if there is any deduction to be had.

Types of Medical Expense You Can Deduct

Deductible medical care expenses include the cost of diagnosis, cure, mitigation, treatment, and prevention of disease as well as treatments affecting parts or functions of the body. Expenses incurred expressly for cosmetic reasons are not allowed as deductions, nor are expenses beneficial to one's general health but not specifically incurred to alleviate or prevent a physical defect or illness.

Caution   *Aspirin and other over-the-counter medicines are not deductible. Your medicine must be obtained with a prescription or not be available over the counter for the IRS to accept the expense as a deduction.*

Figure 7-2 is a checklist of deductible medical expenses that should give you a good idea of the types of expenses that are allowed as deductions. These items are deductible if not reimbursed by insurance.

Medical Expenses

Your adjusted gross income is $60,000.00, so the first $4,500.00 of your medical expenses is not deductible. Did you pay more than $4,500.00 in deductible medical expenses during 2000?

Your medical expenses must total more than 7.5% of your adjusted gross income before you can begin to deduct them. You can deduct expenses not only for yourself, but also for your spouse, your dependents, and in some cases, even non-dependents.

Figure 7-1 • Enter medical expenses if you think your total expenses will exceed the number shown on this screen.

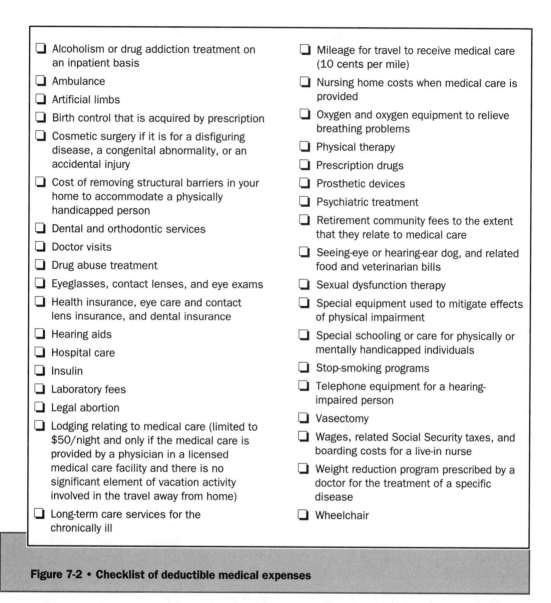

- ❏ Alcoholism or drug addiction treatment on an inpatient basis
- ❏ Ambulance
- ❏ Artificial limbs
- ❏ Birth control that is acquired by prescription
- ❏ Cosmetic surgery if it is for a disfiguring disease, a congenital abnormality, or an accidental injury
- ❏ Cost of removing structural barriers in your home to accommodate a physically handicapped person
- ❏ Dental and orthodontic services
- ❏ Doctor visits
- ❏ Drug abuse treatment
- ❏ Eyeglasses, contact lenses, and eye exams
- ❏ Health insurance, eye care and contact lens insurance, and dental insurance
- ❏ Hearing aids
- ❏ Hospital care
- ❏ Insulin
- ❏ Laboratory fees
- ❏ Legal abortion
- ❏ Lodging relating to medical care (limited to $50/night and only if the medical care is provided by a physician in a licensed medical care facility and there is no significant element of vacation activity involved in the travel away from home)
- ❏ Long-term care services for the chronically ill
- ❏ Mileage for travel to receive medical care (10 cents per mile)
- ❏ Nursing home costs when medical care is provided
- ❏ Oxygen and oxygen equipment to relieve breathing problems
- ❏ Physical therapy
- ❏ Prescription drugs
- ❏ Prosthetic devices
- ❏ Psychiatric treatment
- ❏ Retirement community fees to the extent that they relate to medical care
- ❏ Seeing-eye or hearing-ear dog, and related food and veterinarian bills
- ❏ Sexual dysfunction therapy
- ❏ Special equipment used to mitigate effects of physical impairment
- ❏ Special schooling or care for physically or mentally handicapped individuals
- ❏ Stop-smoking programs
- ❏ Telephone equipment for a hearing-impaired person
- ❏ Vasectomy
- ❏ Wages, related Social Security taxes, and boarding costs for a live-in nurse
- ❏ Weight reduction program prescribed by a doctor for the treatment of a specific disease
- ❏ Wheelchair

Figure 7-2 • Checklist of deductible medical expenses

Enter your medical expenses in TurboTax in the spaces provided. To prepare an itemized list of any type of expense, double-click the area for the expense amount, then enter the details supporting that expense.

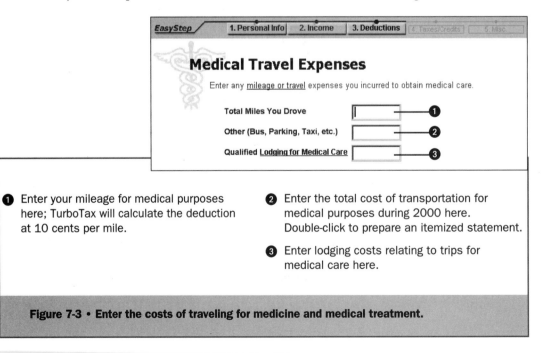

Mileage Expenses for Medical Purposes

You can deduct travel costs for going to the hospital or clinic, trips to the doctor, quick trips to the pharmacy to pick up prescription medicine, and trips to any other facility where a deductible medical procedure is taking place.

If you transport yourself in your own vehicle, keep track of and enter your miles. You can deduct your medical-related mileage—TurboTax will multiply your miles by 10 cents per mile for an additional medical deduction (see Figure 7-3).

❶ Enter your mileage for medical purposes here; TurboTax will calculate the deduction at 10 cents per mile.

❷ Enter the total cost of transportation for medical purposes during 2000 here. Double-click to prepare an itemized statement.

❸ Enter lodging costs relating to trips for medical care here.

Figure 7-3 • Enter the costs of traveling for medicine and medical treatment.

Be sure to keep track of your mileage on paper. Use your calendar or keep a notepad in the glove compartment of your car to document the miles you drive for medical purposes. Include a description of where you went, for what purpose, and the date when you indicate miles driven.

Deductible transportation cost includes airfare, train, bus, taxi, parking, and tolls. Use the TurboTax category for Other (Bus, Parking, Taxi, etc.) to enter all transportation other than your own driving.

Lodging, limited to $50 per night at a medical care facility where a physician is caring for the patient, is allowed as a deduction as well.

Deducting Health Insurance Premiums

Health insurance premiums that you pay yourself are allowed as a medical deduction. Enter the amount you paid during 2000 on the Medical Insurance Premiums screen (see Figure 7-4). Do not include health insurance paid by your employer, health insurance paid by you with after-tax dollars, health insurance paid for anyone other than yourself, your spouse, and your dependents. If you entered self-employed health insurance on Schedule C, TurboTax will automatically carry 40 percent of the amount you entered to your itemized deductions, so don't enter this amount again.

Long-Term Care Insurance

Premium payments for a qualified long-term care policy can be included as deductible medical expenses on Schedule A. Enter the deductible amount of your premium in the area for Qualified Long-Term Care Premiums in TurboTax (see Figure 7-4). The deductible amount of the premium is based on your age, and it increases as you get older. The allowable deductible amounts are shown in Table 7-1 (note that these amounts are 2000 rates and may change next year).

Age of Insured Person	Deductible Amount
Up to 40	$210 per year
41 to 50	$410
51 to 60	$820
61 to 70	$2,200
Over 70	$2,750

Table 7-1 • Limits on Long-Term Care Premiums You May Deduct

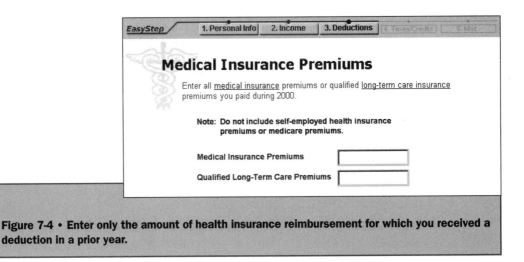

Figure 7-4 • Enter only the amount of health insurance reimbursement for which you received a deduction in a prior year.

To be deductible, the long-term care policy must provide care for the chronically ill. You may also deduct any unreimbursed expenses for qualifying long-term care services as a result of your (or your spouse) being chronically ill. Qualifying long-term care services include diagnostic, preventive, therapeutic, curing, treating, mitigation, and rehabilitative services, and maintenance or personal care services.

A chronically ill person is defined as a person who, for a period of at least 90 days during the preceding 12 months, is unable to perform at least two of the following activities without substantial assistance: eating, toileting, dressing, bathing, continence, or transferring.

Insurance Reimbursements

If you took a medical deduction in a prior year for an amount for which you received an insurance reimbursement in 2000, you must include the insurance reimbursement in your income for 2000. Before you enter a reimbursment for amounts deducted in a prior year, examine the tax return on which you took the deduction and make sure you received the benefit of the deduction. If you were unable to deduct your medical expenses in that year, you do not have to take the reimbursement for those expenses into your income in 2000. If you were only able to deduct a portion of your medical expenses in the prior year, do not take back into income any insurance reimbursement that exceeds the amount of medical expenses you were able to deduct in the year to which the reimbursement applies.

Medical Expenses for Dependents and Others

There are a few special rules that relate specifically to medical expenses you pay on behalf of dependents and others:

- To take a deduction for medical expenses paid for someone else, that person must have been your dependent either when the medical expenses were incurred or when they were paid. For example, your child, who is your dependent, is hospitalized for an injury. The next year, the child gets married and is no longer your dependent. You pay the hospital bill after the child is married. You get to take the medical deduction because the child was your dependent when the hospitalization occurred.

- If you are divorced and your ex-spouse has custody of your dependent child, you are still entitled to claim a deduction for any medical expenses you paid for on behalf of this child.

- If you help an ailing relative with medical expenses, and that relative is not your dependent, not only do you not get to take a deduction for the medical expenses, your relative does not get to take the deduction either, because he didn't pay for the expense himself. You might consider making a gift or a loan of the cash to the relative and letting him pay for his own expenses; that way at least one of you will get the benefit of a tax deduction.

- Health insurance reimbursements for medical expenses reduce the amount of the expense you can deduct. If you pay $500 for a medical procedure, and then receive an insurance reimbursement for $400, you are only entitled to deduct $100 for the procedure.

- If the cost of health insurance is withheld from your income at your job, and that amount is used to reduce the wages reported on your W-2 form, you are not entitled to take a deduction for the insurance premiums you paid. The deduction has already occurred—your income has been reduced by the amount you paid and no tax will be assessed on that amount. Taking an itemized deduction for the medical insurance premiums would amount to a double deduction.

Taxes You Paid

You are allowed to take an itemized deduction for certain taxes you paid during 2000. The types of tax payments you can deduct are payments for state and local income taxes, foreign income taxes, real estate taxes, and personal property taxes. There are plenty of other types of taxes that you pay throughout the year, but they are not allowed as itemized deductions.

State and Local Income Taxes

Unless you live in one of the states that doesn't assess income tax (Washington, Florida, Texas, Connecticut, Nevada, or South Dakota), you probably pay income tax to your state each year, and you may pay local tax to a city or county as well. The amounts that you pay for state and local income tax are deductible on your 2000 income tax return to the extent that they were paid during 2000. Sometimes it can be confusing to figure out in which year to deduct a tax that was paid *for* the year 2000 when it was actually paid in a different year.

The following sections describe the circumstances under which you may have paid income tax during 2000.

State Tax Paid with 1999 Tax Return

If you owed income tax for 1999 that you paid with your state tax return when you filed in the spring of 1999, you can enter the amount that you paid and also identify the state or locality to which you paid the tax. If your locality is not on the drop-down list, or if you paid to more than one locality, choose the XXX option. If you paid taxes to more than one state, choose the XX option.

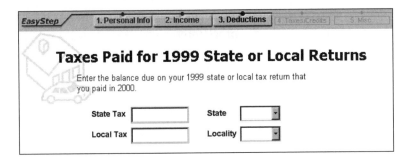

Caution Several states solicit taxpayers for contributions right on the tax form. If you write a check for taxes and the amount includes a contribution to a charity, be sure to include that contribution with your other charitable contribution payments— but don't mistake the amount for a tax payment! This amount is not a deduction for state income taxes.

1999 Refund Applied to 2000 Taxes

Sometimes it's easier to leave your money with the government than it is to get a refund, only to turn around and pay the money right back again. If you had a refund owing to you on your 1999 state or local tax return, and you chose to let the government keep the money and apply it to your 2000 tax return, the amount is an itemized deduction for 2000.

EasyStep	1. Personal Info	2. Income	3. Deductions	4. Taxes/Credits	5. Misc

State and Local Refunds Applied to 2000 Taxes

Enter the amount of any 1999 state or local tax refunds (or "overpayments") you asked to be applied to your 2000 tax returns.

State Refund Applied [   ]   State [▾]

Local Refund Applied [   ]   Locality [▾]

The logic is that even though you never had your hands on the money, you could have received it if you had wanted to, which is the same as having the money as far as the IRS is concerned. The money was in your control. Had you received the refund in April 2000 and then written a check for the same amount to pay taxes to the state, it would be clear than you made a payment during 2000. Leaving the money with the state has the same effect.

State and Local Estimates Paid for 2000

Enter all the estimated payments you made for your state, and then your local income taxes for the year 2000. It is *very important* that the date that appears next to each payment is correct. Not only are these dates used in the computation of any potential penalty for not paying taxes on time to your state or local government, these dates will advise TurboTax of in which year you are entitled to take a federal itemized deduction for the estimated tax payments.

SAVE MONEY   Here's a tax planning tool you can use. Typically, the fourth quarter payment for state taxes is due in January of the year after the year for which the tax is due, so the fourth quarter 2000 payment will be due in January 2001 (if that is not the case in your state, this tip may not apply to you). If you are looking for ways to lower your 2000 income, one method to follow is to make your fourth quarter payment early, in December 2000, and thus take a deduction on your 2000 tax return for that fourth quarter payment.

GET SMARTER Here's another time the early payment of your fourth quarter state income taxes may come in handy: If you plan on itemizing in 2000, but don't expect to have enough deductions to itemize in 2001 (for example, you sold your house and moved into an apartment in 2000), try to get as many deductions as possible into the 2000 return while you can still itemize. You have every right to control the timing of payments made near the end of the year, choosing in which year to pay them. But don't go overboard. If you pay all of your monthly health insurance for 2001 in 2000 to take a medical deduction in 2000, the IRS will frown on the activity, claiming you were trying to manipulate your income and deductions to reduce your taxes. Of course that is your goal, but you aren't supposed to be so obvious about it. The IRS has the right to disallow any deductions that it thinks are unreasonable.

If you paid more than four quarterly payments for 2000, for example if you send in your payments every month instead of every quarter, you can click the Enter More Payments option (see Figure 7-5) to open a screen where you can enter additional estimated payments.

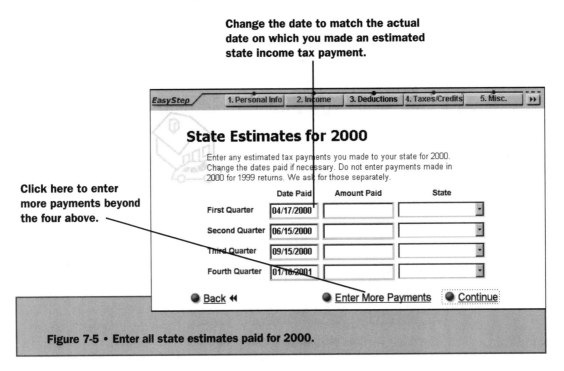

Figure 7-5 • Enter all state estimates paid for 2000.

State and Local Estimates Paid for 1999

Often the fourth quarterly payment for a state or local government isn't due until January of the year following the tax year. For example, your fourth quarter 2000 payment may not have been due until January 2001. Then again, some people like to pay that fourth quarter payment in December, to take advantage of a deduction in the current year.

The payment is deductible when you actually make the payment, not when it is due. If you made a payment for your fourth quarter 1999 tax return in January 2000 (or at any time in 2000), enter the amount of the payment on the screen shown below. If you made your fourth quarter 1999 payment in 1999, the amount qualified for a deduction on your 1999 tax return, but not your 2000 tax return.

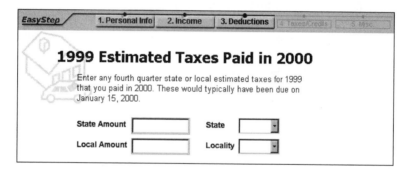

State and Local Extensions

If you were unable to file your 1999 state or local income tax return on time, and filed for an extension of time in which to file the return, and if you made a tax payment with that extension, the amount of tax you paid with the extension is deductible in 2000.

Any amounts paid in 2001 for an extension of time to file your 2000 state or local income tax return are allowed as itemized deductions on your 2001 federal income tax return. If you use TurboTax to prepare your income tax return next year, and you transfer information from your 2000 return to your 2001 return, this extension information will transfer as well, and the extension amount you pay in 2000 for your 2001 state tax return will be treated as a deduction on your 2001 federal income tax return.

GET SMARTER   You are not allowed to take a deduction for state and local income taxes to the extent that the tax is on income that is exempt from federal tax, unless that exempt income is interest income—for example, if you are in the military and you receive a cost-of-living allowance that is exempt from federal income tax but taxed in the state. You must reduce your deduction for state income tax by the amount of tax that applies to the cost-of-living allowance. Calculate this amount by filling in your state tax return excluding the cost-of-living allowance and determine the tax, then add the cost-of-living allowance and determine the tax again. The difference between the two tax amounts is the amount by which you must reduce your deduction for state income tax on your federal tax return.

Other State and Local Taxes

If there are any other situations in which you made payments of state or local income taxes during 2000, you will have an opportunity to enter this information after all the other state income tax information has been entered.

EasyStep	**1. Personal Info**	**2. Income**	**3. Deductions**	4. Taxes/Credits	5. Misc

Other State or Local Taxes Paid in 2000

If you paid any overdue state or local income taxes in 2000, enter the totals below. For example, you may have filed an earlier year's return late, filed an amended return, made payments under an installment agreement, or received a letter requiring payment from a state or local income tax agency.

Enter the tax portion only. Do not enter any interest or penalties included in your payment.

Total State Amounts Paid [   ]   State [▾]

Total Local Amounts Paid [   ]   Locality [▾]

Examples of other state and local income taxes you might have paid include:

- Tax paid for a prior year as a result of a notice of assessment from the state department of revenue

- Tax paid for a prior year as a result of a tax return from the prior year being filed late

- Tax paid as a result of amending a state tax return

- Tax payments from a prior year that were paid during the current year as part of an installment agreement

Taxes on Property

You can take a deduction for the property taxes you pay. Taxes on real property are taxes you pay on your home and the land on which it sits, as well as taxes on other real property you own, such as a vacation home or a condominium. Taxes on personal property include automobile excise tax and any other personal property taxes that you may have to pay.

Real Estate Taxes

Real estate taxes include property tax paid on your personal residence, vacant lots you may own, and a vacation home. If you have a mortgage with a financial institution, the mortgage holder will often pay your real estate taxes for you with money from your mortgage payment that is set aside for this purpose. The amount of tax paid by the mortgage company will appear on your year-end statement for your mortgage. If you changed mortgage companies during the year you may have to combine amounts from two mortgage statements to get the total amount of real estate tax that was paid during 2000.

TurboTax would like you to break out the real estate taxes you paid into the amount relating to your principal residence, and all other amounts. You can double-click the area for Other Real Estate if you want to prepare an itemized statement describing the source of your other real estate taxes.

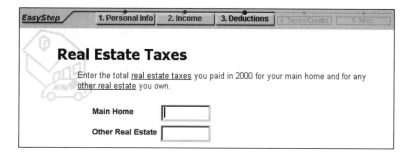

Taxes on a Home You Bought or Sold   If you bought or sold a house during the year, check your closing statement(s). There's an excellent chance that you paid real estate taxes at the closing. If you paid real estate taxes at closing that you owe for the current year, you may take the tax as a deduction on your 2000 tax return. Verify with your mortgage company that this amount has not already been included in your year-end statement summarizing your mortgage costs. If the seller pays taxes that you owe and you reimburse the seller for the taxes, you may deduct that amount as well. Add these amounts to the deduction for real estate taxes on your primary home.

If you pay real estate taxes at closing that are owed from a previous year, your payment is added to the basis of the house but is not a current tax deduction. If the seller pays some of your real estate taxes at closing and you do not reimburse the seller, you must reduce your basis in the house by the amount of taxes paid by the seller.

Taxes on Part of a Cooperative Housing Unit   If you own a condominium or are part of a cooperative housing unit where each member pays a portion of the taxes, your share of real estate taxes for the association is allowed as a deduction on your tax return. The association should provide you with a year-end statement showing how much of your payments for the year represent real estate taxes. These taxes are considered taxes on your primary home for purposes of entering them in TurboTax.

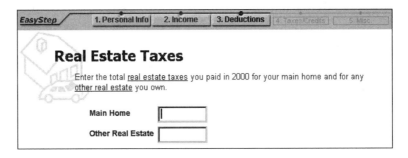

Taxes on a Second Home   The deduction for real estate taxes is not limited to your primary home. All real estate taxes that you pay on all land and homes that you own may be deducted. Enter real estate taxes on all but your primary home as Other Real Estate.

Interest on Local Assessments   If you are assessed for street repairs, sidewalks, streetlights, sewers, or a similar city or neighborhood improvement, and you decide to pay for the assessment over time instead of all in a lump sum, the interest that is included with your time payments is allowed as a deduction—as real estate tax! Include the amount of interest with your other real estate taxes on your primary home.

Personal Property Taxes

The most common form of personal property tax is tax paid on your automobile or other vehicle. Not everyone pays this type of tax—the assessment of this tax is determined on a state-by-state basis.

If your state assesses a personal property tax on vehicles, you will most likely pay the tax when you register the vehicle. The fee will be combined with your license plate renewal fee and should be easily identifiable on the receipt you receive for your registration. Note that the portion of your license fee that represents property tax is the only part of the fee that is based on the value of your car and is thus deductible as property tax. The rest of the registration fee is not allowed as an itemized deduction.

If you own a boat or airplane and pay property taxes on these items, the amount of tax you pay can be included with your other personal property tax deduction.

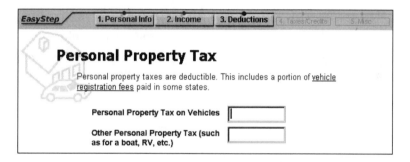

Interest You Paid

There was a time when any type of interest you paid, including interest on revolving credit cards and interest paid on car loans, entitled you to a tax deduction. Now the allowable deductions for interest include only a few types of interest: home mortgage interest, interest on student loans (this is an adjustment, not an itemized deduction, and is covered in Chapter 6), interest on investment property, and interest on business property.

To take a deduction for interest, the following requirements must be met:

- You have to have paid the interest
- You should have a statement supporting your claim for the deduction
- The interest must be assessed on debt that belongs to you
- The interest has to be of a type the IRS will allow you to deduct

Home Mortgage Interest

The most common form of interest that you can deduct is the home mortgage interest expense. Mortgage interest is only deductible on your primary home and a second home (such as a vacation home, or a condominium in another city where you go to work). If you own more than two homes, the interest on money borrowed to finance the additional homes is not allowed as a deduction.

The mortgage interest deduction is subject to some limitation. Although this is not an issue for most taxpayers, the interest deduction will be limited if, at any time during 2000, the total amount of your mortgages exceeds $1,000,000 or the total amount of your interest exceeds $100,000.

Information You Need to Provide

When deducting interest paid on a mortgage, you should list the name of the lender and indicate whether or not you received a 1098 form. The 1098 form is a year-end statement that financial institutions send to mortgage holders summarizing the interest and other expenses paid by the borrower during the year.

The 1098 form may include amounts for the following types of payments you made during the year:

- **Mortgage interest** is allowed as an itemized deduction if the home is your primary residence or your second home.

- **Points** are allowed as an itemized deduction if the home is your primary residence, or you may opt to amortize (spread evenly) the points over the life of the loan. Points must be amortized over the life of the loan if the home is a secondary residence.
- **Real estate taxes** are deductible as itemized deductions.
- **Homeowner's insurance** is not deductible unless the home is used in part as business or rental property.
- **Private mortgage insurance** is not deductible.

Tip   *If you paid a finance charge to the lending institution during the year for late mortgage payments, you are entitled to deduct the finance charge as additional mortgage interest.*

Mortgage Interest Paid to a Person

If you are paying a person for your mortgage instead of a lending institution, you will be required to enter the name of the person, the Social Security number, and the address of the person. The IRS requires this information so that it can cross-reference with the other person's tax form where the interest income will be reported.

Mortgage Interest Paid at Closing

If you purchased or sold your home during 2000, you will receive a closing statement at the time of the sale, and there may be some mortgage interest reflected on that statement. Some of the interest may have been paid by the buyer and some by the seller. Find the mortgage interest that applies to you. You may deduct this amount along with the other mortgage interest you deduct on your home, but see accompanying caution.

Caution *The bank or other financial institution that holds your mortgage may have included the interest amount from your closing statement on your year-end 1098 statement. You can make a call to the issuer of the statement to find out if the interest paid at closing is included on your year-end statement so you don't take the deduction for the same amount twice.*

Points

Points are extra fees paid for the privilege of borrowing money. A single point, which may be referred to as a loan origination fee or loan discount, is generally equal to 1 percent of the loan amount. If you initiated a mortgage in 2000, you may have paid one or more points. Points may be deducted on your tax return if they meet the following requirements:

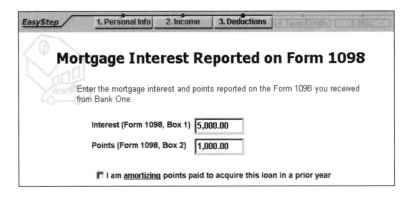

- The points must be designated as points (or loan origination fee or loan discount) on the closing statement.
- The points must be calculated as a percentage of the loan amount.
- The points must be paid in connection with the acquisition of the taxpayer's principal residence and the residence must be designated as collateral for the mortgage.
- The points must be paid by the taxpayer and may not be paid with money from the proceeds of the loan (but see the accompanying caution about points paid by the seller).

- The points must conform to an established business practice in the community and the amount of points must be consistent with the amount generally charged in that area.

Caution   *If the seller of a house agrees to pay the points for the buyer as part of the conditions of the house sale, the points are treated as points paid by the buyer only if the buyer subtracts the points from the purchase price of the home when computing the adjusted basis.*

Points Paid on Refinancing

If you refinance your home mortgage or take out an equity loan on your house, and you pay points on this financing, the points are not deductible in the year of the financing, as they would be if paid in association with a first mortgage (but see accompanying tip). Instead, the points are to be amortized over the life of the loan.

Tip   *Points paid on money from a home equity loan or second mortgage that is used for the purpose of improving the home are treated like points paid on a first mortgage and is fully deductible in the year paid. If only a portion of the loan proceeds is used for home improvements, you must prorate the points based on the portion of the loan used for home improvements, deduct that portion of the points, and amortize the balance.*

For example, if the loan is a 15-year loan and you pay $1,500 in points in association with the loan, you will be entitled to deduct $100 per year for the 15 years of the loan.

To record these amortized points in TurboTax, check the box indicating that you are amortizing points (Figure 7-6). Then on the next screen, indicate the total points paid, the date of the loan, and the number of years over which the loan is financed. TurboTax will calculate the correct amount of points for you to deduct this year.

Should you pay off the loan in a shorter period of time than the original loan period, you may deduct the remainder of the undeducted points in the year you pay off the loan.

Points Paid on Second Home

Points paid on a second home are never deductible in the year of the loan. Instead, they must be amortized evenly over the duration of the loan. If the loan is paid off in a shorter period of time than the original loan period, you may deduct the remainder of the undeducted points in the year you pay off the loan.

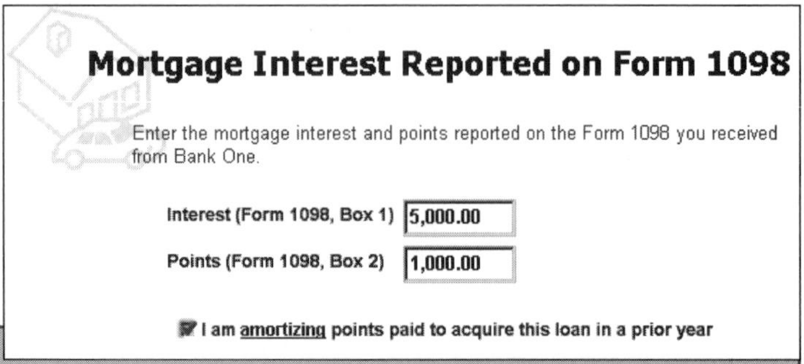

Mortgage Interest Reported on Form 1098

Enter the mortgage interest and points reported on the Form 1098 you received from Bank One.

Interest (Form 1098, Box 1) [5,000.00]

Points (Form 1098, Box 2) [1,000.00]

☑ I am <u>amortizing</u> points paid to acquire this loan in a prior year

Figure 7-6 • Check the box if you are amortizing points this year or deducting this year's portion of points that were amortized in a previous year.

Charitable Contributions

The IRS allows a deduction for charitable giving. You are entitled to deduct as much as 50 percent of your adjusted gross income as gifts made to authorized charities.

What Is an Authorized Charity?

To qualify as a charitable deduction on your tax return, your contribution must be to a charity authorized by the federal government. If you have any doubts about the tax exempt status of the organization to which you are donating, just ask the IRS and they will let you know whether or not the organization qualifies as tax exempt. You can go to http://www.irs.ustreas.gov/prod/search/eosearch.html (see Figure 7-7) on the Internet to search through the IRS's vast list of qualified exempt organizations.

Tax exempt status is granted by the IRS to private and public charities that are nonprofit organizations and perform certain types of service deemed appropriate by the federal government. Qualified charitable organizations include churches, schools, medical facilities, government units, museums, service organizations such as the Red Cross, the Salvation Army, Boy and Girl Scouts, humane activities, file preservation groups, public television, and symphony orchestras.

Charitable contributions to any qualified organization count as deductible contributions. Donations paid directly to needy individuals do not qualify.

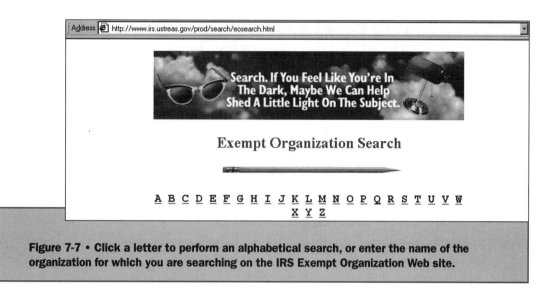

Figure 7-7 • Click a letter to perform an alphabetical search, or enter the name of the organization for which you are searching on the IRS Exempt Organization Web site.

Cash Contributions

Contributions of cash, including checks, paid to qualified organizations should be listed on the screen provided in TurboTax (see Figure 7-8). You can itemize all of your contributions, or you can group them together under one listing, such as "Miscellaneous Organized Charities." If you list all the organizations, the list will transfer forward and be available to you when you prepare next year's tax return, so this could be a timesaver if you contribute to the same organizations year after year.

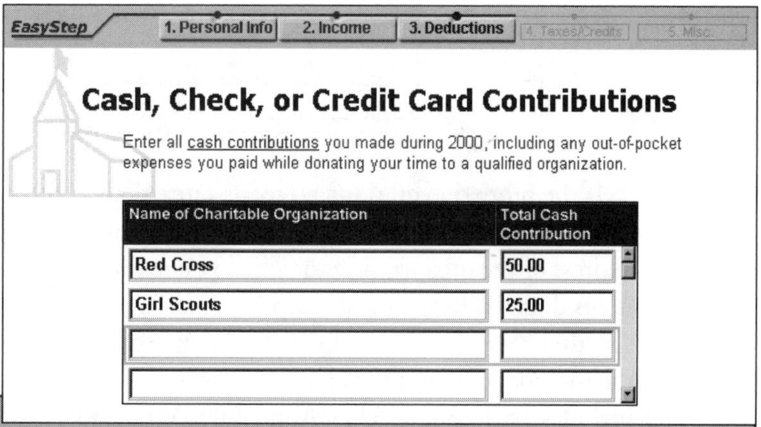

Figure 7-8 • Enter all of your cash contributions here.

Included in cash contributions should be out-of-pocket expenses that you incurred on behalf of charitable organizations, such as parking and tolls, postage, and supplies.

Get a Receipt

You are required to obtain a receipt for all donations valued at $250 and higher. Receipts should include the date of the contribution and the name and address of the charity. The receipt should also include a statement to the effect that you did not receive anything in exchange for the property you donated.

Non-Cash Contributions

If you donated clothing, household goods, books, stock, automobiles, or other items that you own to a charitable organization, you can take a deduction for the fair market value of the property. The fair market value is the amount that a buyer would be willing to pay for the item. When entering donated property, provide the name of the organization and the value you have placed on the property. For information on how to value donated property, see Appendix B.

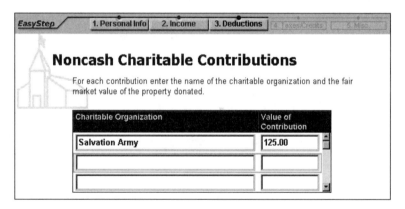

If the property you donated totals more than $500, TurboTax will ask you to supply additional information, as shown in Figure 7-9. You will need to supply the address of the organization to which you made the donation, a description of the items donated (a general description such as clothing, household goods, books, sporting equipment is acceptable), the date on which you made the donation, and the method you used to value the property (choose from a drop-down list that includes Thrift Shop Value, Appraisal, Comparable Sales, and more).

Use these lines to provide a
general description of the property.

Additional Noncash Contribution Information

Charity's Name — Goodwill

Charity's Address — 123 West Street, Indianapolis, IN

Unique Description of Property You Donated — 1994 Dodge Omni

Description, Continued —

Date Donated — 07/15/2000

How did you determine the value? — Catalog

Thrift shop value
Comparable sales
Catalog
Dealers' price
Appraisal
Average stock price
Present value
Arm's length offer
Other

Choose from this list of methods used for valuing the donated property.

● Back ◀◀   ● Continue

Figure 7-9 • Use this screen to enter information about donated property if the value of the property exceeds $500.

You are also expected to enter information about the original cost of the donated property (Figure 7-10). You can estimate this amount if you don't have exact information. Enter the date on which you acquired the property—you can enter a ballpark date if you don't remember the exact date, and you can enter "various" if you acquired the property at different times. You are expected to enter the method by which you acquired the property (purchase, gift, and so on).

When you make donations of items, make sure you keep a list of the items you donate. You don't have to specifically itemize each item (red shirt size 4, book: Gone With the Wind), but you should prepare a list with general information (12 shirts, 8 hardbound books). In addition to your list, you need to obtain a signed receipt from the organization to which you donate indicating the date of the donation, address of the organization, and a general description of donated items (for example, 3 bags of clothing, 1 television). The list and the receipt stay with your tax records—they do not get attached to the tax return.

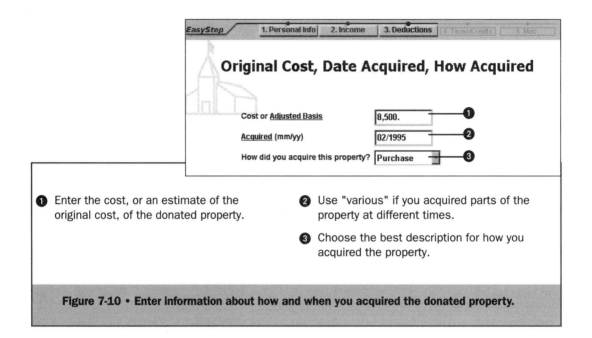

Figure 7-10 • Enter information about how and when you acquired the donated property.

Donating Property That Has Appreciated in Value

You can take a deduction for the fair market value of donated property that has appreciated in value. An item for which you paid a small amount may generate a giant deduction for you. Donating appreciated property is a tool that can be used to avoid the tax on capital gains and generate a deduction at the same time. Instead of selling the property and paying tax on the gain, then donating the cash to an organization, simply donate the property and you'll save on taxes all around.

To take a donation for the appreciated (increased) value of property, you have to have owned the property for at least one year and it has to be property that would generate a taxable gain for you if you sold it. Donated property that does not meet these requirements should be valued at fair market value less the amount that would be ordinary income. Typically this means that your deduction is limited to your adjusted basis in the property. For example, if you donate stock that you purchased for $500 and it is now worth $520, the fair market value ($520) less the income ($20) leaves $500 for your deduction.

Donating Property Valued at More Than $5,000

Donations of property that exceed $5,000 in value must be accompanied by a signed appraisal and this appraisal must be attached to your tax return. The IRS has a special

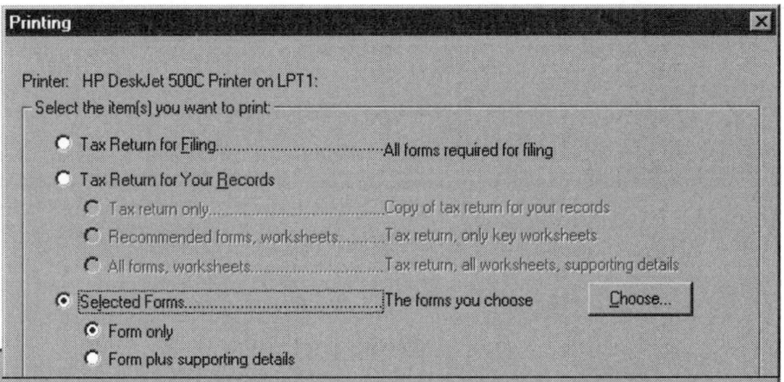

Figure 7-11 • **Click the Choose button to view a list of all tax forms in your tax return.**

form for this purpose (Form 8283). You can print out a copy of this form from your TurboTax program, then take the form to the appraiser for a signature. After entering the information about the contribution, choose File | Print from the TurboTax menu, then click Selected Forms and click the Choose button that appears to the right of this option (see Figure 7-11). In the list that appears, click Form 8283, and then click the OK button and finally the Print button.

Note that when you print your final tax return, this form will print out again. You can discard the unsigned page that prints with the final tax return and replace it with the copy that has been signed by the appraiser.

Limit of Deduction for Contributions

Most deductions for contributions that you make are subject to a 50 percent limit, meaning that you can deduct all of your contributions to the extent that they don't exceed 50 percent of your adjusted gross income. There are, however, certain contributions that are limited to 30 percent and 20 percent of your adjusted gross income. If TurboTax attempts to limit your contribution deduction, here are the reasons why this can occur:

30 Percent Limit   Contributions that are limited to 30 percent of your adjusted gross income include:

- Gifts of capital gain property. This property would be subject to the lower, capital gain tax rates if you were to sell the property. (You can circumvent the 30 percent limit if you reduce your deduction by the amount that would have been long-term gain had you sold the property.)

- Gifts for the use of any organization. For example, if you donate an automobile to an organization for their use, rather than for them to sell or give to a needy family, the contribution deduction is limited to 30 percent of your adjusted gross income.
- Gifts to veterans' organizations, fraternal societies, nonprofit cemeteries, and certain private non-operating foundations.

20 Percent Limit Contributions that are limited to 20 percent of your adjusted gross income include:

- Gifts of capital gain property to veterans' organizations, fraternal societies, nonprofit cemeteries, and certain private non-operating foundations.

Unused Contributions Deduction

If you are unable to deduct all of your charitable contributions, due to the limitations specified in the previous section, you are entitled to carry forward the excess contributions for five years. TurboTax will keep track of this information for you, bringing forward the unused amounts each year until the amounts are either used up or they expire.

Donations of Travel

If you travel on behalf of a charitable organization and perform services for that organization, the money you spend traveling translates into a tax deduction. The IRS warns that the travel is deductible only if there is no significant element of personal pleasure in your activity—this doesn't mean, however, that you have to be miserable to turn the trip into a tax deduction. The premise behind the IRS statement is that to deduct your travel costs, the trip should not be mistaken for a vacation. Your time should be spent performing duties for the charitable organization.

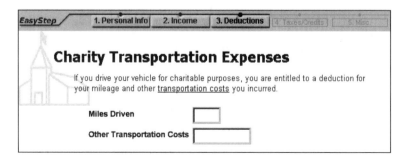

Enter all of your travel and related expenses (including meals) on the Other Transportation Costs line in TurboTax. Deductible transportation expenses include:

- Air, train, bus, and taxi transportation
- Out-of-pocket expenses for your vehicle
- Overnight lodging
- Meals (there is no 50 percent limit on meals as there is for business-related meal expenses)

You are also entitled to deduct mileage driven for charitable purposes. Enter the number of miles you drove for charity and TurboTax will calculate your deduction at 14 cents per mile.

Donations of Time

Your time has value—just ask your employer. But when it comes to donating your time to charity, the IRS doesn't provide an option for you to deduct the value of your time. Donations of your time are made strictly out of the goodness of your heart and your benefit is your sense of satisfaction for time well spent.

Nondeductible Contributions

Certain contributions are not allowed as deductions on your income tax return. You can't take a deduction for contributions to individuals, no matter how needy they may be. Donations to needy people must be made through an organization that supports these people if you want to take a tax deduction for your contribution. If you donate to an organization and specify your donation is to go to a particular person or family, you will not get a tax deduction. This is not to say you can't adopt a needy family and make donations—you simply won't get a tax deduction for doing so.

You also cannot take a deduction for contributions to organizations that are not qualified to accept tax-deductible contributions. These organizations include:

- Political organizations, including communist organizations, and candidates for public office
- Business leagues, including Chambers of Commerce
- Civic leagues
- Country clubs and social clubs

- Foreign organizations
- Homeowners' associations
- Labor unions (however, dues to these organizations may be used as a miscellaneous itemized deduction)

In addition, you cannot take a deduction for a contribution to the extent that you benefit from the contribution. If you attend a charity event where the cost of your ticket includes dinner and entertainment, you must separate the value of the dinner and entertainment from the contribution portion of the ticket. The organization sponsoring the event will usually do this for you. If it is impossible to separate the contribution from the rest of the ticket, you are not entitled to take a deduction.

You are not entitled to take a charitable contribution deduction for the cost of raffle tickets purchased from a charitable organization; however, you can include the cost of such tickets as gambling expenses, which may be deducted as an itemized deduction if you have reported offsetting gambling winnings as income (see Chapter 5 for more information on reporting gambling winnings as income).

Casualty and Theft Losses

If you lose something due to theft or if you suffer damage due to some unforeseen event, you may be able to qualify for a deduction on your federal income tax return. A casualty is defined by the IRS as one of the following:

- **A sudden event** that is swift, not gradual or progressive
- **An unexpected event** that is ordinarily unanticipated and unintended
- **An unusual event** that is not a day-to-day occurrence and that's not typical of the activity in which you were engaged

Disasters such as earthquakes, storms, tornadoes, fires, cyclones, plane crashes in your backyard, volcanic eruptions, ice storms, and hail are the stuff of deductible casualties. A casualty can also include a government-ordered condemnation and demolition of property. Disasters that take time to occur, such as termite infestations and erosion, don't count as casualties as far as the IRS is concerned.

A theft is the unlawful taking and removing of your belongings with the intent to deprive you of those items. If a friend comes to visit and accidentally puts on your coat instead of his own when he leaves, that doesn't count as theft. But if the same "friend" slips your CD player under his arm on the way out the door, you've got yourself a deductible theft.

How Much Did You Lose?

The amount of your casualty or theft loss is the lesser of your adjusted basis in the property (usually your cost plus the cost of improvements to the property) or the difference between the fair market value of the property (the amount you would expect to pay to purchase the property you lost) before and after the casualty.

For example, if someone steals your computer for which you paid $4,000, but in today's market the machine is only worth $500, your loss is considered to be $500, not $4,000. Four thousand dollars is your adjusted basis in the property, but the property was only worth $500 before it was lost, and now, since it is gone, it is worth $0. The difference between $500 and $0 is $500, and $500 is less than $4,000, so $500 is the amount of your loss.

Proving the Loss Occurred

To qualify for the casualty and theft loss deduction on your tax return, you have to convince the IRS that you've suffered a loss. Proving that you've incurred a casualty means proving three things:

- Identifying the type of casualty and when it occurred
- Showing that your loss was a result of the casualty
- Showing that you owned the property that was damaged

Gather all the evidence you can—it's always better to have too much rather than not enough evidence. Prove the casualty occurred with newspaper reports, photographs, and insurance reports. Before and after pictures are excellent evidence of property damage.

To prove that you owned the item, find evidence of your original purchase, such as a bill of sale for the car that got smashed under a falling tree, or a receipt for the CD player that was stolen.

If you suffered a theft, you probably have a police report and should keep a copy of that report with your tax records. The report also provides exact evidence of the date the theft was discovered, which will help tie the casualty to the current tax year. When you enter the casualty information in TurboTax, you will also be asked to identify the date on which the casualty occurred.

EasyStep	1. Personal Info	2. Income	3. Deductions	4. Taxes/Credits	5. Misc

Casualty or Theft Event

This is the casualty or theft you described as "Theft."

Description | Theft
Date | 07/15/2000

How Much Can You Deduct?

The IRS sets strict rules as to how much can be deducted in this area. Each separate casualty and theft deduction gets reduced by $100. In addition to the $100 reduction, each deduction is further reduced by 10 percent of your adjusted gross income, so only the portion of your loss that exceeds $100 plus 10 percent of your adjusted gross income is allowed as a deduction.

Beyond the limitations on your tax return, you must reduce your casualty loss by any insurance reimbursement that you receive. If you had a tree fall on your house and suffered damage of $3,500, and the insurance company paid $3,000, reflecting a $500 deductible on your policy, that would leave you with a $500 loss. Take $100 off the $500 loss and you're left with $400. If your adjusted gross income is $35,000, you will reduce the $400 loss by $350 (10 percent of adjusted gross income), and your deductible loss (if you are eligible to itemized deductions) is $50.

You only have to enter information about the date, type, and amount of the loss. TurboTax will take care of the computations and will enter any allowable deduction on your tax return.

Insurance Coverage for a Loss

Insurance coverage for your loss tends to negate the need for a tax deduction. Tax deductions are for actual losses for which you don't receive any reimbursement or for which the reimbursement is partial. If your insurance doesn't cover the loss, or if it only covers part of the loss, you can claim a deduction on your tax return for the unreimbursed portion of the loss.

If you anticipate an insurance reimbursement but haven't received the insurance money by the time you file your tax return, you shouldn't take a deduction for the part of the loss that will be covered by the reimbursement.

If you're not sure if part of your casualty or theft loss will be reimbursed by insurance, it is recommended that you don't take a deduction for the loss until you find out that you're definitely not receiving a reimbursement. If you took a deduction for a loss and were reimbursed by insurance in a later year, you will have to include the reimbursement in your income in the year in which you receive it.

Including an Insurance Reimbursement as Income

If you took a deduction for a casualty or theft loss in a prior year and received a reimbursement from your insurance company in 2000, you need to record a portion of that reimbursement as income on your 2000 tax return. If you missed the screen where you were asked to record reimbursements for expenses deducted in prior years, you can get there from the EasyStep Navigator by selecting the Other Income option.

One of the Other Income questions relates to Items From A Prior Year. Choose Yes to the first question to indicate you received a reimbursement for something you deducted in a prior year. On the next screen you see, check the box to indicate you received a reimbursement for a casualty or theft loss.

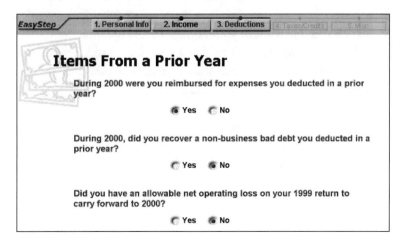

You will be asked to enter the amount of reimbursement you received in 2000. Remember, you only have to enter this information if you actually took a deduction for the loss in a prior year. If you attempted to take a deduction, but the limitations (as described in the previous section, "How Much Can You Deduct?") prevented you from actually getting any tax benefit from the deduction, you have nothing to add back in your income this year.

Taxable Gain from Insurance Reimbursement

There might be an occasion when you receive an insurance reimbursement for your casualty and the reimbursement is for more than your basis in the item that was lost or damaged. For example, if you purchased a diamond ring for $800 and that ring today is worth $3,000, and your insurance company paid you $3,000 when the ring was stolen, not only do you get no tax deduction for any part of the loss, but you have a gain to report.

An exception to the rule stating that you must report this gain is that, if you replace the property with a similar item within two years, and the new item costs at least as much as the insurance payment you received, you will postpone paying tax on the gain. The new item you purchase takes on the basis of the old, and at some point in the future if you choose to sell the replacement item, you will pay tax at that time.

Tax on an item of this nature will be applied at the lower, capital gain tax rates.

Other Deductions

A number of expenditures fall into the category of miscellaneous itemized deductions. Most of these deductions are subject to a limitation based on your adjusted gross income such that the only amounts you are able to deduct are those that exceed 2 percent of your adjusted gross income.

Miscellaneous deductions that are subject to this 2 percent limitation include job expenses, education costs, tax preparation fees, certain legal and accounting fees, certain investment fees, and safe deposit box rental. Not subject to the 2 percent limitation are losses from gambling, to the extent that they are offset by income from gambling reported on page 1 of your tax return, federal estate tax on income from an estate that you include as income on your tax return, and impairment-related work expenses.

Job-Related Expenses

The category of employee business expenses takes into account automobile and travel expenses, entertainment, business gifts, professional dues, subscriptions, continuing education, union dues, uniforms, and other expenditures that constitute money you spent on behalf of your job and for which you weren't reimbursed.

EasyStep	1. Personal Info	2. Income	3. Deductions	4. Taxes/Credits	5. Misc.

Job-Related Expenses

Enter any non-reimbursed job-related expenses you paid during 2000. Union dues are sometimes reported to you on a W-2 in box 14.

Union or Professional Dues	
Professional Subscriptions	
Uniforms or Protective Clothing and Their Upkeep	
Job Search Expenses	

If you were reimbursed for your employee business expenses and your reimbursement equals your expenses, you don't have to report any of your expenses or your reimbursement on your income tax return.

If you used your personal vehicle for your job (commuting from home doesn't count, but making sales calls or running errands for your employer does), you can take a deduction for vehicle expenses either by deducting your actual expenses including gas, oil, repairs, and so on, prorated for the business portion of your automobile usage, or you can deduct a flat rate (computed at 32.5 cents per mile for the actual miles you drove).

Other job-related expenses include:

- Parking and tolls (however, daily parking at your regular place of work does not count)
- Overnight travel expenses
- Business gifts, limited to $25 per person per year
- Uniforms that look like uniforms and not street clothes
- Union dues
- Dues to professional organizations
- Subscriptions to business publications
- Cost of small tools used in your work

- Professional license costs
- Continuing education costs for maintaining a professional license
- Job-related insurance, such as malpractice insurance

Job-Hunting Costs

The cost of looking for a job is a deductible expense in the miscellaneous deductions section of your itemized deductions, even if you don't get a new job. The job search must be for a job in the same profession in which you are currently working. Job search expenses relating to a first job are not deductible. Job search expenses are entered as a lump sum in TurboTax, as shown in Figure 7-12.

The types of expense you can deduct relating to your job search are costs that specifically and exclusively relate to searching for a new job, which include:

- Employment agency fees
- The cost of preparing and printing a résumé
- Mileage and other travel expenses to go to interviews
- Parking
- Postage
- Purchase of publications that list job offerings in your profession
- Long-distance telephone calls

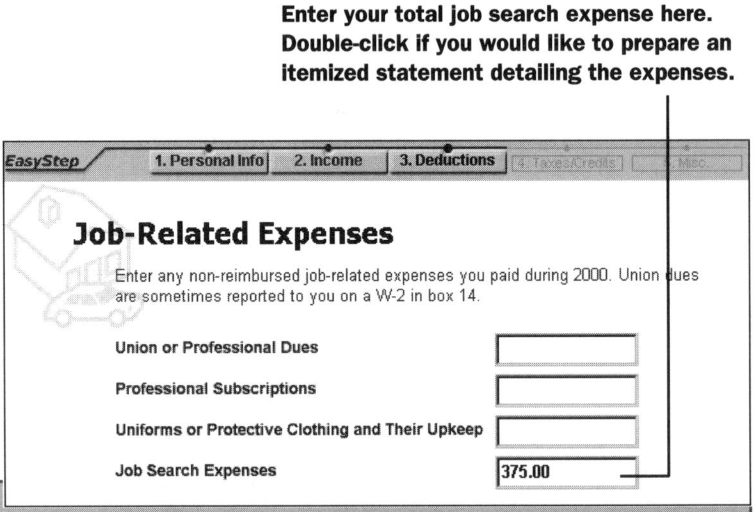

Figure 7-12 • Enter the cost of looking for a new job.

Education Costs

If you pay for the cost of going back to school for additional education after you're employed, that cost can be a miscellaneous itemized deduction. There are certain strict requirements that you must meet to qualify for an education expense deduction.

To take a deduction for educational expense, the education must be required by your employer in order for you to keep your job, or the education must help maintain or improve your skills at your current job level. For example, if your employer wants you to take a computer class to keep current on the latest version of the program you use in your job, the cost of the course is a deductible expense.

Education that trains you for a new job doesn't qualify for the miscellaneous expense deduction. A person who is a salesperson by day and enrolled in law school at night is studying for a new profession. The cost of the law school classes is not deductible.

Also, education that meets the minimum requirements of your job isn't deductible education. For example, if you're a law school graduate and are hired by a law firm to work as a lawyer, it is expected that you will pass the bar exam. The cost of a bar review course is not deductible—passing the bar exam is a minimum requirement of being a lawyer.

If you meet the requirements to deduct education expense, enter your expenses in the space provided in the EasyStep Interview (see Figure 7-13). The types of education expense you can deduct include the following:

- Tuition
- Books
- Supplies
- Laboratory fees
- Travel costs to get to and from the education site

 SAVE MONEY   Keep in mind the new education tax credits that are available. The Hope Scholarship credit and the lifetime learning credit (covered in Chapter 8) are alternatives to deducting education expense and may provide you with a bigger tax benefit.

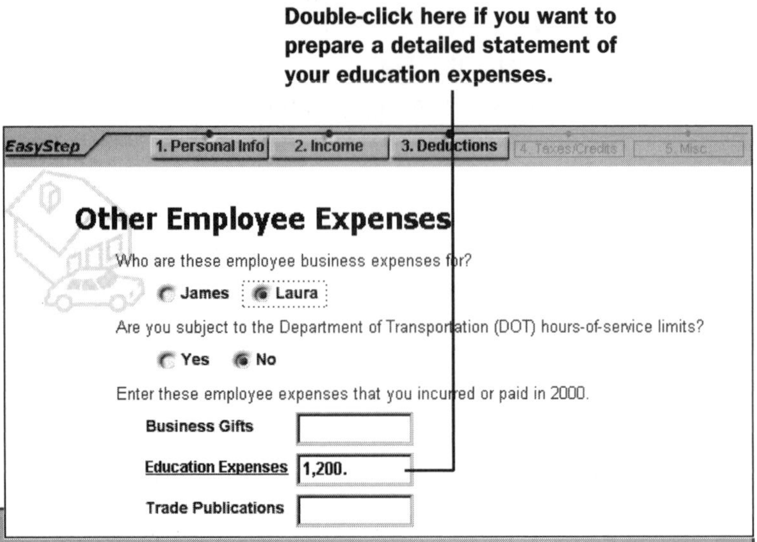

Double-click here if you want to prepare a detailed statement of your education expenses.

Figure 7-13 • Enter deductible education expenses here.

Tax-Related Expenses

The cost of preparing your tax return is a deductible expense, if you have enough miscellaneous expenses to get over the 2 percent of AGI threshold. Tax preparation costs include:

- The cost of your TurboTax program
- The cost of this book
- Electronic filing fees
- Professional tax preparation services or advice
- Tax publications
- Postage for mailing your tax return
- Transportation relating to acquiring any of the above-listed items or services
- Appraisal fees relating to claims for casualty loss or deductions for charitable contributions
- Legal and accounting fees relating to an examination of your income tax return by a taxing authority
- Legal fees for estate planning if the fees relate specifically to tax advice

Summarize all of the tax-related expenses you incurred and enter them as Tax Preparation Fees and Other Tax-Related Expenses.

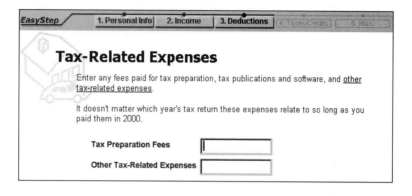

Investment-Related Costs

Expenses related to maintaining your investments are allowed as deductible expenses to the extent that the investments produce taxable income or a taxable loss. The cost of maintaining investments in tax-exempt securities is not a deductible cost. Deductible investment expenses include:

- Fees for brokers to collect income or make investment decisions (commissions on the purchase and sale of stock, however, are added to the cost of the stock or are considered an expense of the sale).
- Safe deposit box rental, if the safe deposit box is used to store documents relating to the production of taxable income, such as shares of stock, bonds, or investment-related papers.
- Subscriptions to investment publications and newsletters.
- Books and magazines you purchase for investment advice.
- The cost of software and the portion of the cost of a computer used to maintain your investments. The computer cost is to be prorated for the business use of the computer, and then depreciated using the straight line method over five years, which spreads the cost of the computer evenly over that time period.
- Trustee fee for an IRA account, if the fee is billed separately and not paid out from the balance in your IRA account.

Gambling Losses

If you report gambling income on your tax return, you are entitled to take a deduction for the losses you incur while gambling, as long as that deduction does not exceed the income from gambling that you report. The gambling losses you deduct are not subject to the 2 percent of AGI limitation on miscellaneous deductions. There is no carryforward available for gambling losses that you cannot deduct in the current year.

When you enter gambling income in TurboTax, you will be presented with a screen on which you can enter your gambling losses. The screen shows you the amount of gambling income you have entered and advises you that you may enter gambling losses only to the extent that they do not exceed this income figure (Figure 7-14).

Be sure to keep a good record of your gambling winnings and losses. Ticket stubs make good evidence, and so does a diary of your gambling exploits. Keep track of the date, location, and amount you spent for each gambling activity, and note also the type of activity and how much you won.

Figure 7-14 • Enter gambling losses for the year, making sure you don't enter more than you won during 2000.

Taking All the Tax Credits You Can

In This Chapter:

- *Claiming the Child and Dependent Care Credit*

- *Taking the Child Tax Credit*

- *Using the Education Credits*

- *Taking Advantage of the Adoption Credit*

- *Cashing In on the Fuel Tax Credit*

- *Claiming the Foreign Tax Credit*

- *Calculating the Earned Income Credit*

- *Taking the Credit for the Elderly or the Disabled*

Tax credits are direct, dollar-for-dollar reductions of your income tax—much better than deductions, which are reductions to the income on which your tax is computed. For example, if you pay tax in the 15 percent tax bracket and you take a deduction of $100, the reduction in your tax is $100 times 15 percent, or $15. Alternatively, if you are entitled to claim a $100 tax credit, the reduction in your tax is $100.

Claiming the Child and Dependent Care Credit

If you pay for care for your child or another dependent, you may be entitled to claim the credit for child and dependent care. This credit entitles taxpayers to a small break in their tax for amounts that were paid to care for dependents while they were out earning a living. The credit follows the same theory that applies to deductions for job-related expenses (see Chapter 7)—if you have to spend money to earn a living, that's an offsetting cost of the job and shouldn't be taxed.

Rather than allow a deduction for dependent care, the IRS lets you take a credit against your income tax. If you have no income tax, you get no credit. If your credit is higher than the income tax, you only get as much credit as you have income tax—there is no refund for unused dependent care credits nor is there a carryover to next year.

Who Qualifies for the Credit?

To qualify for the child and dependent care credit, you need to work and you need to pay a third party for the care of at least one of your dependents.

Who Is a Dependent for Purposes of the Credit?

The people who qualify as dependents for purposes of the child and dependent care credit include:

- Your dependent children (includes all children under the age of 13). If you're divorced or separated, whichever spouse has custody of the child for the longer time during the year may claim the credit.
- Other dependents of yours who can't take care of themselves.
- Your spouse, if that person needs care.

How Much Do I Have to Work?

To qualify for the child and dependent care credit, both you and your spouse (if you are married and filing a joint return) must work while the care is being provided. If one spouse works and the other does not, you are not eligible for the credit.

The credit is based on a percentage of the costs you pay for child or dependent care. The care costs can't exceed the earned income of the lesser-earning spouse.

One exception to the work rule is that one spouse can be a full-time student and the couple will still qualify for the credit. In this situation, the law assumes that the student has earned income of $200 for each month of school attendance, or $400 per month if there is more than one qualifying dependent.

What Types of Expenses Qualify for the Credit?

Expenses for dependent care are expenses paid to the following types of third-party provider:

- **Cost of an in-home care provider.** This cost can include incidental housekeeping expenses if that's part of the care. The in-home care provider can be your own child if that child is at least 19 years of age. The cost of a caregiver includes the cost of food you provide to the caregiver.
- **Cost of day care or other care outside the home.** To apply this cost toward the credit, the dependent must spend at least eight hours per day in your home. (In other words, the costs of constant away-from-home care, such as a hospital or institution, don't qualify for this credit.)
- **Nursery school or kindergarten costs.** These costs qualify for the credit if the school is considered to be providing care in addition to education, and the education cost can't be separated from the child care. (If the two costs are stated separately, only the child care portion qualifies as a dependent care cost.) Kindergarten costs qualify for the credit only in areas where attendance at kindergarten is optional.
- **Cost of summer day camp.** Overnight camp doesn't count toward the credit.

The credit is based on a percentage of the costs you pay for child care. The child care costs can't exceed the earned income of the lesser-earning spouse.

Entering Dependent Care Information

You will first be asked to enter the total amount you paid during 2000 for care for your dependent. Don't worry if the amount you enter exceeds the maximum allowable amount of tax credit. TurboTax will use the information you enter to calculate the proper amount of credit.

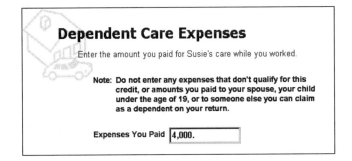

Dependent Care Expenses

Enter the amount you paid for Susie's care while you worked.

Note: Do not enter any expenses that don't qualify for this credit, or amounts you paid to your spouse, your child under the age of 19, or to someone else you can claim as a dependent on your return.

Expenses You Paid | 4,000.

Enter the name of the person or facility that provided the care for your dependent. If you paid more than one caregiver, enter all the information about one caregiver, then you will be given an opportunity to enter information about additional care providers.

Care Providers

Enter the following information for each <u>care provider</u> you paid in 2000.

Name of Provider	ABC Day Care
Name (continued)	
Address	123 Easy Street
City, State, ZIP	Anywhere, IN 47467
EIN or SSN Number (If EIN, Use the format "00-0000000")	35-2929292

Enter the total amount you paid to this provider.

Total Paid | 4,000.00

Caution *Make sure you enter the Social Security number or federal ID number of the person or facility providing care for your dependent. If you leave this number off of your tax return, the IRS may disallow your credit.*

TurboTax will calculate the credit and tell you how much credit you are entitled to receive. The credit is computed by multiplying the care expenses you incurred (up to a maximum of $2,400 for one dependent, $4,800 for two or more dependents) by an applicable percentage. The highest percentage is 30 percent, and that drops to 20 percent as your earned income increases.

The maximum credit allowed is $720 for one dependent ($2,400 in care expenses times 30 percent), $1,440 for two or more dependents ($4,800 in expenses times 30 percent). The maximum credit is only allowed if your earned income is $10,000 or less. As your income increases, the maximum allowable credit decreases, and if your earned income is over $28,000, the maximum credit you can receive is $480 for one dependent (based on 20 percent of your allowable expenses), $960 for two or more dependents (based on 20 percent of your allowable expenses).

Taking the Child Tax Credit

Here's a credit you don't have to answer any questions about—TurboTax will take care of everything that needs to be done to let you take advantage of the child tax credit, with *one exception*: When you enter information about your dependents, make sure you enter the birth date for each dependent. Based on the age of the children you claim as dependents, TurboTax will determine which children, if any, qualify you for this credit and will tell you how much of a credit you are entitled to take.

Child Tax Credit

Your child tax credit for 2000 is $500.

This credit reduces your tax liability.

The child tax credit is $500 per child. A qualifying child is under age 17 as of the end of 2000, and the child must be claimed as your dependent on your tax return.

The child tax credit is reduced by $50 for each $1,000 (or fraction thereof) by which your adjusted gross income exceeds the threshold amount of $75,000 for single or head of household taxpayers, or $110,000 for married filing jointly taxpayers ($55,000 for married filing separately).

GET SMARTER   The child tax credit, like most credits (but see the exception, the earned income credit, described later in this chapter) is not a refundable credit. In other words, if the total tax on your tax return is $850 and you have two children who qualify for the credit, resulting in $1,000 of available credit, you will only be entitled to a credit of $850. However, if you have three or more children who qualify for the credit, the credit is not limited to just your income tax, but to the sum of your income tax and the amount of FICA taxes you paid, reduced by the amount of any earned income credit you are claiming.

Using the Education Credits

Taxpayers who pay tuition and college fees for themselves, a qualifying dependent, or a spouse, are entitled to claim a credit for some of these expenses. There are two education credits: the Hope Scholarship credit and the lifetime learning credit.

The Hope Scholarship Credit

The Hope Scholarship credit is a credit of up to $1,500 per year, calculated by taking 100 percent of the first $1,000 paid in tuition and college fees and 50 percent of the next $1,000 paid during the year for yourself, your spouse, or your dependent. The costs to which the credit applies must be incurred in the first two years (typically, freshman and sophomore years) of post-secondary education.

For example, if you begin school in the fall of 2000 and pay $1,800 per semester for eight semesters, the credit would be calculated as follows:

- **Year 2000.** You began school in the fall, so you only paid one semester of fees, or $1,800, in the first year. The Hope Scholarship credit is 100 percent of the first $1,000 paid, or $1,000, plus 50 percent of the remaining $800, or $400, for a total of $1,400.

- **Year 2001.** You paid $3,600 for the spring (freshman) and fall (sophomore) semesters. The Hope Scholarship credit is the full $1,500 (100 percent of the first $1,000 paid, 50 percent of the second $1,000 paid).

- **Year 2002.** You paid $3,600 for the spring (sophomore) and fall (junior) semesters. For the spring semester, you are a sophomore, so this $1,800 tuition qualifies for the Hope Scholarship credit. Total allowable credit is $1,400 (100 percent of the first $1,000 of the spring semester tuition and fees, plus 50 percent of the remaining $800 of the spring semester tuition and fees).

- **Years 2003 and 2004.** No Hope Scholarship credit, but see the lifetime learning credit information in the next section.

The Hope Scholarship credit is available for each family member attending college. If three members of the family are attending the first or second year of college in 2000, you are entitled to take a maximum of $4,500 for the Hope Scholarship credit.

There are income levels at which the amount of Hope Scholarship credit you can claim is limited. The credit phases out completely when adjusted gross income reaches $50,000 for single filers and $80,000 for joint filers. Married people must file a joint return to claim the credit.

TurboTax will ask you to enter the amount of higher education costs for each member of the family who attended school (see Figure 8-1).

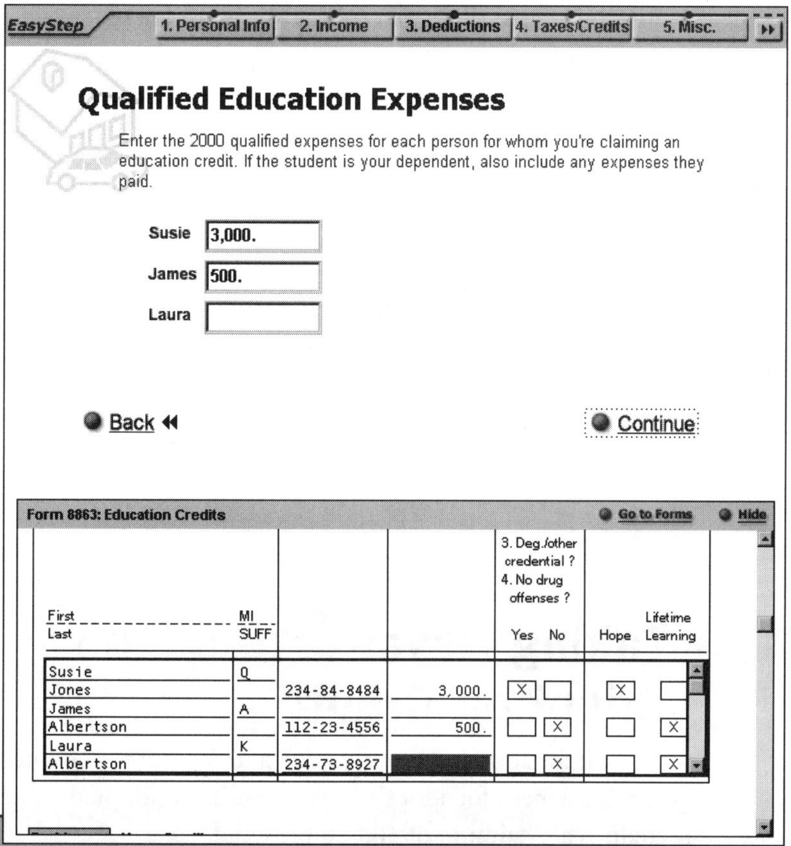

Figure 8-1 • Enter the amount of college expenses you incurred for each family member who attended college. TurboTax will determine how much, if any, and what type of education credit you should receive.

The Lifetime Learning Credit

Another education credit that rivals the Hope Scholarship credit—particularly because you can't take both credits in the same year—is the lifetime learning credit. This credit provides a maximum of $1,000 per year, which is less than the maximum allowed with the Hope Scholarship credit, but the lifetime learning credit is more flexible.

The lifetime learning credit is calculated by multiplying 20 percent times the amount of education costs you incur, up to $5,000 of costs for any or all members of your family. There is no limit on the number of years you can claim the credit—you can keep someone in your family in college forever and claim the credit every year.

The lifetime learning credit applies to education costs for any post-secondary education, including courses to acquire or improve job skills. The course or courses must be offered through a college or vocational school. You don't have to be pursuing a college degree to qualify for this credit.

When you enter your education costs, TurboTax asks you to associate the costs with each of your family members, and it asks you to identify which costs relate to costs from freshman and sophomore years of college. Then the TurboTax program will figure out the most advantageous credit for you to claim.

Years of Education

Check the box for each student who is in the first or second year of education after high school.

☑ **Susie**

☐ **James**

☐ **Laura**

Taking Advantage of the Adoption Credit

A credit for adoption expenses of up to $5,000 per adopted child is available as a reimbursement for adoption expenses. If the adopted child has special needs, the credit is a maximum of $6,000 per child.

The credit may be applied toward any reasonable and necessary adoption costs, such as court costs, legal fees, and other expenses directly related to the legal adoption of a child under age 18 or someone who is physically or mentally unable to care for himself.

The adoption credit is not available to taxpayers who adopt a spouse's child, nor is it available in the case of a surrogate arrangement or an illegal adoption.

To claim the credit, enter the names and Social Security numbers of each adopted child, then enter the amount of expenses you incurred.

Qualified Adoption Expenses

	James
Adoption Fees	2,000.
Court Costs	500.
Attorney Fees	850.
Traveling Expenses	
Other Expenses	

Expenses that qualify for this credit include:

- Adoption fees
- Court costs
- Attorney fees
- Traveling expenses (including meals and lodging)
- Any other expenses directly related to or whose principal purpose is for the legal adoption of an eligible child

Who Qualifies for This Credit?

An eligible child is one who is under 18 years old at the time of adoption or any individual who is physically or mentally incapable of taking care of himself.

According to the IRS, the term "special needs" refers to children who cannot or should not be returned to their parents' home because of ethnic background, age, or membership in a minority group, as well as children who face medical conditions or physical, mental, or emotional handicaps that require special government assistance in the form of this credit. The government of each state is responsible for making the determination as to which children will qualify for this credit. An adoptive child with special needs must be a citizen or resident of the United States if the expenses relating to the adoption are to qualify for the credit.

Note   *This is the last year for the adoption credit to apply to adoptions of individuals without special needs. Beginning in 2001, the credit will only apply to children who are determined by the state government to possess a special needs situation.*

When Should the Adoption Credit Be Claimed?

It would be nice if adoptions were quick and easy, and all the bureaucratic tangle of the process fell into one calendar year. But this is often not the case. An adoption process may be started in one year and not finalized until a later year. So when are you entitled to claim the credit?

The rule is that if the expenses are paid in the year prior to the year in which the adoption is finalized, you should claim the credit during the year the adoption is finalized. This will protect you from having to go back and amend a tax return should the adoption not occur. On the other hand, if you are still paying for adoption expenses in the year after the adoption is made final, you can claim the credit for each year in which you pay for adoption expenses. The credit is calculated on a per child basis, not a per year basis, so if you used $4,000 credit toward an adoption that occurred in 1999, and you finished paying your lawyer the rest of his fee of $1,500 in 2000, you could claim a credit for $4,000 in 1999 and an additional credit of $1,000 (or the entire $1,500 in the case of a special needs child) in 2000.

Cashing In on the Fuel Tax Credit

If you use a non-highway vehicle at least partially for business, such as a piece of farm equipment or some other vehicle that you don't use on normal roads, you can take a credit for the federal tax on gasoline you bought for the vehicle. The cost of the fuel itself is deducted as a business expense.

Note   *If you are a cash-basis taxpayer and took a credit on your 1999 tax return for the federal tax paid on fuels, the amount of that credit gets added into your income for 2000. Report last year's credit as income on your farm or other business tax form.*

In order to qualify for this credit, the vehicle has to be used for a business purpose. Gasoline purchased for a riding lawn mower that is used exclusively to mow the lawn in front of your house doesn't qualify for this credit, but gasoline bought for a tractor used on the farm does. The rule is that the vehicle must be used at least in part for business. The business portion of the tax paid on the fuel will qualify for the credit.

Keep track of the number of gallons of fuel you use for farming and other non-highway business driving. It is the number of gallons, not the exact cost of the fuel, that gets entered on the tax form where the credit is claimed.

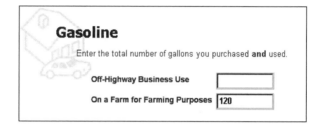

Claiming the Foreign Tax Credit

Do you have investments in countries besides the U.S.? If you are a U.S. citizen and resident of this country and you pay income tax to another country, you can take a credit for that tax. The income from your foreign investments is taxed in this country—taxing it again in another country would be a form of double taxation that citizens of the United States are not required to pay.

If you had taxes from another country withheld from some of your income, you will report the tax as a credit on your U.S. income tax return, and the income from the foreign source will be combined with your other U.S. income and taxed in this country.

Note *You have an option of claiming an itemized deduction in the tax category for the tax you paid to another country. Generally, the foreign tax credit will provide you with a greater tax saving, but you can try taking the itemized deduction in lieu of the credit and seeing which will provide the greater benefit on your tax return.*

In TurboTax, when you enter information from your 1099 form, you can check a box to indicate that the income is from a foreign source (see Figure 8-2).

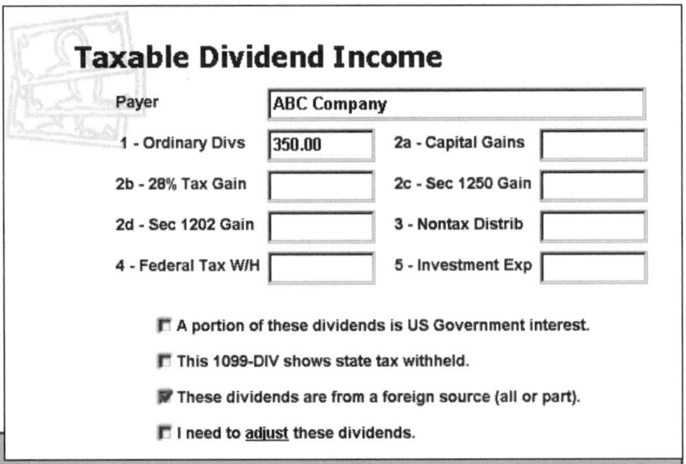

Taxable Dividend Income

Payer	ABC Company		
1 - Ordinary Divs	350.00	2a - Capital Gains	
2b - 28% Tax Gain		2c - Sec 1250 Gain	
2d - Sec 1202 Gain		3 - Nontax Distrib	
4 - Federal Tax W/H		5 - Investment Exp	

☐ A portion of these dividends is US Government interest.

☐ This 1099-DIV shows state tax withheld.

☑ These dividends are from a foreign source (all or part).

☐ I need to adjust these dividends.

Figure 8-2 • Check the appropriate box to indicate the income is from a foreign country.

If you indicated that the income was from a foreign source, you will be asked to identify the amount of the foreign income, the amount of tax you paid, and the name of the country from which the income originated.

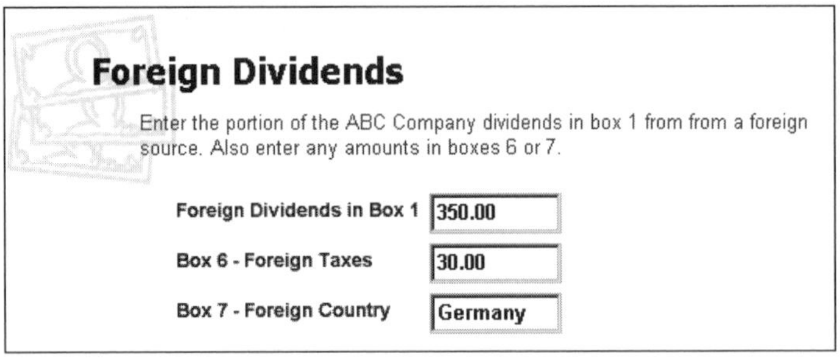

Foreign Dividends

Enter the portion of the ABC Company dividends in box 1 from from a foreign source. Also enter any amounts in boxes 6 or 7.

Foreign Dividends in Box 1	350.00
Box 6 - Foreign Taxes	30.00
Box 7 - Foreign Country	Germany

Calculating the Earned Income Credit

One of the messiest areas of tax preparation seems to be the calculation of the earned income credit. This is a complicated credit to calculate—so complicated that if you are preparing your tax return by hand, you can simply write the letters "EIC" on the line of your tax form where this credit is calculated, and the IRS will figure out the credit for you. Fortunately, you have TurboTax to perform the work for you instead.

The earned income credit is a credit against tax that was devised to help offset income taxes for certain people who don't make very much money. To qualify for the credit, you must meet all of these rules:

- You have to have a dependent child (hereafter referred to as qualifying child) living with you for more than half of the year *or* you must be at least age 25, under age 65, and can't be claimed as a dependent on someone else's tax return.
- You must have earned some income—that is, you have to have a job that pays you for the work you do.
- Your earned income and your adjusted gross income must both be less than $26,928 if you have one qualifying child living with you, $30,580 if you have two or more qualifying children living with you, or $10,200 if you do not have a qualifying child living with you.
- Your investment income for 2000 cannot exceed $2,350.
- If you're married, you must file jointly; you can't use the Married Filing Separately filing status. Any other filing status qualifies for the credit.
- You can't be a qualifying child for someone else who is claiming the earned income credit.
- Your qualifying child can't be the qualifying child of someone else whose adjusted gross income is higher than yours.
- If your qualifying child is married, that child has to be claimed as your dependent.
- If you work abroad and claimed an exclusion from U.S. tax for your foreign earned income, you may not claim the earned income credit.
- You can't be a nonresident alien for any part of 2000, unless you're married to a U.S. citizen or resident and elect to be taxed as a U.S. resident for all of 2000.

If you meet all of these requirements, you are entitled to take an earned income credit on your tax return. TurboTax will figure all of this out for you and tell you the result of its computation.

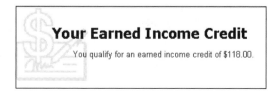

Your Earned Income Credit

You qualify for an earned income credit of $118.00.

One nice feature about the earned income credit is that this is a refundable credit. That means that even if you don't owe any tax on your tax return, you can still take the credit and receive a refund. With most credits, the credit lowers your tax liability, but if your tax isn't as high as the credit, you simply lose the credit. Not so with the earned income credit.

Taking the Credit for the Elderly or the Disabled

The credit for the elderly or disabled is available to taxpayers who meet one of these two tests:

- Your 65th birthday is on or before January 1, 2001
- You're under the age of 65 at the end of 2000 and retired because of permanent and total disability, and you received taxable disability income in 2000 from your former employer's disability plan

Meeting one of these tests doesn't guarantee that you will get the credit, but not meeting one of them guarantees that you won't get the credit.

There are also income levels that limit your access to this credit. To qualify for the credit for the elderly or disabled, you must have income lower than the income limits shown in Table 8-1, and you must not have Social Security payments equal to or greater than the Social Security limits shown in this table. If you meet one of the first two tests, check Table 8-1 to see if your income and Social Security allows you to be eligible for this credit.

If you are married filing a separate return, the credit is only allowed if you and your spouse have lived apart for the entire year. TurboTax will calculate the amount of credit, if any, to which you are entitled, based on the other entries you make in the tax return.

Credit for the Elderly and the Disabled

Your credit for 2000 is $32.00 based upon the information you've entered so far. If you enter additional information in your return, we will automatically recalculate your credit.

Filing Status	Adjusted Gross Income Limit	Limit on Nontaxable Social Security or Pension
Single	$17,500	$5,000
Married Filing Jointly (just one spouse is eligible to claim the credit)	$20,000	$5,000
Head of Household	$17,500	$5,000
Married Filing Jointly (both spouses are eligible to claim the credit)	$25,000	$7,500
Qualifying Widow(er) with dependent child	$17,500	$5,000
Married Filing Separately (you did not live with your spouse at any time during the year)	$12,500	$3,750

Table 8-1 • Income Limits for the Credit for the Elderly or the Disabled

Paying Additional Taxes

In This Chapter:

- *Paying the "Nanny Tax"*

- *Paying the "Kiddie Tax"*

- *Paying the Alternative Minimum Tax*

- *Paying Taxes on Tips*

- *Paying Self-Employment Tax*

- *Paying the Penalty on Early Withdrawal from an IRA*

Chapter 9

There's more to the 1040 than income tax, as you will find if any of these extra taxes apply to you. People who hire domestic workers, people with children who have income, people who have sheltered some of their income from the income tax, and self-employed people are all subject to extra taxes, the calculations of which can tax the mind. Thank goodness TurboTax takes care of figuring out these taxes based on your answers to basic questions.

The Nanny Tax on Household Employees

If you employ someone in your home, such as a caregiver, a private nurse, a grounds person, a cook, a maid, a butler, or a personal secretary, you are required to report the wages for this person to the IRS and you are also required to make sure the proper payroll taxes—income tax, Social Security tax, and Medicare—have been paid for this person.

If you paid a domestic employee age 18 or older more than $1,200 during 2000, or if you paid wages of more than $1,000 in any calendar quarter of 1999 or 2000, or if you withheld federal income tax on your employee during 2000, you're required to file a tax form (Federal Schedule H), and pay Social Security and Medicare on that employee. Although withholding of income tax on the employee's wages is optional for the employer, any amounts withheld must be reported to the IRS.

Because preparing and mailing tax forms can be difficult and confusing, the IRS has made the process of paying taxes on household employees quick and easy. Instead of filling out and mailing separate forms and paying taxes for your employee throughout the year, you can prepare the tax report and pay the taxes right with your federal income tax return.

When you indicate that you pay someone who may qualify for the "nanny tax" (see Figure 9-1 below), TurboTax will then ask you whether you paid the wages yourself or with your spouse and ask for your federal identification number. Then you will be asked to enter the amounts you paid to your employee.

Next, you will be asked to enter the wages you paid to your employee that are subject to Social Security and Medicare taxes, and you will need to indicate if you withheld any income tax for the employee. As shown in Figure 9-2, TurboTax will compute the amount of Social Security and Medicare tax you owe (both the employee and the employer share, which comes to 15.3 percent), and will enter this information on Schedule H, Household Employment Taxes, which will result in additional tax that you pay with your income tax return.

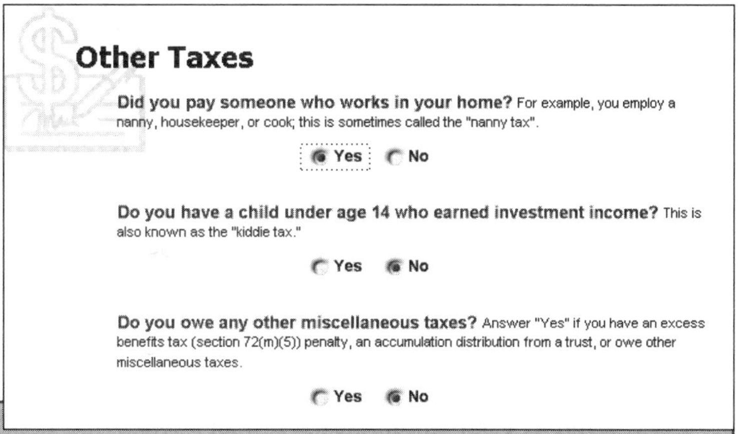

Other Taxes

Did you pay someone who works in your home? For example, you employ a nanny, housekeeper, or cook; this is sometimes called the "nanny tax".

    ● Yes   ○ No

Do you have a child under age 14 who earned investment income? This is also known as the "kiddie tax."

    ○ Yes   ● No

Do you owe any other miscellaneous taxes? Answer "Yes" if you have an excess benefits tax (section 72(m)(5)) penalty, an accumulation distribution from a trust, or owe other miscellaneous taxes.

    ○ Yes   ● No

Figure 9-1 • Click the Yes option to indicate that you have employed and paid wages to someone who worked in your home.

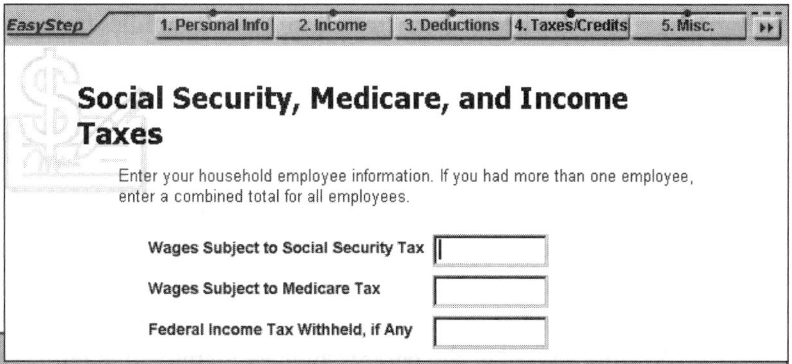

| EasyStep | 1. Personal Info | 2. Income | 3. Deductions | 4. Taxes/Credits | 5. Misc. | ▶▶ |

Social Security, Medicare, and Income Taxes

Enter your household employee information. If you had more than one employee, enter a combined total for all employees.

Wages Subject to Social Security Tax   [   ]

Wages Subject to Medicare Tax   [   ]

Federal Income Tax Withheld, if Any   [   ]

Figure 9-2 • Enter the taxable wages of your household employee and any federal income tax you withheld.

It is not a requirement that you withhold income tax from your employee—you should speak to the employee to find out if he or she prefers to have you withhold tax during the year or prefers to pay the entire tax on his or her tax return at the end of the year.

Preparing an Income Tax Return for Your Child

If you elect not to report your child's income on your return, you will answer No when asked if you wish to do so (see below). You must then prepare a separate tax return for your child.

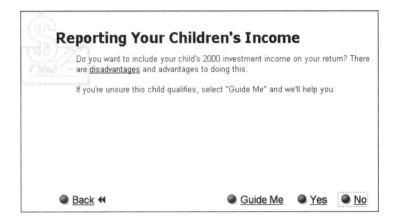

If you choose to file a separate tax return for your child (recommended—see the previous Save Money sidebar), you should complete the parents' tax return first so you will have the correct information to transfer over to the child's return. When asked (see Figure 9-3), you will enter the parents' taxable income in the child's tax return, then TurboTax will ask for information about capital gains and losses reported on the parents' return. If the parents' tax return is completed, you can find this amount by either looking at line 39 of the parents' 1040 form, or by placing your mouse over the tax/refund indicator in the upper-right corner of the interview window in the parents' TurboTax file. After you enter taxable income, TurboTax will ask for information about capital gains and losses reported on the parents' return.

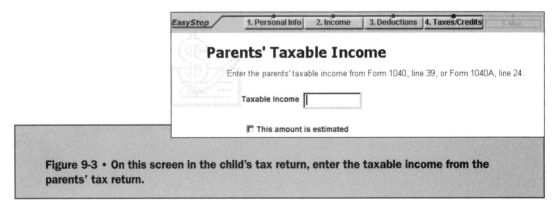

Figure 9-3 • On this screen in the child's tax return, enter the taxable income from the parents' tax return.

Adding the Child's Income to the Parents' Tax Return

As an alternative to filing a separate tax return for your child, you can add the child's income to the parents' tax return and pay tax on both the incomes in one return. You may want to take the time to calculate the child's tax both ways (on the parents' return and on a separate return for the child) to determine if there is a difference in total tax and, if so, how much.

If you are adding the child's income to that of the parents', you will enter the child's interest, dividend, and income from capital gain distributions on the appropriate screens in TurboTax.

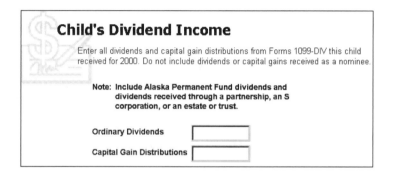

TurboTax will provide you with a nice summary of how the child's income will affect the tax on your tax return (see Figure 9-4). If you decide to calculate the child's tax on a separate tax form to compare the tax effects of both procedures, be sure to eliminate the child's income from the parents' tax return before copying the taxable income amount from the parents' return to the child's return.

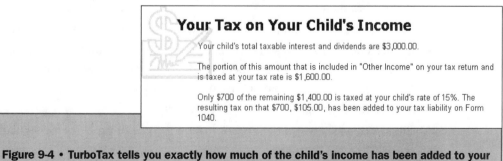

Figure 9-4 • TurboTax tells you exactly how much of the child's income has been added to your return and the tax effect of that income.

The Alternative Minimum Tax

One of the most confusing aspects of federal income taxation is the alternative minimum tax (AMT). This tax was originally targeted at people with high incomes who have opportunities to shelter some of their income from tax. Because of rising incomes and changes in the tax laws, the AMT has become a burden to many taxpayers, not just the most wealthy.

The AMT was instituted to ensure that taxpayers who are eligible to take advantage of preferential treatment with certain types of deductions and credits will pay at least a minimum tax. The tax effectively eliminates many deductions and credits and produces a tax liability for individuals who otherwise might pay little or no income tax.

The AMT tax affects married taxpayers filing jointly with incomes over $45,000, single and head of household taxpayers with incomes over $37,750, and married taxpayers filing separately with incomes over $22,500.

Note Although the amount of income that gets taxed at the lower marginal tax rates increases each year, thus giving the appearance that the tax rates overall are decreasing, more and more taxpayers are finding they are subject to the AMT, which has the effect of raising total tax liability.

If you take adjustments or receive preferential treatment on your tax return, or if any of the tax documents you receive from your various income sources refer to amounts that are for alternative minimum tax purposes, you might have a responsibility to include Form 6251, Alternative Minimum Tax, with your income tax return. The most common types of adjustments and deductions that can trigger the AMT include:

- Personal exemptions (everyone, except dependent children filing their own tax returns, has these)
- The standard deduction (everyone who doesn't itemize has a standard deduction)
- Itemized deductions for state and local taxes, including income and property taxes, certain interest, miscellaneous deductions, and medical deductions that do not exceed 10 percent of adjusted gross income
- Accelerated depreciation on business property
- The difference between the gain or loss on the sale of property for regular versus AMT tax purposes
- Income from incentive stock options
- Passive losses

> **Note**   *In 1990, 132,000 taxpayers were subject to the alternative minimum tax. It is projected that more than ten times that amount—1,141,000 taxpayers—will pay this tax in 2000, and if current trends continue, more than 8 million taxpayers will be subjected to this tax in another ten years. The main reason for the proliferation of taxpayers subject to this tax is that the personal exemption and standard deduction amounts for regular income tax purposes are indexed for inflation and thus increase each year. The exemptions allowed for alternative minimum tax are not indexed and thus remain stable each year. As more people reduce their taxes with increased exemptions and deductions, these same people will have to increase their taxes to make up for these exemptions and deductions. Income tax rates appear to continue to be lowered each year, when actually the total tax burden is increasing annually.*

TurboTax will ask you a few questions to help determine if you qualify for this tax, and then the program will take care of filling out the form for you. When the AMT is calculated, the result is compared to your regularly calculated income tax, and the AMT is only used if it exceeds your regular income tax. If the AMT is higher, the difference between the AMT and your regular tax is added to your regular tax as an additional tax (see Figure 9-5), and the total is the amount you are required to pay.

Recover Your AMT Tax with a Credit

If you are required to pay the AMT in any year, the amount of AMT you pay will be allowed as a credit in any subsequent year in which your regular tax exceeds your AMT tax liability. TurboTax will compute this AMT credit if you used TurboTax in a prior year in which the AMT was paid and if that information has been carried forward into your tax return.

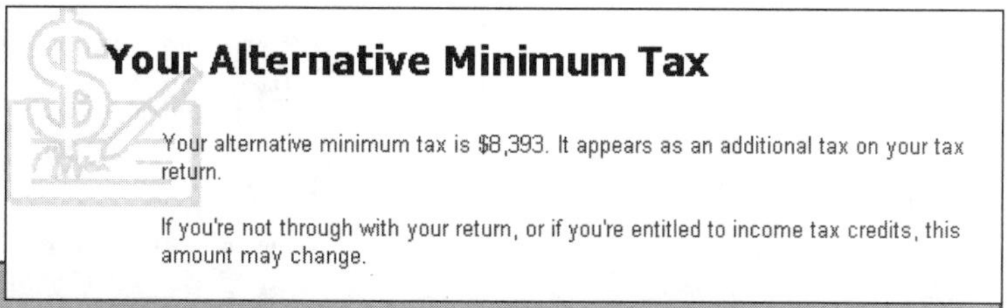

Your Alternative Minimum Tax

Your alternative minimum tax is $8,393. It appears as an additional tax on your tax return.

If you're not through with your return, or if you're entitled to income tax credits, this amount may change.

Figure 9-5 • TurboTax calculates the AMT and then advises you about how much AMT tax will be added to your other taxes on this tax return.

If you didn't use TurboTax in a prior year when you paid the AMT, you must enter the prior year AMT information into your TurboTax program so that TurboTax will have the proper information to see if you will benefit from the credit.

On the Which Other Credits Apply screen, indicate that you want TurboTax to calculate the Credit for Alternative Minimum Tax Paid.

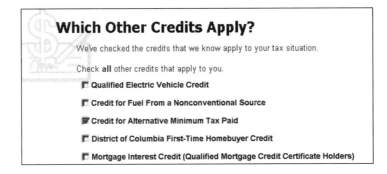

Which Other Credits Apply?

We've checked the credits that we know apply to your tax situation.

Check **all** other credits that apply to you.

☐ **Qualified Electric Vehicle Credit**

☐ **Credit for Fuel From a Nonconventional Source**

☑ **Credit for Alternative Minimum Tax Paid**

☐ **District of Columbia First-Time Homebuyer Credit**

☐ **Mortgage Interest Credit (Qualified Mortgage Credit Certificate Holders)**

You will be asked to enter the information from your 1999 return reflecting either the amount of AMT paid in 1999 or the amount of AMT paid in a prior year that was carried forward to 1999 (see Figure 9-6). Once entered, TurboTax will maintain this information and carry it forward to apply to future credits if you are ineligible for a credit in 2000. Even if you don't qualify for the minimum tax credit, you should enter this information so that it will carry forward to future tax returns.

Credit for Prior Year AMT

You might qualify for a tax credit this year if you

- Paid alternative minimum tax in 1999, or
- Have a minimum tax credit carryover from 1999, or
- Have a nonconventional source fuel credit, or a qualified electric vehicle credit not allowed in 1999.

To find out, look at your 1999 tax return. If there is an amount on either of the following lines, enter them here.

1999 Form 8801, Line 26	
1999 Form 6251, Line 28	651.

Figure 9-6 • Enter any minimum tax credit carryover or AMT tax from your 1999 tax return.

Paying Tax on Tips

This section assumes that you receive tips and don't turn them in or report them to your boss. Keep in mind, however, that many employers expect their employees to tell how much they collect in tips, even if they keep all the money for themselves, and then the employer will include the amount on your W-2 form.

If you are going to take the responsibility for reporting your own tips, keep a very clear record of the tips you receive. The easiest way to record your tip income, and the method the IRS prefers, is to keep a notebook or diary where you track your tips on a daily basis. The IRS always likes paper records, so keeping the diary will be extremely useful evidence for the tips you collect. Even if you plan to report the tips to your employer, the diary provides the best method for keeping track of all that you collect.

To the extent that you have paper evidence of your tips, such as credit card receipts or restaurant checks, you should also keep this information. The more evidence you can provide to support your daily reportings of your tips, the more authentic your records will be.

Tip   *Here's a nice "tip" for you—the IRS publishes a document that you can use to keep track of your tip income. Form 4070A, otherwise known as Employee's Daily Record of Tips, is available from the IRS. You can download the form, which is included in Publication 1244, at the IRS Web site, http://www.irs.gov/. Choose the Forms and Publications option, then choose Publications, and select Publication 1244 from the list. This publication not only includes instructions for filling out Form 4070A, but it includes a copy of the form, which you can duplicate and use for the entire year.*

As far as the IRS is concerned, tips aren't just the cash you receive. Tips also include non-cash items such as tickets to events, passes, or other items of value. Anything you receive for your services that has value is subject to tax, and the value of the amount you receive should be listed on your report of daily tips you receive.

When it's time to file your tax return, your tips that aren't included in your W-2 form should be added to the amount of wages you report on line 7 of your 1040 form (if you are reporting tips that aren't on your W-2, you can't use a 1040A or 1040EZ). TurboTax provides you with an opportunity to enter this income, right after you finish entering your W-2 income (see Figure 9-7).

Figure 9-7 • **Enter the total of tips that weren't reported to your employer, and TurboTax will calculate the appropriate tax on this amount.**

Not only will you be subject to income tax on these tips, but, because your employer didn't withhold any tax, you will also have to pay Social Security and Medicare tax on the tip income. TurboTax will compute the tax by multiplying 7.65 percent times the amount of tip income, and the tax will be added to the amount on the line that reads "This is your total tax" on your tax return.

Paying Self-Employment Tax

If you have self-employment income of at least $400 for 2000, you will probably owe self-employment tax on that income, in addition to the income tax you pay. Self-employment tax is a combination of Social Security tax and Medicare tax. The difference between the Social Security tax and Medicare tax that employees pay and the self-employment tax is that employees only pay half of the tax (their employer is responsible for the other half), and all of the tax is withheld from their pay, so they never have the feeling of having owned that money in the first place.

Self-employed taxpayers pay both halves of the Social Security and Medicare taxes, and they have to write the checks themselves to pay the tax, taking the money from their own bank account, unlike their employed counterparts.

How Much Do You Have to Pay?

Self-employment (SE) tax is computed at the rate of 15.3 percent of your self-employment income up to a maximum of $76,200 in income for 2000. If you have both income earned as an employee and self-employment income, the income you earned as an employee is used to reduce your income from self-employment for purposes of computing this tax.

In other words, if you earned $30,000 as an employee, you will have paid Social Security tax on that $30,000 at your workplace. If you are showing $80,000 as the net income on your Schedule C, you can first reduce this number to $76,200 for purposes of computing the SE tax, because $76,200 is the maximum amount on which this tax is applied. But before the SE tax is calculated, the self-employment income is again reduced by $30,000, the amount on which you have already paid the Social Security tax, so the SE tax will only apply to $76,200 minus $30,000, or $46,300 of income.

Medicare tax on self-employment income is 2.9 percent (this amount is included in the 15.3 percent that is used to calculate SE tax). But unlike Social Security tax, Medicare tax has no ceiling. Long after your self-employment income has exceeded $72,600, you'll still be paying Medicare tax on the total amount. The taxpayer who earned $30,000 as an employee will pay Social Security and Medicare tax on that amount, then will pay 15.3 percent SE tax on the next $46,300, and then 2.9 percent Medicare tax on all remaining SE income.

TurboTax will compute this tax for you—you don't have to fill out the SE form yourself—but it's important for you to be aware of the amount of tax you are required to pay, especially if you make payments of your tax with quarterly estimates.

Quarterly Estimated Payment Considerations

Self-employment tax, just like income tax, is required to be paid throughout the year instead of all on April 15. If you are self-employed and are making a profit in your business, you are required to make quarterly payments for both the income tax and the self-employment tax on this profit.

TurboTax will help you calculate your quarterly payments and will give you the forms to send with your payments. See Chapter 15 for more information about how to make quarterly estimated payments.

Paying the Penalty on Early Withdrawal from an IRA

You can take money out of your IRA account—after all, it's your money—but you pay a price when you do this. If you withdraw money from your IRA before age $59^{1}/_{2}$, the amount you withdraw from your IRA account may get added to your income as an IRA distribution. If you took a deduction for your contributions to your IRA, the entire amount you withdraw is subject to income tax. If you didn't deduct your IRA contributions or only deducted some of the contributions, the portion of your IRA withdrawal that represents previously untaxed income will be subject to income tax.

The trustee that administers your account will provide you with a 1099-R form after the end of the year, summarizing the amount of your withdrawal from the IRA and any tax that was withheld. The amount you withdraw from your IRA prior to age $59^1/_2$ gets subjected to a 10 percent penalty for early withdrawal (but see exceptions to the penalty, in the next section).

Exceptions to the Penalty on Early Withdrawal

Although the previously untaxed money you withdraw from your IRA will always be subject to income tax, there are certain circumstances in which you are entitled to withdraw money early from your IRA without having to pay the 10 percent early withdrawal penalty. The penalty does not apply if you meet one of these requirements:

- You have incurred medical expenses for which you will not be reimbursed and those expenses are more than 7.5 percent of your adjusted gross income (in other words, you have medical expenses that you will be entitled to deduct if you itemize your deductions).
- The amount you receive from your IRA is not more than the cost of your medical insurance.
- You are disabled.
- You are the beneficiary of a deceased IRA account owner.
- You are receiving distributions from the account in the form of an annuity.
- You are attending college or vocational school and the distributions you receive from your IRA account are not more than your qualified higher education costs.
- You use the IRA distributions to buy, build, or rebuild a first home. First home, in this situation, is considered to be any home, as long as this is the first home you have purchased within two years. Withdrawals for this purpose may not exceed $10,000 in a lifetime.
- The IRA distribution is a return of same-year contributions made before the due date of your tax return.
- The IRA distribution is required as a result of an IRS levy on the account.

After you enter the information from your 1099-R form, TurboTax will ask you to identify if any exceptions apply to your withdrawal. Enter the amount that applies in the field associated with any applicable exception, as shown in Figure 9-8.

Unless amounts are withdrawn for any of the situations described above, your IRA withdrawal is subject to a 10 percent penalty, which TurboTax will calculate and add to your other taxes on your tax return.

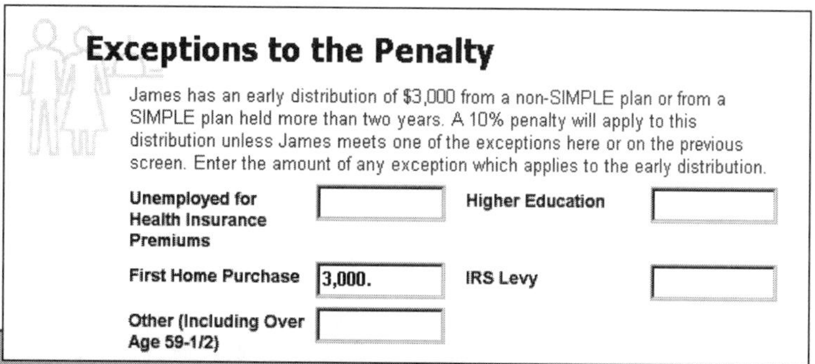

Exceptions to the Penalty

James has an early distribution of $3,000 from a non-SIMPLE plan or from a SIMPLE plan held more than two years. A 10% penalty will apply to this distribution unless James meets one of the exceptions here or on the previous screen. Enter the amount of any exception which applies to the early distribution.

Unemployed for Health Insurance Premiums		Higher Education	
First Home Purchase	3,000.	IRS Levy	
Other (Including Over Age 59-1/2)			

Figure 9-8 • Enter any amounts that are protected from the 10 percent early withdrawal penalty.

Preparing Your
State Tax Return

In This Chapter:

- *Reviewing New State Tax Laws*

- *Entering State Information*

- *Paying State Taxes When You Move During the Year*

- *Paying State Taxes When You Live/Work in Multiple States*

Chapter 10

One thing you can say about every state that has a state income tax is that that state's income tax is different from the tax structure in every other state. No two states are identical in the items they tax, the rate at which they apply tax, or the requirements for who has to file a state tax return. There are different colors and sizes of forms, different due dates, and different requirements for what needs to be attached to the state form.

Because it would be impossible to incorporate the tax rules for every state into a book this size, and because TurboTax does such a nice job of keeping track of all those laws for you, this chapter will focus on how to use TurboTax to prepare your state tax return and the answers to common questions that arise regarding filing state tax returns.

Reviewing Changes to Your State's Tax Laws

As you begin working with your state tax program (see Appendix A for information about purchasing and installing your state tax program), TurboTax will present you with pertinent information about changes to the state tax laws in your state.

For more detailed information about issues affecting your state, you may want to pay a visit to your state's Web site—each state has one—where you can find press releases and documentation regarding new developments in tax laws. The state Web sites are listed here:

Alabama: http://www.ador.state.al.us/

Alaska: http://www.revenue.state.ak.us/

Arizona: http://www.revenue.state.az.us/

Arkansas: http://www.state.ar.us/dfa/

California: http://www.ftb.ca.gov/

Colorado: http://www.state.co.us/

Connecticut: http://www.drs.state.ct.us/

Delaware: http://www.state.de.us/revenue/

District of Columbia: http://www.dccfo.com/

Florida: http://sun6.dms.state.fl.us/dor/

Georgia: http://www2.state.ga.us/departments/dor/

Hawaii: http://www.state.hi.us/tax/tax.html

Idaho: http://www2.state.id.us/tax/

Illinois: http://www.revenue.state.il.us/

Indiana: http://www.ai.org/dor/

Iowa: http://www.state.ia.us/government/drf/

Kansas: http://www.ink.org/public/kdor/

Kentucky: http://www.state.ky.us/

Louisiana: http://www.rev.state.la.us/

Maine: http://janus.state.me.us/revenue/

Maryland: http://www.comp.state.md.us/

Massachusetts: http://www.magnet.state.ma.us/dor/

Michigan: http://www.treas.state.mi.us/

Minnesota: http://www.taxes.state.mn.us/

Mississippi: http://www.treasury.state.ms.us/

Missouri: http://dor.state.mo.us/

Montana: http://www.state.mt.us/revenue/

Nebraska: http://www.nol.org/revenue/

Nevada: http://tax.state.nv.us/

New Hampshire: http://www.state.nh.us/

New Jersey: http://www.state.nj.us/treasury/taxation/

New Mexico: http://www.state.nm.us/tax/

New York: http://www.tax.state.ny.us/

North Carolina: http://www.dor.state.nc.us/

North Dakota: http://www.state.nd.us/taxdpt/

Ohio: http://www.state.oh.us/tax/

Oklahoma: http://www.oktax.state.ok.us/

Oregon: http://www.dor.state.or.us/

Pennsylvania: http://www.revenue.state.pa.us/

likely need to file two state tax returns. You will report the income from your job in the state where you work, filing a nonresident tax return in that state, and you will report all of your income, including the income from your out-of-state job, in the state where you live. Then you will claim a credit in your resident state for taxes paid to another state. TurboTax can prepare the state returns you need. You will need to acquire two state tax programs (see Figure 10-1), and TurboTax will help you split your income between the two states.

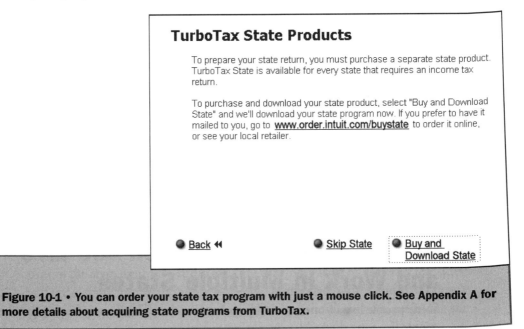

Figure 10-1 • You can order your state tax program with just a mouse click. See Appendix A for more details about acquiring state programs from TurboTax.

Finalizing Your
Tax Return

In This Chapter:

- *Checking the Return for Errors*

- *Printing Your Tax Return*

- *Filing Your Return Electronically*

- *Mailing Your Tax Return*

You've worked hard to prepare your tax return, and now it's time to look over the return for the last time, then get it out the door and on its way to the IRS. If you're expecting a refund, you're probably in a hurry to get this tax return dispatched. If you owe tax, you may decide to wait until April (tax returns are due April 16, 2001) before you send in your tax return and your payment. In either case, however, it makes sense to complete everything now and get the return ready to go on its journey to the tax authorities.

Updating Your TurboTax Software

Before getting ready to file or print your tax return, you should always check for an update to the TurboTax program. Late tax law changes do happen and this ensures that you will always have the latest version of the program prior to filing.

You can check at any time to see if there is an updated version of TurboTax available by opening the Online menu and choosing One-Click Updates (you must have Internet access to perform this step). A connection will be made to the TurboTax Web site, and any current changes to the program will automatically be loaded onto your computer.

Check Your Return for Errors

TurboTax is a great help in checking to see if there are any errors in your tax return. In fact, if you don't check for errors and you try to print your tax return, TurboTax will give you a gentle reminder that there is some unfinished business to take care of before your return is completed.

There are two ways to view the errors on your tax return: you can either view the errors through the regular interview process, or you can go directly to the forms and produce an error report. Either method provides you with the same error information. If you use the interview to view errors, you will be presented with interview-type questions to help you solve the problems that are creating errors. If you go directly to the forms, you will see a description of the error and a view of the actual form where the error occurs, and you can enter corrected information right on the form. The preferred process is to use the EasyStep Interview, where the problems causing the errors will be explained in more detail.

Running the Final Review

When you finish preparing your federal tax return, the next step in TurboTax's EasyStep Interview is the planning session. Indicate that you want to check for errors and TurboTax will examine your tax return and present errors and omissions to you, one by one, as shown in Figure 11-1.

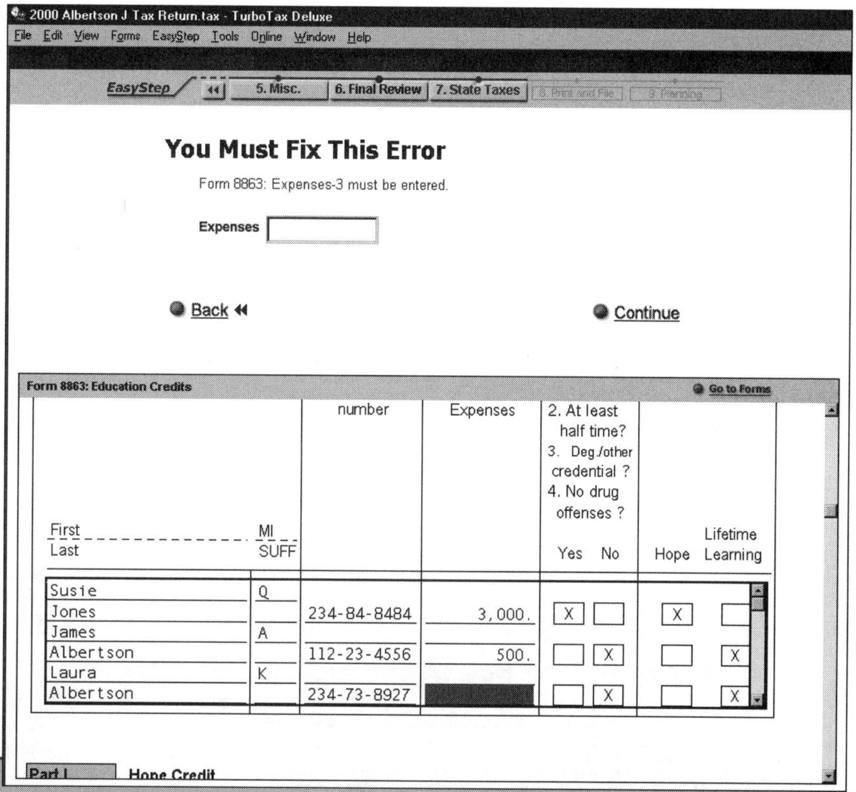

Figure 11-1 • Enter the missing information as TurboTax uses the bottom part of the screen to display the form containing the error or omission.

After responding to each item in the error check, you should run the error check again to make sure that the information you entered and the responses you made during the preliminary error check didn't generate any additional errors.

Error Check Complete

Congratulations! We found no errors in your return.

● Back ◀◀   ● Continue

Finding Errors Using the Forms Method

If you are looking at the actual tax return forms instead of using the TurboTax EasyStep Interview, you can still check to see if there are any errors in your tax return. Click the Form Errors button at the top of the screen.

A small section will open near the top of the screen offering you a list of errors and omissions that are in your tax return. In the list of errors, you can click any error, one at a time. The form will be displayed, and the section of the form requiring information will be highlighted.

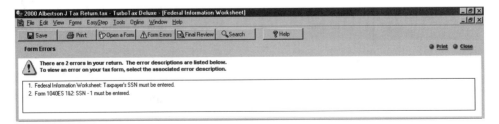

When all errors have been corrected, the error box will appear empty. Click the Close button in the upper-right corner of the error box to remove the box from your screen.

Printing Your Tax Return

Should you choose to file your tax return by mail (as opposed to filing electronically, which is covered in the next section), the EasyStep Interview will give you an opportunity to print your tax forms. Choosing the option in the interview to Print Selected Returns, having checked the box for your federal tax return, will result in your complete tax return being printed with every accompanying form and schedule that is required to be mailed to the government.

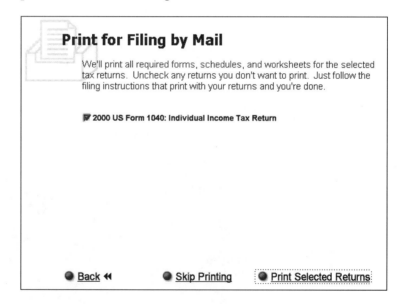

If you only want to print certain forms and not the entire tax return, or if you want to print not just your entire tax return but also all of the supporting statements and detailed schedules that you prepared as you entered your tax information, you should instead use the menu and choose File | Print (or press CTRL-P).

A window will appear in which you can select exactly which parts of your tax return you want to print.

Print Return for Filing

The first option in the Printing window, Tax Return For Filing (see Figure 11-2), produces the same results as selecting the Print Selected Returns options on the TurboTax interview screen. The entire tax return will print, ready to be signed and sent to the government.

Figure 11-2 • Choose Tax Return For Filing to print a tax return ready to mail to the government.

Tax Return for Your Records

There are three options from which you can choose when it comes to printing a copy of your tax return for your personal records (see Figure 11-3).

- **Tax Return Only.** This option produces a copy of the tax return, which is just like the tax return for filing, except for the omission of payment vouchers or other forms that are required to be attached to the tax return you mail, but that don't need to be saved in your records.

- **Recommended Forms, Worksheets.** This option produces the same forms of your tax return as the Tax Return Only option, and also prints the worksheets that support the final numbers in your tax return.

- **All Forms, Worksheets.** This option prints every form of your tax return, as well as every worksheet you prepared and all supporting details you created.

Personally, I like to print out one copy of the All Forms, Worksheets option when I'm sure that everything has been entered properly in my tax return. This option produces a *lot* of paper. The reason I like this option is that it provides me with a complete picture of everything I entered in the TurboTax program. Should anything happen to the tax file where my return is stored (an unlikely event), I will have a hard paper copy of everything that was entered.

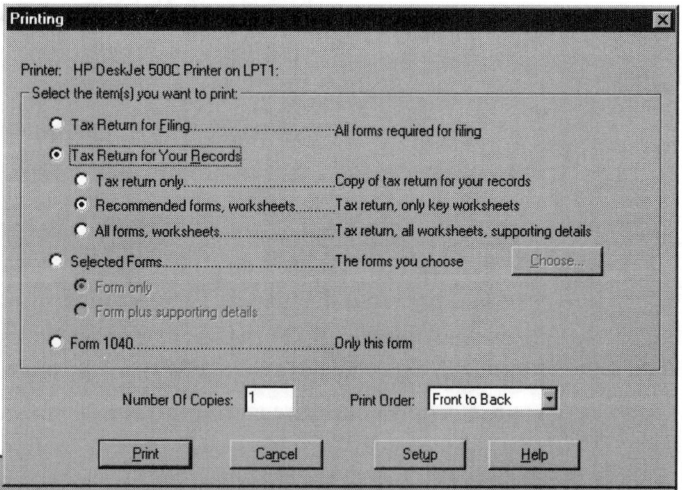

Figure 11-3 • Choose from the three options for printing documents for your records.

Printing Selected Forms

Sometimes you only need to print one form or a few pages of the return. You may not need to print the entire tax return. For example, if you are applying for a bank loan, you may need to produce a copy of your 1040 or your Schedule C, but your banker may not need to see all the supporting schedules. Or maybe you noticed that you made an error entering the federal identification number of your caregiver on the child and dependent credit form, and you only need to change and reprint this form. To print just one or more forms, but not the entire tax return, choose the Selected Forms option (see Figure 11-4).

If you only need to print part of your tax return, you can choose the Selected Forms option. When you choose Selected Forms, you must then click the Choose button. This opens a window that lists all the forms and worksheets that go with your tax return. Click on any form you want to print.

To select more than one form, hold down the CTRL key on your keyboard while you click on each form you want to print. Click OK when you have finished selecting forms.

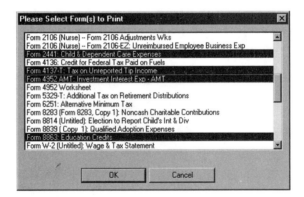

If you prepared detailed lists to accompany any of the amounts on your tax forms, and want to print the detailed lists with the tax forms, click the Form Plus Supporting Details option in the Printing window. When you have made your selections, click the Print button to print the forms you indicated.

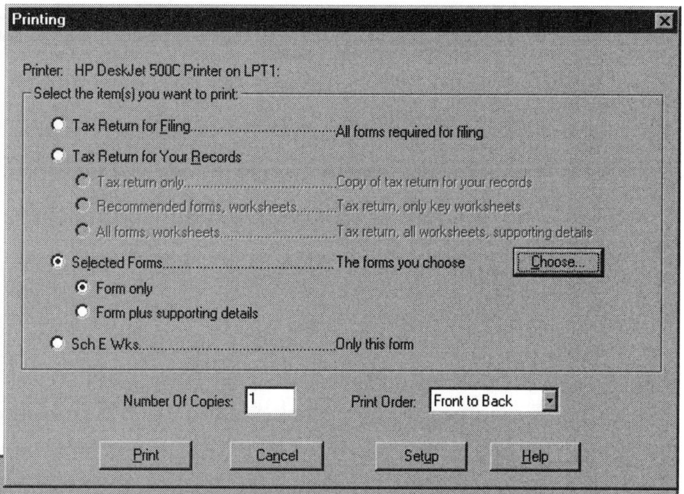

Figure 11-4 • Click the Choose button to indicate which forms you want to print.

Print the Form You're Working On

One other option exists in the Printing window. When you are working on a particular form, either in the TurboTax interview or on the actual forms screens, and you choose Print from the File menu, a fourth option appears, offering you the opportunity to quickly print the form on which you are working, and only that form.

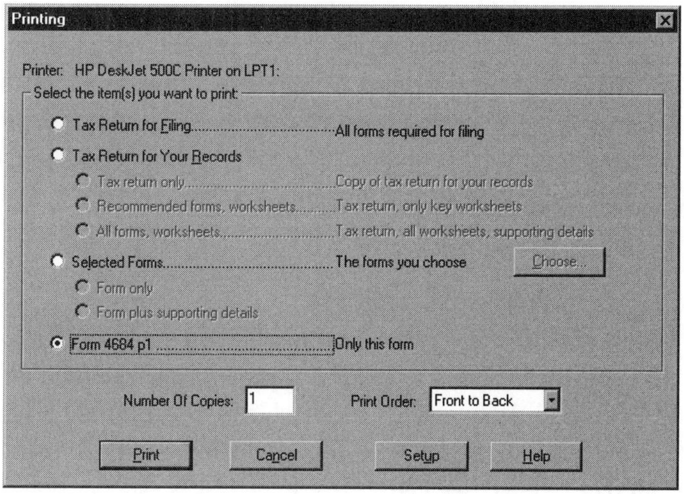

Filing Your Return Electronically

There are some significant advantages to filing a tax return electronically instead of using the traditional paper method:

- You can expect your refund several weeks earlier than if you file a paper return.
- You don't have to worry about getting your return to the post office on time.
- You don't have to be concerned that every required form is included with your return.
- You can count on your return being more accurate than a paper return. The IRS will not have to enter your numbers manually; instead, the numbers will automatically be uploaded to the IRS computer. Statistics show that electronically filed tax returns are 20 to 40 percent more accurate than manually filed returns.

If you choose to file electronically, by clicking the Continue With Electronic Filing option when TurboTax asks you how you want to file your return, and if you owe tax, TurboTax will ask you how you want to pay the tax due with your return:

- **Discover card.** You can use a Discover card to charge the tax due.
- **Direct debit.** You can enter information about your bank account so that the government can go right to your account to take the money you owe on your tax return.
- **Check.** You can write a check for the amount you owe and mail the check, even though you are filing the tax return electronically. If you choose this option, you will still have to pay Intuit for processing your electronically filed tax return before the return is sent. The next screen you see will ask you to indicate which type of credit card you want to use (you are not limited to the Discover card when paying Intuit) and then you will enter information about the card. After your return has been accepted by the IRS, which you will determine when you open your TurboTax program 24 to 48 hours after filing your return, you will be instructed to print a 1040-V voucher form that you can send to the IRS with your payment.

Sign Consent Form

In order to file your return electronically, you must "sign" a consent form that gives your consent for Intuit to send your tax return to the IRS. The consent also indicates that you realize that you are responsible for the information presented in the form. You don't have to sign a piece of paper; you can sign the consent online by giving your date of birth (see Figure 11-5).

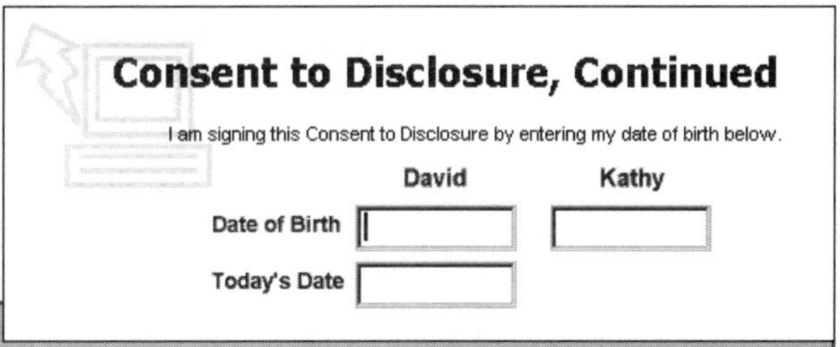

Consent to Disclosure, Continued

I am signing this Consent to Disclosure by entering my date of birth below.

	David	Kathy
Date of Birth		
Today's Date		

Figure 11-5 • You must provide your exact date of birth for the IRS to accept your consent of the terms of electronic filing.

From this point, TurboTax will take over and dispatch your tax return(s) to the IRS and, if you chose to file a state return electronically, the state government.

Checking on the Status of an Electronically Filed Return

Wait at least 24 and preferably 48 hours after electronically filing your tax return to check the status of the return. This will provide the IRS with enough time to begin processing your tax return. When you open your TurboTax program, after having electronically filed your return, the program should open to a screen where information is displayed about the status of your tax return.

You must be online to receive the tax return status report. If you don't see the status information, choose File | Electronic Filing | Check Electronic Filing Status from the menu and you will be taken to the proper screen. If the filing status does not appear, you can click the Get Status option to update your screen.

When your return has been accepted, TurboTax will give you instructions for printing some paperwork to keep for your records. If your return is rejected, you will receive information regarding the reason for the rejection. It is important that you check back soon after you file your return to see the status of the electronic filing. If your return has been rejected, you only have until April 21 to correct the problem and still have your return considered to be filed on time.

Electronic Tax Return Due Date

Your electronic tax return is due by midnight, April 16, just as with a paper return. The paper return must have a post office postmark in order to identify the time it was mailed. An electronic return receives an electronic postmark. Intuit is authorized to issue an electronic postmark as soon as it receives your tax return. You will receive a message from Intuit indicating that the company has received your return and the date and time when it was received. Print this information and save it, as this is your proof that the return was filed on time.

The electronic postmark is issued at approximately the same time as you file your tax return, but don't wait until the last minute! If you have a problem with your computer or your Internet service, you might miss that deadline.

Mailing Your Tax Return

The tax return must be postmarked by no later than midnight, April 16, 2001, unless one of the following exceptions is met:

- You filed a Form 4868 on or before April 16, 2001, indicating your desire for an extension of time to file the tax return, in which case your tax return must be postmarked by midnight August 15, 2001.
- Your state postal service is on holiday April 16, in which case your tax return must be postmarked by midnight April 17, 2001.

Don't Forget!

Here are a few tips for getting the right information into the mail on time:

- There is a right and wrong way to assemble your tax return! When you print your tax return in TurboTax, the forms come out in the order in which they are supposed to be assembled. The best way to keep your forms in order is to staple the tax return forms together right after they are printed, before the forms get mixed up. If it's too late for that, the trick to ordering the forms in your tax return is to look at the Attachment Sequence Number (see illustration below) that appears in the upper-right corner of your forms. Each form (other than the 1040, 1040A, or 1040EZ, which go on the top of your packet) has one of these numbers. This sequence number is the clue to the order in which you should assemble your tax forms.

- Don't forget to attach your W-2 forms. These get stapled to the front of the tax return. Also, if you had taxes withheld from a source other than jobs (such as retirement income reported on Form 1099-R), attach the other forms that show how much tax you had withheld.
- Sign and date the tax return at the bottom of page 2 of the 1040 or 1040A, and page 1 of the 1040EZ.

Where Does the Tax Return Get Mailed?

When you print your tax return, you will see a cover page of filing instructions. This page includes the address to which your tax return should be mailed. The IRS changed the addresses of its service centers this year, so you may be mailing your return to an address different from the one you have used in the past. To verify the mailing address, you can check the IRS addresses inside the back cover of this book.

Internet Resources to Help You File Your Taxes

This part of the book tells you about ways in which you can take advantage of the vast resources of the Internet, both to find out information about taxes and to actually prepare your income tax return. You get an introduction to some of the tax-related Web sites that are available as well as information about what you can expect if you choose to prepare your entire tax return online at the TurboTax Web site. This part includes the following chapters:

Chapter 12: *Exploring Tax Sites*

Chapter 13: *Using TurboTax for the Web*

Exploring Tax Sites

In This Chapter:

- *Using Intuit's TurboTax Web Site*

- *Using the IRS's Web Site*

- *Using Your State's Web Site*

- *Exploring Other Internet Tax Sites*

- *Assessing Internet Security*

Chapter 12

The Internet provides a vast collection of constantly changing information. You can find just about anything you need to know about taxes and tax preparation by scouring the Web.

Using the TurboTax Web Site

You can find your way to the TurboTax Web site by entering its URL, http://www.turbotax.com/, in the Address bar of your Web browser, as shown here:

Address 📄 http://www.turbotax.com	▼

Once there (shown in Figure 12-1), you'll find the following:

- Options for downloading the TurboTax federal and state tax return preparation programs
- Product updates (occasionally there will be an update to the TurboTax program during the tax season)
- Press releases where you can read the latest news regarding the TurboTax program
- Weekly tax tips that answer common questions about tax return preparation
- A tax estimator for estimating your tax liability before you actually prepare your tax return—a great tool for determining what your quarterly estimated payments should be
- An opportunity to actually prepare your tax return online (see Chapter 13 for more information about online filing)
- An option for obtaining online technical support for TurboTax and the state tax programs
- A link you can use to check on the status of the tax return you filed electronically

From the main TurboTax Web page, click Quicken Tax Center (see below) and you will find a wealth of tax-related information.

> **Quicken Tax Center**
> Great tips and quick answers to your tax questions.

**Purchase federal and
state tax preparation
programs.**

Get the latest update.

**Estimate your tax liability
before you prepare your
tax return.**

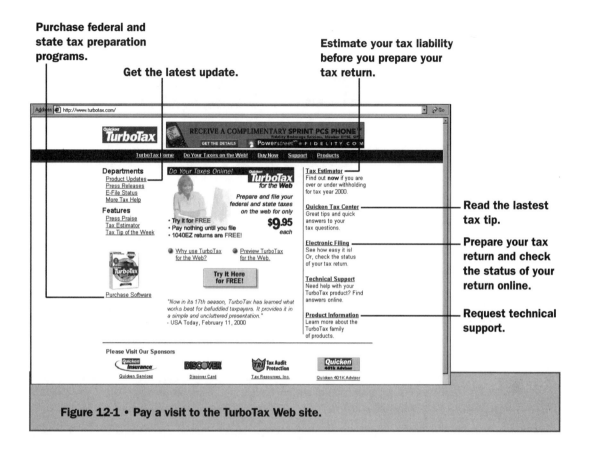

**Read the lastest
tax tip.**

**Prepare your tax
return and check
the status of your
return online.**

**Request technical
support.**

Figure 12-1 • Pay a visit to the TurboTax Web site.

The Quicken Tax Center (see Figure 12-2) includes such useful tools as:

- Tax calculators to help you determine the tax effects of major investment decisions
- A Roth IRA planner that will help you decide if a Roth IRA is for you
- Access to tax forms and IRS publications
- Tax rates on various types of income and limits on tax deductions and credits
- Message boards where you can post a question and read answers to hundreds of questions posted by others

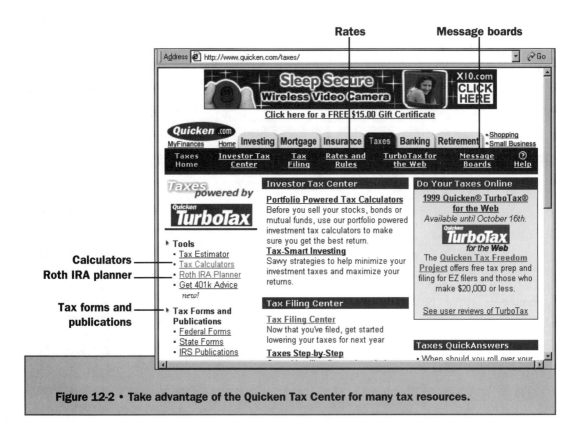

Figure 12-2 • Take advantage of the Quicken Tax Center for many tax resources.

Using the IRS's Web Site

You can find federal tax forms, tax publications, and the latest news from the IRS at http://www.irs.gov/ (see Figure 12-3). What's more, you'll be amazed to discover that someone at the IRS has a sense of humor!

Hyperlinks at the bottom of the IRS Web page provide access to tax statistics from previous years, tax forms and publications, news, information about electronic filing services, and information about how to contact the IRS.

For example, click the Tax Stats option at the bottom of any IRS page and then choose Number of Returns. From the reports that appear (summarized in Table 12-1), I learned that the number of annual income tax returns filed electronically in the United States has grown astronomically over the past decade.

Year	Number of Returns Filed Electronically
1990	4,193,242
1991	7,515,861
1992	10,923,895
1993	12,341,683
1994	13,509,688
1995	11,142,582
1996	14,977,123
1997	19,152,498
1998	24,599,870

Table 12-1 • Number of U.S. Federal Income Tax Returns Filed Electronically 1990 to 1998

Figure 12-3 • The IRS combines humor with information at its Web site.

I also discovered, by clicking the Tax Stats option at the bottom of any IRS page and then choosing Refunds, that the number of refunds issued for federal individual income tax returns hardly changed at all for the period 1995 to 1998 (see Table 12-2). Over two-thirds of the nation's taxpayers overpay their tax and receive a refund after filing their tax return.

Year	Number of Refunds Issued
1995	88,736,980
1996	85,468,010
1997	88,095,262
1998	87,703,895

Table 12-2 • Number of Refunds Issued for U.S. Federal Income Tax Returns 1995 to 1998

Checking on the Latest Changes to Tax Rules

Click the What's Hot option at the bottom of the IRS Web page to gain access to news about recent changes in the tax rules that may affect you.

Also, click IRS Newsstand for links to press releases and news about a variety of tax-related topics, including modernization of the IRS, news from IRS offices around the nation, and goals of the IRS.

Get a Head Start on Next Year's Taxes

You can start planning early for 2001 taxes. The IRS will make the 2001 tax return forms available on its Web site as soon as the forms have been approved, probably in the fall of 2001. Click the Forms & Pubs option at the bottom of the IRS Web page, then click Forms and Instructions. A list of all available tax forms (including next year's forms, when they are ready) appears.

To download a tax form that you can examine and print, click the form name, then click Review Selected Files. When the link to the form you selected appears, click the link and the form will be downloaded to your computer via Adobe Acrobat Reader, a software program that you will be prompted to acquire (for free) if it isn't already on your computer.

Using Your State's Web Site

Each state has a Web site and includes links to information about taxes and tax forms for that state. Some states permit tax returns to be filed electronically right from the Web site; others do not offer this service.

Many sites on the Internet provide tax-related links to all the states. Here's one site that lists each state: http://www.funwithtaxes.com/State_Tax_Forms.htm (shown in Figure 12-4). Click a state name and you will get a link to the state's home page as well as a link to direct information about taxes for that state.

Most of these state Web pages provide information about filing due dates, tax news, electronic filing options, and tax forms. In addition to information about income tax, you can also find information about property, payroll, and sales taxes for your state. Mail addresses, telephone numbers, and email information are also generally available on the state Web sites.

Other Internet Sites Relating to Taxes

The Internet is full of fascinating places to go for information about income taxes. Some sites are full of useful tax information; other tax sites are gateways that provide links to other sites containing resources, rather than providing resources themselves. Here is a sampling of some of the tax sites that are available for research, news, forms, chat, commentary, training, tax professionals, regulatory agencies, tax law, and tax books and other publications:

Internet Law Library/Federal Register (http://www.priweb.com/internetlawlib/ 7.htm)   The Internet Law Library, shown in Figure 12-5, is the place to go for heavy reading—a search for "tax" will provide you with links to federal tax regulations and regulations for all the states.

Ryan SALT Gateway (http://www.ryanco.com/salt.html)   SALT stands for State And Local Tax. Use the Ryan SALT Gateway, shown in Figure 12-6, as a jumping off point for links to all the states where you can find information about state and local taxes.

Tax and Accounting Sites Directory (http://www.taxsites.com/state.html) You can use the Tax and Accounting Sites Directory, shown in Figure 12-7, to find links to state and federal taxing authorities, tax news, accounting firms and organizations, and tax rates.

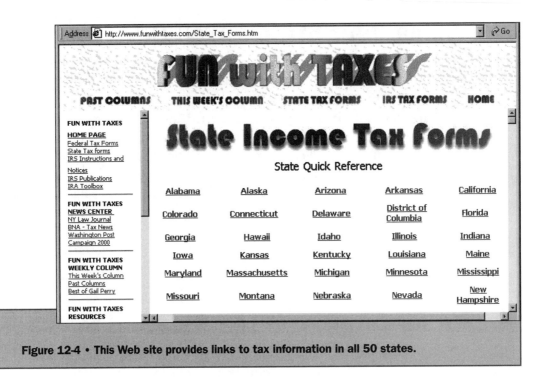

Figure 12-4 • This Web site provides links to tax information in all 50 states.

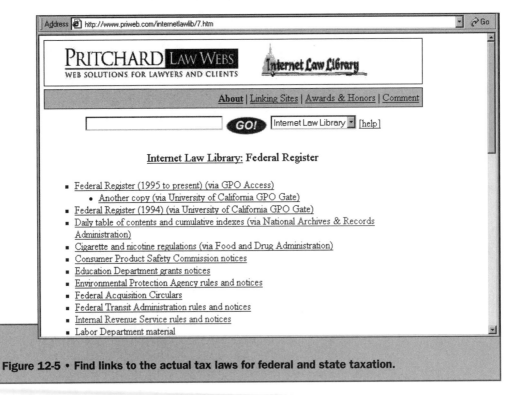

Figure 12-5 • Find links to the actual tax laws for federal and state taxation.

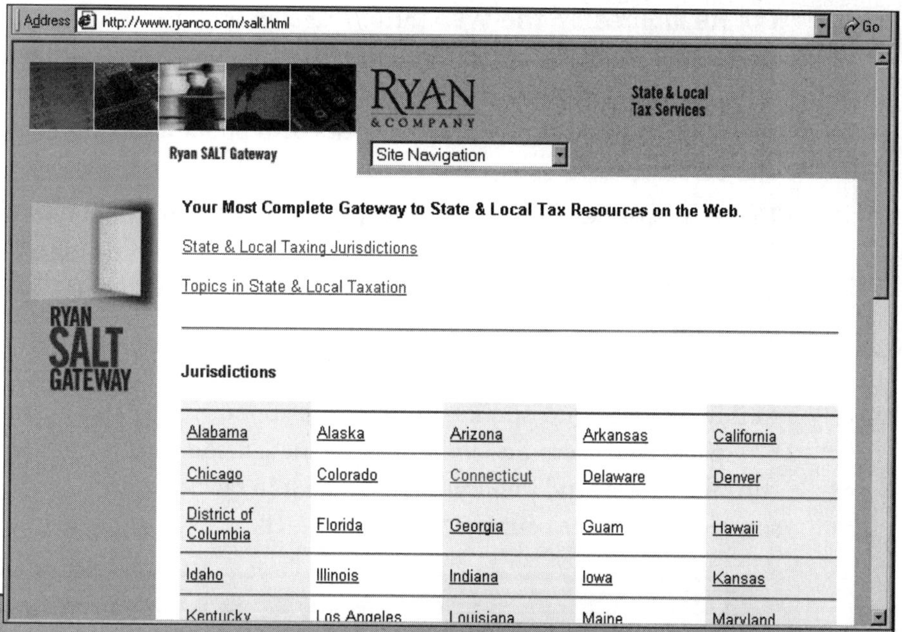

Figure 12-6 • The place to go for information about state and local taxes across the country.

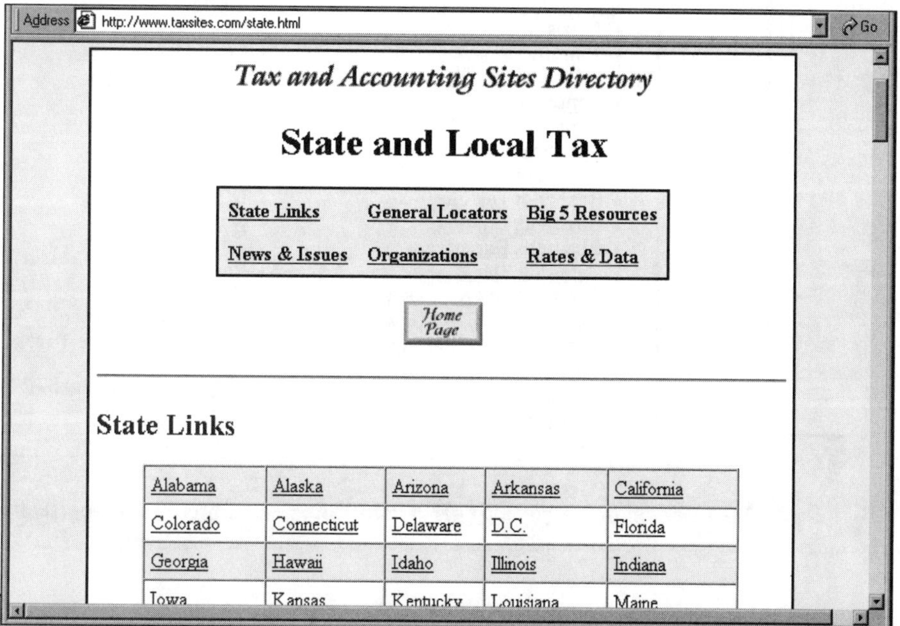

Figure 12-7 • Use this site as a source for tax news, and accounting firms and organizations.

Tax Resources on the Web (http://pages.prodigy.net/agkalman/)   If you have a question about taxes and want to search by tax topic, the Tax Resources on the Web site shown in Figure 12-8 provides a topical list, arranged alphabetically. Click on a topic and see a list of links to articles, IRS publications, and other Internet tax sites on the chosen topic.

The Tax Prophet (http://www.taxprophet.com/)   In addition to state and federal tax resources, you can read the proprietor's bimonthly tax Q&A column that appears in the *San Francisco Examiner* newspaper at Figure 12-9.

Fun with Taxes (http://www.funwithtaxes.com/)   In addition to state and federal tax resources, you can read the proprietor's (also known as this author) weekly tax Q&A and opinion column that appears in the *Indianapolis Star* newspaper. You'll also find links to all the state income tax forms and instructions, federal tax forms and publications, the latest in tax news, and links to CPA societies around the country. See Figure 12-10.

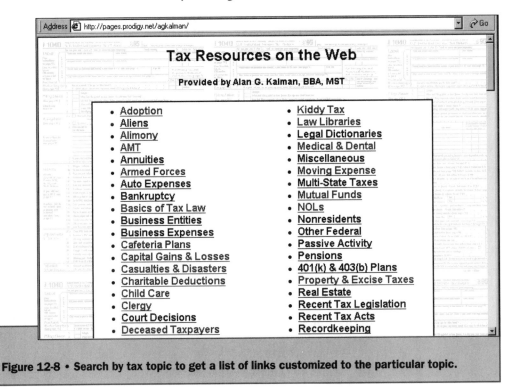

Figure 12-8 • Search by tax topic to get a list of links customized to the particular topic.

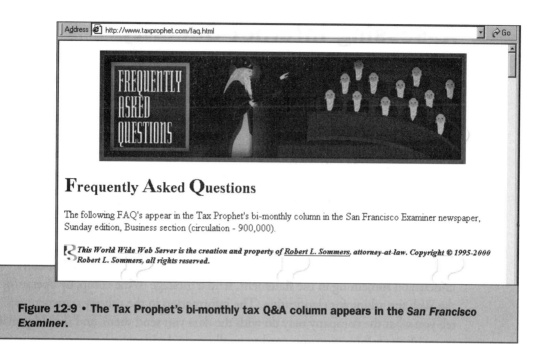

Figure 12-9 • The Tax Prophet's bi-monthly tax Q&A column appears in the *San Francisco Examiner*.

Figure 12-10 • Can't get enough of my take on taxes in this book? Check out my Web site and read my weekly newspaper columns that appear in the *Indianapolis Star*.

Using TurboTax for the Web

In This Chapter:

- *Information to Gather Before You Begin*

- *What to Expect from Your e-Experience*

- *Filling in the Blanks*

- *Printing Your Return for Your Records*

- *Filing the Return*

- *Checking Your Status*

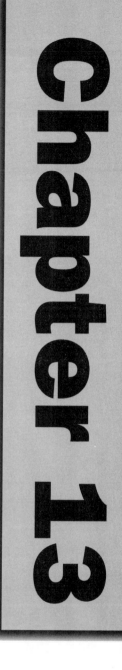

Chapter 13

Preparing and filing your tax return with TurboTax for the Web takes tax preparation to the next higher level. Now, not only can you use your personal computer to prepare your tax return with speed and accuracy unheard of for handwritten returns, but you can go right to the TurboTax Web site on the Internet, bypass purchasing the TurboTax software program, and prepare your tax return online.

The TurboTax for the Web program works much like the traditional TurboTax program in that you respond to questions posed in an interview format. However, instead of working from a software program that resides on your computer, you are using a program that resides on the Internet. The process of preparing your tax return online has many advantages over the traditional format. These advantages are described later in this chapter in the section entitled "Advantages to Using TurboTax for the Web."

Information to Gather Before You Begin

The experience of preparing your tax return using the TurboTax for the Web program is similar to the experience of preparing your tax return using the traditional TurboTax program.

Table 13-1 is a checklist you can use to make sure you have all your documents in order. You should gather as many of these documents as possible prior to beginning to use the online TurboTax for the Web program.

What to Expect from Your e-Experience

TurboTax for the Web offers taxpayers the opportunity to prepare and file their tax returns easily and quickly, without having to download or install any software. The experience of preparing your tax return on the Web is similar to preparing your tax return off the Web. You will proceed through the EasyStep Interview process, answering questions and filling in blanks. You can stop or go back to different parts of your tax return at any time, knowing that TurboTax is providing you not only with impeccable accuracy in calculations, but an advanced level of security to ensure your confidence in submitting confidential information via a Web site.

✓	Tax Preparation Checklist
❏	W-2 forms (reporting income from your jobs)
❏	1099 forms (reporting income from interest, dividends, rents, retirement, and miscellaneous sources)
❏	Year-end mutual fund statements
❏	Year-end bank statements
❏	Income and expense records from your own business
❏	Log of auto mileage
❏	Statements from brokers
❏	K-1 forms (showing your participation in partnerships, trusts, and small business corporations)
❏	Income and expenses from rental properties you own
❏	Prize winnings and gambling transactions
❏	Statements from employers regarding fringe benefits you received
❏	Medical expenses
❏	Real estate tax statements
❏	Vehicle registration form (if you live in a state that charges property tax for registering your vehicle)
❏	Record of contributions
❏	Unreimbursed expenses relating to your job
❏	Child or dependent care costs when both parents work
❏	Name and federal ID number for dependent care providers
❏	Exact birth date of person for whom the return is to be filed (remember to get this information if you are filing a return for a relative or someone else—the IRS compares the birth date to the Social Security number to verify that the return is being filed for the correct person)

Table 13-1 • Checklist of Items to Organize Your Online Tax Preparation

TurboTax for the Web and Security

Intuit, the company that makes TurboTax, uses state-of-the-art 128-bit SSL encryption to secure transmission of tax data. Once a user files a tax return at the TurboTax Electronic Filing Center online, Intuit sends all tax returns directly to IRS computers. There is no third-party transfer involved in data transmission.

Advantages to Using TurboTax for the Web

There are several points to recommend about the TurboTax for the Web tax return preparation and filing experience:

- You can prepare your tax return and check on its status after it has been filed, from any computer that has Internet access, anywhere, at any time.
- There is no need to go to a store to purchase the TurboTax program, nor is there any need to download or install the program. You aren't required to use space on your hard drive for the TurboTax program.
- Refunds arrive more quickly when you file electronically—estimates are that a refund may be received within ten days of filing using TurboTax for the Web.
- If you owe money, you can still file your tax return at the TurboTax Web site and use your Discover card to pay the tax.
- Satisfaction is guaranteed or you will get your money back.
- When you file electronically, you receive an acknowledgement that the IRS has received your tax return.
- Electronically filed tax returns are date and time stamped when they are filed, meaning you have proof of the date and time the return was filed—no more relying on postmarks that only the IRS can see.
- Taxpayers who file electronically will receive a personal identification number (PIN)—automatically from the IRS in some cases, in other cases you will have to apply for the PIN at the TurboTax Web site, and submit information from their 1999 tax return as proof of their identity. This PIN serves as an electronic signature, thus eliminating the need for taxpayers to sign and mail a form along with their electronically filed tax return.
- No more need to prepare and mail a paper tax return.
- A quick cash loan based on your refund is available from the TurboTax Web site, with loan fees to be deducted from the refund when it arrives.

Filling in the Blanks

Preparing your tax return using TurboTax for the Web is fast, easy, and accurate. To access TurboTax for the Web, log on to the Internet and go to http://www. turbotax.com/. There you will see a link to do your taxes online using TurboTax for the Web.

When you decide to begin preparing your tax return at the TurboTax Web site, you will find that, although there is a nominal fee (the amount is to be announced in January 2001) for electronically filing or printing your return, there is no fee for simply experimenting with the TurboTax for the Web program and entering tax information. You are not billed until you determine that your tax return is in final form and you are ready to electronically file or print your return.

> **Note**   *There is no fee for filing a tax return if your adjusted gross income is $20,000 or less, no matter which tax forms you file. This free filing is offered as part of the Quicken Tax Freedom Project, which was enacted in 1998 to benefit lower income individuals and families. In 1999, more than 764,000 federal tax returns and more than 375,000 state tax returns were prepared and filed at no charge through this philanthropic project.*

Prepare Your State Tax Return

You can also prepare your state tax return using TurboTax for the Web. This program covers all states that impose an income tax. If your state supports electronic filing (at the time this book went to press, 38 states allowed electronic filing), you can file your state return right from the TurboTax Web site. If you cannot file electronically in your state, you can print your state tax return and mail it to the proper authorities.

Print a Test Copy of Your Tax Return

Whether you decide to actually file your tax return electronically or mail the return yourself, you can print copies of your return from the TurboTax Web site. Print at any time to examine a paper copy of your return—you don't have to wait until you have completed the return to print it.

Follow the Interview

Enter information in the TurboTax for the Web program by answering questions and filling in the blanks provided by the TurboTax EasyStep Interview, a descriptive onscreen process that leads you through the tax return preparation, step by step.

You can stop your preparation at any time and resume at a later time—you are not required to prepare the entire tax return in one sitting. Your data will be password protected so that only you can access the information and it will be there for you when you return to the TurboTax Web site.

Use the Automated Tax Return Process

New to TurboTax for the 2000 tax year is the Automated Tax Return system. This feature (described in Chapter 5) enables taxpayers to automatically transfer information from W-2 and 1099 forms directly into the tax return. Your W-2 and 1099 forms will state that this feature is available if the company preparing the forms is a participating company.

If you choose to use this feature, your preparation time will be slashed even more. When asked to enter W-2 and 1099 information in your TurboTax for the Web program, you will be given an option to indicate that you have qualifying tax records for the Automated Tax Return system. Then you can select the name of the company that prepared your W-2 or 1099 (this information is printed on the form), and TurboTax will transfer your tax information for that form—you won't have to enter anything!

The Automated Tax Return process simplifies the most common task relating to tax return preparation: entering information from your W-2 and 1099 forms. Data entry time is saved and accuracy is ensured. Military-grade encryption security is provided so you don't have to worry about your personal financial data getting into the wrong hands.

If you use Quicken or QuickBooks to keep track of your financial records, you will be given the opportunity to directly import information from these programs to your tax return. For the process to work, you must have entered tax line information for all the income and expense categories in Quicken or QuickBooks from which you want to transfer information to your tax return. More information about this coding is provided in Chapter 4.

Printing Your Tax Return for Your Records

At any time during the preparation process, you can print a copy of the tax return you are preparing. Whether or not you print the return during preparation is your choice. Once you have finalized the tax return you should definitely print your return. The tax return information you enter *will not* be available indefinitely on the TurboTax Web site.

After October 15, 2001, the last day for filing 2000 tax returns with extended due dates, the information you entered for your 2000 tax return will no longer be accessible to you at the TurboTax Web site. After this date, TurboTax recommends that you contact the IRS at (800) 829-1040 to request a printed copy of your tax return.

Filing the Return

After you have entered all of your information in TurboTax for the Web, filing your return is a matter of clicking on an option to file your return, entering billing information so that you will be charged for the tax preparation fee, and confirming that you are ready to file the return. You will be given an opportunity to print your tax return (both federal and state). It is recommended that you do this so you will have your own copy of the return.

TurboTax will dispatch the return to the IRS and, if you prepared a state tax return, to the proper state taxing authority. The IRS and state tax agencies communicate directly with TurboTax as soon as their computers have received your return and verified that the return is eligible for processing. The IRS will compare the birth date you entered to the Social Security number to verify that it is recording information for the correct person. If the birth date is not entered or does not agree with the birth date on file for the Social Security number you entered, the tax return will be rejected until you supply the correct information. If any other required information is not entered, the tax return will be rejected and you will be informed of the information that is necessary before the return can be processed.

Checking Your Status

Return to the TurboTax Web site at any time after your return has been filed (it is recommended that you wait at least 24 hours) and you will receive verification that the return has been accepted by the IRS and, if applicable, the state government where you are filing.

You should check on the status of your return within 48 hours of filing to make sure that the return wasn't rejected. If rejected, the IRS or state revenue agency will provide a reason for the rejection, such as an incorrect birth date. You can enter the correct information right at the TurboTax Web site and the tax return will be dispatched once again.

Dealing with the IRS

This part of the book addresses the various situations, besides filing your tax return, when you may have to communicate with the IRS. Sometimes you will want to contact the IRS yourself, other times you may be responding to a communication from them. This part includes the following chapters:

Chapter 14: Waiting for Your Refund

Chapter 15: Paying Tax to the Government

Chapter 16: Amending Your Tax Return

Chapter 17: Communicating with the IRS

Waiting for
Your Refund

In This Chapter:

- *Waiting for Your Return to Be Processed*

- *Checking on Your Refund*

- *Checking on an Electronic Refund*

- *Getting a Refund for the Wrong Amount*

- *Making Money on Your Refund*

- *Dealing with Refunds That Don't Come at All*

One aspect of filing a tax return that makes the process tolerable is the opportunity to receive a refund. Approximately two thirds of all tax return filers receive a refund each year. Even though getting a refund technically means you paid too much in tax during the year, somehow the prospect of receiving a check in the mail or a deposit in your bank account is much more appealing than the thought of having to write a check to the IRS on the 15th of April.

How Long Should You Wait?

Wouldn't it be nice if you could receive your refund the same day you put your tax return in the mail? After all, the IRS expects you to send in your payment along with the tax return if you owe money. But sometimes it seems as if the IRS is taking an extraordinary length of time to send home those refunds.

A delay in receiving your refund is not difficult to understand. The IRS has approximately 126 million tax returns to process each spring, and most of those returns arrive in the weeks closest to April 15. Open the envelopes, examine the returns to make sure all the proper forms are attached, perform a quick math check, request that the check or deposit be prepared—all of this takes time, and multiply that time by millions.

Tip   *When using the direct deposit feature to have your refund dispatched directly to your bank account, keep in mind that you must take the responsibility of checking in with the bank from time to time to find out exactly when the deposit has arrived. Direct deposit gets your refund working for you (earning interest or being available to pay bills) more quickly—by three to ten days over traditional mail.*

The IRS actually works pretty quickly, all things considered, and the process is sped up considerably if you file your return electronically. With electronic returns, a computer takes care of much of the work that was formerly performed by hand, and the tax refund is processed much more quickly. On the average, you will receive your refund about ten days after you file electronically. Compare this to the following information.

It is estimated that the typical tax refund for a tax return prepared on paper and mailed to the IRS, assuming there are no obvious problems associated with the tax return, will take approximately six weeks to process. The amount of time increases somewhat if the return is mailed near the April 15 deadline. A taxpayer who mails a tax return in January or February could well see a tax refund in fewer than six weeks.

Checking on Your Refund

You don't have to wait forever, and if you're getting impatient you can contact the IRS to find out if there is a problem with processing your refund payment. The IRS suggests that you wait at least four weeks (three weeks if you file electronically) and preferably six weeks before you start searching for your refund.

Tip   *If you filed your tax return electronically, the processing time is shorter and you can begin searching for news of your refund after three weeks have passed.*

You should have a copy of your tax return with you when you call the IRS, and you will be asked for the following information:

- Your Social Security number
- Your filing status
- The exact whole-dollar amount of the refund you anticipate receiving

To check on your refund, call the IRS's TeleTax service at (800) 829-4477. The TeleTax service is completely automated, and you can call from any touch-tone phone to access this service. Because this is recorded information, you can call 24 hours a day, 7 days a week.

The IRS TeleTax service will provide you with the most current information available regarding the status of your tax refund, including the date on which the refund was or is expected to be issued. If information is not yet available when you make your call, be a bit patient—the recorded telephone information for refunds is only updated every seven days, so there's no need to call every day for new information.

Checking on an Electronic Refund

The electronically filed tax returns speed up the process of tax return processing enormously. You can check to see if your tax return has been received and accepted by the IRS after only one or two days, and refund status will be available within three weeks.

Refund Status If You Used the TurboTax Program

If you filed your tax return electronically using TurboTax, you can check the status of your refund right in your TurboTax program. You are advised to wait at least 24 and preferably 48 hours before checking on the refund of an e-filed tax return.

When you are ready to check your tax e-refund status, there are two ways in which you can proceed in TurboTax:

- Open your TurboTax program. If you used the Interview method of preparing your tax return, you will automatically be asked if you would like to check the status of your tax return. Answer Yes and TurboTax will proceed to access and present the information for you.
- If you are not automatically asked if you want to check the status, click the File menu and choose Electronic Filing | Check Electronic Filing Status (shown below). A window will appear giving you the options to get the status onscreen or print the status.

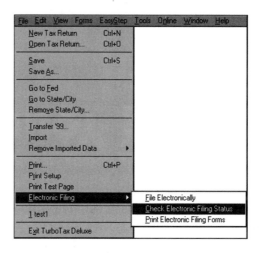

Refund Status If You e-Filed at the TurboTax Web Site

If you filed your tax return completely on the Internet, go to the TurboTax Web site at http://www.turbotax.com/, and follow the onscreen instructions to determine if your electronically filed tax return was accepted or rejected by the IRS. It is recommended that you wait 24 to 48 hours before performing this status check.

Once your tax return has been accepted, you can call the IRS's electronic TeleTax service, as described previously in this chapter, to verify the status of your refund.

when the refund payment is issued. If the payment is made within this 45-day time frame, there is no interest paid to the taxpayer. You could file your tax return in February and receive your tax refund in May and there would be no interest owing to you because the payment was made within 45 days of the due date of the tax return.

If the IRS misses the 45-day deadline and still hasn't issued a refund payment, the refund you eventually receive will include interest calculated from the due date of the tax return or the date on which you filed, whichever is later. If 45 days passes before you receive your refund and the refund you eventually receive does not include interest, contact the IRS at (800) 829-1040 for information about why the interest was not included.

Choosing to Let the IRS Keep Your Refund

When you prepare your tax return, you have the option of applying your tax overpayment to the tax for the following year. If you anticipate owing more tax than you will have withheld next year, or if you normally make estimated payments and want to use your 2000 overpayment as part of your 2001 estimated payments, you can request right on your tax return that the IRS hold this money.

There is a drawback, however, to leaving your tax money with the IRS. The money is safe—no problem there—but the money will spend the next year at the IRS and you will not receive any interest on the money.

Caution   *Be aware of the fact that once you decide to leave your money with the IRS, there it will stay. If you indicate on your tax return that you want your tax overpayment to be applied to next year's taxes, you cannot, at a later date, change your mind and get your money back from the IRS.*

Saving Your Refund for a Rainy Day

It's best to cash or deposit your tax refund check soon after you receive it. If you let too much time pass before you cash or deposit the check you receive from the IRS, you may lose the money altogether. A check issued by the IRS for a tax refund is good for twelve months. If the check is older than twelve months, it no longer holds any value.

All is not lost, however. Should this happen to you, you can contact the IRS and request that they issue a new check to replace the one that expired.

e-Refund Status by Telephon

Doesn't it sound so very *last century* to use a telepl
your electronically filed tax return? If you don't ha
program or if you aren't near a computer with Int
status of your electronically filed tax return by call
Information Center at (520) 901-3236.

This automated electronic filing status informat
a day.

Refund for the Wrong A

It's possible that the IRS will make a mistake when y
receive a refund check that is for more than the amo
advised by the IRS to not deposit the check, but to c
resolve the discrepancy. You can reach the IRS at (80
representative who will assist you.

If you receive a refund check for less than you expec
with the refund describing the discrepancy. Generally n
same envelope as the check, but sometimes the two are
recommends that, if you receive no notice with your ch
two weeks before contacting the IRS about the discrepai
mailed separately from the check will arrive within a few

If you receive a refund check for less than the amou
up your right to contest the amount you received by d
check. You can hold the check until the matter is resolv
choose to deposit the check while still preserving your
discrepancies with the IRS.

Interest Earned on Late R

The IRS does not pay interest on the tax money that it h
will, however, pay interest on refunds that are paid late, i
problems with your tax return.

The IRS gives itself 45 days from the due date of your
date on which you file your tax return (if you file after th

Refunds That Never Come

In recent years, the IRS has instituted a plan by which your refund may be redirected to cover certain outstanding payments you might owe. The types of past due payments covered by this program include:

- Past due federal income tax
- Other federal debts such as student loans
- Unpaid state income tax
- Child and spousal support payments

If your tax refund has been redirected to pay one or more of these amounts, you will receive a notice from the IRS describing what has been done.

If you file a joint tax return and only one spouse owes one of the previously described amounts, the other spouse can be considered an *injured spouse* and as such will not be considered liable for the past due payment. In a situation like this, the injured spouse may still be entitled to receive half of the tax refund while the other half is redirected to the outstanding payment.

For the injured spouse rule to apply, the following circumstances must occur:

- The spouses must have filed a joint tax return.
- There must have been income reported on the tax return.
- There must have been tax payments reported on the tax return or a refundable earned income credit.
- There must be a refund owing on the tax return.

If the injured spouse status applies to you, you need to attach a completed Form 8379, Injured Spouse Claim and Allocation, to your tax return. In the upper-left corner of page 1 of your tax return, write the words, "Injured Spouse." On the injured spouse form, you will list the income and deduction amounts from your tax return, then show which amounts apply to you and which to your spouse. The IRS will then take past due payments only from the other spouse's share of the federal income tax.

Note *Filing the injured spouse form may cause some delay in your tax return processing. The IRS indicates that your refund may be delayed for six to eight weeks due to the extra attention that must be given the return.*

Paying Tax to the Government

In This Chapter:

- *Paying Tax with Your Tax Return*

- *Options for Withholding Tax*

- *Calculating and Paying Quarterly Estimated Payments*

- *Installment Agreements with the IRS*

- *Making an Offer in Compromise*

Chapter 15

It may not be one of your most enjoyable tasks in life, but paying taxes is certainly an inevitable task. One way or another, you need to find a way to get a share of your earnings to the government. Alternatives for tax payment include having the tax withheld from your wages, making quarterly estimated payments, making a payment with your tax return, or making arrangements with the IRS to pay your taxes after your tax return has been filed. Whatever arrangement you make, keep in mind the fact that technically, taxes are due as you earn your money, and you should expect to make payments of your taxes, one way or another, throughout the year.

Tax Due with Your Tax Return

When you prepare and file your income tax return, you may feel lucky if you are owed a refund. But the tax return doesn't always provide good news. Sometimes you will owe additional tax with your tax return. In fact, one in three taxpayers owes money with the tax return.

If additional income tax is owed with your income tax return, this situation is typically a result of your not having enough taxes withheld from your job income during the year, or not having made sufficient quarterly estimated tax payments to cover the amount of tax you owe.

A number of situations can contribute to there being additional tax owing on your tax return, including:

- You earned more income in 2000 than in 1999.
- You received some income, such as dividends or interest, which was not subject to withholding.
- Your tax situation changed—for example, you lost an exemption or changed your filing status.
- Your higher income resulted in a phase-out of anticipated exemptions or deductions.
- You own your own business and didn't anticipate having to pay the self-employment tax.

Your Income Increased in 2000

It is a common occurrence in our present economy to have one's income increase from one year to the next. In fact, the opportunity to watch your income rise is typically viewed as a positive event. The negative side of increasing your income is that typically taxes increase simultaneously. A sharp rise in income, particularly a rise that occurs outside the job place, as in a surge in the performance of your investments or an unexpectedly profitable day at the track, can cause an unanticipated increase in income tax that can surprise you in April.

Tip *If you find that you owe additional tax when you prepare your income tax return, the first thing you should do is attempt to determine why your tax withholdings or estimated payments were not sufficient to meet your tax obligation. If the increase in income is expected to continue, you can adjust your ongoing tax payments for the rest of the year so that you don't find yourself with a tax debt on next year's tax return.*

Some of Your Income Is Not Subject to Withholding

One of the most frequent reasons why people owe additional tax with their income tax return is that they have earnings outside the workplace that are not subject to income tax withholding. Earnings of this nature can come from sources such as these:

- Investments that generate dividends or interest
- The sale of capital assets such as stocks or a piece of investment property
- A bonus or cash award that is not subject to withholding
- Money earned at odd jobs

Any income you receive that is taxable should be considered when planning your withholding or estimated payments. The sections in this chapter on withholding options and estimated payments will provide some guidance on how to incorporate the tax on your additional income into your year-round tax planning.

Your Tax Situation Has Changed Since Last Year

A common cause for an unexpected increase in tax is that your actual tax situation may have changed. As your children grow, you are no longer eligible to claim them as exemptions and you see a slight rise in tax as a result of this. If you change your filing status from single to married, or from married to head of household, you may also see an increase in your tax.

Other changing situations that can cause a noticeable change in your income tax include the following:

- You are no longer paying mortgage payments and thus lose the mortgage interest deduction.
- You begin renting your home and no longer pay property tax.
- Your medical expenses decrease, perhaps in conjunction with a child no longer needing orthodontics, or perhaps you take a job with a health plan that covers costs you previously paid yourself.
- Your child, who is still your dependent, no longer qualifies you for the child tax credit or the child and dependent care credit.
- You begin withdrawing money from a taxable retirement plan or annuity.

As you can see, there are many life-changing situations that can result in a change in your tax liability. If any of the above situations occur during the year, you should attempt to calculate the change that will occur in your tax so you can be sure the amount of withholding or estimated payments you make is sufficient.

Your Income Is Too High for Certain Tax Benefits

When your income reaches certain levels, some of the tax benefits available to many taxpayers are no longer available to you. Table 15-1 illustrates some situations where the amount of adjusted gross income you report will reduce or eliminate your ability to claim some deductions and adjustments.

Type of Reduction	Married Filing Separately	Single	Head of Household	Married Filing Jointly	Qualifying Widow(er)
Personal exemptions	$96,700	$128,950	$161,150	$193,400	$193,400
Itemized deductions	$64,475	$128,950	$128,950	$128,950	$128,950
Student loan interest	$40,000	$40,000	$40,000	$60,000	$40,000
IRA contributions	$0	$32,000	$32,000	$52,000	$52,000
Child tax credit	$55,000	$75,000	$75,000	$110,000	$75,000
Education credits	$40,000	$40,000	$40,000	$80,000	$40,000

Table 15-1 • Income Level at Which Certain Tax Benefits Begin to Be Phased Out, Based on Filing Status

You Own Your Own Business

One of the biggest surprises to affect taxpayers who own their own businesses is the self-employment tax. Adding a hefty 15.3 percent tax on your net business income to the rest of the tax you compute on your tax return can turn even the staunchest entrepreneur into an hourly wage-earner.

If you are liable for self-employment tax, you are required to pay this tax throughout the year by increasing your estimated tax payments accordingly, just as you pay your income tax. The first year you are in business, this tax will no doubt come as a shock. Once you get in the groove, you may not like it, but you will get used to paying this tax for your share of Social Security and Medicare.

Options for Withholding Tax

Now that you've learned many of the ways in which your tax can be increased, you need to consider the ways in which you can pay the tax. The worst method is to not make any payments during the year but wait until you file your tax return on April 15 and pay the full amount at that time.

Besides being a shock to your bank account, paying the tax all at once when you file your return is strongly discouraged by the IRS, and you will find yourself assessed with interest and penalties to make up for the fact that you waited so long to pay your tax.

As an alternative to waiting until the end of the year to pay your taxes, you can work with your employer to ensure that your withholding meets your fiscal needs. The next section explains how this can be accomplished.

Claim More Withholding Allowances

When you take a new job, you prepare a W-4 form for your employer. This form provides your employer with the information needed to withhold a proper amount of tax from your pay. It is up to you, however, to determine how many withholding allowances you will claim, which in turn tells the employer how much tax to withhold.

On the W-4 form, you indicate how many withholding allowances you want to claim for your family. Typically, people claim one allowance for themselves, one for their spouse, and one each for the children in the family who are reported on the tax return as dependents. If you like, you can claim more allowances than just one for each member of your family. *The more allowances you claim on Form W-4, the less tax will be withheld.*

If you typically receive a large refund and wish to reduce your withholding, so that you will have access to more of your own money during the year, it makes sense to file a new W-4 form with your employer and increase the number of allowances.

Besides claiming an allowance for each member of your family, the W-4 form, as shown in Figure 15-1, provides options for claiming additional allowances for these reasons:

- You are single.
- You are married and your spouse does not work.
- Your annual wages from a second job (or your spouse's wages) are $1,000 or less.
- You use the Head of Household filing status.
- You plan to claim a credit for child or dependent care.
- You plan to claim the child tax credit.
- You plan to itemize deductions.

Remember that each allowance you claim means you will take home more pay on your paycheck, but you will reduce the amount of tax going to the IRS during the year. If you adjust your W-4 form to claim more allowances, you may want to estimate your tax during the year to make sure your withholding will be sufficient.

Personal Allowances Worksheet (Keep for your records.)

A   Enter "1" for **yourself** if no one else can claim you as a dependent . . . .   A _____

B   Enter "1" if: • You are single and have only one job; or
                   • You are married, have only one job, and your spouse does not work; or
                   • Your wages from a second job or your spouse's wages (or the total of both) are $1,000 or less.   B _____

C   Enter "1" for your **spouse**. But, you may choose to enter -0- if you are married and have either a working spouse or more than one job. (Entering -0- may help you avoid having too little tax withheld.) . . . .   C _____

D   Enter number of **dependents** (other than your spouse or yourself) you will claim on your tax return . . . .   D _____

E   Enter "1" if you will file as **head of household** on your tax return (see conditions under **Head of household** above) .   E _____

F   Enter "1" if you have at least $1,500 of **child or dependent care expenses** for which you plan to claim a credit . .   F _____

G   **Child Tax Credit:**
    • If your total income will be between $18,000 and $50,000 ($23,000 and $63,000 if married), enter "1" for each eligible child.
    • If your total income will be between $50,000 and $80,000 ($63,000 and $115,000 if married), enter "1" if you have two eligible children, enter "2" if you have three or four eligible children, or enter "3" if you have five or more eligible children   G _____

H   Add lines A through G and enter total here. **Note:** *This may be different from the number of exemptions you claim on your tax return.* ➔ H _____

For accuracy, complete all worksheets that apply.
    • If you plan to **itemize** or claim adjustments to income and want to reduce your withholding, see the **Deductions and Adjustments Worksheet** on page 2.
    • If you are **single**, have more than one job and your combined earnings from all jobs exceed $34,000, OR if you are **married** and have a **working spouse** or **more than one job** and the combined earnings from all jobs exceed $60,000, see the **Two-Earner/Two-Job Worksheet** on page 2 to avoid having too little tax withheld.
    • If **neither** of the above situations applies, **stop here** and enter the number from line H on line 5 of Form W-4 below.

Figure 15-1 • Fill in this area of the W-4 form to calculate the number of allowances you plan to claim.

Claim Fewer Withholding Allowances

If, instead of dealing with a refund each spring, you find yourself paying extra tax to Uncle Sam in April, you can file a new W-4 form with your employer and decrease the number of withholding allowances you claim. *The fewer allowances you claim on Form W-4, the more tax will be withheld.*

Tip *When making adjustments to your W-4 form, it is recommended that you ask the payroll supervisor at your job to explain the exact effects of the change in withholding on your take-home pay and on the total amount of tax you will have withheld for the year.*

You can calculate the number of allowances you are eligible to claim on your W-4 form, as shown in Figure 15-1, but that doesn't mean you have to claim all those allowances. The number of allowances you calculate is a good starting point, but from that point forward, you can reduce the number you actually place on line 5 of the W-4 form (see Figure 15-2), thus increasing your tax withholding.

You can also claim more allowances than the number you compute on the W-4 form if you believe it will provide a better determination of your proper withholding. Note that if the number of withholding allowances exceeds ten, your employer must send a copy of your W-4 form to the IRS. The number of allowances you claim over ten may be legitimate, but know that the IRS may be looking at your tax return in the spring to determine if you are instructing your employer to withhold properly.

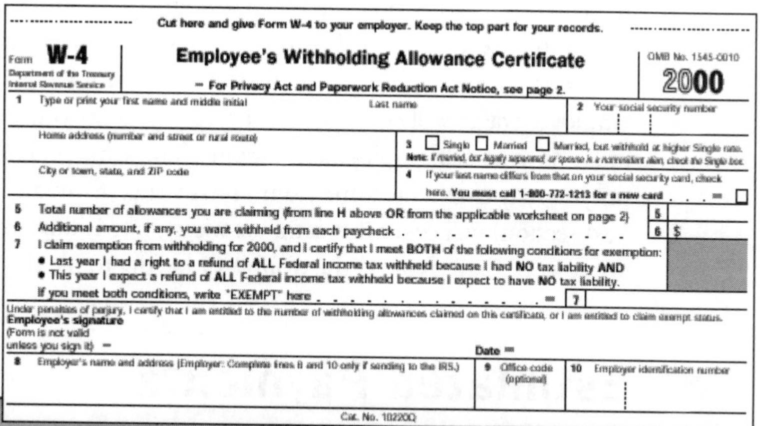
Cut here and give Form W-4 to your employer. Keep the top part for your records.

Form **W-4** Department of the Treasury Internal Revenue Service

Employee's Withholding Allowance Certificate

For Privacy Act and Paperwork Reduction Act Notice, see page 2.

OMB No. 1545-0010 **2000**

1 Type or print your first name and middle initial — Last name — 2 Your social security number

Home address (number and street or rural route) — 3 ☐ Single ☐ Married ☐ Married, but withhold at higher Single rate.
Note: *If married, but legally separated, or spouse is a nonresident alien, check the Single box.*

City or town, state, and ZIP code — 4 If your last name differs from that on your social security card, check here. **You must call 1-800-772-1213 for a new card** . . . ☐

5 Total number of allowances you are claiming (from line H above **OR** from the applicable worksheet on page 2) — 5

6 Additional amount, if any, you want withheld from each paycheck . . . — 6 $

7 I claim exemption from withholding for 2000, and I certify that I meet **BOTH** of the following conditions for exemption:
- Last year I had a right to a refund of **ALL** Federal income tax withheld because I had **NO** tax liability **AND**
- This year I expect a refund of **ALL** Federal income tax withheld because I expect to have **NO** tax liability.

If you meet both conditions, write "EXEMPT" here . . . — 7

Under penalties of perjury, I certify that I am entitled to the number of withholding allowances claimed on this certificate, or I am entitled to claim exempt status.
Employee's signature (Form is not valid unless you sign it) — **Date**

8 Employer's name and address (Employer: Complete lines 8 and 10 only if sending to the IRS.) — 9 Office code (optional) — 10 Employer identification number

Cat. No. 10220Q

Figure 15-2 • Enter the number of withholding allowances you plan to claim on line 5.

Claim Extra Withholding

You can go one step further with your W-4 form if you really want to make sure you've had enough tax withheld from your pay to cover your tax liability. On line 6 of the W-4 (see Figure 15-2), there is an opportunity to enter an additional amount that you wish to have withheld from your pay. The dollar amount you enter here will be deducted from each of your paychecks.

Stagger Your Withholding

One last option for controlling the amount of tax withheld from your paycheck is to adjust the withholding amount during the year. Depending on your preference, you can have excess tax withheld during the early months of the year and get the bulk of your withholding over with. You can then file a new W-4 form midyear to increase the number of exemptions you claim and thus decrease the amount of withholding, or you can adjust the W-4 during the year to increase the tax withholding so that more tax is taken out later in the year.

If you plan to alter your withholding during the year, taking care of your tax withholding in bulk, it makes economic sense to hold off until the end of the year for your withholding and have the use of your money early. The alternative of paying your tax early and getting it over with means that the IRS gets to have your money, interest free, for most of the year. It is more logical to lower your withholding early in the year, and put the money into an account where it can earn some interest. You will then have that money (plus the interest it earned) to help defray living expenses at the end of the year when you increase your withholding.

If you have a business of your own in addition to being employed, you can increase your withholding at your job to the point where the tax taken from your employee wages will cover the estimated payments you would otherwise have to make on your self-employment income. The same potential exists for covering the tax you may owe on income from investments. Estimated payments (discussed in the next section) will cover this extra tax nicely, but asking your employer to take out the tax at work may save you the trouble of having to file the quarterly forms altogether.

Estimated Payments

Estimated taxes are a means of paying income tax during the year when tax withholding from a job is nonexistent or insufficient to cover your taxes. Estimated taxes are paid quarterly, on the 15th of April, June, September, and January of the next year. If the 15th falls on a weekend or a holiday, the tax is due the next business day.

Paying quarterly estimates is not just an option or a choice that you make if you feel like being generous with the IRS. The quarterly payments are a requirement if, after withholding, the following conditions are met:

- You expect to owe more than $1,000 on your tax return after your withholding has been applied to the tax liability.
- Your withholding and any tax credits for which you qualify are less than the smaller of 90 percent of the tax on your tax return or 100 percent of the tax shown on your tax return from last year.

How Much Should You Pay?

When calculating your quarterly payments for 2001, you should plan on paying at least the smaller of:

- 90 percent of your anticipated 2001 tax
- 100 percent of your 2000 tax (your 2000 tax return must have covered all twelve months of 2000 and your adjusted gross income for 2000 must have been $150,000 or less; $75,000 or less if married and filing separately)
- 106 percent of your 2000 tax if your adjusted gross income for 2000 was over $150,000 or $75,000 if married and filing separately (this percentage will be 112 percent in 2001 and 110 percent in years thereafter)

Calculate Your Actual Tax

Another way to estimate the amount of tax to pay quarterly is to calculate your net taxable income to date, *annualize* that amount, calculate the tax on the annualized income, and then pay the appropriate amount ($\frac{1}{4}$, $\frac{1}{2}$, $\frac{3}{4}$, or all) of the calculated tax as your estimated payment.

Note   *The method for annualizing your net taxable income is as follows. Calculate your net taxable income (taxable income less allowable deductions and adjustments) for the quarter. The "quarter," according to the IRS, ends on the last day of the month prior to the month in which the quarterly payment is due. Therefore the first quarter ends March 31, the second ends May 31, the third ends August 31, and the last quarter ends December 31. Divide the net taxable income that you calculated by the number of months in the quarter, then multiply the result by 12. This will give you the annualized income on which you will calculate the tax.*

Performing this annualization calculation can be confusing, so don't hesitate to contact a professional for some advice in this area.

Installment Agreements

Taxpayers who can't pay all their tax when they file their federal income tax return are encouraged to send as much money as they can with their tax return, and attach Form 9465, Installment Agreement Request, to the tax return. On this form you are to indicate how much you will be able to pay on your taxes each month, and the day of the month on which you wish to make these installment payments.

The IRS is required to accept your installment agreement request if all of the following points apply:

- Your total taxes do not exceed $10,000.
- In the past five years you have not failed to file a tax return, failed to pay your tax, or entered into another installment agreement.
- You can't pay your tax when it is due.
- The tax will be paid in three years or less.
- You agree to comply with tax laws while the agreement is in effect.

Tip   *If you don't meet all of the criteria for an installment agreement, that doesn't mean the IRS won't accept your agreement, it only means that they are not required to do so.*

After filing an installment agreement request form, you should hear from the IRS within 45 days of filing your tax return, accepting or altering your payment plan, and you can send your monthly payments until the taxes are paid in full. There are of course penalties and interest that continue accruing until all the taxes are paid. You don't have to calculate your own penalty and interest, however. Just make your regular payments and the IRS will contact you with information about penalties and interest.

Once your plan is accepted, you will receive a monthly notice from the IRS reminding you of your payment. Send this notice with your payment to the address indicated on the form.

Offer in Compromise

One method of dealing with debt to the IRS is an offer in compromise. If you owe a large quantity of money and you can't foresee paying it off in any reasonable time, you can make an offer to the IRS to make a lump sum payment of an amount that is less than the total liability.

When you make an offer in compromise, you will prepare detailed financial statements setting out everything you own and everything you owe. The IRS may want to make contact with your creditors to verify the information on your statements.

If the amount you offer is better than the amount the IRS expects it will be able to collect, the offer may be accepted. You can consider borrowing money from a family member or business associate in order to put together an offer, as an alternative to trying to keep the IRS at bay.

If you plan to pursue an offer in compromise, it is strongly recommended that you seek the assistance of a tax or legal professional who has had some experience in negotiating with the IRS.

When you send your tax return in the mail or dispatch it electronically, you may think you've said the final word about your income, deductions, and taxes for the year. But wait! You still have time to make changes. The IRS allows taxpayers to file an amended tax return if there is a mistake or an omission on the original return you filed.

Situations That Require Amending

There are several situations that can give rise to the need to amend a tax return. Here are a few:

- You forgot to take some tax deductions. Perhaps an envelope full of tax-related receipts surfaced after you filed your tax return, or perhaps you didn't realize you were supposed to take a deduction (the depreciation expense on your home office, for example). You can amend your tax return and include the deductions that were left off the first time around.

- You neglected to record some income. Perhaps a wayward W-2 form for a temporary job got misplaced when you were preparing your tax return, or you may have received an unexpected K-1 or 1099 form in the mail after the return had already been mailed. It's possible your employer made a mistake on your original W-2 form and sent a corrected form after your return had been filed. Or maybe you received income, such as prize or gambling winnings, and you were unaware that this income gets taxed, but have discovered this fact since you filed your tax return.

- You decide to change your filing status or the number of exemptions you claimed on your original tax return. It may be the case that you realize after filing your tax return using the Married Filing Separately status that you actually qualified for the Head of Household status. Or perhaps you are divorced and claimed your child as an exemption only to realize that your former spouse made the same claim—one of you will have to amend.

> **Tip**   *If you discover, after filing, that you made a mathematical error on your tax return—added up your deductions incorrectly or miscalculated the income tax—you don't have to file an amended return. The IRS checks for all math errors and you can assume that they will catch the error and send you a notice of the change they are making to your return.*

How Far Back Can You Go?

The IRS allows you to amend a tax return if you file the amended return within three years after the date on which you filed your original tax return, or within two years after the date on which you paid the tax on that return, whichever is later.

GET SMARTER   There are exceptions to the rule of amending a return within three years of the due date.

If the reason for amending a return is because a bad debt or a security became worthless, you have seven years after the due date to amend a return. Losses from bad debts or securities of insolvent companies may only be deducted in the year in which the debt became worthless. If you discover you overlooked a bad debt from a prior year, or if you were seeking verification of the worthlessness of the debt or security, you can still amend your return for up to seven years.

If the reason for amending a return results from a carryback of a general business credit or a net operating loss, you can amend for three years from the due date of the return for the tax year generating the loss or credit. A net operating loss can occur when a business form, such as a Schedule C or Schedule F, generates a loss that is greater than your other income. When this occurs, the excess loss is carried back and applied to income in the past two years. If there is still some unused loss, the remaining loss gets carried forward and applied to future years, up to twenty years. In the situation where you are carrying back a loss, the years to which the loss is carried back are eligible for amending for the same years as the tax year that generated the loss. So if you have a business loss in 2000 that will be carried back to 1999 and 1998, you will be able to amend the 1999 and 1998 tax returns until April 15 of 2004.

If you filed your original return prior to April 15 of the year in which it was due, the IRS considers your return is filed on April 15, even if you file earlier, for purposes of determining how long you have to amend the return. Therefore, if you filed your 1997 tax return on March 3, 1998, you will have until April 15, 2001 to amend the 1997 return.

Amending Your Return

You can prepare your amended return right in TurboTax, and the program will take care of filling in most of the information required for this form.

Where in TurboTax Do I Amend My Return?

During the TurboTax Interview you will be given an opportunity to prepare an amended return. If you miss that screen, or aren't ready to amend a return at the time you see the option, here's how you can get back to the screen that launches the amended tax return portion of the interview.

Follow these steps to begin amending a tax return in TurboTax:

1. From the TurboTax Interview screen, click the Personal Info option. A drop-down menu will appear, as shown below:

2. Scroll down until you see the option for Which Return Do You Need to File? and click this option. This option appears almost at the bottom of the Personal Info section, just before the Income section begins, as shown below:

3. On the screen that appears, click the option for An Amended Return for 2000 or a Prior Year, as shown below:

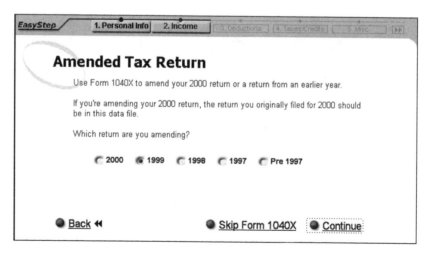

4. On the Amended Tax Return screen that appears, select the year for which you want to amend a return, then click the Continue option, as shown below:

   At this point you will be ready to prepare the Form 1040X, the form to use for an amended tax return. TurboTax will pose questions about all the areas of your original tax return and you will be expected to enter any changes you want to make on your original return.

Entering Information for the 1040X

The TurboTax interview will walk you through the complete process of entering information for your amended tax return. The final result will be a 1040X that is ready to be mailed to the IRS.

Answer Some Questions

TurboTax presents you with a series of questions, the answers to which will appear on the amended tax return. One of the questions has to do with your filing status. One of the reasons you can amend a tax return is to change your filing status. Generally you can change your original decision about your filing status to any other status, but there is one exception. You cannot change from Married Filing Jointly to Married Filing Separately unless the original due date for the tax return has not yet passed. If you determine, after the original due date has passed, that you could have saved on taxes had you filed using the joint status, you're out of luck.

Enter Original Amounts

On the screen shown in Figure 16-1, enter the amounts exactly as they appeared on your original tax return. If you are amending the current year's return, TurboTax will take care of entering these amounts.

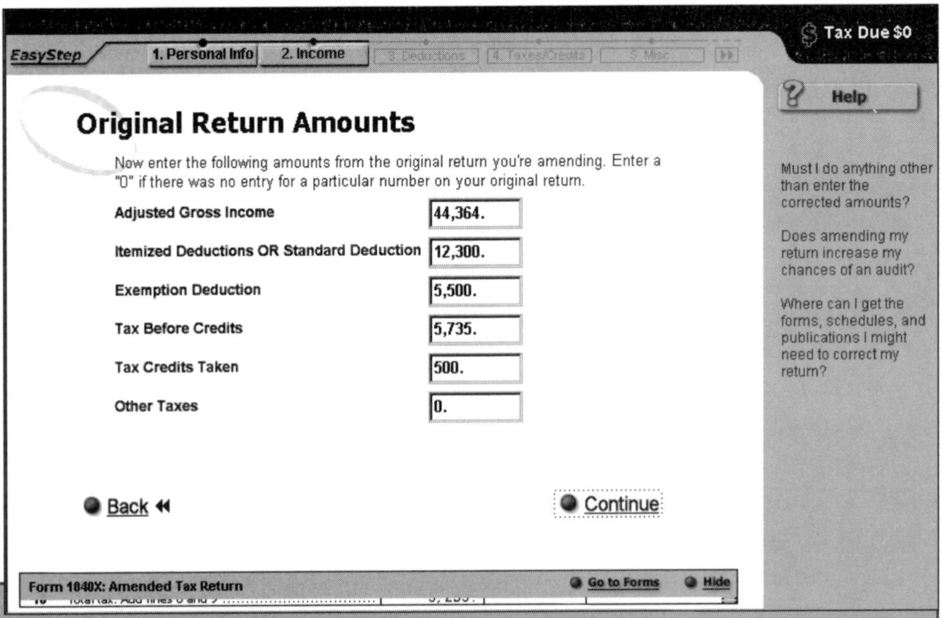

Figure 16-1 • Enter amounts as they originally appeared on your tax return.

Enter the Payments You Paid

You must enter the amounts you paid with and for your original tax return (see Figure 16-2). These entries will include the following types of payments:

- Payment made with an extension of time to file your return
- Withholding tax that was reported on your original income tax return
- Estimated payments you made for the year
- Any additional payment made when you filed the return
- Overpayment reported on your original return that was to be retained by the IRS and applied toward future taxes

It's your choice: you can enter the amounts by which your original tax return numbers are changing, or you can enter the corrected amounts that should actually appear on your tax return. Whichever method you choose (see Figure 16-3), TurboTax will calculate the other. For example, if your original itemized deductions totaled $12,500 and you realize you forgot to deduct a $500 contribution, you can enter the *net change* of $500, or you can enter the *corrected amount* of $13,000. You only need to enter one of these numbers; TurboTax can figure out the other one.

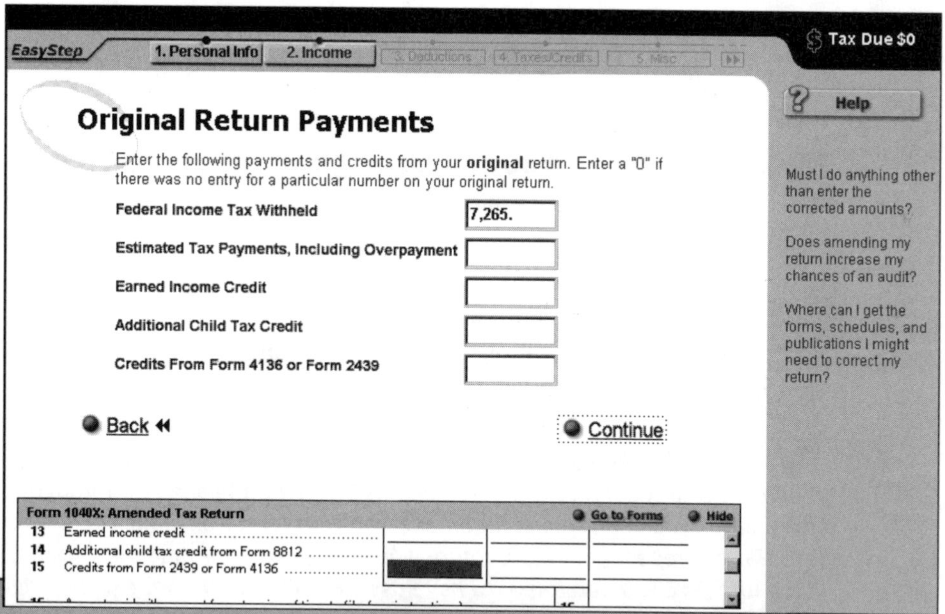

Figure 16-2 • Enter all the payments you made for the tax return you are amending.

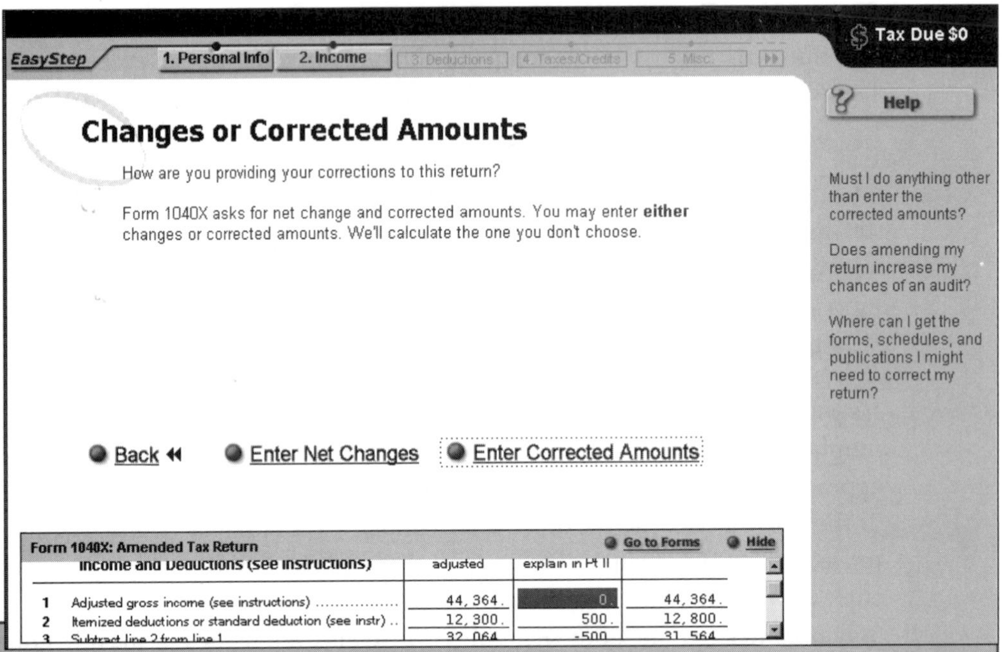

Figure 16-3 • Choose the method you prefer: changes or corrected amounts.

Make Any Other Needed Changes

If necessary, you can make other changes to your amended return, including changing the number of exemptions you claimed when you originally filed the return, changing the amount of exemptions you deducted on the original return, and changing the dependent information you entered on your original return. TurboTax presents a screen for each of these options where you can fill in the appropriate information.

Tip   *Don't forget that you may need to amend your state return as a result of a change to your federal return. If the changes you are making flow through to your state return, you can request an amended return form from your state. If you used TurboTax to prepare your state return, you can prepare an amended state tax return using TurboTax. You don't have to have used TurboTax in the year of the original return—the amended tax return form for each state applies to any year.*

Enter Explanations

One of the most important parts of amending a tax return is entering the explanations for your changes. TurboTax provides a screen for entering explanations, and on this screen you need to enter a narrative explanation for each change that occurs on the return.

For example, if you amended your return to take into account a $500 cash contribution you forgot to deduct previously and to report a reduction in the number of dependents and exemptions you claimed due to the fact that your ex-spouse also claimed your child as a dependent, your explanation screen would look something like this:

> Line 2: Net increase in itemized deductions of $500 due to charitable cash contribution made to St. Paul's Episcopal Church, which I neglected to include on the original return.
>
> Line 4: Net decrease in exemptions of $2,750 due to fact that ex-spouse, John Jones, Social Security number 234-56-7890, is claiming our daughter, Jennifer Jones, Social Security number 345-67-8901, as a dependent.

Your explanation should include the line number on which the change occurs, the amount of the change, and any detailed information that will help satisfactorily explain the change in your return.

TurboTax will take care of computing the change in the tax and any other adjustments that need to be completed on your 1040X.

Attachments to the 1040X

The IRS requires that you attach the revised copy of any tax schedule or form that is changing as a result of your amendments. For example, if you are changing your itemized deductions, attach a copy of Schedule A. If you are changing something on your business form, attach the revised Schedule C. If your tax computation changes, attach a revised 1040.

Across the top of any revised form you are attaching to the 1040X, write "Amended" so the IRS will know that this is the new version of the form.

You do not need to attach any forms from your original 1040 to the 1040X.

Mailing Your 1040X

Keeping in mind the due dates mentioned previously in this chapter (see "How Far Back Can You Go?"), the amended tax return gets mailed to the same address that you use for your federal income tax return.

If your mailing address has changed since you filed your original tax return, the mailing address for your 1040X may be different than the address you used on your original return. Mail the 1040X to the IRS service center that covers the area where you now live. All addresses for mailing federal tax returns to the IRS are located inside the back cover of this book.

When you print the tax return from TurboTax, the mailing address will appear on your filing instructions that print with the return. Mail your 1040X to the appropriate address. You don't need to attach any sort of cover letter, just the form and the attachments described previously in this chapter.

The 1040X doesn't get processed by the IRS with the alacrity of the annual 1040 returns—those returns get the top priority service. The IRS claims that it often takes two to three months to process the 1040X. You won't hear from the IRS during this period. When the IRS begins reviewing your amended return, you will only be contacted if any information or forms are missing.

Communicating with the IRS

In This Chapter:

- *Receiving IRS Requests for Information*

- *Explaining the Different Kinds of IRS Examinations*

- *Preparing Yourself for an Audit*

- *Disagreeing with the IRS*

Chapter 17

Most people harbor a fear of the IRS—a fear born of the mystery and power that surrounds this federal agency. The IRS knows it has the power to intimidate, and that power helps them collect taxes. With this chapter I hope to give you the ability to think of the IRS as you would any other entity to which you owe a payment. If the local department store sent you a bill and you disagreed with the amount owing, you wouldn't simply pay the amount and hope they leave you alone. Instead you would get to the bottom of the issue, resolve any disputes, and vow to pay only what you rightfully owe. Taxes should be regarded the same way. If you receive communication from the IRS, or if you disagree with an amount they say you owe, get to the bottom of the matter and resolve the issue amicably.

IRS Letters Requesting Information

You may feel the only welcome correspondence a person can receive from the IRS is a refund check, and you may be right. Be that as it may, there are some other types of correspondence that you might receive from the IRS. This chapter will provide some guidance as to how to react to and respond to the letters you may receive from your favorite Uncle Sam.

The Incomplete for Processing Letter

The IRS has a standard form letter that covers requests for a variety of information that wasn't included with your tax return. The letter is entitled "Individual Return Incomplete for Processing." The standard letter contains 35 separate sections requesting information that could be missing from a tax return. The IRS agent preparing the letter for a taxpayer uses a computer to choose which sections apply, then prints the letter containing only the sections appropriate to the taxpayer.

With this incomplete for processing letter, the IRS can request such information as a missing W-2 form, a missing Social Security number of a taxpayer or dependent, a missing signature, a resubmission of an illegible form, supporting detail for an amount on your tax form, or a choice of filing status. This letter is not to be construed as notification that your tax return is being examined or that there is a mistake on your return. Instead, this is simply a request for missing information, information that will enable the IRS to finish processing your return, send you your refund if applicable, and put the tax return away for good. Complete the missing information and return the form in the accompanying envelope, and chances are you won't hear from the IRS again regarding this tax return.

The Notice of Tax Due and Demand for Payment

This is a notice that the IRS sends indicating that they've disagreed with the amount of tax you show owing on your tax return, or there is a penalty due, or perhaps you didn't make the full payment of tax owing with your tax return. The IRS, with this notice, is requesting full payment immediately.

Be sure to double-check and recalculate the amount of tax the IRS has assessed. Don't assume the IRS is correct. If you find an error on the notice, call the IRS at the number that appears on the notice and explain your disagreement. You will probably be able to work out your disagreement over the telephone, or the agent may ask you to send some documents that support your claim.

Statement of Changes to Your Account

This notice announces a change in the amount of refund that you expected to receive and the reasons for the change. For example, the amount of payments you thought you made during the year may not agree with the amount of payments recorded by the IRS, or there may have been a mathematical error on your tax return.

Always be sure when you receive a notice like this that you double-check the IRS calculations and contact the IRS immediately if you disagree with their calculations.

Other information that may be included on this form is a notice that your refund, though perhaps calculated correctly, will not be sent to you because the money is being applied to an amount you already owed the IRS. You may also receive notice that your refund is being diverted to pay off government-funded student loans or delinquent child support payments.

Respond to the statement of changes in one of these three ways:

- Do nothing if the IRS indicates a revised refund and you agree with the amount. You don't have to respond if you plan to accept the revised calculations.
- Send the additional payment that the IRS has calculated, along with a copy of the letter.
- Send a letter to the address on the letter or place a telephone call to the number on the letter indicating any IRS error that may have occurred. Include supporting documentation for changes you are making. For example, if the IRS indicates that your interest income from your bank should be $500 and

your 1099 form shows $50, send a copy of the 1099 form along with your letter in response. Or if the IRS indicates it has no record of estimated payments you sent, have your cancelled checks handy when you telephone the IRS and you may be able to settle the discrepancy on the phone.

IRS Letters Associated with an Audit

It's one of those perfect days—the sun is shining, the temperature is warm, the birds are singing in the trees, children are playing in the yard, you're happy in your work, all is right with the world. And then, you open the mailbox. Nestled in among the bills and ads and magazines is an envelope that makes your heart beat a little faster. Glaring at you from the return address corner are the words, "Internal Revenue Service."

Should your tax return be selected for an audit, there are some basic forms of communication that you will receive. The initial communication will be an announcement of the examination. Later communication will cover results of the audit.

The Audit Letter

When you receive a letter from the IRS notifying you that your return has been selected for an audit, your first thought may be to book a flight to a foreign country and leave no forwarding address. Whether or not this is an extreme reaction depends in part on how confident you are about the accuracy and legality of the numbers you used on your tax return. For most people, leaving the country is not a viable option and so it makes sense instead to find out what the IRS wants and provide them with the answers to their questions as best you can. If it turns out you owe additional tax, take your medicine, work out a payment arrangement, and get on with your life.

Keep in mind that your tax return has been selected, along with a million or so others, by the very fallible IRS computer, which most of the time is making no judgment other than to state that some of your deductions may be out of line with the national average. You, personally, are not the subject of the examination— only the tax form on which you wrote your numbers.

Before you head for the airport, try to grasp the fact that an audit of your tax return is simply an attempt to clarify your numbers.

The audit letter will ask for one of these things:

- You will be asked to mail in receipts that substantiate one or more numbers on your tax return.
- You will be asked to call your local IRS office (the telephone number will be provided) and set up an appointment to discuss particular items on your tax return.
- An appointment date and time will be designated in the letter.

An audit letter contains check boxes for the various items on your tax return. The checked items are the items being examined, nothing more.

If your examination letter includes a specific date and time for your appointment, you have the right to request a change if you will be unable to attend on the date listed. See the section "Preparing for an Audit" later in this chapter for information on how to get yourself ready to meet with the IRS face to face.

The 30-Day Letter

The situation is starting to get a little sticky when you receive a 30-day letter. This is a letter from the IRS providing you with information regarding the results of your audit. The 30-day letter is so named because you are given 30 days in which you may officially disagree with the findings of the IRS as stated in this letter. See the section "How to Appeal" later in this chapter for what to do if you disagree with the information in the 30-day letter.

If you simply don't respond to this letter within 30 days, the next correspondence you may receive from the IRS is a 90-day letter.

The 90-Day Letter

Ignore the IRS when you receive a 30-day letter, and you will be in line for a Statutory Notice of Deficiency, otherwise known as 90-day letter. The IRS is finished wasting time at this point and is making a demand for payment. If you receive this letter, you have 90 days in which you may appeal the decision of the IRS to the U.S. Tax Court.

You will need to be represented by an attorney if you plan to disagree with the IRS at the level of the Tax Court and if the amount in dispute is more than $10,000. You may be represented by a CPA or you may even represent yourself if the disputed amount is $10,000 or less. The lesser amount is considered to be a small claim in Tax Court.

Preparing for an Audit

What is an audit, why do audits exist, and why do taxpayers fear them so much? We're told the tax system is a voluntary system. The government sends out millions of tax forms each December and then crosses its fingers and hopes the millions of taxpayers will send the forms back. The main method the IRS has of ensuring that taxpayers file tax returns is its power to perform audits.

Keeping Taxpayers in Line

Think back to the days when you were in school. Would you have completed all your homework, night after night, if you knew the teacher wouldn't notice if you didn't turn in your papers? Sometimes you might have done the work, but without the threat of poor grades, humiliation in front of your classmates, and other indignities, chances are you might have skipped an assignment from time to time.

The IRS audit process is similar to the teacher who grades homework. If you knew no one was checking, would you voluntarily send in a tax return each year, and if so, would you always report all of your income and not stretch the truth on any deductions?

Determining National Averages

Besides making sure the taxpayers turn in their homework each April, another reason the IRS performs audits is to find out what to expect of the average taxpayer. By auditing tax returns of various employment groups and analyzing the results, the IRS determines the average amounts that various types of taxpayers report as income and deductions.

Every few years the IRS chooses a handful of professions and randomly selects tax returns filed by members of those professions in order to gain insights as to what constitutes normal income and expenses of the profession. Audits of those tax returns provide the IRS with information about the earnings and deductions of the typical doctor, lawyer, teacher, editor, musician, and so on.

In addition to studying the habits of professionals, the IRS also performs totally random audits from different income levels, again attempting to discover what average American taxpayers earn and spend. These exhaustive audits are called TCMP audits, which stands for Taxpayer Compliance Measurement Program audits, and are comprehensive examinations that encompass every number on the tax return.

Types of Audits

There are three types of audit examinations: an office examination, a correspondence audit, and a field examination.

The Office Examination

An examination that takes place at an IRS office near you is called a desk or office examination. About half of the audits conducted are of this type. You will be notified of a date and time and given the location of the IRS office at which you are to appear. When the IRS contacts you, you will receive an explanation of the office examination process.

The Correspondence Audit

In a correspondence audit, you receive a letter requesting additional information to support items reported on your tax return. You make copies of the requested information and the IRS makes decisions about how the items should have been reported on your tax return. It is possible that the entire audit will be handled by mail and you will reach agreement without ever having to meet an IRS agent face to face.

The Field Examination

A field examination takes place at your own place of business, which might even be your home, if that is where you conduct your business. You will receive a notice from the IRS informing you of your field audit date. The IRS may choose this type of audit when the transactions reported on the tax return are very complex, when there are a lot of records for the business that need to be examined, or when it is useful to the audit to examine the business premises, such as in a situation when inventory is present. In an office examination, the agent provides you with a list of questionable items and normally doesn't stray from the list. In a field audit, it isn't uncommon for the entire tax return to be reviewed, making all the transactions contained in the tax return fair game for questioning.

Stay Calm

One of the most important things to remember if the IRS invites you in for an examination is to not get panicky about it. All the IRS wants to do is ask you some specific questions about the numbers on your tax return. Pretend you're explaining to your spouse or your tax accountant where the numbers come from. Try not to think of the IRS agent as your enemy.

Assuming you did your best job of gathering information for your tax return and you believe the numbers you presented represent the actual financial activity in your household for the year under examination, you have nothing to fear.

If you realize that there is a mistake on your tax return, or if you omitted information or exaggerated your deductions, you may not be quite so comfortable about preparing for your audit. Hiding from the inevitability of the examination process, however, will not benefit your situation. You still need to go forward with the meeting and help the IRS agent determine what the correct tax liability should be for you.

What Should You Bring to an Audit?

The better prepared you are for your audit, the more confident you will be and the easier the audit experience will be.

Bring the items requested by the IRS. Along with your audit notice, you will receive a list of items the IRS wants to see. If the IRS has requested specific documents or forms, you must bring those with you to your audit if you can. For example, if you've been asked to bring evidence to support the deductions on your Schedule C, bring the cancelled checks or receipts marked "Paid" with your company name on them.

Note   *If it turns out the documentation you bring with you for your meeting with the IRS isn't sufficient to support the amounts on your tax return, you will be given an opportunity to reschedule your appointment in order to collect additional support for your tax return number.*

What Shouldn't You Bring to an Audit?

Don't provide the IRS with original documents. If you can't make copies of your checks or documents, bring them with you and ask the IRS representative to make copies. You don't want to leave your only evidence of tax return numbers with the IRS—if the document gets misplaced, you do not have another one.

Don't bring documents that support any part of your tax return other than the information requested by the IRS. If you don't have any extra documents with you, you won't be tempted to open up and share information that is not part of the audit. Bring only the items requested by the IRS. For example, if they ask for substantiation of your business income, don't bring receipts supporting your business deductions.

Your Appearance and Mannerisms

A basic rule for any business meeting is to dress nicely and be polite. If you take the time to care about your appearance and your mannerisms, you will be taken more seriously than if you dress casually and act like you don't care. The IRS audit is not a black tie affair, but standard business attire is appropriate.

Sending Someone in Your Place

You have the right to not represent yourself in front of the IRS. You may bring a tax accountant or a lawyer or even a friend or a family member to your audit, and you may authorize that person to answer questions on your behalf.

You also have the right to send a tax accountant or a lawyer in your place to the audit. You don't even have to go! To be represented by someone at the audit, the person you choose must be approved to practice before the IRS, and you must sign a Power of Attorney form (IRS Form 2848) designating that person as the person who can answer tax-related questions on your behalf. Most practicing CPAs and lawyers and many non-CPA accountants are approved to practice before the IRS, and all of them have Power of Attorney forms you can sign.

When should you bring someone with you and when should you send someone in your place? Use your judgment. If you are comfortable talking about your tax return and are confident that you have all the documentation you need to support your income and deductions, you may not need anyone to accompany you. If you are afraid you won't understand some of the questions you are asked, you may want to bring someone with you who can speak the same language as the IRS representative. If you feel very awkward about the audit, even if you are confident about your documentation, and if you have someone you trust implicitly who can represent you, you may rest more easily if you stay home and send someone in your place.

Tip *If you attend the audit unaccompanied and decide once you get there that you don't understand the questions you're being asked, or if you feel the agent is intimidating you, you can ask that the meeting be rescheduled for a later date and bring someone with you when you return.*

Appealing IRS Decisions

After you finish your audit, you will likely receive a notice from the IRS indicating changes that they want to make in your tax return and perhaps an additional amount of tax that you owe.

Try to Settle Without an Appeal

If you agree with the changes, you'll be asked to sign a Form 4549, Income Tax Examination Changes, which allows the IRS to assess your deficiency. You then pay your tax and put the entire experience behind you. Keep in mind that by signing the Form 4549, you're giving up your right of appeal to the IRS Appellate Conference and the Tax Court. However, you can still file a refund suit in federal district court or the Court of Federal Claims. If you want to object to the changes, you have that right as well. If you disagree with the proposed audit changes, don't sign this form. Instead, if you disagree with the proposed changes, follow these steps:

1. If you do not agree with the results of the audit meeting, your first step is to tell the auditor with whom you had your meeting that you don't think the assessment is correct. Discuss the areas of disagreement over the phone or arrange for another meeting. Ask if there's more information you can bring in that would help establish your case. Maybe there was some misunderstanding. The auditor wants this situation cleared up as much as you do, so talk it out and see if you can reach an agreement.

2. If the auditor won't budge, ask for either a telephone or a personal audience with a manager. The auditor can't refuse this request. This manager has the right to override the auditor's decision. Maybe you just didn't explain things well enough to the auditor, or maybe there was a personality conflict and you'll get along better with the manager. Know that the manager will want to back the auditor, but that doesn't mean the manager won't listen to your story and give you a chance to explain your disagreement with the auditor.

3. If you can't reach an agreement between the auditor and the auditor's manager, your next step is the appeal process.

How to Appeal

If you do not agree with the changes offered by the IRS, you can refuse to sign the changes letter. You will next receive a 30-day letter, as described previously in this chapter. You have the following four options in responding to this letter:

- Sign an agreement form and pay the tax
- Send new information within 15 days
- Ask for an office meeting
- Ask for an appeals hearing

If you disagree with the auditor's findings, as set out in the 30-day letter, don't sign the agreement. Instead, go right to option three and ask for an office meeting. Ask to meet with your auditor's supervisor. You can present any additional information and documentation that you have at this meeting. Be sure to schedule this meeting within 30 days of the date on your letter.

If you still disagree with the IRS examination results after your meeting, request an appeals hearing. *You must make this request before your 30 days run out.*

An appeals hearing will be scheduled for you, much like the audit hearing, but with a different, higher-up person. This person has the right to negotiate and settle cases. When you attend the hearing, bring all your documentation supporting your side of the story, and present your case clearly and concisely. Unless you are very confident of your ability to explain your position, you may want to bring a tax professional with you to this meeting.

If the appeals officer agrees with you, you're finished. The appeals officer won't disagree with you without explaining the law behind his decision. Make sure you understand the law as the officer explains it. If you don't understand, ask to have the law explained in layman's terms. Write down all the information provided by the appeals officer, including legal citations.

There may be more evidence you can bring to the appeals officer that will support your claim—for instance, your word or testimony. One of the major differences between an auditor and an appeals officer is that an appeals officer can and will consider your oral testimony in determining a settlement. In other words, the more credible you are, the greater the chance of a favorable settlement. Once the two of you understand each other, if the IRS still thinks you owe more tax, you can suggest a settlement. You might be able to work out a payment amount and arrangement that's mutually acceptable.

Your avenues of protest don't stop with the appeals officer. In some situations, you can settle with the IRS attorneys prior to actually showing up in court. If you can't reach a settlement and feel you have a strong case, you can to go Tax Court, district court, and even to the U.S. Supreme Court to argue your case. As you progress up through the court system, you will need to be represented by a tax professional.

Keep in mind, however, that the IRS is interested in reaching a settlement early. It is costly and time-consuming to continue disputing taxpayer claims. New taxpayer services organizations within the IRS are positioned to help taxpayers resolve disputes in a timely fashion.

Good Tax Sense for the Future

If you want to pay the lowest possible taxes, then tax planning should be a year-round event. Good tax planning includes keeping good records and thinking beyond current year taxes. You can make tax-related decisions today that will affect your taxes for years to come. This part includes the following chapters:

Chapter 18: Recordkeeping

Chapter 19: Long-Range Tax Planning

Chapter 20: Using TurboTax for What-If Scenarios

Part Five

Recordkeeping

In This Chapter:

- *Saving Your TurboTax File*

- *Keeping a Copy of Your Tax Return*

- *Keeping Supportive Documentation*

- *Identifying Documents You Don't Need to Keep*

Chapter 18

The hard part is finished! Your tax return has been completed, and it's on its way to the IRS for official scrutiny. At this point, you may feel like you never want to see any of your tax documents again, but before you put them out of sight, read this chapter to find out just what you need to keep and how long you need to keep it.

Keep Your TurboTax File in a Safe Place

Before deciding which documents to keep and which to throw away, think about saving the file on your computer that contains your tax return. Here are some reasons why you should be concerned about saving your tax return file:

- If you plan to use TurboTax next year, you can take advantage of its ability to import information from a prior year's tax return directly into the next year's tax return. This way you won't have to reenter information that repeats from year to year, like your name and address, your employer's name, and information about your dependents.
- Your tax return file contains sensitive data. You may want to limit access to the file if others use your computer. You can do this by removing the file from your computer's hard drive and placing the file on a disk for future use.
- Technology changes quickly. Next year you may have a new computer. If you change computers, you will need to make a copy of your tax return from the old computer so you will have it available next year on the new computer.

Note *If you filed your return on the TurboTax Web site, be sure to print a copy of the return, as discussed in Chapter 13, so you will have a paper copy of the tax return for your records.*

Same Computer, Next Year

The tax return file stays on your computer, even if you uninstall your TurboTax program. If you use the same computer next year, TurboTax will find your prior year tax file and carry forward the necessary information.

Making a Copy of Your Tax File

With technology changing as quickly as it does, there's a chance you may upgrade to a new computer between now and next spring. If you do acquire a new computer, you'll probably want to make copies of a lot of the data on your old computer so you can transfer information to the new computer without having to recreate data files.

Make sure one of the files you copy and transfer to your new computer is your tax return file. If you make a copy of all the information on your old computer, this file will be included with that copy. If you selectively copy information to transfer to the new computer, make sure you include the tax return file as one of the files you copy.

Even if you plan to use your same computer next year, you may feel a need to remove the tax return file so that no one else can have access to this confidential information. When you are completely finished with your tax return and don't have a need to examine the file again until next year, you can copy the tax file and place it on a disk for safekeeping, and, if you like, remove the original file from your computer. To copy your 2000 tax return file to a disk for purposes of transferring the file to your new computer or keeping the file safe in a remote location, follow these steps:

1. Insert a floppy or zip disk in your computer. This is the disk onto which you will transfer your tax file.
2. Open Windows Explorer or the My Computer window, which will display all the folders on your hard drive.
3. Click the Tax00 folder, which should be located right off of your C:\ drive (it is not a subfolder of any other folder). Among the files displayed in this folder is a file named 2000 *yourname* Tax Return (your name appears in place of *yourname*). This is the file that contains your tax return information.
4. Right-click the file containing your tax return information. Choose Copy from the pop-up menu that appears.
5. Click the drive name for the drive containing the disk to which you will transfer your tax file.
6. Right-click the drive name, and then choose Paste from the pop-up menu. When the paste operation is completed, the filename will appear as part of the contents of the floppy or zip disk.

Once you have made a copy of the file, if you have a reason to remove the tax file from your computer, you can return to the listing of the tax file on your hard drive, right-click the filename, and choose Delete. Next spring, when you are ready to prepare your tax return, you can return the file to the hard drive from its remote location, or you can access the file from the disk on which it was stored.

Keeping Good Records

In Chapter 2, you learned what types of documents you will need to support the income and expense numbers on your income tax return. Most of these documents do not get attached to your tax return form. Instead, they are used in the preparation of the return, and then you are expected to keep these records in case your tax return gets examined.

IRS Recordkeeping Guidelines

There are specific guidelines set out by the IRS regarding how long you are supposed to keep tax records:

- Keep records that support items of income and deductions for three years from the date you filed the tax return. A return filed prior to the due date should be considered as having been filed on the due date for purposes of saving records.

- If you didn't pay your entire tax liability when you filed your tax return, keep these receipts for three years from the date you filed your return or two years from the time you made your last payment, whichever is later.

- If you neglected to report income on your tax return and this unreported income represents at least 25 percent of the income shown on the original tax return, the period for saving receipts is extended to six years after the original return was filed.

- If you fraudulently misrepresented information on your tax return, or filed no tax return at all, there is no time limit on how long the IRS has to examine your data for the tax year, so plan on holding on to receipts in this situation for a long time!

Records of Property Purchases

There are specific rules when it comes to saving documents that relate to purchases of property. You may purchase a home, a vacation cottage or time-share, stock, bonds, mutual funds, or other investment property that will be reported on your tax return when you ultimately sell the property. You could have purchased a piece of investment property forty years ago, and when you finally get around to selling it, you are going to need the original purchase documents to help you prepare your tax return. Furthermore, the IRS will expect you to retain these documents in case your tax return is examined.

W-2 Forms

The IRS recommends that you save your copies of your W-2 forms for all the years of your employment. This type of recordkeeping goes beyond what is necessary for your income tax returns. By keeping your W-2 forms until you retire, you will have accurate records of your wages earned over your lifetime and will have ready access to this information when it is time to calculate your Social Security benefits. By using your own records, you will be able to perform your own calculations and ensure that you are receiving the benefits to which you are entitled.

Prior Year Tax Returns

It is imperative that you keep your current tax return as a current record to compare to when you receive your refund or if you should have any correspondence with the IRS. You can also use your current tax return as a financial record when applying for a loan or for any other circumstance in which you might need to document your financial status.

Tip *Missing a tax return? You can request a transcript of a prior year's tax return from the IRS by calling (800) 829-1040.*

The current tax return will also act as a guide in the preparation of next year's tax return.

Because the IRS has the right to go back and examine the past three years of tax returns, you should also keep at least three years of tax returns on file along with the supporting records that document the numbers in your return.

Beyond three years, saving tax returns is a matter of personal preference. Many people keep a file or large envelope where they store tax returns for long periods of time. Even when you have long since discarded the receipts and other slips of papers that provide support for your tax numbers, you may want to hang on to old tax returns in case you are ever asked for financial information from the past. Tax returns provide excellent documentation and an historical record of your past financial endeavors.

Note *Should you ever need to amend a tax return (see Chapter 16), there may be information in that return carrying forward from a prior year. In this situation, you may be required to produce tax returns from longer than three years back. For example, if in 2000 you amended a tax return from 1998, and that 1998 tax return included a carryforward of long-term capital loss from 1995, the act of amending the 1998 tax return in the year 2000 will leave the 1995 return open for examination until 2003.*

Records of Payments

Another item to stash away is evidence of the payments you made to the IRS for any tax returns you filed within the previous three years. For many people, the payment record is the W-2 form, which shows your withholding for the year, and you're saving this form already. For some people, taxes are paid in the form of quarterly estimated tax payments. If you pay your taxes quarterly, you should keep cancelled checks or bank statements to prove that you actually made the payments.

Documents You Don't Need to Keep

For those of you who are always cleaning up and weeding out unnecessary paperwork and other items, here is a list of the tax-related documents you can pitch:

- Cancelled checks that support transactions in tax returns filed more than three years ago (but see the Note about amended returns in the previous section).

- Receipts and other evidence that duplicate records you intend to save.

- Receipts for contributions, lists of contributed items, evidence supporting other deductions claimed on your tax return if the return can no longer be examined by the IRS (this date usually occurs three years after the return filing due date or the date on which you actually filed, whichever is later).

- Bank statements, broker statements, savings institution statements and other evidence of income earned, as long as the three-year time period during which the tax return can be examined has expired.

Tax Planning

In This Chapter:

- *Tax Planning for Next Year's Tax Return*

- *Tax Planning for Life Decisions*

- *Tax Planning for Your Retirement*

- *Tax Planning for Your Investments*

- *Tax Planning for Your Estate*

Chapter 19

Tax planning is not just an event that occurs once a year, on or near April 15. Nor is it simply an event that occurs occasionally, when you engage in a financial transaction and remember that you need to save a receipt for your tax return.

Rather, tax planning is more a state of mind, a method of regarding all of your life events from the perspective of how they affect your taxes. Successful tax planning can result in significant sums of money that you save on your taxes and can then invest to produce more money, comfort, luxuries, and financial choices for you and your family.

When you wait until April 15 each year, fill out your tax return, and pay the tax that is calculated, you are letting the government make decisions about how your money is utilized. When you plan and time your life events from a tax perspective, you take the reins regarding how much money you will have to live on, invest, and make available to your family.

Every taxpayer has different goals and a different family situation, so strict rules for making tax-related choices will not apply universally. Instead, this chapter attempts to provide you with the knowledge of how taxes can be controlled and what questions you can ask and decisions you can make that will reduce your taxes both currently and in the future.

Tax Planning for Next Year's Tax Return

If you plan in advance, there are several decisions you can make during the course of a calendar year that will affect the outcome of your tax return. From planning at the beginning of the year to adjust the amount of withholding that is deducted from your paycheck, to deciding how much and for whom to spend on holiday gift giving in December, you can make a difference in how much tax you owe and how much you will pay with your tax return.

What You Can Do

You can't change when dates like December 31 and April 15 fall on the calendar, but you can exert some control over the way in which financial events occur in your life. For example, when payment due dates fall near the end of the calendar year for items that will be deductible on your tax return, you can choose to make December payments in January, thus pushing deductible items into the next year. If your deductions for 2000 are very close to the standard deduction, there may be some sense in taking the standard deduction in 2000 and sending some of your deductible expenses off to January to be paid with other expenses in 2001 and thus perhaps provide you with enough deductions to itemize in 2001.

Or perhaps your child is entering college in 2001 and you want to lower your adjusted gross income for 2001 to the level that will permit you to claim one of the college tax credits. The Hope Scholarship credit and lifetime learning credit are available to taxpayers with income under $50,000 (single) or $100,000 (joint). More detail on how the credits work is available in Chapter 8. If you are close to being eligible to claim these credits, you may be able to lower your income for 2001 by moving end-of-the-year 2000 business expenses into 2001, or alternatively, you may be able to lower your 2001 income by shifting some of your 2001 income into 2000. For example, your customers who owe you money in early 2001 may be willing to pay you in December 2000, thus lowering your 2001 taxable income.

⬤ **Note** | *In order for end-of-the-year money-shifting schemes to be successful, you must be a cash basis taxpayer. Most taxpayers report their income and expenses on the* cash basis, *meaning they report income when they receive or have access to it and report expenses when they actually pay the bills. Some taxpayers, particularly those with their own businesses, are* accrual basis *taxpayers, meaning they report their income when they earn it, even if it isn't collected right away, and they report their expenses when the expenses are incurred, even if the bill isn't paid until some time in the future. Shifting the payments and receipt of cash from one year to the next won't affect the tax for accrual basis taxpayers.*

Whether you're trying to reduce income this year or next, raise income in one of those years, or you just want to pay the lowest tax, this chapter provides you with information about some situations in which you may be able to control the timing of income and expense reporting.

The Tax Events You Can Control

Some taxable events are out of your control. For example, your employer decides when you will receive your paychecks, your bank decides when it is going to pay interest on your savings account, and the year in which you are classified as an elderly taxpayer is completely out of your hands.

But look beyond the obvious tax-related events that occur whether you ask for them or not, and you'll find that you actually have some control over the timing of income and deductions in many forms. The following sections give some examples of the choices that you can make throughout the year that will affect the outcome on your tax return.

Employment

You can establish a withholding plan with your employer that will affect your refund or the tax due on next year's tax return. Discuss how to fill out Form W-4, Employee's Withholding Allowance Certificate, with your employer or with the payroll supervisor at your place of employment, and make choices about the number of exemptions you claim to determine whether you want more or less tax withheld from your pay. The decision you make can be changed annually, or even more frequently if you need to alter the amount of tax withheld from your paycheck.

Note *If you plan to change your withholding more frequently than once a year, confirm with your employer how long it takes to execute a change in your withholding. If you decide on December 15 that you want to change your withholding for your last paycheck of the year, there may not be time to get this change in place before the final paycheck is issued.*

For example, consider the situation of a single employee making $30,000 per year, with no dependents, currently claiming one exemption (himself) on his W-4 form. During 2000, this employee's federal income tax withholding will be approximately $3,670. If that single person has only one job and can itemize his deductions, he can consider increasing his exemptions to three, in which case his federal income tax withholding for the year will be approximately $2,830. Changing the number of exemptions claimed on the W-4 form (see example in Figure 19-1) will increase the amount of take-home pay for this employee by about $840 for the year.

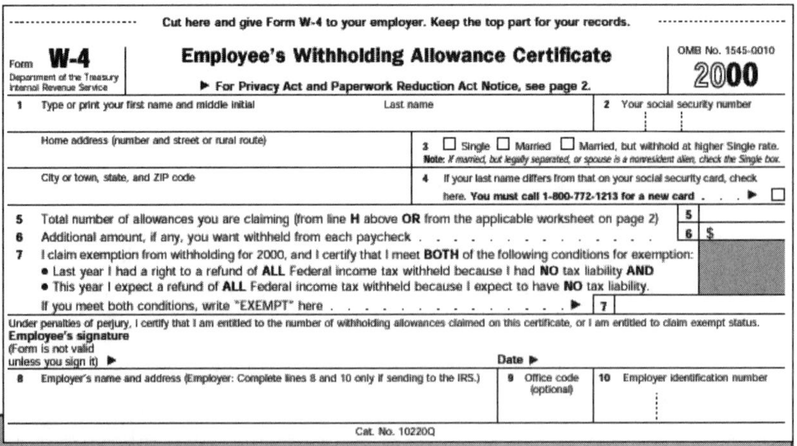
Cut here and give Form W-4 to your employer. Keep the top part for your records.

Form **W-4** Department of the Treasury Internal Revenue Service

Employee's Withholding Allowance Certificate

▶ For Privacy Act and Paperwork Reduction Act Notice, see page 2.

OMB No. 1545-0010 **2000**

1 Type or print your first name and middle initial — Last name — 2 Your social security number

Home address (number and street or rural route) — 3 ☐ Single ☐ Married ☐ Married, but withhold at higher Single rate. Note: If married, but legally separated, or spouse is a nonresident alien, check the Single box.

City or town, state, and ZIP code — 4 If your last name differs from that on your social security card, check here. You must call 1-800-772-1213 for a new card . . . ▶ ☐

5 Total number of allowances you are claiming (from line H above OR from the applicable worksheet on page 2) 5

6 Additional amount, if any, you want withheld from each paycheck . . . . 6 $

7 I claim exemption from withholding for 2000, and I certify that I meet BOTH of the following conditions for exemption:
- Last year I had a right to a refund of ALL Federal income tax withheld because I had NO tax liability AND
- This year I expect a refund of ALL Federal income tax withheld because I expect to have NO tax liability.

If you meet both conditions, write "EXEMPT" here . . . . ▶ 7

Under penalties of perjury, I certify that I am entitled to the number of withholding allowances claimed on this certificate, or I am entitled to claim exempt status.

Employee's signature (Form is not valid unless you sign it) ▶ Date ▶

8 Employer's name and address (Employer: Complete lines 8 and 10 only if sending to the IRS.) — 9 Office code (optional) — 10 Employer identification number

Cat. No. 10220Q

Figure 19-1 • Fill out a new W-4 form for your employer if you need to change the number of exemptions you claim.

You can use TurboTax to prepare a W-4 form for your employer. From the Planning section of the interview, choose Form W-4, Withholding Certificate, and Form 1040-ES, Estimated Taxes.

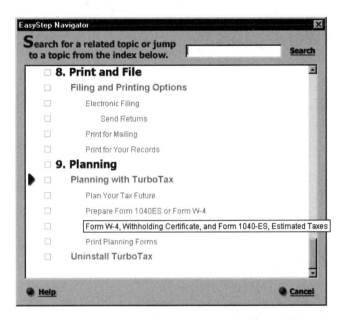

Indicate your filing status and if you are over 65 or blind, then enter the number of exemptions you want to claim. The questions about estimated income and deductions relate to preparing vouchers for estimated taxes. If you are not required to pay estimated taxes, you can leave these screens blank (if you do pay estimated taxes and want to calculate your payments here, see Chapter 15) and continue to the screen where you can indicate that you want to Prepare Form W-4.

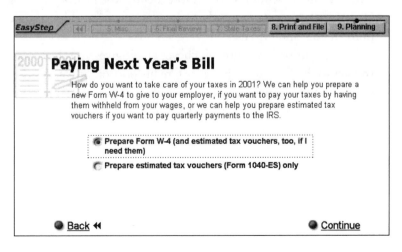

A few more screens, and you will have the opportunity to print the Form W-4, which you can then take to your employer.

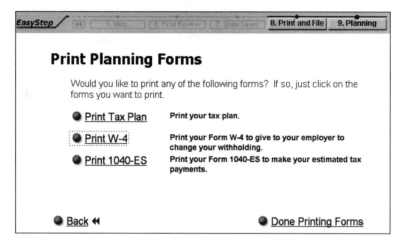

College Education

Schedule the timing of tuition payments and college loan payments for yourself or a family member to take advantage of the lifetime learning credit, the Hope Scholarship credit, the Education IRA, and the deduction for student loan interest. Keep in mind that there are income limits that may affect your ability to claim the education tax credits and the student loan interest deduction.

The lifetime learning credit and the Hope Scholarship credit are mutually exclusive, meaning you can only take one on any tax return. Both of these higher education credits are not available to taxpayers with income over $50,000 ($100,000 if married filing jointly). Furthermore, neither the lifetime learning credit nor the Hope Scholarship credit may be claimed in a year in which a student is using funds from an Education IRA.

You are entitled to claim whichever credit gives you the better tax benefit. When you get to the Education Expense Credits portion of your TurboTax program (found in the Deductions section of the EasyStep Navigator), you will be asked if the family member is in the first or second year of college.

Then you will be asked to enter the amount of higher education costs you incurred for each member of your family. From that point forward, TurboTax will compute which credit will benefit you the most and fill out your tax forms accordingly.

Lifetime Learning Credit   This credit, explained more fully in Chapter 8, is a tax credit for college-level courses. The credit can be taken each year and applies to the cost of education for all members of the family, whether the students are full-time college students, adults attending a business seminar sponsored by an institution of higher learning, or graduate students. The maximum credit is $1,000 per year, calculated by taking 20 percent of up to $5,000 in qualified tuition paid for all family members in a year. (The credit increases to 20 percent of up to $10,000 in 2003.)

Hope Scholarship Credit   This credit, explained more fully in Chapter 8, is available for only the first two years of college costs, and applies to each member of the family individually, as opposed to the lifetime learning credit, which applies to all costs for the entire family. The Hope Scholarship credit is a maximum $1,500 per year credit, calculated by taking 100 percent of the first $1,000 and 50 percent of the second $1,000 spent on post-secondary school education. A qualifying student must be at least a half-time student for one academic period (semester or term) during the year.

Education IRA   The Education IRA, which is explained in detail in Chapter 6, is a savings vehicle whereby a taxpayer with income below $110,000 ($160,000 if married filing jointly) can contribute up to $500 per student per year. The tax benefit to the donor is negligible as the only tax savings is in the form of tax-free earnings on the account. The beneficiary of the account will be able to withdraw the funds in the account, tax-free, to pay for tuition, fees, books, and supplies at an educational institution. Room and board may be covered by funds in an Education IRA if the student is pursuing a degree and is at least a half-time student at the school.

Student Loan Interest   Another tax break for college students, the student loan interest adjustment, is explained more completely in Chapter 6. In general, students or their parents who are paying off college loans may be entitled to reduce income on their tax returns by the amount of loan interest paid, up to a maximum of $2,000 in 2000, and $2,500 per year each year thereafter. The deduction is allowed only for the first 60 months of interest paid, and the ability to take such a deduction is phased out when income exceeds $55,000 ($75,000 if married filing jointly). You do not need to itemize to take this deduction, and you are not precluded from claiming this deduction if you are claiming a higher education credit (discussed above) in the same year.

Move to a New Home

Learning the tax rules for distance and length of employment will enable you to take advantage of the tax benefits associated with a change in personal residence. The IRS allows a deduction for moving expenses, if certain tests are met. You don't need to itemize your deductions to get the benefit of the moving expense deduction.

The first test of whether you qualify to take the moving expense deduction is that your new place of work must be at least 50 miles further from your old home than was your old place of work. The second test is that, if you are an employee, you must maintain full-time employment for at least 39 of the 52 weeks following your move. If you are self-employed, you must work full-time for at least 78 of the 104 weeks following your move. By controlling these events, you can ensure that you will be able to deduct your moving expenses from your income.

For example, if your new job is 100 miles away from your old home and you decide to move so that you will be closer to that job, you can assume some of your moving costs will be deductible. But what if you were taking the train into the city at your old job and your commute was actually 60 miles from your home? For you to qualify to take a deduction for moving expenses, the location of your new job would have to be at least 110 miles from your old home. In this situation, you would not be entitled to a moving deduction.

Here's another example. You've moved to a new home to take a new job, and we'll assume the mileage test has been met. But for whatever reason, you lose your job after 30 weeks. You've got 13 weeks in which to find another job, and you must hold that job for at least nine weeks, or you lose your moving expense deduction. If you wait 14 weeks before taking a new job, 44 weeks have passed since you moved, and in 8 weeks, your move will have occurred 52 weeks ago, and you won't have worked for 39 of the 52 weeks. No deduction for moving expenses will be allowed.

When you use TurboTax to calculate your moving expense deduction, you will be asked if you meet the 39- or 78-week test. If you meet this test, TurboTax will help you with the calculation for the mileage test. Then you will be asked to enter your moving expenses and TurboTax will figure out the allowable deduction.

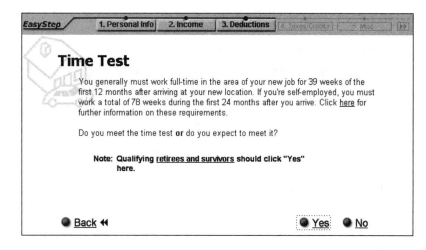

Day-to-Day Expenses

Knowing what types of expenses are deductible as itemized deductions will empower you with the knowledge of which expenditures you need to track, and you will also be able to consider timing year-end and beginning-of-the-year payments to coincide with years in which the tax advantage will be the greatest. Major categories of deductions over which you can exercise some control regarding the timing and amount of payments you make include the following:

- Medical expenses
- State income and property taxes
- Mortgage interest
- Investment interest
- Charitable contributions
- Miscellaneous expenses

Chapter 7 covers these deductions in detail.

Retirement

While you are working, making contributions to retirement plans can create tax benefits through investment funds that produce tax-deferred or tax-free earnings. In addition, in many cases the contributions to such plans are not subject to income tax in the year in which you contribute. See "Planning for Your Retirement" later in this chapter for more information on this subject.

Investments

Learn how the timing of investment decisions affects the tax on your investment earnings and the sales of investments. Make purchases and sales decisions that will provide you with the lowest possible tax.

Selling Shares of Stock   When you make a decision to sell shares of stock, you should calculate the gain or loss you will experience on the sale and consider the impact this would have on your tax before you make the sale. For example, stock held more than one year and sold at a gain will be taxed at no more than 20 percent (10 percent if your income is in the lowest tax bracket), but if you sell the stock before a year has passed, you could pay as much as 39.6 percent income tax on the profit from the sale.

Another consideration when selling stock or any investment is to keep in mind that the money going into your pocket is not all necessarily taxable. The proceeds from the sale of an investment get compared to your *basis* in the investment, and the difference is taxed.

GET SMARTER Calculating the Basis on an Investment Whenever you sell an item that results in a taxable transaction, you must report not only the sales price of the item but the "cost or adjusted basis." The cost of an item is what you paid for it. The adjusted basis is the cost, adjusted by any amounts that relate to the cost, including broker commission, shipping, and sales tax. If you inherited an item, you didn't incur any cost, but your adjusted basis is the value of the item on the date of death of the original owner. If you receive an item as a gift, calculating the adjusted basis gets a bit trickier. See the next Get Smarter sidebar, "Your Basis in a Gift," for the details of this computation. If you spend any money to improve an item, that cost gets added to the adjusted basis. For example, if you purchase an antique vase for $1,000, then pay $200 to have the vase restored to its original splendor, the adjusted basis would be $1,200.

If you are considering selling some investments in the year to come, one way to experiment with different tax scenarios is to create a new TurboTax file, by choosing File | New from the menu. Use this sample file during the year to test different transactions and gauge their impact on your income tax.

Selling Shares in Mutual Funds   Many investors purchase shares in mutual funds over time, reinvesting earnings each month to purchase additional shares, including fractional shares. When it comes time to sell those shares, calculating your basis may seem like an accounting nightmare. To make the calculation a little easier, the IRS gives you the right to average the cost of your mutual fund shares (the average basis method). Many brokers will perform this calculation for you and include the average cost of your shares right on your year-end broker statement.

Although averaging the cost of shares is usually much easier than calculating the specific cost of each share you sell, you may find that the tax savings from specifically identifying and costing your shares are well worth the time it takes to perform this task. If you keep a nice worksheet where you track all the shares you purchase and the cost of those shares, you may find that it isn't so difficult after all to figure out how much each of your shares costs (the cost basis method).

When you sell shares in a mutual fund, you have the right to choose the method for reporting the cost of the shares that will provide you with the greatest tax saving. Furthermore, you have the right to direct your broker as to exactly which shares are sold. Depending on whether you are trying to generate a gain, which you can offset against other losses you may have this year, or maximize your tax savings with a loss, the best way to keep control of your finances in this area is to keep thorough records of your share purchases and sales. You can choose between using the average basis method or the cost basis method when determining your basis in mutual fund shares that you sell.

The Average Basis Method   When you choose to use the average basis for determining the basis of shares sold from a mutual fund, you must choose between the single category method (the more common) and the double category method.

The single category method dictates that you average all shares together, without any consideration for the length of time you have held the shares. Add the purchase price of all the shares in the fund, then divide by the number of shares you own at the time of sale. The resulting average per-share price is the price you will use to calculate gain or loss on the sale.

The double category method instructs you to determine whether shares fall into the short-term (held less than one year) or long-term category at the time you sell the shares. You average all the short-term shares together in one group and all the long-term shares in another group. The basis you use for determining your gain or loss depends on the group from which you are selling shares. Each time you sell additional shares you must perform this calculation again, because the long- and short-term status of shares will change as time passes.

GET SMARTER   **Your Basis in a Gift**   The general rule is that when you receive a gift, your basis in the gift is the same as that of the donor. So if you receive a gift of stock that cost the original purchaser $5,000, your basis in that stock is $5,000 also—right? Maybe not. The IRS says that special basis rules apply when you receive a gift:

- If you sell the stock for more than $5,000, your basis is $5,000, and you will pay tax on the amount by which the sales price exceeds $5,000. So if you sell the stock for $7,000, you will report a gain of $2,000 on your tax return.

- If you sell the stock for less than the fair market value of the stock on the day on which you receive it, your basis is not the cost, $5,000, but instead it is the fair market value of the stock on the day on which you received it. (You can check with the reference desk at your library to find out the value of stock on a particular day.) So, if the fair market value is $3,000 when you receive the stock, and you sell the stock for $2,500, your basis is $3,000, and you will report a loss of $500 on your tax return.

- If you sell the stock for something in between the original cost of the stock ($5,000 in this example) and the fair market value at the time you received it ($3,000 in this example), no gain or loss is reported on the sale. So, if you sell the stock for $4,000, the sale has no effect on your taxable income or on your tax.

If you choose to use an average basis method for calculating the basis of your shares, you must indicate this information on your tax return either in a notation on your Schedule D or in a separate statement attached to your Schedule D. **Once you begin using the average basis method, you must continue doing so for all future sales from that fund.** You may use different methods for different funds.

The Cost Basis Method   This is a more time-consuming method for calculating cost of shares in a mutual fund, but ultimately you may find it more satisfying. You must track the cost of all shares purchased, including fractional shares and reinvested dividends, along with the date on which each share or fractional share was acquired. This method provides you with the most control because you can choose exactly which shares you want to sell. You must tell your broker if you intend to select the shares to sell. If you simply tell your broker to sell shares, without indicating which shares to sell, the shares you have owned the longest are the shares that will be sold.

> **Note** | *If you own shares in a mutual fund and the cost of those shares varies only slightly over the years, it may not be worth your time to use the cost basis method. The average cost method will probably produce results that will be so close to the cost basis method that a sale using either method may result in very little difference in your tax liability. In this situation, the average cost method is advised.*

Gifts and Estates

Estate is a term generally associated with the wealthy. Actually, every person who dies with assets greater than liabilities owns an estate, and you will want to make sure that as much of your estate as possible passes to your family and friends, not the taxing authorities. Control the amount of tax that is assessed on your estate. Know the annual gift-giving limits, the estate tax exclusion, and alternatives that are available for limiting the tax on estates.

See "Preparing for Taxes on Gifts and Estates" later in this chapter for more specific information on this topic.

Planning for Your Retirement

For many, retirement plan contributions represent just one more amount taken from your paycheck—another piece of your earnings that you don't get to use currently. Retirement planning lets you have a long-term perspective on the contributions you make, and when you are planning for the future, the amounts you contribute today will have a purpose.

Most people do not want to burden their family with their care, nor do they want to reach an age when they can no longer work and have nothing set aside to live on. A long-range retirement plan will provide you with peace of mind that you and those you care about will be comfortable as you age.

There are several types of retirement accounts, each a bit different from one another from a tax perspective. Some of the most common types of accounts are explained here.

Company-Sponsored Retirement Plans

Many companies provide workers with the opportunity to route some of their earnings to a retirement plan. These plans have names like 401(k) or 403(b), depending on the type of company you work for. The plan types are named for the section of the Internal Revenue Code that defines these plans and permits employees to make tax-deferred contributions to the plans.

These employee-funded retirement plans are part of a class of plans known as defined-contribution plans, so named because the amount contributed to the plan is fixed. Typically, the allowed contribution amount is a percentage of your salary, up to a maximum amount ($10,500 in 2000). Sometimes employers will make a contribution to the plan as well.

The contributions you make to the plan reduce your taxable income, so that in the year in which you make a plan contribution you don't pay income tax on the amount you pay into the retirement plan. When you retire and begin withdrawing money from your retirement plan, you will be subject to income tax on the amount you withdraw. The theory is that you will be deferring income that will be taxed at higher rates to later years when it will likely be taxed at a lower rate.

It is generally assumed that you will not make as much income when you retire as you do when you work, and thus the amounts you withdraw will be taxed at a lower rate than the tax rate you pay when you are working. Keep in mind that, even if the tax rate is the same when you retire as it was when you worked, by deferring the tax on your retirement contributions, you have had the opportunity to invest that money you would have spent on taxes, and the earnings on your investment may well cover all the taxes on your retirement income.

If you have access to a retirement plan such as the ones described here, and if you can afford to make the contributions, it is an excellent savings and tax-deferment investment vehicle. The money is yours—you don't have to worry about any risk of losing it. If you change jobs, you will have the option of transferring the money into a similar tax-deferred account.

Often there will be investment options for the funds in your retirement account and you will have an opportunity to choose the option you believe is right for you. You can monitor your investments to ensure that you receive the best return on the investment options available to you. Some companies provide their employees with opportunities to choose the level of risk associated with the retirement funds, and you should analyze your choices as they might apply to your age and any other investments you have.

Traditional IRA

A traditional Individual Retirement Account (IRA) is an account much like the 401(k) except that you set up the account yourself instead of having an employer set up and administer the account. You need to set up the account through an authorized financial institution, such as a bank or credit union, or through a stockbroker. You cannot simply open a savings account and declare that the account is an IRA. The financial institution or brokerage becomes the trustee of the account, and is responsible for reporting your account activity to the IRS.

Your annual contributions to an IRA are limited to a maximum of $2,000, but see Chapter 6 for rules on when and how much you can contribute. Also see Chapter 1 for the latest information regarding legislative changes to the IRA contribution rules.

An IRA is an account that you control fully, so you can determine how the money in the account is invested, and you can monitor the performance of the investments. The interest and dividend income that is earned annually in your IRA, as well as any capital gain income for sales of IRA investments, is tax-deferred until such time as you draw the money from the account.

An IRA is prohibited from investing in collectibles, such as stamps and antiques; however, there are certain gold, silver, platinum, and state-issued coins that are allowed as investments.

Withdrawals of money from an IRA are subject to a 10 percent early withdrawal penalty if you are under age $59\frac{1}{2}$ when you withdraw the money. There are some exceptions to this rule, which are described in Chapter 6.

Your tax planning decisions while you own an IRA will include:

- How much to contribute
- How frequently to contribute
- How the money in the account should be invested
- When to sell shares of stock or mutual funds owned in the account

- Whether to begin withdrawing at age 59$^{1}/_{2}$, the earliest age, or wait until age 70$^{1}/_{2}$, the latest age at which you can start withdrawing funds, or choose some time in between
- Which funds, in which order, to withdraw when you reach retirement age
- Whether to convert all or a portion of the traditional IRA account to a Roth IRA
- Whether to make an untimely (early) withdrawal of funds that may be subject to a penalty

The Roth IRA

The Taxpayer Relief Act of 1997 brought many major changes to the tax landscape, not the least of which was the Roth IRA. The Roth IRA is similar to a traditional IRA, the primary differences being:

- No contribution to the Roth IRA can be tax-deferred.
- You can continue to contribute throughout your entire life.
- There is no required age at which you must begin withdrawing funds.
- No withdrawals from the Roth IRA will ever be subject to income tax.

See Chapter 6 for details about when and how much you can contribute to a Roth IRA, and see Chapter 1 for information about recent legislative action affecting the Roth IRA. Also, there is a plethora of information about the Roth IRA available on the Internet. A particularly good Web site for Roth IRA information is http://www.rothira.com/.

Tax planning options involving the Roth IRA include all of the points listed in the section about the traditional IRA except you are not required to begin withdrawing funds at any age.

Many decisions you make about IRAs are not permanent. For example:

- You can alter the investment mix as the market changes.
- You can invest in a traditional IRA and then switch your funds to a Roth IRA.
- You can change the beneficiary arrangement of your IRA.
- In any year you can change your mind about how little or how much (up to the $2,000 limit) you want to contribute to an IRA.

For more extensive information about the Roth IRA, and other types of retirement plans that are available through employers and individual financial planners, you can turn to http://www.quicken.com/ on the Internet (shown in Figure 19-2). Click the Retirement tab to display a wide array of resources and planners.

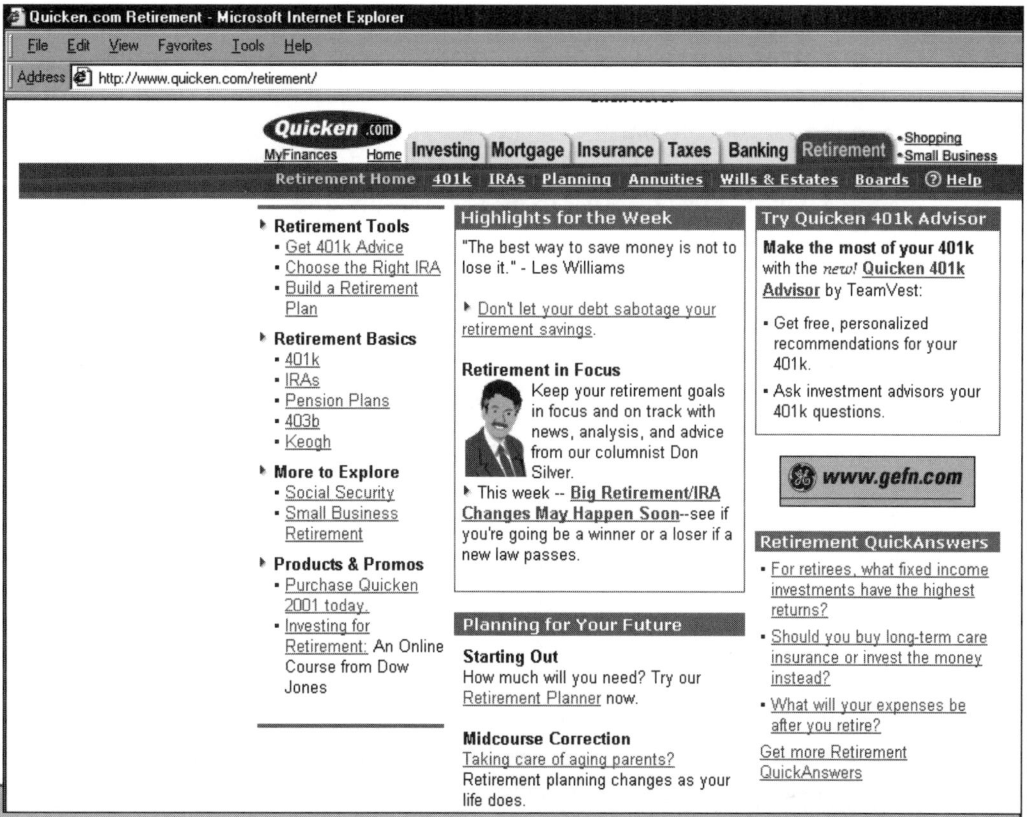

Figure 19-2 • Display a full range of retirement resources at the quicken.com Web site.

Making Investment Decisions

Decisions you make about how and when you will invest your money play a large role in tax planning. Although it's fun to decide to put some extra cash in a money market fund where it will earn a bit more than it would in your savings account, or to buy a block of shares in the stock of a new company that you're certain will be the next Microsoft, making long-range investment decisions involves careful thought and planning.

There are several separate decisions you need to make about investing, including how much and when to invest. Here are some issues to think about when making some long-range plans for investing.

How much can you afford to invest?   The best investment plans often involve committing to invest a particular percentage of your income or a specific amount on a regular basis. Even a very small amount, such as $10 per paycheck or 2 percent of your annual pay will get you started on an investment plan. If you get over the initial hump of beginning to make regular investments by starting with a small amount, it will be easier to increase the amounts you invest later on.

For example, if you earn $30,000 per year and decide to invest 2 percent or $600 per year for 10, 20, or 30 years, Table 19-1 shows you what you can expect in the way of savings, much of which results from compounding interest.

Year	Total Invested	Invested at 5%	Invested at 7.5%	Invested at 10%
5	$3,000	$3,481	$3,746	$4,029
10	$6,000	$7,924	$9,125	$10,519
15	$9,000	$13,595	$16,846	$20,970
20	$12,000	$20,832	$27,932	$37,811
25	$15,000	$30,068	$43,846	$64,909
30	$18,000	$41,856	$66,693	$108,566

Table 19-1 • Effect of Compounding Interest on a $600 per Year Investment

From a tax standpoint, keep in mind that although investing increases the value of your money, provides you with long-term income potential, and relieves family members of having to care for you in your old age, investments can represent risk. One rule of thumb is that you shouldn't invest money in risky ventures unless you can afford to lose the money. Make sure you can afford to set aside the money you want to use for investment, without letting other necessary costs (including taxes) slide.

How frequently will you invest?   The easiest method for making investments is to invest on a regular basis. You pay the electric bill every month, right? And your rent or mortgage too. Waiting until the end of the year to pay the entire year's rent would be a real financial hardship for most people. Monthly or even more frequent payments are much easier on the budget. You might argue that you want to wait to invest until you have enough money to make a minimum investment in a mutual fund or purchase a large block of stock. That's fine—but you should still consider putting aside the money on a regular schedule, perhaps in a savings account or some other very liquid account that can be cashed out quickly. When you have enough saved, you can make your purchase.

Tax considerations when deciding how frequently to make investments include:

- If the amount of your investment is going to result in tax-deferred income (such as investing in a company-sponsored retirement plan or an IRA), you have until the due date (including extensions) of your tax return in order to make the contribution to the plan.

- Making investments on a monthly basis—for example, placing money in a mutual fund each month—may be easier on your budget, but you will have some significant bookkeeping ahead of you. You should keep track of each investment you make and the date on which the investment is made. When you sell the investment, you will need to know which portions are short-term (held less than one year) and which are long-term.

What will you invest in?   There are more choices for investing than you can count. If you choose to go the route of mutual funds, there are thousands from which to select. An excellent resource on the Internet for examining the history and performance of mutual funds is the Morningstar Web site at http://www.morningstar.com/cover/funds.html. Morningstar provides rankings of mutual funds (five-star being the highest) that are used by brokers for analyzing investment options.

If you want to purchase stocks, again, there are thousands to pick from. Quicken.com's stock screener, on the Internet at http://www.quicken.com/investments/stocks/search/, provides a set of 33 criteria to help you choose the stock investment that is right for you. The Internet has opened a new world of online stock purchasing for bargain-rate commissions. Purchase and sell stocks for under $20 a transaction at sites such as E*TRADE (http://www.etrade.com/), Ameritrade (http://www.ameritrade.com/), and Datek Online (http://www.datek.com/).

You can also consider purchasing government or corporate bonds, investing in real estate, buying a stake in a partnership, buying life insurance, or purchasing a long-term annuity. Although deciding what to invest in is perhaps the toughest decision you will make, you don't have to make it alone. There are investment advisors available who can help you design your investment portfolio to meet your investing needs. Stock brokerage houses like Charles Schwab (http://www.schwab.com/), Morgan Stanley Dean Witter (http://www.msdw.com/), and Salomon Smith Barney (http://www.smithbarney.com/) all charge a fee for services, but offer individual investment counselors, investment seminars, and research services that exceed the services available on free Internet sites.

When you choose the investments where you want to place your money, consider some of these tax and investment angles:

- Spreading your investment dollars over several types of investments protects you from an overwhelming loss if one investment fails to perform in the manner you had hoped.

- You can make investments that will result in tax deferment on the amount you invest, such as contributions to a retirement fund.

- You can invest in tax-free obligations such as municipal bonds or tax-free municipal funds. These investments typically pay a smaller return on investment than their taxable counterparts, but if your tax bracket is high, the tax savings will more than make up for the lower income you receive.

- You can invest for short-term income, long-term growth, or somewhere in between. Investigate how stocks or funds have performed in the past, how much of their earnings produces current taxable income and how much will be taxed later.

- You can choose to acquire investments that will result in either ordinary income (such as dividend income or short-term capital gain) or long-term capital gain, which is taxed at a lower rate than other income.

- Some mutual funds limit their trading so as to avoid capital gains that are passed on to the investor on an annual basis, other funds trade extensively during the year and generate significant capital gains for the investors. Investors in funds that report capital gains end up paying tax on these gains even though they don't receive any cash proceeds from the trading transactions.

When will you sell your investments?   Purchasing investments is only half of the investment cycle. The other half occurs when you decide to sell your investments, either to have access to the cash yourself, or to change your holdings to something different. You need to make decisions about how long to hold your investments, and then how to apply the proceeds from your sale.

Tax considerations when selling your investments include:

- The holding period for long-term capital gain treatment on the sale of an investment is one year. Sell your investment at a gain before a year ends and you will be subject to short-term capital gain treatment, which means the investment will be taxed at your regular (ordinary) income rates. Hold the investment for at least one year and you pay a maximum of 20 percent tax on your gain (10 percent if you are in the lowest tax bracket).

- Selling investments at a loss can help your tax situation (sometimes). If you have a lot of capital gains, especially gains that are being taxed as short-term gains, you can sell some investments at a loss and offset the taxable gain income. If there are investments that you are fairly certain are only going to continue to lose money, it may make sense to go ahead and sell those now, cutting your losses where possible. Keep in mind that you are only allowed to deduct up to $3,000 per year in losses from sales of investments.

- In other words, if you sell stock for a gain (sales price less your purchase price) of $6,000 and you sell stocks at a loss of $11,000, providing a net loss of $5,000, only $3,000 of the loss will be deductible this year. The remaining $2,000 loss will carry forward to next year's tax return.

Preparing for Taxes on Gifts and Estates

When you make a gift to someone, you don't typically think about paying tax on the gift, nor does the recipient expect to report the gift on his or her tax return. The IRS, however, has some rules about gift giving that involve taxation on gifts over a certain level.

If you give a gift to one person that is valued at more than $10,000 in a single year, you are responsible for reporting that gift on a gift tax return, and you may be liable for gift tax.

The way the gift tax works is this:

- You are allowed to give up to $10,000 per year, tax free, to as many people as you like. The gifts can be to family members, friends, or anyone else you choose.

- If you give more than $10,000 to any person during a calendar year, you must report the gift on Form 709, United States Gift Tax Return.

- You are allowed to exclude from tax, under the uniform estate and gift tax credit, up to $675,000 in gifts that do not fall under the $10,000 rule. If you choose to use some of this credit, you will indicate that on Form 709. The $675,000 cap on the tax credit is a lifetime cap. Once you have used it up, you have no more allowance for tax-free gifts.

- Keep in mind that if you use some of the $675,000 tax credit to avoid paying gift tax on gifts that exceed $10,000, you are chipping away at the amount of exemption allowed from estate tax. The $675,000 credit applies to both your estate and your excess gifts, so as you use this up in your lifetime, you are reducing the credit available to apply to your estate.

Note   *Current law will increase the uniform estate and gift tax credit to $1,000,000 over the next five years. Congress has been trying to do away with the estate and gift tax altogether, but successful passage of such a bill in the House and Senate during 2000 met with a veto from President Clinton. It remains to be seen if this tax will continue in effect in future years.*

Because the uniform estate and gift tax credit applies to gifts over $10,000 per year per person and to estates, it is important to include gift planning in your estate planning. If you have assets that put you in contention for paying the estate tax, you should consult with a professional during your lifetime to explore means of protecting your estate from tax and lengthy probate.

Leaving your estate to your heirs to sort out may result in the estate not being disbursed in the manner you intend, due to taxes and legal fees. There are measures you can take in your lifetime to protect the value of your estate, to keep the assets available for your loved ones, and to reduces taxes. If you expect to have an estate that will be taxed, it is worth the time and money to meet with a tax or legal professional who specializes in the area of estate law and taxation, who can provide you with knowledge of your options and give you guidance as to how to protect your estate and how to make sure that the people you designate as beneficiaries receive what you intend for them.

Using TurboTax for What-If Scenarios

In This Chapter:

- *Using the Life Events Planner*

- *Using the Tax Planner*

- *Using the IRA Planner*

Chapter 20

In the previous chapter, you learned of many ways in which tax planning can affect the outcome of your income tax. TurboTax provides you with the tools to actually view how changes in your life and long-range planning can affect your taxes. Starting with your current year income and deductions as a base, TurboTax gives you the opportunity to indicate changes that either will or might occur in your life, and then displays the specific impact these changes will have on your tax return.

Use these planning tools to arm you with the knowledge of how your taxes are going to change when you make certain decisions. This way, when next April 15 rolls around, you'll know exactly what to expect.

Planning for Life Changes

When you have finished entering your 2000 tax information into TurboTax, you can use the Planning section of the program to peek into the future.

Note   *Although you can skip over to the planning section of TurboTax at any time, the feature works best if all of the information for your 2000 tax return has been entered.*

If you haven't arrived at the Planning screen through the EasyStep Interview, you can click the Planning topic at the top of the Interview screen, then select Planning in the box that appears, shown below, to go to the Planning section of TurboTax.

When you continue past the introductory Planning screen, you are given the choice of the following three planners (see Figure 20-1):

- **Life Events Planner** enables you to project your taxes based on major changes in your life, such as having a child, changing your filing status, making a significant change in your income, beginning a career, purchasing or selling a home, or retiring.

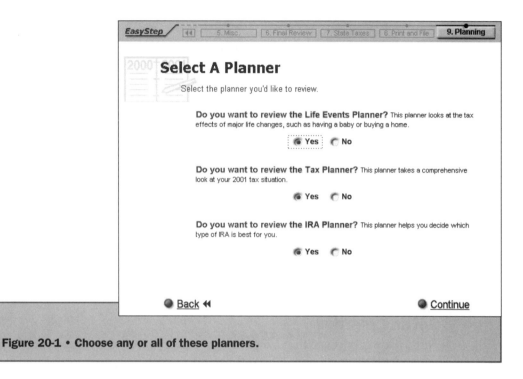

Figure 20-1 • Choose any or all of these planners.

- **Tax Planner** gives you the opportunity to estimate how you think the amounts in your 2000 tax return might change in 2001, and then see the detailed results of those potential changes.
- **IRA Planner** helps you determine what type of IRA contribution you are eligible to make, and assists you in deciding which type of IRA, traditional or Roth, would be best for your financial situation.

Click the Yes option on any of these planners that you want to try.

Tax Effects of Life Events

When you use the Life Events Planner in TurboTax, you are given seven options, shown on the next page, for determining the tax effects of major changes in your life. Choose one option at a time, then click the Continue option and TurboTax will ask for information that will enable the program to calculate the tax effect of the life change you have chosen.

Getting Married

TurboTax will calculate the change in your income tax as it switches your filing status to Married, Filing Jointly. You are asked to enter your spouse's birth date so TurboTax can determine if certain age-related tax modifications will apply. You'll also enter information about any additional family members brought by the marriage (for example, if you're marrying someone who has children or a dependent parent). TurboTax will ask you to indicate the types and estimated amounts of income and deductions that the new spouse will bring to the joint tax return so it can calculate your income tax with the new modifications, as shown here:

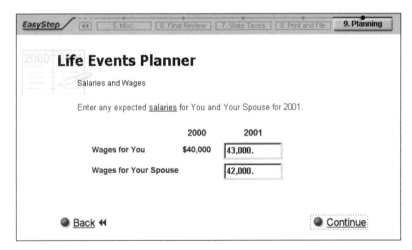

If you don't know exact amounts, feel free to estimate in this section. The point of the exercise is to give you a ballpark idea of how your tax is going to change—you don't need to know the changes down to the penny.

Adding Family Members

You may be expecting a child or perhaps you are going to start caring for an older relative. You may be divorced or separated and you and your former spouse alternate the years in which you can claim your children as dependents. When you acquire new family members, there is a ripple effect on your tax return. Dependents generate tax exemptions, which lower your taxes. Dependents can require care while you work, and that care expense can translate into a tax credit. Children can make you eligible for the child tax credit, which is discussed in Chapter 8.

Tip *New family members can also add expenses to your personal budget, such as the cost of food, medical care, clothing, entertainment, and so on. These costs are not relevant in the TurboTax Tax Planner, but are issues you should consider when budgeting for the coming year.*

When you request the planner for adding family members, you will be asked to enter the number of new family members expected for 2001, as shown below. You should specify if new family members are under age 17, in which case you may be eligible for the child tax credit. Enter negative numbers if family members are decreasing in any category. You can also enter the amount you anticipate spending on care for your dependents. The care expense you enter should be only the expense of care while you (and your spouse, if applicable) work. For more information on the dependent care credit, see Chapter 8.

Losing a Dependent

From a tax standpoint, the flip side of adding a member to your family is having a dependent lose dependency status. If a dependent moves away from home and becomes self-supporting, or if a dependent child over age 19 is no longer a full-time student, you will no longer be able to claim the person as a dependent, and your taxes will reflect this change.

TurboTax will ask for the number of dependents by which your family is decreasing. If you will still have at least one dependent, you will be asked to indicate the amount of dependent care expense you will incur while working. Then TurboTax will present you with the estimated amount by which your taxes will change next year and a detailed summary of the estimated amounts that will appear on your tax return.

Change in Earnings

If you anticipate a significant change in any area of your earnings, such as wages, investment income, income from your own business, or retirement income, you can provide an estimate of the expected amount (or percent) of change, and see a calculation of how the change will affect your income tax.

When contemplating a change in earnings, remember to take into account any change in your marital status that may affect the earnings reported on your tax return.

Along with calculating a change in earnings, this section of the program will allow you to indicate an expected change in the adjustments section of your tax return, which includes deductions for IRA and other retirement plan contributions, interest paid on student loans, health insurance paid by self-employed persons, moving expenses, alimony, and medical savings account activity.

Purchasing or Selling a Home

If you plan to sell or purchase a home in 2001, you can use the Life Events Planner to help you anticipate the tax effects of changes in your deductions for real estate tax and mortgage interest, as shown on the next page. These amounts will be eligible for inclusion with your itemized deductions.

EasyStep | ◄◄ | 5. Misc | 6. Final Review | 7. State Taxes | 8. Print and File | **9. Planning**

Deductions for Mortgage Interest and Points

Does the amount shown below reflect the amount of mortgage interest and points you expect to pay during 2001? If not, change it now.

Mortgage Interest and Points   12,350.

● Back ◄◄   ● Continue

The gain on a sale of a personal residence is no longer subject to income tax due to changes in the tax law in 1997, as long as you meet certain criteria:

- You must have owned the home for at least two of the five years leading up to the date of the sale.
- You must have lived in the home, using it as your principal residence, for at least two of the five years prior to the date of the sale.
- You cannot have sold another home and excluded the gain on the home from your taxes in the two years prior to the date of the sale.

If you meet all of the above requirements, you are entitled to exclude from taxation the gain on the sale of your house, up to $250,000 (or $500,000 if you are married and filing a joint tax return). Any gain over the specified amounts is taxable.

Gain on your house is defined in simple terms as the sales price of the house less the cost of the house. Cost and sales price, however, are not always simple numbers to calculate.

The cost or adjusted basis of your home is calculated as follows:

1. Begin with the original purchase price, including any fees and costs associated with the purchase that are not allowed as deductions on your tax return. Deductible portions of the purchase that are not added to your cost basis would include mortgage interest and points, real estate tax, and any amounts

you were able to deduct as part of a moving expense deduction. (Costs associated with the purchase of a home are no longer allowed as deductible moving expenses, but if your house was purchased prior to 1994, you may have been eligible to claim many of the expenses of your home purchase as moving expenses. If your home was purchased prior to 1994, you should examine a copy of your tax return from the year of purchase to determine which if any expenses have already been deducted.)

2. Add the cost of any permanent improvements you have made during the time you owned the house. An improvement increases the value of your home (or the land on which the home rests), extends its life, or adapts it for another use. Improvements would include adding or remodeling a room, upgrading plumbing or wiring, planting trees, building a fence, or restoring damaged property. Improvements also include assessments from the city for sidewalks, sewers, street lights, and so on. Improvements do not include painting, cleaning, or performing minor repairs.

3. Deduct from the cost of your home any casualty loss deductions you may have claimed on prior tax returns, and any depreciation you have claimed on any portion of the home.

The sales price of your home is calculated as follows:

1. Start with the purchase price for which a buyer has agreed to purchase your home.

2. Deduct from the price any costs of the sales transaction that you must pay, such as realtor commission, title verification fee, legal fees, advertising fees, and any loan charges that you pay on behalf of the purchaser to finalize the sale. Do not deduct any mortgage interest or real estate tax that you pay at the time the sale is finalized. These amounts will be included with your itemized deductions for the year, but they will not affect calculation of your gain or loss on the sale of your home.

The amount you get when you deduct the adjusted basis of your home from the sales price is the gain (if positive) or loss (if negative) on the sale. Losses are not deductible, and a gain typically is not subject to income tax unless it exceeds the thresholds mentioned earlier. Special rules can apply when you have used a portion of your home as a business location. See "The Effects of Depreciating Your Home" in Chapter 5 for more information on the business use of a home.

Start or Quit Working

Another part of the Life Events Planner involves entering anticipated changes in your income for 2001. If you plan to begin, end, or change a job, or if you plan to operate a business or farm, you can select the Start Working or Quit Working option and you will be given an opportunity to enter anticipated changes in your income for 2001.

Planning to Retire

If you plan to retire in 2001, the Life Events Planner will give you the option of entering your anticipated change in your income from jobs and businesses, and the taxable amount you expect to receive from retirement and pension plans, as shown below. Participants in tax-deferred retirement plans such as 401(k) plans and IRAs are required to begin withdrawing funds from their plans, based on a set schedule (see the "Retirement Income" section of Chapter 5), starting at age $70^{1}/_{2}$. Most people are eligible to begin withdrawing amounts from these self-funded retirement plans at age $59^{1}/_{2}$. Social Security benefits may begin arriving at age 65.

All these sources of revenue produce income that may be subject to tax. By using the planner provided by TurboTax, you will be able to see in advance how a new source of income is going to affect your tax.

Using the Tax Planner

TurboTax's Tax Planner lets you examine your entire 2000 tax return and experiment with making changes in any area of the return, just to see what the tax effect will be. Perhaps you are contemplating starting a business of your own and want to know how the additional income will affect your taxes, or maybe you are thinking about refinancing your mortgage and are curious about the effect of deducting additional mortgage interest payments. Perhaps you've always been curious about how the tax would change if you and your spouse filed using the Married Filing Separately status instead of the Married Filing Jointly status.

You can try out tax scenarios with the Tax Planner, just to see what the effect will be.

Answering the Questions

One method of using the Tax Planner is to answer the interview questions in this area as TurboTax provides them. You will be asked about your filing status, your dependents, and your income and deduction amounts. Fill in the blanks and watch TurboTax prepare a mock-up of your tax return at the bottom of the screen (Figure 20-2).

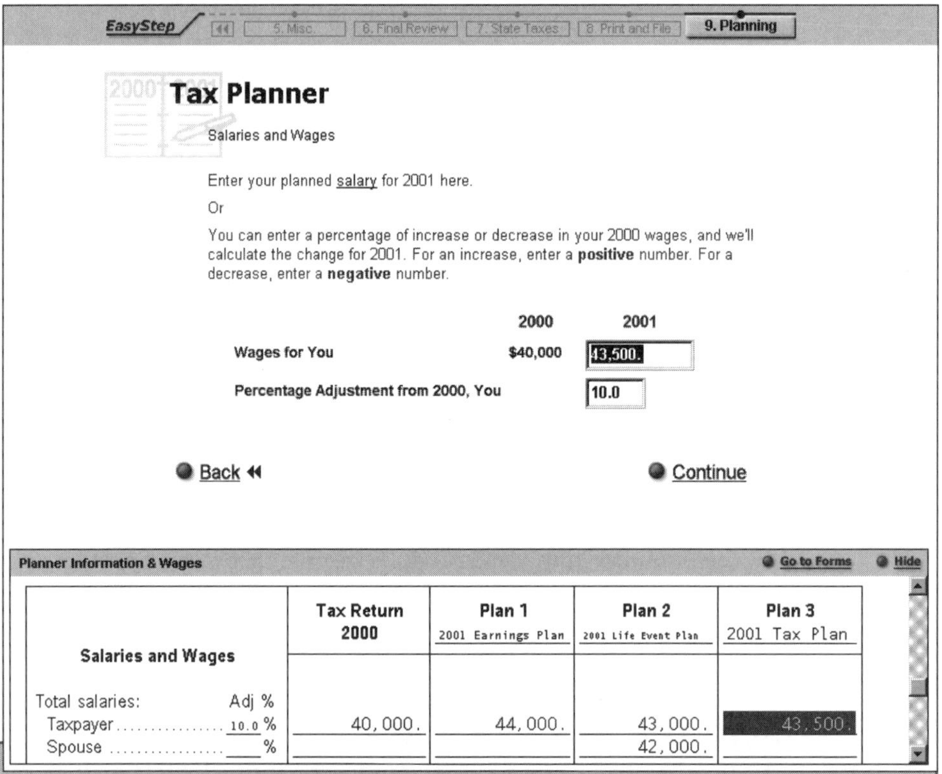

Figure 20-2 • TurboTax calculates your tax projection as you enter information.

Another method of experimenting with tax planning scenarios is to click the Go To Forms button near the bottom of the screen (see below). Clicking this option will take you directly to the form on which the tax scenario is played out.

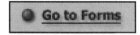

On the Tax Planning Worksheet that appears, you can scroll down the form, viewing all the pertinent parts of your tax calculation, and make changes right on the form. Working with the Tax Planning Worksheet like this gives you a more thorough perspective of how the changes will affect your tax return, as you can see most of the tax return information at once, while you are entering the projected changes.

From the Forms window, where you are operating if you chose Go To Forms, you can gain access to a variety of calculations for your tax return. Click the Open A Form button, and scroll down in the list provided, shown below, to choose from a variety of Planner Summary Information forms. For example, you can choose the Itemized Deductions form and view your tax scenarios as they affect your itemized deductions. Make changes right on this form to experiment with the effect of increasing your charitable contributions, or making your January mortgage payment in December so as to get the benefit of an extra month of mortgage interest deduction.

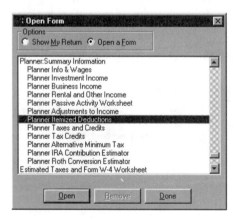

Choose Planner Taxes and Credits from the Open Form list in the Forms window and you will see how your changes affect the bottom line.

You can easily return to the interview at any time by clicking the Back To Interview option at the top-right corner of the screen. You will be returned to the precise place where you left off in the interview.

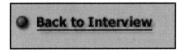

Using the IRA Planner

One area of taxes and financial planning that confuses many taxpayers is the subject of IRA plans and contributions. Traditional IRAs now compete with Roth IRAs for taxpayers' dollars, and the IRS administers the rules for who can and cannot contribute, and when those contributions result in a tax deduction.

TurboTax's IRA Planner sheds some light on the process of deciding which type of IRA is best for you. Indicate that you want to review the IRA planner, then choose the IRA Contribution Estimator or the Roth Conversion Estimator, and TurboTax will provide you with the opportunity to compare IRA alternatives.

To get to this part of TurboTax quickly, click the Planning option on the top of the EasyStep Interview screen, then choose the Plan Your Tax Future option in the Navigator window. Click Select a Planner, and choose Yes for the option of reviewing the IRA tax planner. You will see the screen illustrated below; check one or both of the boxes on your screen, and click Continue to open the planner(s).

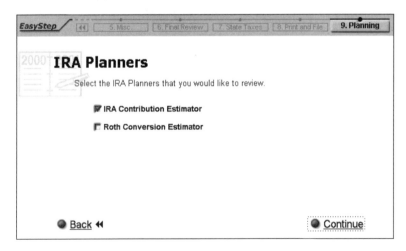

There are two IRA considerations that TurboTax will help you with. The first is the IRA contribution planner, which will help you decide if and how much you can contribute to an IRA. The second planner is the Roth conversion planner, which will assist you in determining if you should consider converting money you hold in a traditional IRA to a Roth IRA account. Use these planners to gain an excellent perspective on the IRA options that are available to you.

The IRA Contribution Planner

You will be asked to enter your filing status and estimated adjusted gross income. These factors play a part in determining your eligibility for making IRA contributions. The planner will tell you how much and to which type of account you are eligible to contribute.

After asking about the amount you intend to contribute and over how long a period of time, the results you will see will show you how much you can expect to receive in income each year from your IRA, and will compare the amounts between traditional and Roth IRAs, if you qualify for both types of accounts.

To make this comparative calculation, you must enter the same information regarding the number of years you plan to contribute and the year in which you expect to begin withdrawing funds for both a traditional and a Roth IRA. This calculation may prove to be limiting, since Roth IRA participants are not required to stop contributing nor are they forced to begin withdrawing funds at a particular age. The program will not allow you to indicate that you plan to contribute to an IRA after age 70, nor will it allow you to indicate you plan to begin withdrawing funds at any age past age 71, and neither of these stipulations applies to a Roth IRA.

A better place to look for a more comprehensive IRA planner, if you are contemplating contributions to a Roth IRA, is at the Quicken Web site, where the options let you enter precise ages for your estimated life expectancy, the number of years you plan to contribute to an IRA, and the age at which you expect to begin taking withdrawals. You can also run calculations that will show the difference between whether you expect to spend the money you withdraw or reinvest it. Go to http://www.quicken.com/retirement/RIRA/planner/ (Figure 20-3) for a detailed look at the Roth IRA and how it can benefit you.

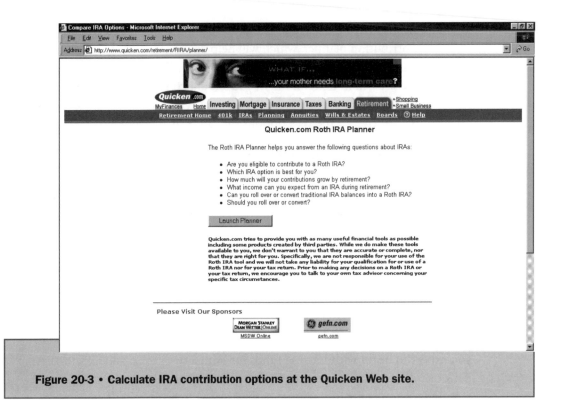

Figure 20-3 • Calculate IRA contribution options at the Quicken Web site.

Converting to a Roth IRA

The benefit of converting traditional IRA funds to a Roth IRA is that, from this point forward, the amount of money in the Roth IRA account will grow, tax-free. The down side of a conversion is that you must pay tax currently on any amounts converted from your traditional IRA that have not previously been taxed.

TurboTax's Roth Conversion Estimator lets you project the tax effect of converting a traditional IRA to a Roth IRA account. The estimator gives you the tax cost of converting to a Roth IRA, and the amount by which your retirement income will be affected depending on whether or not you make the conversion.

A limitation of the TurboTax estimator is that it only calculates the tax cost of a conversion in 2001 and doesn't give you the option of calculating the cost of a conversion to a Roth IRA over a period of years. Many traditional IRA holders are reluctant to make a conversion to a Roth IRA because of the large tax bite, but a conversion over a period of years, paying the tax as you can afford it, can be much more palatable.

When using the TurboTax estimator, you can run one scenario in which you estimate the cost of converting the entire balance of your traditional IRA to a Roth IRA, then you can go back and run a separate calculation to determine the cost of converting only a portion of your IRA in this year.

Appendixes

The information included in this last part of the book gets you started with acquiring and installing your TurboTax program, and also provides you with pointers for some contemplative thinking about how taxes impact your life. Install the program, prepare your tax return using the rest of this book as a guide, then come back here and start thinking about how you can take control of your taxes by making decisions with the help of the planners and worksheets provided here. This part has the following appendixes:

Appendix A: Purchasing and Installing Your TurboTax Program

Appendix B: Bonus Tax Worksheets

Purchasing and Installing Your TurboTax Program

In This Appendix:

- *Purchasing a TurboTax Federal Tax Program*

- *Installing Your Federal Program*

- *Purchasing a TurboTax State Tax Program*

- *Installing Your State Program*

Appendix A

I f you've used TurboTax in previous years, the information in this appendix will probably bring back memories, because the purchase and installation process really hasn't changed much from the past. If you are new to the program, if it has been a few years since you used TurboTax, or if the whole getting-started process has confused you in the past, you may find that there are some options for purchasing and installation about which you might not be aware.

Purchasing TurboTax for Federal Tax Returns

You can acquire the federal TurboTax program, which will produce your 1040, 1040A, or 1040EZ, in a variety of stores throughout the winter months. Bookstores, computer stores, office supply stores, even some grocery stores stock the program.

If you have access to the Internet, you can order a copy of the TurboTax program by logging on to http://www.turbotax.com/. Choose from TurboTax Federal for $29.95 or TurboTax Deluxe Federal for $39.95. The Deluxe version provides you with more resources for looking up answers to questions than are provided with the non-deluxe version, a free electronic filing option (an $11.95 value—also provided with the non-deluxe version), and one free state tax download (a $29.95 value). If you intend to use TurboTax for your state taxes, the Deluxe version is definitely the better deal.

You can download the basic TurboTax Federal program if you purchase it online. When you order TurboTax Deluxe Federal online, you will receive the program in the mail. Accompanying the program is an installation guide.

If you live in a remote area and don't have access to the Internet, you can order a copy of the program by telephone at (800) 224-1047.

Installing the TurboTax Federal Program

When you acquire the CD for your TurboTax Federal program, installation is simply a matter of placing the CD in your CD drive and closing the drive door. Your computer should read the CD and display the following message:

If an installation message doesn't appear on your screen, you can order the installation by following these steps:

1. Click the Start button on your computer. A menu will appear, as shown here:

2. Choose Run from the Start menu. A small window will appear, as shown here:

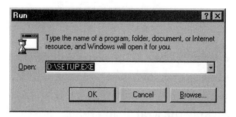

3. Click the Browse button, and in the Browse window that appears, change the Look In location to your CD drive, as shown here:

4. Double-click the Setup option that appears in the list of files.

5. Click OK to begin the setup.

Once the setup process begins, you will be asked to verify the location where the program will be stored, and then the program will load. An icon will be added to your desktop during the installation process, so you can access the program easily by double-clicking the icon at any time.

Purchasing TurboTax for State Tax Returns

TurboTax has two separate programs for federal and state tax returns. You must have the TurboTax Federal program in order to use a state program, and you can purchase a state program that is specifically designed for your particular state.

If you ordered the TurboTax Deluxe Federal program directly from Intuit (either from the Web site or by calling them), you can download one state program at no additional charge. If you purchased the federal program in a store, you will receive a mail-in coupon that will provide a rebate for the purchase price of the TurboTax State program.

The TurboTax State programs are often available in stores at the same location where you purchased your federal program. California and New York have their own separate state program available on a single CD. In other states, and on the TurboTax Web site, you can purchase the TurboTax Multistate program, which includes all 45 states that have an income tax on one CD. Note that you may be required to download an update to your state program if the state is late in its forms release. TurboTax will advise you of the need for such an update, and the download process will be free.

Although all states are available on the CD, each state carries a separate fee. If you need a state program from another state (if you moved during the year, or if you live near a state border and work in another state), you will have access to any state return on your Multistate CD. After installing the first state, additional states can be unlocked for $29.95 each, a fee that will be paid to Intuit. You can pay this fee either on the TurboTax Web site or by phone, and in either case you will receive a code that will enable you to have access to the additional state.

You can download state TurboTax programs from the http://www.turbotax.com/ Web site. If you don't qualify for a free promotion, the charge for the state program is $29.95, and Intuit will bill this amount to your credit card. Indicate the state you want to order and the program will be downloaded to your computer in an executable file that looks like this:

    wili900144.exe
    wini900144.exe

Note | *The sample filenames listed here represented Illinois and Indiana tax files from 1999. The filenames may differ slightly for 2000 versions.*

The second two letters of the filename represent the state. Intuit has tax files available for every state in which there is an income tax.

Intuit recommends that you save a copy of the file in a location other than your computer hard drive (on a zip drive or floppy disk, for example) for safekeeping.

Installing Your TurboTax State Program

If you download your TurboTax State program from the TurboTax Web site, you can install the program by finding the program file (described above) in your My Computer window or in Windows Explorer, and double-clicking it. The file will install itself, and the next time you use TurboTax, the state return pages will be available to you.

If you purchased the state program at a store, you should follow the same process described earlier for installing your federal program from a CD.

You don't have to take any special measures to tell the TurboTax Federal program that a state tax program has been installed. TurboTax will find the state program and activate it immediately.

You can install as many states as you like or need on your computer, and TurboTax will recognize all of them. If you have installed more than one state program, when you are using the TurboTax Federal program and indicate that you want to go to the state program, you will be asked which state's program you want to use.

Bonus Tax Worksheets

In This Appendix:

- *Five-Year Automobile Lease versus Buy Worksheet*

- *Effects of Home Office Depreciation Worksheet*

- *Converting Traditional IRA to Roth IRA Worksheet*

- *Roth IRA Effects of Compounding Interest Worksheet*

- *Non-Cash Charitable Contributions: Valuation Guide*

The worksheets in this appendix are designed to help you in the preparation of your tax return and also to help you make decisions that will impact your taxes for years to come. Use these worksheets, fill in the blanks, use the instructions where necessary to help you perform the calculations, and go forward to future tax returns with the knowledge of what effect your choices will have on tax returns down the road.

Automobile, Buy versus Lease

If you don't take a deduction for the business use of a vehicle, you can still use this section to determine the actual cost differential between buying and leasing a vehicle. You will simply leave the sections requiring a tax calculation blank.

Taking the process one step further, if you use your vehicle for business and you qualify to take a deduction for your mileage, either as unreimbursed employee business expense (Form 2106) or, more likely, on your Schedule C or Schedule F, this section should give you an idea of the part taxes play in your decision to buy or lease.

Are you uncertain as to whether you qualify to take a vehicle expense deduction? As an itemized deduction, vehicle expenses fall into the category of miscellaneous itemized deductions. These deductions are only allowed by the IRS to the extent that the amount of the deductions exceeds 2 percent of your adjusted gross income. For example, if your adjusted gross income is $40,000, the first $800 of your miscellaneous itemized deductions is not used. Only the amount that exceeds $800 will be allowed as a deduction.

General Considerations for Vehicle Decisions

When calculating automobile expenses for a tax deduction, you may have the option of either deducting a flat rate for every mile driven (for 2000, that rate is 32.5 cents per mile) or deducting the proportionate share of your actual vehicle expenses. More information about deducting vehicle expenses, including the rules for when you should use one of these methods or the other, is included in the "Entering Auto Expenses" section of Chapter 5.

The worksheet for determining whether you should lease or purchase a vehicle anticipates that you will be calculating your vehicle expenses by using the actual expense method as opposed to the mileage method.

Another consideration when deciding whether to lease or buy involves certain terms of the lease. Most auto leases provide for a fixed number of miles that can be driven each year, for example, 25,000 per year. Any miles driven that exceed this amount result in excessive per-mile fees that increase the lease cost. Also, any damage to the leased vehicle must be repaired before the vehicle can be turned in at the end of the lease, and you may find you are at the mercy of the leasing company when it comes to defining damage.

If you think you might want to purchase the vehicle you are leasing, keep in mind that the price to buy a vehicle at the end of a lease, combined with the lease payments over the term of the lease, is usually substantially higher than the cost of buying a vehicle and financing it over the same amount of time as the lease term.

The Lease versus Buy Worksheet

Use Worksheet B-1 to compare the costs of leasing and buying a vehicle over a five-year period. The worksheet doesn't take into account costs of repairs, licenses, car washes, gas, oil changes, and other expenses that would be the same whether you leased or purchased the vehicle.

Note   *The worksheet is available online at http://www.osborne.com/ if you would like to experiment with various scenarios using your computer.*

Year 1	Lease	Buy
a. Down payment		
b. Monthly payment × number of months		
c. Number of miles driven for business		
d. Total number of miles driven		
e. Percentage of business use (c/d)		
f. Deductible expense (a + b) × e		n/a
g. Depreciation (cost of vehicle × appropriate rate—33.33% if using accelerated depreciation, 16.67% if using straight-line) × e, limited to $3,060 in 2000	n/a	
h. Deductible interest (interest paid on vehicle loan × e)	n/a	
i. Leased vehicle add-back for vehicles with fair market value over $15,500 (see IRS publication 463, "Travel, Entertainment, Gifts, and Car Expenses")		n/a
j. Highest marginal tax rate that you pay		
k. Tax saving (f + g + h − i) × j		
l. Cash out of pocket (a + b − k)		

Worksheet B-1 • Lease versus Buy

You can extend the Lease versus Buy worksheet for five years (or whatever is the term of your lease) to gain a long-term view of how your decision will play out in future tax returns. In the final year, you will increase your lease payments (monthly payment) by the amount of additional mileage and repairs that you have to pay to conclude the lease.

Home Office Depreciation Deduction

Taking a deduction for a home office is optional. Deducting depreciation on the home office, if you deduct other home office expenses, is not optional. When you choose to deduct expenses for operating an office from your home, the IRS requires that you take a deduction for depreciation on the home. When you take a deduction for depreciation on your home, the basis in your home (see footnote 2 beneath Worksheet B-2) is reduced by the amount of the depreciation, thus widening the gap between the basis and your sales price, and generally resulting in a larger gain on the house sale. Furthermore, the business portion of the home can result in a taxable gain, even when the rest of the gain is not subject to tax.

When Are You Taxed on the Sale of a Home?

If you claim a deduction for business use of your home for more than three of the five years leading up to the date on which you sell your home, you will be required to pay tax on the business portion of any gain on the sale of the home. Not only are you required to pay tax on the gain, but the portion of the gain that represents a recapture of your previously deducted depreciation is taxed at ordinary income rates instead of capital gain rates. The depreciation you took over the years comes back to haunt you, all in one year, when you sell the house.

Because you have a choice about whether you want to take a deduction for a home office or not, you should think ahead to the future and determine how much time will pass before you intend to sell your house. Also, try to estimate what you expect to sell the house for and how much gain (and related tax on the business portion of the house) that sale will generate. By using the worksheet provided here, you can compare the tax benefits of a home office deduction to the tax disadvantage of selling a home that you have used for business at a gain.

Note that the depreciation on the house itself is not the only factor that affects the tax treatment of the gain when you sell the house. If you added improvements to the house—for example, built-in bookshelves and wiring for access to the Internet in your workspace, a security system for the house, or a private entrance for clients—and you have depreciated or taken deductions for any of these improvements on your tax returns, your adjusted basis in the house will be reduced by the amount of deductions you have claimed, and thus your gain will increase.

It is advisable to do as much long-range planning as possible before choosing to take a home office deduction, so that you have a clear picture of how these current year deductions will affect your taxes in the future.

The Home Office Depreciation/Sale of Home Worksheet

Use Worksheet B-2 to calculate the tax effect of claiming a home office deduction and the tax resulting from the sale of the home. Use this worksheet to help you decide whether it is worthwhile to take the home office deduction and for how many years.

Tax Savings from Home Office Deduction	
a. Business percentage of home (square footage of business space divided by square footage of home, or number of rooms used for business divided by total rooms in home)	
b. Annual deductions for home office that would not be allowed as itemized deductions, such as utilities, repairs, home maintenance, and insurance	
c. Depreciation allowed on home [1]	
d. Highest marginal tax rate that you pay	
e. Tax benefit of home office deduction (b + c) $\times$ a $\times$ d	
Tax Effect of Home Sale	
f. Anticipated selling price of home, less expenses of sale	
g. Adjusted basis of home [2]	
h. Anticipated gain on home sale (f – g)	
i. Business portion of gain (a $\times$ h)	
j. Depreciation taken (total of all amounts in c for the number of years you take a deduction for business use of home)	
k. Tax on portion of gain representing prior depreciation (d $\times$ j)	
l. Balance of tax (i – j) $\times$ 20% (or 10% if d = 15%)	
m. Total tax on sale (k + l)	
n. Comparison of tax savings versus tax cost (e – m)	

[1] Depreciation on the business portion of your home is calculated over a period of 39 years. See the section in Chapter 5 on "The Effects of Depreciating Your Home" for specific information about calculating your depreciation.

[2] The adjusted basis of your home is calculated by determining the original cost of your home, including nondeductible purchase costs, adding the cost of improvements, and deducting any allowable depreciation expense. For a more detailed summary of calculating adjusted basis, see the section "Selling Your Home" in Chapter 5.

Worksheet B-2 • Home Office

Note   *The worksheet is available online at http://www.osborne.com/ if you would like to experiment with various scenarios using your computer.*

Converting Your Traditional IRA to a Roth IRA

The IRS has encouraged Americans to convert traditional IRA accounts to Roth IRA accounts, and the process seems to be a win-win situation. The IRS benefits by getting tax money up front that would have taken 20 or more years to acquire. The American citizens benefit in the long-run by being able to create retirement accounts that are not subject to any further taxation, and that can be passed on to heirs tax-free.

IRA to Roth IRA Conversion Rules

The rules for converting funds from a traditional IRA to a Roth IRA are as follows:

- Adjusted gross income (not including the IRA conversion amount) for the year of the conversion cannot exceed $100,000.
- Taxpayers using the Married Filing Separately status are not eligible to convert.
- The rollover of funds must take place within 60 days of removing the funds from the traditional IRA.
- Should the withdrawal of funds from a traditional IRA to a Roth IRA begin before the end of the year but not culminate until the next calendar year, the conversion will be deemed to have occurred in the year of the withdrawal.
- When a conversion occurs, all converted funds that have not previously been taxed are subject to income taxation at ordinary income tax rates.

IRA Conversion Worksheets

There are some complicated calculations involved in determining whether it makes sense to convert funds from a traditional IRA to a Roth IRA or to leave them where they are. If you have Internet access, here are some site links that provide online calculators that will help you determine the best route to take.

- *SmartMoney* magazine provides a nice little calculator that helps you decide if you should convert to a Roth IRA or stick with the traditional IRA. http://smartmoney.com/retirement/roth/index.cfm?story=convert
- Banksite.com has a calculator that provides charts and tables that will demonstrate the long-term difference between keeping your money in a traditional IRA and switching over to a Roth IRA. http://www.banksite.com/calc/rothira/

When you go to these Web sites, you should be ready to provide the following information:

- Current IRA balance
- Percent of your IRA balance that is taxable
- Your current age
- Your expected annual IRA contribution
- Desired starting age for withdrawals from IRA
- Estimated current return on your investments
- Estimated return on your investments at retirement age
- Estimated inflation percent (4 percent is a good estimate in today's economy)
- Amount of annual income you expect to require upon retirement, beyond Social Security payments
- Current marginal tax rate
- Anticipated marginal tax rate at retirement

If you do not have access to the Internet, you can contact your IRA account holder and ask for estimates like the ones described here.

Roth IRA: Long-Term Investment Worksheet

To show the compounding powers of a simple investment in a Roth IRA, the example in Table B-1 shows how the value of a small IRA investment—$2,000 per year for five years, beginning at age 20—will grow exponentially over the adult life of the account holder.

 GET SMARTER   A $10,000 investment beginning at age 20 will grow to over $200,000 by age 85 if invested at 5 percent, over $500,000 by age 72 if invested at 8 percent. Invest at 10 percent and that $10,000 will grow to over $1,000,000 by the time the owner of the account reaches age 70! Can you think of any better gift to leave as a legacy for your child or grandchild? As soon as a child enters the workforce (the child must have earned income in order to make deposits into a Roth IRA), a Roth IRA should be established and funded. Five years of funding and the child will be well cared for in retirement. Fund for more than five years and the amounts will increase even more. (Editorial comment: Now if only we could get our government to consider private retirement accounts instead of fighting the losing battle over Social Security, the cost to care for today's children when they retire would be remarkably small.)

In this example, it is estimated that the investment will earn approximately 8 percent per year. Different rates of return over the years will naturally produce different results. This small investment of $10,000, when held in the Roth IRA account until the owner reaches age 65, has turned into an account worth $297,313, which is increasing in value at over $22,000 per year. Wait another five years, until the owner reaches age 70, and the account is worth $436,851, and is increasing in value at over $32,000 per year. Invest $2,000 per year for more than five years and the numbers grow even higher. The point here is that a relatively small commitment to funding a retirement account at a young age can result in a significant and TAX-FREE retirement income.

Note   *The worksheet that was used to calculate the compounding interest in Table B-1 is available online at http://www.osborne.com/ if you would like to experiment with various scenarios using your computer.*

Table B-1 • An Example Showing the Power of Compounding Interest

Year	Number of Years	Age	Contribution	Balance	Growth per Year
2000	1	20	$2,000	$2,160.00	$160.00
2001	2	21	$2,000	$4,492.80	$332.80
2002	3	22	$2,000	$7,012.22	$519.42
2003	4	23	$2,000	$9,733.20	$720.98
2004	5	24	$2,000	$12,671.86	$938.66
2005	6	25		$13,685.61	$1,013.75
2006	7	26		$14,780.46	$1,094.85
2007	8	27		$15,962.89	$1,182.44
2008	9	28		$17,239.92	$1,277.03
2009	10	29		$18,619.12	$1,379.19
2010	11	30		$20,108.65	$1,489.53
2011	12	31		$21,717.34	$1,608.69
2012	13	32		$23,454.72	$1,737.39
2013	14	33		$25,331.10	$1,876.38
2014	15	34		$27,357.59	$2,026.49

Table B-1 • An Example Showing the Power of Compounding Interest (*continued*)

Year	Number of Years	Age	Contribution	Balance	Growth per Year
2015	16	35		$29,546.20	$2,188.61
2016	17	36		$31,909.89	$2,363.70
2017	18	37		$34,462.69	$2,552.79
2018	19	38		$37,219.70	$2,757.01
2019	20	39		$40,197.28	$2,977.58
2020	21	40		$43,413.06	$3,215.78
2021	22	41		$46,886.10	$3,473.04
2022	23	42		$50,636.99	$3,750.89
2023	24	43		$54,687.95	$4,050.96
2024	25	44		$59,062.99	$4,375.04
2025	26	45		$63,788.03	$4,725.04
2026	27	46		$68,891.07	$5,103.04
2027	28	47		$74,402.35	$5,511.29
2028	29	48		$80,354.54	$5,952.19
2029	30	49		$86,782.91	$6,428.36
2030	31	50		$93,725.54	$6,942.63
2031	32	51		$101,223.58	$7,498.04
2032	33	52		$109,321.47	$8,097.89
2033	34	53		$118,067.19	$8,745.72
2034	35	54		$127,512.56	$9,445.37
2035	36	55		$137,713.56	$10,201.00
2036	37	56		$148,730.65	$11,017.09
2037	38	57		$160,629.10	$11,898.45
2038	39	58		$173,479.43	$12,850.33
2039	40	59		$187,357.78	$13,878.35
2040	41	60		$202,346.41	$14,988.62

Table B-1 • An Example Showing the Power of Compounding Interest (*continued*)

Year	Number of Years	Age	Contribution	Balance	Growth per Year
2041	42	61		$218,534.12	$16,187.71
2042	43	62		$236,016.85	$17,482.73
2043	44	63		$254,898.20	$18,881.35
2044	45	64		$275,290.05	$20,391.86
2045	46	65		$297,313.26	$22,023.20
2046	47	66		$321,098.32	$23,785.06
2047	48	67		$346,786.18	$25,687.87
2048	49	68		$374,529.08	$27,742.89
2049	50	69		$404,491.40	$29,962.33
2050	51	70		$436,850.72	$32,359.31

Non-Cash Charitable Contributions: Valuation Guide

One of the most frequently asked questions tax preparers encounter is, "How should I value my donated goods?" Used clothing and other donated items vary in value based on the quality of the item and the location—donated items in larger cities often fetch a higher resale price than in small towns. This valuation guide, provided by the Salvation Army, provides a sample range of values that are used for pricing goods in their stores across the country. The best method for determining the value of your donated items is to go to the local resale shops in your area and see what similar items are selling for. If you don't have any resale shops nearby, try visiting the garage sales in your neighborhood and make price comparisons in that manner.

The checklist in Table B-2 should provide you with a starting point for determining the value of your donated items. For the most current version of this valuation guide, please go to the Salvation Army Web site at http://www.180095truck.com/.

 Note *You can also call (800) 95TRUCK if you would like to arrange for the Salvation Army to pick up your donations. The Salvation Army does not set a valuation on your donation. That is the privilege and responsibility of the donor. For professional advice please consult your tax advisor.*

Table B-2 • Valuation List, Copyright the Salvation Army, 1996 to 2000

Ladies' Clothing	Low Range	High Range
bathing suits	$4	$12
bathrobes	$2.50	$12
blouses	$2.50	$12
boots	$2	$5
bras	$1	$3
coats	$10	$40
dresses	$4	$19
evening dresses	$10	$60
foundation garments	$3	$8
fur coats	$25	$400
fur hats	$7	$15
handbags	$2	$20
hats	$1	$8
jackets	$4	$12
nightgowns	$4	$12
pant suits	$6.50	$25
shoes	$2	$25
skirts	$3	$8
slacks	$3.50	$12
slips	$1	$6
socks	$0.40	$1.25
suits	$6	$25
sweaters	$3	$15

Table B-2 • Valuation List, Copyright the Salvation Army, 1996 to 2000 (*continued*)

Men's Clothing	Low Range	High Range
belts, ties	$3	$8
jackets	$7.50	$25
overcoats	$15	$60
pajamas	$2	$8
pants, shorts	$3.50	$10
raincoats	$5	$20
shirts	$2.50	$12
shoes	$3.50	$25
slacks	$5	$12
suits	$15	$60
sweaters	$2.50	$12
swim trunks	$2.50	$8
tuxedos	$10	$60
undershirts	$1	$3
undershorts	$1	$3

Children's Clothing	Low Range	High Range
blouses	$2	$8
boots	$3	$20
coats	$4.50	$20
dresses	$3.50	$12
jackets	$3	$25
jeans	$3.50	$12
pants	$2.50	$12

Table B-2 • Valuation List, Copyright the Salvation Army, 1996 to 2000 (*continued*)

Children's Clothing (cont.)	Low Range	High Range
shirts	$2	$6
shoes	$2.50	$8.75
skirts	$1.50	$6
slacks	$2	$8
snowsuits	$4	$19
socks	$0.50	$1.50
sweaters	$2.50	$8
underwear	$1	$3.50

Dry Goods	Low Range	High Range
bedspreads	$3	$24
blankets	$2.50	$8
chair covers	$15	$35
curtains	$1.50	$12
drapes	$6.50	$40
pillows	$2	$8
sheets	$2	$8
throw rugs	$1.50	$12
towels	$0.50	$4

Furniture	Low Range	High Range
air conditioners	$20	$90
bar stools	$10	$20
bars	$30	$75

Table B-2 • Valuation List, Copyright the Salvation Army, 1996 to 2000 (*continued*)

Furniture (cont.)	Low Range	High Range
beds (double), complete	$50	$170
beds (single), complete	$35	$100
bicycles	$15	$65
carriages	$5	$100
chairs (upholstered)	$25	$75
chests	$25	$95
china cabinets	$85	$300
clothes closets	$15	$50
coffee tables	$15	$65
convertible sofas (w/ mattress)	$85	$300
cribs (w/ mattress)	$25	$100
desks	$25	$140
dressers w/ mirror	$20	$100
dryers	$45	$90
electric stoves (working)	$75	$150
end tables (2)	$10	$50
figurines (large)	$50	$100
fireplace sets	$30	$90
floor lamps	$7.50	$40
folding beds	$20	$60
gas stoves	$50	$125
heaters	$7.50	$22
hi-risers	$35	$75
high chairs	$10	$50
kitchen cabinets	$25	$75

Table B-2 • Valuation List, Copyright the Salvation Army, 1996 to 2000 (*continued*)

Furniture (cont.)	Low Range	High Range
kitchen chairs	$2.50	$10
kitchen tables	$25	$60
mattresses (double)	$35	$75
mattresses (single)	$15	$35
organ consoles	$75	$200
pianos	$75	$200
pictures and paintings	$5	$200
ping pong tables	$15	$40
playpens	$15	$30
pool tables	$20	$75
radios	$7.50	$50
record players (components)	$30	$200
record players (stereo)	$30	$90
refrigerators (working)	$75	$250
rugs	$20	$90
secretaries	$50	$140
sofas	$35	$200
trunks	$5	$70
TVs, b/w (working)	$25	$60
TVs, color (working)	$75	$225
wardrobes	$20	$100
washers (working)	$50	$150
waterbed headboards	$30	$90
waterbeds (complete)	$150	$325
waterbeds (frame)	$15	$40

Table B-2 • Valuation List, Copyright the Salvation Army, 1996 to 2000 (*continued*)

Sporting Goods	Low Range	High Range
bicycles	$15	$65
fishing rods	$5	$25
ice/roller skates	$10	$40
skis	$15	$100
sleds	$5	$20
tennis rackets	$5	$40
toboggans	$15	$90
Miscellaneous	**Low Range**	**High Range**
adding machines	$20	$75
broiler ovens	$15	$25
Christmas trees	$15	$50
copiers	$100	$200
home computers	$150	$500
mannequins	$25	$200
mimeograph machines	$100	$200
mixers	$5	$20
mowers (auto)	$10	$100
mowers (riding)	$100	$250
power edgers	$5	$25
rototillers	$25	$90
sewing machines	$15	$75
snow blowers	$50	$150
telephone answering machines	$25	$75
typewriters	$7.50	$35
vacuum cleaners (working)	$20	$60
wigs	$5	$25

Index

F

K

L

M

N